# The Book of Religions & Dynasties

## Or: On the Great Conjunctions

by Abū Ma'shar

The Complete Edition from Arabic

TRANSLATED & EDITED BY
BENJAMIN N. DYKES, PHD

---

The Cazimi Press
Minneapolis, Minnesota
2025

Published and printed in the United States of America
by The Cazimi Press
Minneapolis, MN 55414

© 2025 by Benjamin N. Dykes, Ph.D.

All rights reserved. No part of this publication may be reproduced, stored in or introduced into a retrieval system, or transmitted, in any form or by any means (electronic, mechanical, photocopying, recording or otherwise), without the prior written permission of both the copyright owner and the above publisher of this book.

The scanning, uploading, and distribution of this book via the Internet or via any other means without the permission of the publisher is illegal and punishable by law. Please purchase only authorized editions and do not participate in or encourage electronic piracy of copyrighted materials. Your support of the author's rights is appreciated.

ISBN-13: 978-1-934586-55-6

# Also available at www.bendykes.com:

Designed for curious modern astrology students, *Traditional Astrology for Today* explains basic ideas in history, philosophy and counseling, dignities, chart interpretation, and predictive techniques. Non-technical and friendly for modern beginners.

One of the most famous medieval books on astrological theory and basics is now available in an affordable edition. Abū Ma'shar's *Great Introduction* is foundational for later astrologers, comprising fixed stars, elemental qualities, degrees, configurations, Lots, and more.

This new translation of six works by Sahl b. Bishr is a required text for Benjamin Dykes's traditional natal astrology course, and is the first translation of Sahl's huge *Book of Nativities* from Arabic.

Dorotheus's *Carmen Astrologicum* is a foundational text for traditional astrology. Originally written in a lost Greek version, this is a translation of the later Arabic edition. It contains nativities, predictive techniques, aspect and house combinations, and a complete approach to elections or inceptions.

This excellent and popular introduction to predictive techniques by contemporary Turkish astrologer Öner Döşer blends traditional and modern methods, with numerous chart examples.

The first two volumes of this medieval mundane series, *Astrology of the World*, describe numerous techniques in weather prediction, prices and commodities, eclipses and comets, chorography, ingresses, Saturn-Jupiter conjunctions, and more, translated from Arabic and Latin sources.

Two classic introductions to astrology, by Abū Ma'shar and al-Qabīsī, are translated with commentary in this volume. *Introductions to Traditional Astrology* is an essential reference work for traditional students.

The classic medieval text by Guido Bonatti, the *Book of Astronomy* is now available in paperback reprints. This famous work is a complete guide to basic principles, horary, elections, mundane, and natal astrology.

This first English translation of Hephaistion of Thebes's *Apotelesmatics* Book III contains much fascinating material from the original Dorotheus poem and numerous other electional texts, including rules on thought-interpretation.

The largest compilation of traditional electional material, *Choices & Inceptions: Traditional Electional Astrology* contains works by Sahl, al-Rijāl, al-'Imrānī, and others, beginning with an extensive discussion of elections and questions by Benjamin Dykes.

The famous medieval horary compilation *The Book of the Nine Judges* is now available in translation for the first time! It is the largest traditional horary work available, and the third in the horary series.

*The Search of the Heart* is the first in the horary series, and focuses on the use of victors (special significators or *almutens*) and the practice of thought-interpretation: divining thoughts and predicting outcomes before the client speaks.

*The Forty Chapters* is a famous and influential horary work by al-Kindī, and is the second volume of the horary series. Beginning with a general introduction to astrology, al-Kindī covers topics such as war, wealth, travel, pregnancy, marriage, and more.

The second volume of *Persian Nativities* features a The second volume of *Persian Nativities* features a shorter, beginner-level work on nativities and prediction by 'Umar al-Tabarī, and a much longer book on nativities by his younger follower, Abū Bakr.

*Astrological Magic: Basic Rituals & Meditations* is a basic introduction to ritual magic for astrologers. It introduces a magical cosmology and electional rules, and shows how to perform ritual correctly, integrating Tarot and visualizations with rituals for all Elements, Planets, and Signs.

Expand your knowledge of traditional astrology, philosophy, and esoteric thought with the *Logos & Light* audio series: downloadable, college-level lectures on MP3 at a fraction of the university cost!

# Short Table of Contents

Table of Abbreviations ............................................................. VIII
Table of Figures ........................................................................ IX
Translator's Introduction ....................................................... 1

## The Book of Religions & Dynasties

Introduction ............................................................................. 70
**Book I**: Principles & Prophets ................................................ 72
**Book II**: Dynasties & Kings ................................................... 109
**Book III**: Mutual Aspects of all Planets .............................. 186
**Book IV**: Each sign as an Ascendant, Profected Ascendant, or Profection from a Conjunction ................................. 201
**Book V**: Each Planet as a Time Lord, in all Signs ................ 221
**Book VI**: The Planets' Transits over Each Other, in all Signs ................................................................................. 276
**Book VII**: Profected or Revolutionary Ascendants, on Places of Prior Charts, & Planets in them ....................... 337
**Book VIII**: Disasters, Wars, Foundational Charts, & *Fardārs* ............................................................................. 364

Appendix A: Al-Kindī's *Forty Chapters* ................................ 388
Bibliography ........................................................................... 392
Index ....................................................................................... 394

# Long Table of Contents

Table of Abbreviations ................................................................. VIII
Table of Figures ............................................................................. IX
Translator's Introduction ............................................................. 1
    §1: The current volume & the Astrology of the World series ...................... 1
    §2: Evaluation of BRD ............................................................................. 3
    §3: *BRD*'s initial theory of mundane astrology (Ch. I.1) ............................ 6
    §4: Persian model of politics ................................................................... 10
    §5: Conjunctions, shifts, & ingresses (Chs. I.1-I.2) ................................... 11
    §6: "What does the chart say?" A few words on chart interpretation ....... 23
    §7: Overview & structure ........................................................................ 28
    §8: Prophets (Chs. I.3-I.4) ....................................................................... 35
    §9: Kings & dynasties (Book II) ............................................................... 36
    §10: Predictive techniques ...................................................................... 38
        §10.1: General approach to mundane prediction ................................. 38
        §10.2: The red herring of the Flood ..................................................... 41
        §10.3: The Turn (or 360s) & the Quarters (BRD I.1, **71-91**) ............. 43
        §10.4: Sets of 10 Saturn cycles (II.8, **146-57**) .................................. 45
        §10.5: The Sixties (BRD II.8, **139-45**) ............................................. 47
        §10.6: Annual & quarterly ingresses .................................................... 48
        §10.7: *Fardārs* (BRD VIII.2, **40-65**) ............................................... 49
        §10.8: Mundane profections ................................................................ 51
        §10.9: Saturn-Mars conjunctions in Cancer (BRD II.8, **1, 4-30, 174-75**) ......................................................................................... 52
    §11: Special victors ................................................................................ 57
    §12: Mundane Lots ................................................................................ 58
    §13: Mundane indications of the places & planets ................................. 60
    §14: Chorography & peoples ................................................................. 64
    §15: Colors of the signs & places ........................................................... 67
    §16: Abū Ma'shar's charts ..................................................................... 67

## THE BOOK OF RELIGIONS & DYNASTIES

**INTRODUCTION** .................................................................. 70
**BOOK I: PRINCIPLES & PROPHETS** ...................................... 72
    Chapter I.1: On setting forth the universal Beginnings which are of great usefulness ................................................................ 73
    Chapter I.2: On knowing the strongest of the conjunctional signs of the triplicities, & the appearance of their indications in the regions attributed to them .................................................. 92
    Chapter I.3: On knowing the conjunctions indicative of the nativities of prophets & conquerors, their morals & character, the marks coming to be on them, the tokens of their prophethood, the timing of their appearance, the locating of each one of them, & the extent of the quantity of their years ................................................. 97
    Chapter I.4: On knowing their customs & ordinances, their dress, & transport ................................................................................. 105
**BOOK II: DYNASTIES & KINGS** ........................................... 109
    Chapter II.1: On how to know the shift of the dynasty from nation to nation, & to which nation it passes .......................................... 110
    Chapter II.2: On how to know to which of the regions the dynasty shifts, & the locations of the cities of its kings ............................ 116
    Chapter II.3: On how to know the length of the duration of rulership among the people of the religious community to whom it has shifted, their strength & weakness, the number of their kings, & what the people of the kingdom to which it has shifted will do to the people of the kingdom from which it has withdrawn .............. 118
    Chapter II.4: On how to know the nativities of the kings of the people of that religious community in accordance with the alighting of the [planetary] bodies in the Ascendants of the shift of the conjunction in the triplicities ............................................................... 121
    Chapter II.5: On how to know the length of their terms ................ 134
    Chapter II.6: On what their ailments are, indicating their disasters ....... 149
    Chapter II.7: On knowing the manner of their disasters, & the day on which that will be, & to whom the rulership will pass after them ...... 151

Chapter II.8: On the indications of the uniting of the two infortunes in all of the signs, & their alighting in the triplicities, for the lower events coming to be from their influences, & what resembles that...162
    II.8.1: Saturn-Mars conjunctions in Cancer ............................................162
    II.8.2: Saturn-Mars conjunctions in other signs ....................................169
    II.8.3: Saturn-Mars in the exaltation signs............................................171
    II.8.4: Saturn-Mars in the triplicities ....................................................172
    II.8.5: Saturn-Mars in the divisions or places .....................................179
    II.8.6: The Sixties .................................................................................180
    II.8.7: Sets of 10 Saturn cycles .............................................................181
    II.8.8: Dynasties by the planets' greatest years.....................................183
    II.8.9: Trepidation theory .....................................................................184

**BOOK III: MUTUAL ASPECTS OF ALL PLANETS........................................186**
  Chapter III.1: On the combinations of the planets with Saturn.............187
  Chapter III.2: On the combinations of the planets with Jupiter .............192
  Chapter III.3: On the combinations of the planets with Mars.................195
  Chapter III.4: On the combinations of the planets with the Sun.............197
  Chapter III.5: On the combinations of the planets with Venus ...............198
  Chapter III.6: On the combinations of the Moon with Mercury............199

**BOOK IV: EACH SIGN AS AN ASCENDANT, PROFECTED ASCENDANT, OR PROFECTION FROM A CONJUNCTION ............................................201**
  Chapter IV.1: On the indications of Aries for lower events if it was the Ascendant of one of the revolutionary periods, or the years terminated at it from one of the Ascendants of the preceding Beginnings, or from the positions of the conjunctions ........................202
  Chapter IV.2: On the indications of Taurus in the same way..................204
  Chapter IV.3: On the indications of Gemini in the same way .................206
  Chapter IV.4: On the indications of Cancer in the same way.................208
  Chapter IV.5: On the indications of Leo in the same way .......................209
  Chapter IV.6: On the indications of Virgo in the same way.....................210
  Chapter IV.7: On the indications of Libra in the same way .....................212
  Chapter IV.8: On the indications of Scorpio in the same way.................214
  Chapter IV.9: On the indications of Sagittarius in the same way ............216
  Chapter IV.10: On the indications of Capricorn in the same way..........217
  Chapter IV.11: On the indications of Aquarius in the same way ............218

Chapter IV.12: On the indications of Pisces in the same way.................219
**BOOK V: EACH PLANET AS A TIME LORD, IN ALL SIGNS ..................... 221**
Chapter V.1: On knowing Saturn's indications by himself if he had the victorship over the Ascendants of one of the Beginnings, or he had lord-of-the-yearship or distributorship, or upon his being parallel with all of the signs, in the sense of mixture.............................................222
Chapter V.2: On how to know the indications of Jupiter in the same way.................................................................................................................231
Chapter V.3: On how to know the indications of Mars in the same way 240
Chapter V.4: On how to know the indications of Venus in the same way.................................................................................................................248
Chapter V.5: On how to know the special property of the indications of Mercury, in the same way ....................................................................254
Chapter V.6: On how to know the special properties of the indications of the Moon, in the same way ................................................................262
Chapter V.7: On how to know the indications of the two Nodes (the northern & southern) & the appearance of the tailed stars, during their parallelism with all of the signs, in the sense of mixture .............266
**BOOK VI: THE PLANETS' TRANSITS OVER EACH OTHER, IN ALL SIGNS 276**
Chapter VI.1: On judging the transits of the planets above one another during their parallelism with the sign of Aries.........................................278
Chapter VI.2: On judging the transits of the planets above one another during their parallelism with the sign of Taurus......................................284
Chapter VI.3: On judging the transits of the planets above one another during their parallelism with the sign of Gemini ....................................289
Chapter VI.4: On judging the transits of the planets above one another during their parallelism with the sign of Cancer.....................................293
Chapter VI.5: On judging the transits of the planets above one another during their parallelism with the sign of Leo ..........................................298
Chapter VI.6: On judging the transits of the planets above one another during their parallelism with the sign of Virgo .......................................303
Chapter VI.7: On judging the transits of the planets above one another during their parallelism with the sign of Libra.........................................308
Chapter VI.8: On judging the transits of the planets above one another during their parallelism with the sign of Scorpio ....................................313

Chapter VI.9: On judging the transits of the planets above one another during their parallelism with the sign of Sagittarius.................318

Chapter VI.10: On judging the transits of the planets above one another during their parallelism with the sign of Capricorn...............322

Chapter VI.11: On judging the transits of the planets above one another during their parallelism with the sign of Aquarius................327

Chapter VI.12: On judging the transits of the planets above one another during their parallelism with the sign of Pisces.....................332

**BOOK VII: PROFECTED OR REVOLUTIONARY ASCENDANTS, ON PLACES OF PRIOR CHARTS, & PLANETS IN THEM ......................... 337**

Chapter VII.1: On the indication of the sign of the terminal point or the Ascendant of the revolution for lower events, if it was the Ascendant of one of the preceding Beginnings, or the sign of the conjunction, or the direction, or one of the upper bodies was in it or in the Ascendant of the revolution............................................................338

Chapter VII.2: On the indication of the second house, in the same way 341

Chapter VII.3: On the indication of the third house, in the same way ..343

Chapter VII.4: On the indication of the fourth house, in the same way 346

Chapter VII.5: On the indication of the fifth house, in the same way....348

Chapter VII.6: On the indication of the sixth house, in the same way...350

Chapter VII.7: On the indication of the seventh house, in the same way..................................................................................................................352

Chapter VII.8: On the indication of the eighth house, in the same way 354

Chapter VII.9: On the indication of the ninth house, in the same way .356

Chapter VII.10: On the indication of the tenth house, in the same way 358

Chapter VII.11: On the indication of the eleventh place, in the same way..................................................................................................................360

Chapter VII.12: On the indication of the twelfth house, in the same way..................................................................................................................362

**BOOK VIII: DISASTERS, WARS, FOUNDATIONAL CHARTS, & FARDĀRS 364**

Chapter VIII.1: On knowing lower events from the revolutions of years .......................................................................................................365

Chapter VIII.2: On knowing the terminal points in the transit of the years from the Ascendants, the positions of the conjunctions, &

their indications, & how to know the *fardārs*, their lords, & their indications for all lower events..................................................................374
APPENDIX A: AL-KINDĪ'S *FORTY CHAPTERS* ........................................ 388
BIBLIOGRAPHY ............................................................................................. 392
INDEX ............................................................................................................. 394

## TABLE OF ABBREVIATIONS

| | |
|---|---|
| Arab Rule | Al-Kindī, *The Length of Arab Rule* (in Appendix III of *BY*) |
| AW1 / AW2 | Dykes, *Astrology of the World* Vols. 1-2 |
| BRD | Dykes's edition of Abū Ma'shar, *The Book of Religions & Dynasties* (the present volume) |
| BY / **BY** | Burnett and Yamamoto's edition of Abū Ma'shar, *The Book of Religions & Dynasties* |
| Conjunctions | Māshā'allāh's *Book of Conjunctions*, in *AW2* |
| Flowers | Abū Ma'shar's *Flowers of Abū Ma'shar*, in *AW2* |
| Forty | Al-Kindī's *The Forty Chapters* |
| Fulfilment | Mūsā b. Nawbakht, *The Book of Fulfilment* |
| Gr. Intr. | Abū Ma'shar, *The Great Introduction to the Science of the Stars* |
| History | Al-Ṭabarī's *The History of Prophets & Kings* |
| Leopold | Leopold of Austria, *A Compilation on the Science of the Stars* |
| LeStrange | Guy LeStrange, *The Lands of the Eastern Caliphate* |
| Periods | Mūsā b. Nawbakht, *The Book of Periods & Epochs* |
| PN4 | Abū Ma'shar, *Persian Nativities IV: On the Revolutions of the Years of Nativities* |
| Revolutions | Sahl b. Bishr's *On the Revolutions of the Years of the World* |
| RYW | Māshā'allāh, *On the Revolutions of the Years of the World*, in *AW2* |
| Scito | Abū Ma'shar (attr.) *Scito horam introitus*, in *AW2* |
| Tet. | Ptolemy, Claudius, *Tetrabiblos* (Robbins edition) |
| Thousands | David Pingree, *The Thousands of Abū Ma'shar* |

## TABLE OF FIGURES

Figure 1: General theory of mundane astrology (*BRD* I.1) ............... 8
Figure 2: Time lords and conjunctions classified ............... 12
Figure 3: Abū Ma'shar's triplicity shift after 13 conjunctions ............... 13
Figure 4: Earthy triplicity shift and conjunctions (Twenties) ............... 14
Figure 5: List of modern Sixties ............... 15
Figure 6: 1901 mean conjunction ............... 17
Figure 7: Complete table of mean conjunctions and distances ............... 18
Figure 8: Illustration of mean conjunctional period ............... 19
Figure 9: Modern tropical & sidereal triplicity shifts compared ............... 20
Figure 10: Abū Ma'shar's parameters for Saturn-Jupiter conjunctions ............... 22
Figure 11: Effects in which conjunction ............... 23
Figure 12: 1901 conjunction ............... 39
Figure 13: Profection to 1903 ............... 40
Figure 14: 1903 ingress ............... 41
Figure 15: Two Flood conjunctions ............... 42
Figure 16: Sets of 10 Saturn cycles ............... 46
Figure 17: Sets of 10 Saturn cycles ............... 47
Figure 18: The Sixties in early Islam (*BRD*) ............... 48
Figure 19: Mundane *fardārs* in Mūsā (Ch. 5) ............... 50
Figure 20: General indications for mundane profections (*BRD* I.1) ............... 51
Figure 21: Saturn-Mars conjunctions in Cancer ............... 56
Figure 22: Mundane Lots in *BRD* ............... 60
Figure 23: Mundane significations of the planets ............... 62
Figure 24: Mundane significations of the places ............... 64
Figure 25: Bounds assigned to people and regions ............... 65
Figure 26: Religious indications of the planets ............... 66
Figure 27: Colors of the signs and places ............... 67
Figure 28: Five charts in *BRD* ............... 69
Figure 29: General theory of mundane astrology ............... 73
Figure 30: Six types of mundane chart ............... 77
Figure 31: Abū Ma'shar's triplicity shifts ............... 79
Figure 32: Abū Ma'shar's triplicity shift after 13 conjunctions ............... 81
Figure 33: Flood and Islam Turns of Māshā'allāh and Abū Ma'shar ............... 85

Figure 34: Key planets and positions for early Islam .................................................. 86
Figure 35: General indications for mundane profections ........................................... 89
Figure 36: Strength and direction of signs .................................................................. 92
Figure 37: Effects in which conjunction ..................................................................... 93
Figure 38: Second rotation of profection to conjunction (I.3, 3) ............................... 97
Figure 39: Time of appearance (of prophet [BRD] or acceder [Musā]) ................... 102
Figure 40: Triplicity shift to fire (809 AD) and appearance of al-ʿAlawī al-Basrī ................................................................................................................................. 103
Figure 41: Approximation of II.2, 10, in the Fagan-Bradley sidereal zodiac ... 117
Figure 42: Planetary indicators of Caliphs .............................................................. 132
Figure 43: Zodiacal directions of 90° ....................................................................... 154
Figure 44: Solar eclipse, 841 AD: ............................................................................. 157
Figure 45: Aries Ingress of year of Hijrah (622 AD) ............................................... 164
Figure 46: Modern approximation of BRD's Hijrah ............................................... 166
Figure 47: Modern approximation of 652 AD revolution for Saturn-Mars conjunction ............................................................................................................ 167
Figure 48: Six configurations of ............................................................................... 172
Figure 49: The Sixties in early Islam ........................................................................ 181
Figure 50: Planetary years ........................................................................................ 183
Figure 51: 1902 ingress Ascendant (outer) ............................................................. 343
Figure 52: Triplicity shift to Islam (571 AD) ........................................................... 375
Figure 53: Modern approximation of Abū Maʿshar's shift to Islam ..................... 376
Figure 54: Dynasty shift to ʿAbbāsids (749 AD) .................................................... 377
Figure 55: Modern approximation of Abū Maʿshar's dynasty shift to ʿAbbāsids ................................................................................................................................. 378
Figure 56: Triplicity shift to fire (809 AD) .............................................................. 379
Figure 57: Triplicity shift to fire (809 AD) .............................................................. 380

# Translator's Introduction

## §1: The current volume & the Astrology of the World series

This book is a translation of Abū Ma'shar's *Book of Religions and Dynasties* (*BRD*), which was more popularly known in the Latin West as *On the Great Conjunctions*.[1] It is the first of a new group of translations in my mundane series, *Astrology of the World* (*AW*), and represents a new start within it. As such, I will begin with a brief introduction to basic principles of mundane astrology.

Mundane astrology (from the Lat. *mundanus*, "pertaining to the world") seems to have been the earliest branch of astrology stemming from the Babylonians, and deals with people and events which affect broad swathes of the earth and its peoples: cultures, governments, agriculture, economics, disease, weather, and natural disasters. In most cases, mundane astrologers cast charts for distinctly mundane times (e.g., Solar ingresses into Aries), or for distinctly mundane events (e.g., eclipses), and interpret them in light of people represented astrologically as groups (such as Jupiter for the wealthy, or Venus for Muslims), or as individuals who represent institutions or affect the people as a whole (such as Saturn for a king), and for other similarly broad groups and phenomena (such as Taurus for livestock, or Libra for certain crops or weather patterns). Certain parts of an astrological chart are furthermore reinterpreted for a mundane context, such as treating Mars in terms of war instead of merely personal conflicts, or the second and eighth places as trade and exchanges instead of a native's own personal money and debts.

In order to put some order to this complex branch of astrology, in my two previous volumes I distinguished broadly between two different approaches to events and time. In *AW1* I described the "episodic" approach to mundane astrology. This is based on techniques mainly found in Ptolemy, such as chorography (assigning planets and signs to regions of the world), eclipses and

---

[1] I have used Burnett and Yamamoto's (**BY**) critical edition of 2000 as the basis of my translation.

comets,[2] annual and quarterly ingress charts, and lunation charts. In these cases, the charts generally stand alone or describe isolated "episodes," in that they might not form parts of general, long-term patterns: such as weather, prices, crop and livestock effects, and short-term political events.

In *AW2* I introduced "historical" astrology as developed later by the medieval Persians and Arabs (with input from the Indians). Historical astrology embeds certain short-term techniques within a hierarchy of longer-term charts and time lord schemes, which are largely taken from natal astrology: mundane profections, mundane distributions, *fardārs*, and so on. Historical astrology adds to mundane astrology broader political trends such as the rise and fall of dynasties, and the appearance of historical individuals such as prophets (or would-be prophets) and leaders.

The next few volumes of *AW* are meant to begin this process anew, focusing on practical interpretation and advice, within a more elaborately articulated historical framework. They will comprise:

- *AW3*: Abū Ma'shar's *Book of Religions and Dynasties* (*BRD*). The present volume.
- *AW4*: Mūsā b. Nawbakht's two books on mundane astrology, *The Book of Fulfilment on the Secrets of the Stars* (*Fulfilment*) and *The Book of Periods and Epochs* (*Periods*).
- *AW5*: Sahl b. Bishr's *On the Revolutions of the Years of the World* (*Revolutions*).
- *AW6*: Abū Qumash's *The Book on the Judgments of the Stars*.

The present volume by Abū Ma'shar addresses historical astrology in a general way, and provides basic rules for how certain techniques and charts may activate latent promises in more foundational charts, such as a mundane profection activating the promise of an earlier triplicity shift chart. (The primary foundational chart Abū Ma'shar is interested in, is that of the Saturn-Jupiter conjunction.) If one understands Abū Ma'shar's theory of natal prediction and its techniques (see my *PN4*), it's easy to see that he is applying them to mundane charts.

---

[2] I realize that eclipses occur in regular cycles over similar areas of the earth, but this is not how the ancients treated them astrologically.

Mūsā's two books (*AW4*) were arranged (and one of them translated into English) by Ana Labarta in 1982 and 2005 respectively. They take historical astrology to a new level of organization and detail. First, *Periods* is a general introduction to mundane astrology (a kind of combination of Sahl and Abū Ma'shar), but Mūsā takes greater care in trying to link "lower-level" charts of ingresses and conjunctions, to greater and more authoritative ones (such as triplicity shifts). Then, *Fulfilment* is a catalogue of over 90 mundane charts with commentary. It is meant to fulfil the promise of the theory in *Periods*, and represents the views of a later compiler and provider of chart examples, which are not always abundant in traditional astrology.

*AW5* by Sahl contains some chart examples as well as other things such as material on eclipses, but is mainly focused on how to interpret individual ingress charts. He makes liberal use of the Arabic version of Māshā'allāh's *RYW*, which can now be almost completely reconstructed separately from the Latin version which I translated in *AW2*.

Finally, in *AW6* a compiler named Abū Qumash (1300s AD) collected and organized, in one huge manuscript, dozens of excerpts from mundane authors. These range from the famous, like Māshā'allāh, to the obscure (such as Indian authors I have not heard of before). This volume will provide additional perspectives on many topics.

As of mid-2025, *BRD* is complete, and *Periods* and *Fulfilment* are in the final editing stages. Sahl is nearing completion and Abū Qumash is still a few years away from readiness.

## §2: Evaluation of BRD

*The Book of Religions and Dynasties* is a product of Abū Ma'shar's old age and was written after 883 AD, due to its mention of the death of an 'Alī b. Muḥammad "the 'Alawite," the leader of a rebellion who was killed in that year.[3] The introductory material in Book I, which stands in parallel to what I

---

[3] This dating presents a problem if we accept Pingree's view (based on al-Nadīm) that Abū Ma'shar was born in 786-87 AD), because that would have made him about 96 years old at the time of writing. (Al-Nadīm said he'd died at the age of 100,

call the "Persian" theory of the superiors, may be an original contribution by Abū Ma'shar, as it is reminiscent of some similar material in his *Great Introduction*.

As for the rest of *BRD*, it is hard to pin down what may be original to Abū Ma'shar. Much of it is a *pastiche* of many other astrologers' opinions, from Ptolemy to Māshā'allāh, al-Kindī, probably Sahl, and others. In these cases, Abū Ma'shar sometimes seems to quote them directly, sometimes he elaborates known passages from them but without always explaining their context. One conspicuous example is his references to the "indicator of the king," which is a term used by Māshā'allāh (and from thence, Sahl).[4]

In other cases, it is fair to say that Abū Ma'shar simply applies natal predictive techniques (such as in *PN4*), to mundane astrology. For example, in Book VII we see if the profected sign of the year or the Ascendant of an ingress chart, is in such-and-such a place (such as the fourth place) of some previous chart, normally a Saturn-Jupiter conjunction. This is exactly like asking if the profected sign of the year or the Ascendant of a natal solar revolution is in such-and-such a place of a *nativity*. Thus, if the profected sign of the year or the revolutionary Ascendant is Taurus, and Taurus was the fourth place of some older conjunctional chart, then the topics of the fourth place (land ownership, construction works, *etc.*) will be activated and relevant during that year. In this way some of Abū Ma'shar's standard methods are just mundane applications of what he already does for nativities.

However, there are certain questions and puzzling trends which arose for me (especially since I have translated both *Gr. Intr.* and *PN4*), and indeed earlier authors doubted *BRD* was even written by Abū Ma'shar at all (see below).

- The first is the aforementioned carelessness in not defining key terms like the "indicator of the king," which he certainly knew were

---

in 886.) I have already argued in *PN4* that I reject the dating of Abū Ma'shar's birth to 786-87 anyway, so I don't have a problem accepting such late authorship.

[4] See *BRD* II.8, **93**, which reflects *RYW* Ch. 45, **4** and Sahl's *Revolutions* Ch. 1.2, **64**. Also VIII.1, **51-54**, which reflects Sahl's *Revolutions* Ch. 1.2, **40-45** (see also his Ch. 8.2, **2**), and *Scito* Ch. 80, **2-5**.

- important in the tradition. But again, this could be chalked up to his simply copying and pasting passages from his predecessors.
- Abū Ma'shar conspicuously uses the word سائر to mean "all" of something (such as "all of the planets"), whereas the usual word is كلّ: سائر normally means "the rest of" something. Indeed, Abū Ma'shar never uses سائر like this in his earlier masterpiece, the *Great Introduction*. To a translator, the difference is so startling that I had to go back to *Gr. Intr.* and compare it with *BRD* to be sure I was not imagining things.
- Despite Abū Ma'shar's apparent application of natal predictive techniques to mundane charts, his instructions are frankly crude and even seem lazy as compared with his earlier work. Let me illustrate this by expanding on one point. In *PN4* (on natal predictive techniques) we distinguish between the features of a "root" (أصل) or earlier foundational chart like the nativity, and ongoing transits later on. And when looking at a particular place in a revolution chart, it makes an interpretive difference whether a planet was there in the root (the nativity) or is only transiting through it at a revolution. But in *BRD*, Abū Ma'shar calls his foundational charts "Beginnings"[5] (بوادئ) rather than roots, and he makes no such careful distinctions between planets which were in places at a Beginning or by transit. So, the standards of instruction differ greatly between the two books.
- There are a number of terms which Abū Ma'shar treats ambiguously, to the detriment of the student (and which again appears as an oddity). First, he routinely uses the same word for a "superior" planet (like Saturn, Jupiter, and Mars), and an "upper" body (i.e., any planet at all). More seriously, he often enough uses the normal word for a primary "direction" (تسيير) when he really means a "profection" or terminal point (انتهاء). This is a mistake he does not make in *PN4*, and this ambiguity can wreak havoc on certain techniques in which primary directions don't make any sense at all. I

---

[5] I have followed **BY** in capitalizing this word to alert the reader that Abū Ma'shar is referring to these special. See VIII.2 for his primary foundational charts.

have footnoted numerous places in the text where the reader could be led astray by his terminology. Third, and most frustratingly, he uses the term دور in a completely equivocal way. This Arabic noun is from a root verb that connotes circular things, like turning, periods, and so on. Abū Ma'shar frequently uses it in four ways, despite having other alternatives in Arabic (indeed, even among other astrologers): as a "circuit" or "cycle" (such as Saturn cycling through the zodiac), as a "period" (such as planetary periods or determinate periods of time), as a profection (sometimes otherwise called "turning"), and as a special mundane time lord technique I call a "Turn" (listed by Mūsā as one of many possible "cycles").

In the notes to their translation,[6] **BY** say that Abū Ma'shar was stated to have written *BRD* (or what seems to be it) for someone named Ibn al-Bāzyār. Upon reading it, one critic named al-Muktafī seems to have doubted Abū Ma'shar could have written it. "The intellect of Abū Ma'shar was not equal to the writing" of it, he sniffed. But as a translator of both *Gr. Intr.* and *PN4*, my impression is just the opposite: if anything, *BRD* is not equal to the intellect of the Abū Ma'shar who wrote those other books. Either way, what we have in *BRD* is a kind of *pastiche* of earlier authors, with little ingenuity but some valuable parts which can help us put develop a program to do historical astrology.

### §3: BRD's initial theory of mundane astrology (Ch. I.1)

In the earliest, Babylonian days of astrology, it seems that all or most planetary phenomena were assumed to be mundane, or at least indirectly mundane because even if they referred only to the person of the king, they would thereby affect the whole nation. But by the time of Claudius Ptolemy (2nd Century AD) astrology had been formally divided into three parts: mundane, natal (birth astrology), and electional or inceptional (the choosing of opportune times for action, and the outcomes of events). Regular and

---

[6] See **BY**, p. *xx*.

seasonal events like lunation charts and eclipses were the most common ways of determining mundane effects.

By the 8th Century in the Islamic empire, some Indian and other theories of historical change were combined with astrology to form new types of mundane astrology, particularly among the Persians. In *BRD*, Abū Ma'shar implicitly asks the following question: what justifies treating certain charts and their planets in an especially mundane way? Ptolemy had already wrestled somewhat with this question when he pointed out in *Tet.* II.10[7] that different cultures reckoned the beginning of the year as being at different times. The Egyptians, for instance, famously associated the beginning of the year with the summer solstice, due to its proximity to the flooding of the Nile and the heliacal rising of Sirius. Thus, if one assumes that we need a special lunar chart to cast for the beginning of the year, namely to act as an annual chart (which Ptolemy suggests), we have a number of choices. Which chart should we use?

Abū Ma'shar approaches this question in a somewhat different way, which is related to what I call the "Persian" theory of superiors (see below), but also in line with something he had attempted in his *Gr. Intr.* IV.4. There, he suggested that (for instance) the very structure and speed of Saturn's planetary system suggested the types of things that Saturn indicates astrologically: things that move slowly, are difficult to change, and so on. This is because of the slow movement of his mean position and (probably) the small size of his epicycle, which allows only a small range of degrees for his retrogradation. In *BRD* he returns again to the Aristotelian principles he had used in *Gr. Intr.*, but now to present a different model. I render his general argument as follows, from Ch. I.1.

If the planets are to represent changes in the world as a whole, then we should associate the planets with the types of motion (i.e., change) that are universally possible. Following Aristotle's *De Caelo* I.2, 268b, 11-25 (approximately), there are three natural motions if we assume the basic shapes of a line and a circle. We can treat the center of the earth as a point at the center of the universe, and draw a line from it out into the universe: this accounts for motions to and from the earth, particularly the motion of the elements to

---

[7] Robbins, pp. 195-97.

their "natural places": fire and air up high, water and earth down low and close to the center of the earth. We can also use a compass to draw a circle around the earth or center point, which accounts for circular motion. This means there are three basic types of motion: away from the center, towards the center, and around the center. Now since the planets can be divided into three categories (superiors, inferiors, and the Sun between them), we can start to associate planetary motions and meanings with these three categories. Moreover, within the categories of superiors and inferiors, he perceives a process much like the quadruplicities: beginnings (like the convertible signs), consolidations and maturity (like the fixed signs), and corruption and change (like the double-bodied signs). The following table illustrates what he means.

| Motion | Planet | Time period | Stages | Indications |
|---|---|---|---|---|
| Around center | ♄ | Long | Beginning | Religions, dynasties |
| | ♃ | | Completion | Laws |
| | ♂ | | Breakdown | War, struggle |
| From center | ☉ | Medium | | Kings, overlords |
| Towards center | ♀ | Short | Beginning | Marriage, garments |
| | ☿ | | Completion | Writing, calculation |
| | ☽ | | Breakdown | Migration, travel |

Figure 1: General theory of mundane astrology (*BRD* I.1)

In this table, the superior planets indicate broad civilizational effects. Saturn indicates something like "the lawgiver," where long-lasting principles of a civilization are set down; this is a beginning. Then this is elaborated and codified through laws, established practices, and accumulated wisdom (Jupiter). Finally, Mars indicates these things' breakdown through conflict, struggle, and the use of violent compulsion.

The inferior planets indicate more day-to-day cultural dynamics. Venus is like a beginning, because marriage relationships establish bonds which transmit the basic culture on to new generations. One might wonder about "garments," but in older societies the colors and types of dress often indicated rank and status, more so than today. Such cultural indicators regulated a lot of social behavior. Mercury is a bit harder to pin down, but seems to indicate transmitted teachings which help codify all of this, as well as calculations about taxes and such which regulate life in various ways. Finally, the Moon indicates forms of migration, travel, and communication, which often instigate or are the result of cultural changes.

In the center is the Sun. In the context of an entire civilization or culture, he represents temporal authority and leaders, who mediate between the foundations of the civilization (the superiors), and its daily operation (the inferiors). This will lead us to a possible conflict or at least ambiguity when it comes to chart interpretation. For, we customarily associate the Sun with authority and a sovereign. However, in both *BRD* and the Persian model, Saturn represents the "lawgiver," who might *also* be a particular person, such as a prophet like Muhammad. And in the Persian model itself, Saturn represents something like "the establishment" or "the permanent administration" or even "the king." (In modern parlance, this might be compared to the bureaucratic "deep state.") So although we might want to seize upon the Sun as representing the king at the center of society, in some of *BRD*'s material the Sun actually acts more as a generic principle of authority as such—so that if some planet is associated with the Sun, that class of people is trying to gain authority, even if they or it do not act exactly as a particular human king. In other words, even though the planetary hierarchy and Aristotelian movements may provide a blueprint for civilization as such, it doesn't mean that in every instance a planet's archetypal meaning will immediately indicate a particular class of people. This is something that we will have to work out in practice.

Finally, although he does not elaborate on this much, the planets which form the beginnings, culmination, and corruption within their own category also correspond to each other: for instance, under the higher conceptual rubric of corruption and change, war (Mars) is often associated with real-time migration and population disruption (Moon).

## §4: Persian model of politics

Above I mentioned that Abū Ma'shar's use of the superiors to justify mundane astrology was probably related to a "Persian" theory of the superiors. With my new translations of Sahl and Mūsā, we can now see its scope and influence, which will appear in more detail in the Sahl volume (*AWS*).

This Persian theory assigns special titles to the superiors, and in the case of Saturn and Jupiter they at first appear to be called the first and second "Lots" (سهم), respectively. One can see this unusual appellation in a number of sources, such as in *Scito*, quotations in al-Rijāl, in Māshā'allāh's *Book of Conjunctions*, and Abū Ma'shar refers to it (while apparently not understanding it) here in Ch. II.5, **102**. Indeed, *BRD* includes several sentences which can be traced back to the theory, either implicitly or explicitly. (And Mūsā uses this theory liberally throughout *Fulfilment*.)

However, it turns out that "Lot" is not the correct translation. The normal word for a Lot in Arabic (سهم) actually means an "arrow," and was adopted to mean a Lot because of the practice of inscribing names on arrows (and in other cultures, other things), which are then drawn as lots for purposes of divination. But in Sahl we can see the full mundane context: Saturn and Jupiter are the two Arrows, and Mars is the Sword, and these three *military* terms together are meant to provide a guide to understanding and predicting the activities of the government, rebels, propaganda, coups, and so on. Saturn is the "First Arrow," and represents the current administration (especially as personified in the current king or Caliph). Jupiter is the "Second Arrow," and represents reformers and moralizers who challenge the current authority (and would like to take authority for themselves). The model for this is pious or even self-righteous public persons who are both powerful in society and want to change it or at least the current administration's practices. Mars is "the Sword," and represents several types of attack upon the regime *or* reformers, from within the government and elites: from actual rebels and armies, to propaganda and fomenting civil unrest, to more legalistic challenges. Within this framework then, the mutual transits and aspects between the superiors trace a kind of political drama unfolding within the realm. For example, if Mars separates from Jupiter and applies to Saturn, then the reformers are attacking (via propaganda, for instance) the king; but if he separates from Saturn and applies to Jupiter, the king is attacking the reformers. All of this is captured within Ch. 8 of Sahl's book, but several passages in *BRD* are implicitly or explicitly drawn from this doctrine and its presentation in Sahl:

- II.1, **17-18**. I don't find this in Sahl, but it matches the Persian approach.
- II.5, **15**: This is very similar to 'Umar al-Tabarī in al-Rijāl's VIII.20, **11**.
- II.7, **2-4**. Not in Sahl, but matches the Persian approach.
- II.7, **9-10**. *Ditto.*
- II.7, **24-28**. *Ditto;* but it starts out similarly to Sahl's Ch. 8.1, **38**.
- VIII.1, **56-57**. This is found in Sahl's Ch. 8.1, **44-45**.

At this point let us turn to the primary historical framework in traditional mundane astrology: conjunctions, their periods and patterns.

## §5: *Conjunctions, shifts, & ingresses (Chs. I.1-I.2)*

The primary way of understanding historical periods and changes was through Saturn-Jupiter conjunctions. Saturn-Jupiter conjunctions occur at regular intervals and form certain patterns which make them ideal for understanding time at the level of short periods or short generations, longer periods of centuries, and middling periods. The following table from my Mūsā book explains what I mean. But the reader should remember that since the symbolic meaning of a conjunction is a change in laws, morals, and culture, when Abū Ma'shar and others interpret them they often speak of them in dramatic and destructive tones: they are not just timing devices.

On the right we see four types of Saturn-Jupiter conjunctions, which are given special names by Mūsā. At the bottom are the "Twenties," so-called because every Saturn-Jupiter conjunctions occur approximately every 20 years. This means that any given conjunction chart taken by itself (and always cast for the Aries ingress of the seasonal year in which it occurs) holds good for 20 years. This is an ideal, short period when considering the terms of rulers, economic trends, and cultural changes. On the far left you can see that Mūsā considers this the "lesser" or smallest type of conjunction—both in its historical importance and its narrowly-defined time period. Underneath it are the annual Aries ingresses, which means that annual ingresses are considered to be part of the process of whatever Twenty they take place in. Thus, let Saturn and Jupiter conjoin in Leo: the conjunction chart stands both for that year and as a thematic chart for 20 years, and the following 19 ingresses act as annual charts which fall under that Leo conjunction chart.

|  | Time lords<br>All begin from 0° ♈ | ♄-♃ Conjunctions |
|---|---|---|
| **Mighty** | **Thousand (360,000 years)**<br>Direct 1° / 1,000 years<br>Profect 1 sign / 1,000 years | ♄♃☌ at 0° ♈ (960y)<br>☌ returns to fiery triplicity |
| **Following the mighty (the "Turn")** | **The 360 (360-year cycles)**<br>Sign-planet rotation from ♈-♄<br>In 360-year groups and Singles | |
| **Greater** | **Hundred (1,200-year cycles)**<br>Direct 1° / 100 years<br>Profect 1 sign / 100 years | Triplicity shift (240y)<br>☌ shifts to new triplicity |
| **Middle** | **Ten (120-year cycles)**<br>Direct 1° / 10 years<br>Profect 1 sign / 10 years | Sixty (60y)<br>☌ returns to sign of shift |
| **Lesser** | **Single (12-year cycles)**<br>Direct 1° / 1 year<br>Profect 1 sign / 1 year | Twenty (20y)<br>☌ moves to next sign |
| | **Annual ♈ ingress**<br>*Individual years and their subdivisions* | |

**Figure 2: Time lords and conjunctions classified**

As we move upwards from the Twenties, we find that sets of conjunctions fit into a hierarchy of patterns, so that no chart truly stands alone. The first pattern is created within a single triplicity: every Twenty occurs in roughly a backwards trine from the previous one, except that it advances a couple of degrees in whatever the new sign is. The Figure here illustrates Abū Ma'shar's version of this. Let there be

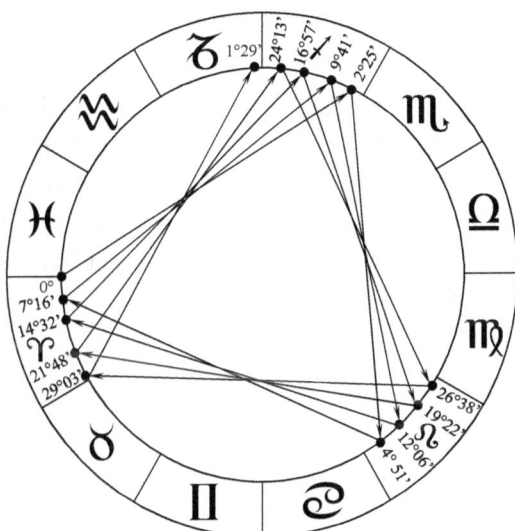

**Figure 3: Abū Ma'shar's triplicity shift after 13 conjunctions**

a conjunction at 0° Aries: this is a Twenty. After about 20 years, they will conjoin in another Twenty, but this time in Sagittarius: a backwards trine, but advancing about 2° 25'. The next Twenty will be in Leo, again a backwards trine but advancing to 4° 51'.

The conjunctions keep occurring in the fiery triplicity, in a kind of slowly-rotating triangle, until they get to the Twenty in 29° 03' Aries. Because each conjunction creeps forward slightly, the next conjunction will not be in Sagittarius, but just at the beginning of Capricorn, an earthy sign: this is the "conjunction of the shift" or a "triplicity shift," which will occur after approximately 10-11 Twenties, or about 200 – 220 years. This is Mūsā's "greater" conjunction.

Figure 4 illustrates how the triplicity system of conjunctions must be understood; I use the recent earthy triplicity as an example. The shift into earth occurred in Virgo in 1802, and lasted until 2000: the chart of the earthy shift theoretically governs 198 years. But within that triplicity, the Virgo conjunction chart also acted as the first 20 years of that series (1802-1822); the Taurus chart (1822-1841) the roughly next 20 years; and so on. So we have conjunctions of lesser duration nested within a master chart of a longer duration.

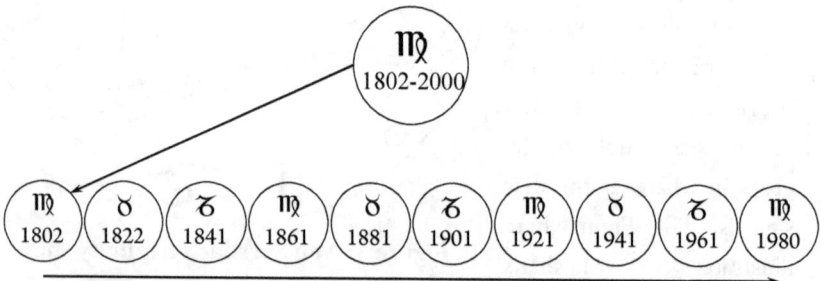

Figure 4: Earthy triplicity shift and conjunctions (Twenties)

Groups of Twenties will continue within a triplicity, and make triplicity shifts, until they return to about 0° Aries every 820 years or so (but in Mūsā and Abū Ma'shar, 960, due to their different astronomical parameters). This is a "mighty" conjunction, which then begins another series of triplicities and shifts.

But between the triplicity shifts and the Twenties are another kind of conjunction that happens within a triplicity: a Sixty, which occurs when the rotating sets of Twenties return to the sign in which the shift occurred. Let a triplicity shift happen at the beginning of Virgo: the Twenties continue until they return to Virgo, 60 years later and every 60 thereafter, in conjunctions #4, #7, and #10. Abū Ma'shar mentions this only briefly in *BRD*, but Mūsā gives them a central place in his system, because the meaning of the entire triplicity series will be reaffirmed at one or more of the Sixties—each one, remember, governing 20 years by itself.

Thus, every conjunction is a Twenty, every third or fourth is also a Sixty, every eleventh or so is a Twenty and also a triplicity shift, and every forty-something conjunction is a Twenty, a triplicity shift, and a mighty conjunction around 0° Aries. All of these charts also comprise about twenty individual years of ingresses under them. In this way, any year can be identified as part of some historical process as well as standing for a year in its own right.

Triplicity shift charts are the dominant charts in both Abū Ma'shar's and Mūsā's schemes. I will return to them below, but the central point is that they must be examined because they indicate the largest and longest changes to cultures and politics, including through war. Because of this, I also offer a warning to the student who would like to dive right in and find historical "hits" for his favored world events: civilizations, countries, and cultures are extremely complicated, and we should expect that mundane astrology requires knowledge of politics, economics, military history, and cultural history. Lucky "hits" for certain events are not enough.

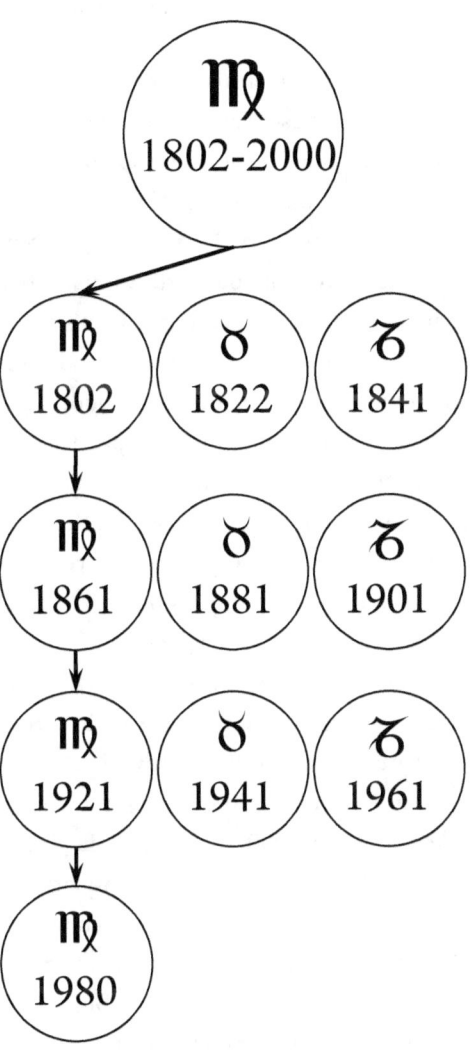

**Figure 5: List of modern Sixties**

## Mean conjunctions and modern parameters

In order to determine the exact distance between conjunctions (their conjunctional distance) and the length of time between them (their conjunctional period), mundane astrologers in the Arabic period standardly used "mean" conjunctions. Now, in everyday astrology, we deal with "true" conjunctions and "true" positions, which means we reckon where the planets actually are, from our earthly perspective, taking retrogradation and daily changes of speed into account. That's where we place the planets in a chart. So a "true" conjunction of Saturn and Jupiter at 15° Gemini means that we could look up and see their very bodies conjoined closely in the heavens at 15° Gemini, from our visual perspective.

But there is a problem with true conjunctions. Since Jupiter is faster and both he and Saturn go retrograde, they sometimes make true conjunctions several times over the period of a year; and if this happens around a sign boundary, it will be impossible to tell whether the conjunction belongs to the current triplicity, a triplicity shift, or even a sign of the past triplicity (if the shift has already happened). This happened in the late 20th Century, when the mean conjunctions were in earthy signs. The mean conjunction of 1980 was in Virgo, still an earthy sign, and the mean triplicity shift to air took place in Gemini in 2000. But by true positions, the 1980 conjunction was in *Libra*, and the 2000 conjunction in *Taurus*. Only in 2020 were both the mean and true conjunctions in Aquarius. This means there was a 40-year period by true conjunctions in which there was not a clear shift from earth to air. Now, it might be that when the two types of conjunction do not match, this has an interpretive meaning. But unless we recognize the difference between them, we cannot tell what it is.

Mean conjunctions are meant to solve this problem, and the diagram of conjunctions above shows Abū Ma'shar's version of them. A planet's "mean" motion or position refers to the idealized position it *would* be at, if it moved at a constant rate and never went retrograde. In fact, the distinction between mean and true motions and positions was key in ancient astrology, because it allowed one to have workable tables. First, the astrologer would calculate the mean or expected position of a planet for some day; then, based on other factors (like knowing when and where retrogradations happen), one could add or subtract certain degrees to get the "true" position we actually observe. These corrections to the mean position were called "equations" and were gotten from a table. (In other words, a mean position, plus an equation or correction, yields the true position. The true position was sometimes called the "equated" position.)

The advantage of mean positions is that one can calculate *exact* distances and periods for planetary conjunctions, over a long period of time (since they involve uniform motion), as long as one is prepared to accept that they are a kind of abstraction and not how the "true" planet behaves. The disadvantage is that the mean position of a planet is invisible: two planets' mean positions might be mathematically conjoined, but in terms of their true, observable motions one of them might be moving more quickly direct, and the other retrograde, so that they don't *appear* to be conjoined. In the Figure here for the actual date of the 1901 mean conjunction, the mean positions of Saturn and Jupiter are at the same degree (15° 12' Capricorn); but because of their motion on their epicycles, their "true," visible positions are quite far away.

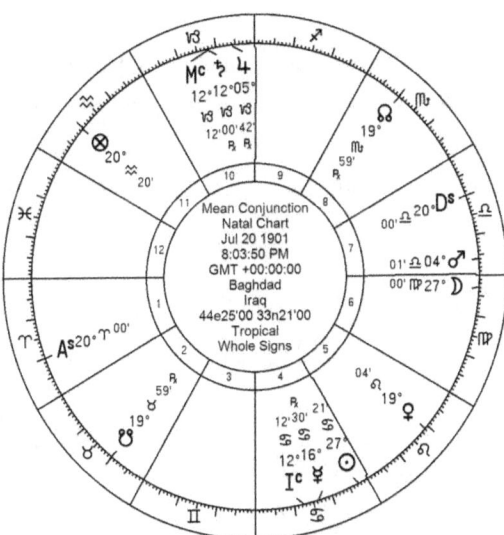

Figure 6: 1901 mean conjunction

Over time then, we know that mean motion is valuable, and mean conjunctions happen regularly and predictably—albeit invisibly. When we look at a particular mean conjunction it will not appear to be "true." On the other hand, turning only to true conjunctions means not being able to tell where triplicity shifts happen at all.[8] So, astrologers took the tropical cycles of Saturn and Jupiter, and combined them in the following formulas in order to tell exactly when and how far away their mean conjunctions occurred. The

---

[8] Al-Battānī rejected mean conjunctions altogether.

"periods" below refer to the mean tropical periods of two planets (namely, Saturn and Jupiter):

**Length of a conjunctional period:**
(Period 1 * Period 2) / (Period 1 − Period 2)

**Distance between conjunctions:**
( ( Conjunctional period - shorter period ) / shorter period ) * 360

By inserting modern period values into the equations, we get the following:

| NASA Tropical Year: 365.24219 days | | | |
|---|---|---|---|
| NASA Sidereal Year: 365.256363 days | | | |
| | Conjunctional period (years) | Conj. distance | Conj. per triplicity |
| *Tropical Period/Years:* Saturn: 29.4241473 Jupiter: 11.85677646 | 19.85929143 | 242.9754326° = advance of 2° 58' 32" | 10-11 |
| *Sidereal Period/Years:* Saturn: 29.45662578 Jupiter: 11.86177556 | 19.8585313 | 242.6982412° = advance of 2° 41' 54" | 11-12 |

Figure 7: Complete table of mean conjunctions and distances

Figure 8 illustrates what I mean. Let's begin with the mean positions of Saturn and Jupiter at 0° Aries (or anywhere), and let them advance at their mean rates. You can see that over the next 19.85 years, they will travel at different rates, with Jupiter finally catching up with Saturn again at about 242° from their original mean conjunction. This is one mean conjunctional period. It happens with such exactness that we can project these cycles out for centuries at a time.

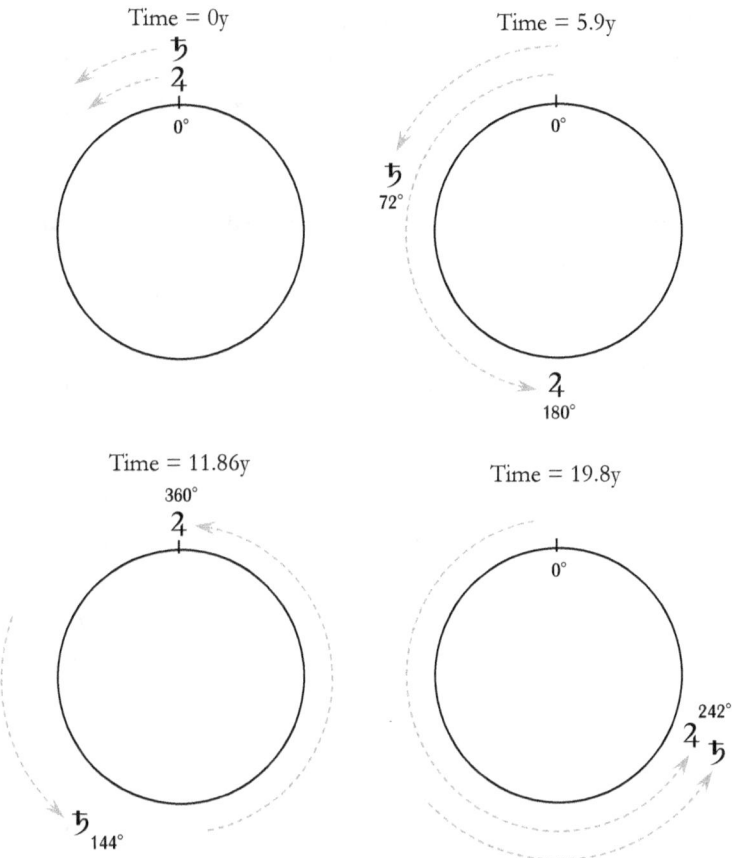

**Figure 8: Illustration of mean conjunctional period**

Unfortunately, Abū Ma'shar's values for the conjunctional period, the triplicity shift, and the exact degrees are all wrong as compared to our modern values for the tropical zodiac and the sidereal zodiac he was using. The table below shows the correct ones. In our modern tropical zodiac, if Saturn and Jupiter conjoined at 0° Aries, the next conjunction in Sagittarius would be at 2.975° (2° 58' 30"), and if we keep the series going you can see it will shift into earth—and actually in Virgo—after only 11 conjunctions, at 2.730° (2° 43' 48" Virgo), not at 1° Capricorn. If we continue, the earthy triplicity will continue only for 10 conjunctions. On the right we can see the modern sidereal values, which would have 12 conjunctions in the fiery triplicity and 11 in the earthy. So, the different zodiacs operate at different speeds. It's important to know this because medieval astrologers tended to simply copy over the rounded-up values they found, and often assumed that these shifts would happen every 12 conjunctions—a nice symbolic number, but inaccurate.

| Tropical Series | Distance | Sidereal Series | Distance |
|---|---|---|---|
| Fire (1) | 0° | Fire (1) | 0° |
| 2 | 2.975° | 2 | 2.698° |
| 3 | 5.951° | 3 | 5.396° |
| 4 | 8.926° | 4 | 8.095° |
| 5 | 11.902° | 5 | 10.793° |
| 6 | 14.877° | 6 | 13.491° |
| 7 | 17.853° | 7 | 16.189° |
| 8 | 20.828° | 8 | 18.888° |
| 9 | 23.803° | 9 | 21.586° |
| 10 | 26.779° | 10 | 24.284° |
| 11 | 29.754° | 11 | 26.982° |
| Earth (1) | 2.730° | 12 | 29.681° |
| 2 | 5.705° | Earth (1) | 2.379° |
| 3 | 8.681° | 2 | 5.077° |
| 4 | 11.656° | 3 | 7.775° |
| 5 | 14.631° | 4 | 10.474° |
| 6 | 17.607° | 5 | 13.172° |
| 7 | 20.582° | 6 | 15.870° |
| 8 | 23.558° | 7 | 18.568° |
| 9 | 26.533° | 8 | 21.267° |
| 10 | 29.509° | 9 | 23.965° |
| | | 10 | 26.663° |
| | | 11 | 29.361° |

**Figure 9: Modern tropical & sidereal triplicity shifts compared**

## Abū Ma'shar's parameters

At this point the reader should understand Abū Ma'shar's astronomical parameters, because there are some flaws in them and we must use modern ones instead. Abū Ma'shar's parameters rest on two different concepts: (1) the sidereal year and zodiac, and (2) his theory of periodic conjunctions over 360,000 sidereal years. Abū Ma'shar lays out his calculations for conjunctions in an interlude at Ch. I.1, **30-63**.

(1) As I explained in *AW2*, Abū Ma'shar does not use a tropical year for measuring conjunctions, but rather a sidereal year of 365.259 days. This is slightly longer than NASA's modern value of 365.256363 days, but close to it. It's important to keep this in mind, because in I.1, **34** he complicates things unnecessarily by noting that the amount of time between conjunctions is a certain number of years and days in "years of the mean Sun," which he explains is exactly 365 days. This is true, but an irrelevant bit of data that can easily confuse the reader.

(2) More importantly, and again as I explained in *AW2*, Abū Ma'shar believes in a theory that all of the planets conjoin (in a mean conjunction) every 360,000 years. If so, then all planets will have made an integer (whole) number of cycles around the zodiac in that time: if they had only made a certain integer number of cycles plus or minus some fraction, they could not be conjoined at exactly that time. Now it so happens that Abū Ma'shar's Indian sources did *not* show an integer number of cycles for Saturn at that time. So, to make the parameters fit the theory, Abū Ma'shar rounded the number of cycles for Saturn up to the nearest whole number. *He altered the data to match his theory.*

Thus, Abū Ma'shar combines the (1) too-long sidereal year with (2) the wrong number of cycles, yielding calculations we cannot use today—especially if we are using a tropical zodiac and year. Following is a summary of Abū Ma'shar's parameters and values as presented in I.1:

- Sidereal year: 365.259 days.
- Saturn cycles in 360,000 sidereal years: 12,214.
- Jupiter cycles in 360,000 sidereal years: 30,352.
- Sidereal period of Saturn: 29.47437367 sidereal years.
- Sidereal period of Jupiter: 11.86083289 sidereal years.
- Conjunctional period: 19.84783328 sid. years (7249.599736 days).
- Conjunctional distance: 242.42143566° (242° 25' 17" 10''' 06'''').
- Number of conjunctions in each triplicity: 12-13.

**Figure 10: Abū Ma'shar's parameters for Saturn-Jupiter conjunctions**

*Conjunctions and elements*

When we read the Arabic material, we find a lack of something we might otherwise expect. Nowadays astrologers put great value in interpreting the elements, so if we put on our interpretive hats, we might expect that this 198 years or so in the earthy triplicity has something to do with what the earthy element "means." But oddly enough, this is not how the Arabic astrologers thought. The triplicity system is largely a framing and timing device, and they did not interpret the whole period according to the elements.[9] They didn't think, for example, that the fiery triplicity would be full of wars, the watery triplicity full of emotions, and so on. (I think there are some ways that we can probably do this properly, but I'll leave that for another time.) Instead, they looked at patterns and added some sacred geometry. Thus, if the triplicity shift occurred in Virgo, then we should expect other major changes which are of the theme of the period, in subsequent Virgo conjunctions (the Sixties)—or maybe they might be experienced or glimpsed in a year whose Ascendant was Virgo. In Ch. I.2 Abū Ma'shar offers three other possibilities based on sacred geometry. In the earthy triplicity, the manifestation of the effects might happen in (1) the 4$^{th}$ conjunction after the return to the sign of the shift, or in (2) the 8$^{th}$ after the conjunction itself, or generally in (3) the Capricorn conjunctions. In the case here, the conjunction re-

---

[9] An exception would be in I.2, **30-31** where Abū Ma'shar uses a traditional classification of social ranks: for example, that watery and earthy signs indicate lower classes. See also *Gr. Intr.* VI.11.

turned to Virgo in 1861. If we count this as the 1ˢᵗ conjunction, then (1) the 4ᵗʰ conjunction is the Virgo conjunction of 1921-41. If we count the triplicity shift as the 1ˢᵗ conjunction, then (2) the 8ᵗʰ overall is the Taurus conjunction of 1941-61. If we use Capricorn, then we are looking at (3) the conjunctions of 1841-61, 1901-21, and 1961-80.[10]

|  | ♂ after return to shift | Or ♂ after shift: |
|---|---|---|
| Fire | 3 | 9 |
| Air | 4 | 8 |
| Earth | 4 | 8 |
| Water | 2 | 6 |

**Figure 11: Effects in which conjunction**

### §6: "What does the chart say?" A few words on chart interpretation

Ultimately, as astrologers we are chart readers: we want to pick up a piece of paper and know, "what does the chart say?" In terms of mundane astrology I have struggled with this for many years, because different authors emphasize different approaches, and there are many factors to consider. It is only in the past few years, as I have finished my natal course and translated Mūsā, that I feel like I can begin to address the matter here. For reasons that should already be clear, chart interpretation in mundane astrology requires some shifts in thinking. I list here some considerations that should help, and I will expand on them in my Mūsā volume, as well as Sahl and probably Abū Qumash.

1. *Approaches we should use (but the older authors rarely or don't describe).* Given that so much of mundane astrology borrows from nativities, here are a few ideas for applying natal techniques which could help structure the order of interpretation:

---

[10] The reason for Capricorn as the dominating conjunction, is because it is the house of Saturn, the superior planet. See Ch. I.2: in fire, the Sagittarius conjunction dominates because it's ruled by Jupiter; in earth, Capricorn as the house of Saturn; in air, Aquarius as the house of Saturn; in water, Pisces as the house of Jupiter.

- *A general appraisal of annual happiness.* In his *Revolutions* Ch. 1.1, Sahl offers some rules for evaluating whether the people are generally happy, confident, and have trust in the government. These include the lord of the Ascendant, the sect light, and other things. However, the ancients already had a natal technique for this, which deals with the native's overall prosperity, happiness, life path, and the support he has for this in life. It is well attested in Dorotheus and Valens, and includes the following: the sect light with its two triplicity lords, combined with the Fortune angles. I think it would be good to use this to formalize the full technique for mundane purposes.
- *The Lot of Fortune and its angles.* Although Fortune is used in the technique above, it seems to me that we should be using Fortune much more in its own right. For Fortune generally describes how many different causes coalesce so as to produce (or hinder) opportunities and choices for the native. Since mundane astrology trades in large-scale processes (such as the economy), we should pay more attention to the Lot.
- *Applying the advanced natal model of topics.* In full-scale natal astrology, there are three classes of things to examine for every (or almost every) topic. First, a natural significator with its triplicity lords; second, a place and its lord; third, a Lot and its lord. Thus when evaluating fertility and children, we look at Jupiter and his triplicity lords, the fifth place and its lord, and the Lot of children and its lord. This should be adapted to the many mundane topics we are interested in. I have already suggested one of these above: the sect light and its triplicity lords, the first place and its lord, and the Lot of Fortune and its lord. But we could probably do something like this for other topics, if they are suitably converted to mundane meanings.
- *Developing checklists for various topics.* This builds upon the previous point. In certain mundane works there are chapters and lists of indications for things like the rise and fall of prices, war, and so on. These should be put into checklists, especially if we have integrated the advanced natal techniques into them. When many astrologers

prepare for clients, there is usually a favored list of "top-line" items which are reviewed, with interesting chart features flagged for further discussion: for example, the Ascendant and its lord, the Midheaven and planets in it, maybe a couple of favored Lots, and then some planetary configuration or condition to be discussed. I myself teach a "fast track" method like this in my course, where we look at a few Lots, the fortune of the sect and the infortune contrary, the most advancing or angular planets, and so on. It should be possible to develop a prioritized list of topics, with their complete method of interpretation.

2. *Some advice.* This is based on traditional texts, as well as my own experience and observations.

- *Embeddedness.* In mundane astrology especially, no chart stands alone. Any ingress chart—even a triplicity shift—is like a solar revolution, which needs to be compared to a previous chart. We will see that Abū Ma'shar and Mūsā have ideas about how the Ascendants of consecutive triplicity shifts may show continuity of rule (or, war and a change of dynasty). Again, any merely annual chart occupies one year in the period ruled by a conjunction, so one must compare an ingress to the conjunctional chart before it. For example, suppose the profected Ascendant of the most recent conjunction comes to the Mars in that chart: we must then see how Mars appears in the current ingress, and whether it actually supports increased Martial influences at that time. Even then, certain events foretold in the shift are supposed to be especially visible in the conjunctions called the Sixties: so one must be aware of which conjunction one is actually in.

- *Regionality.* This is rarely ever discussed, if ever, but I have been raising it in my workshops on eclipses. The fact is that, if one casts ingress charts for the capitals of countries which are close geographically, they will often share the same rising sign. Whether one uses whole signs or quadrant divisions, this means that the charts will often look very similar, and it's hard to tell one country from another. One can see this on a map, if one casts Ascendants for such capitals: for example, at an Aries ingress all or most of Europe might have Gemini rising, which means that the infortunes will be in, squaring, or opposing, virtually the same places in each chart. This astronomical fact reflects the empirical fact that a lot of politics is connected and regional. If there is civil unrest in one country, its neighbors will also feel the effects (and perhaps, reflect them in their charts), even if they do not have civil unrest. Thus, we need to understand what is going on in a whole region, rather than sticking to particular charts. But this leads to two other considerations. First, interpreting the chart of a regional hegemon might be more useful than those of tinier states. For instance, I conjecture that the Beijing chart might be more useful for the region around China, than the Mongolia chart. But second, where we do have large countries (which are often but not always the hegemon), it might be good to cast charts for major cities or the locations where certain decisions are made. The unique politics and culture of the West Coast of the USA suggests that charts for Los Angeles may be more informative for them, than Washington, DC.[11] Likewise, using the chart for Chicago might be more informative for tracking commodities prices (due to the Chicago Board of Trade being located there), than Washington, DC.

- *Layers of interpretation.* We can discern several layers of interpretation which the traditional astrologers followed, even though we obviously need a more comprehensive and disciplined approach. In one layer, they used chorography to describe effects on nations in general: so if Mars squared a certain sign at an ingress, it might affect Khurāsān or Azerbaijān. This use of chorography will be independent of chart details: in the Sasanian-Arabic scheme, certain planets and signs indicated Azerbaijān and so it means something for Azerbaijān no matter where you cast the chart for.

---

[11] Obviously this would be even more important if one is experimenting with weather astrology.

But in France, the very same sign might indicate Germany or Italy, so one does have to get one's chorography straight, at least for the region one is working with. In another layer, they used general significators and their aspects to describe phenomena particular to the country of the chart (or more likely, the regional hegemon or capital of an empire): thus for example if the Sun sextiles Mars, then since the Sun indicates authority and the Mars the army, then the army will be confident, powerful, and so on (but perhaps may suggest uprisings and conflict as a result). This is sometimes combined with the goodness of the places where the Sun and Mars are—one can see this particularly in Mūsā. Third, there is straightforward planet-in-place interpretations, such as Venus in the 11th, or some planet squaring the lord of the fifth. I will have more to say about this in my Introduction to Mūsā. Finally, there are the observations about how the ingress chart relates to earlier charts, which I mentioned above.

3. *Political bias.* This is an extremely important point. Permit me some teasing about the countless times I've heard contemporary mundane astrologers predict a "transformation of consciousness" in the world, which usually involves Leftist fetishes like a revolt against capitalism and the like. How many transformations of consciousness can we count in the past 50 years? Mundane astrology teaches that attitudes about economics, society, culture, and so on actually last for decades and centuries—which is what we should be tracking, not using yesterday's issues of *The Guardian* to predict annual results. Or suppose we have some ingress configuration that appears to some people to indicate a disastrous leader, but to others the collapse and corruption of the establishment? Which is the correct interpretation? Traditional astrologers worked for many administrations and had to navigate these tricky situations, sometimes at the price of their own heads: we can't simply confirm our own biases, especially when they do not yield correct results. Sometimes our favorite policies and leaders are losers, and the people we hate are winners. We must be able to fit events and trends fairly into a historical scheme that will stand up well to time.

## §7: Overview & structure

For the sake of simplicity, *BRD* can be divided into three parts. The first part comprises Books I and II. Here, Abū Ma'shar presents his justification of mundane astrology, special details about Saturn-Jupiter conjunctions, and rules for predicting and interpreting the appearance and careers of prophets, kings, and dynasties. For most people, this will be the "new" and juiciest information.

The second part comprises Books III-VII, i.e., most of the book. Here, Abū Ma'shar presents all manner of interpretive combinations, systematically moving through planetary placements, aspects, and Ascendants. (As in his natal predictive work, there is an emphasis on Ascendants.) However, it is not clear that he handled his source materials in tandem: that is, aspect combinations might have been gotten from one source, planetary placements from another, and so on. Thus, we cannot assume that the various methods and details of interpretation actually cohere with one another. But taken all together, they purport to provide a complete way of interpreting charts.

The third and final part is Book VIII.

*Book I*: This Book begins with the basic principles and techniques of mundane astrology, and then turns to prophets. As for the principles and techniques (I.1), they range from Abū Ma'shar's version of the "Persian" model of political astrology I mentioned above, to the specific predictive techniques and types of chart he will use. Then we turn to some ideas about when the meaning of a chart will manifest (I.3), and identifying and predicting (or tracking) the birth and careers of would-be prophets (I.3-I.4). The reason for beginning with prophets is simply this: that as spiritual and often legal figures, they are primarily responsible for the development of new civilizations, cultures, and religious communities.

*Book II*: This book is devoted to kings and dynasties: when a change of dynasty will occur, where it will be based, and what it will be like (II.1-II.3), and identifying the nativities of kings, their careers, and downfalls (II.4-II.7). Then in II.8, Abū Ma'shar turns to some other ways of timing civil unrest, the downfall of kings, changes of dynasty, and the appearance of prophets: Saturn-Mars conjunctions in Cancer (**3-30**), Saturn-Mars conjunctions in other signs taken individually (**32-60**), in the exaltation signs (**62-68**), the infortunes in the triplicities (**69-129**), the Saturn-Jupiter conjunctions in the Sixties (**139-45**), Saturn cycles (**146-57**), and the greatest years of the planets (**158-62**). A short discussion of trepidation theory ends the chapter.

In a certain sense, Books I-II are the heart of the work. In theory, if one knew the mundane significations of houses and places (including for weather and chorography, not just politics), and how Abū Ma'shar's natal predictive system is being overlaid onto mundane charts, one could possibly reconstruct the rest of the books. But let us turn to them now and make some commentary on them.

The middle of *BRD* really shows how the signs of conjunctions and Ascendants (of all types) play a central role in Abū Ma'shar's approach. There is a constant emphasis on (1) the Ascendants of triplicity shifts, the Twenties, and annual Aries ingresses, which are a kind of solar revolution (SR) for the world, just as a natal SR is for a natal chart. Predictively we also emphasize (2) profection from the Ascendant of a major chart (like a shift), from the Ascendant of a Twenty, and from the sign of the conjunction.

*Book III: Ascendants and what the people are like.* Here Abū Ma'shar considers planets which are combining by conjunction or aspect *in* an Ascendant: the Ascendant of a shift, in the sign of a profected Ascendant (probably, both in the shift chart or in real time later), or in the Ascendant of an ingress. Abū Ma'shar reminds us that the superior planets have a more intrinsic relation to mundane astrology, so their conjunctions will tend to be more long-lasting and notable, especially from the start—whereas conjunctions with inferiors may be more intermittent or take a long time to manifest. Overall, Abū Ma'shar means this to show what the people of a particular religious community or civilization (viz., the ones indicated by the shift) will be like, or do, or be interested in—that is, especially if the planets are applying. But if they are separating, it shows what the people of that culture have little engagement in or even reject.[12] Such configurations in the Ascendants

---

[12] III.6, **10-11**.

of annual SRs show the same thing, but for shorter amounts of time.[13] My sense is that, for charts like a shift, they may not define a culture as such but show some cultural trends which are deeply embedded in the value system; perhaps in a Twenty they show more generational concerns.

The interpretations are rather similar to Dorotheus's in *Carmen*, but are given a mundane slant. The reader should be aware of Abū Ma'shar's use of squares, however: sometimes he may speak of a planet looking at the planet in the Ascendant "from the fourth," which might seem to mean "from the fourth place," which is a square. But the interpretation might fit the *overcoming* square more so than the inferior square, meaning that Abū Ma'shar is perhaps not that picky about which interpretation in Dorotheus he has adapted. There does not seem to be any relationship to the work of Theophilus of Edessa, perhaps because he was a more strictly military astrologer, and not more broadly a mundane one.

*Book IV: The signs as Ascendants; chorography.* Here each sign is interpreted as an Ascendant: of a shift or conjunction, or the profection of an Ascendant or a conjunction, and maybe the Ascendant of any normal ingress. The signs are interpreted in themselves as types of social events and trends, agricultural and weather effects, some politics, and even fashion, particularly for the areas of the earth associated with that sign (such as the province of Fārs for Aries). So, Taurus will have a lot of Taurean-type indications. One should note the prevalence of "Babylon" in many of the chapters: this probably reflects the central influence of this part of Mesopotamia upon the whole region, and that whatever Ascendant is rising in that portion of the world will probably be shared by central and southern Iraq. Also, the last part of each sign is a version of Ptolemy's weather indications for the signs, from *Tet.* II.11; but the mechanics do not make a lot of sense because Ptolemy was not considering them as Ascendants. It does not make sense to say that an Ascendant is in the northern latitude of a sign, for example.

*Book V: Each planet as an Ascendant lord or time lord.* Just as we can consider each sign as an Ascendant of several types, in this Book Abū Ma'shar

---

[13] III.1, **2-3**.

considers each planet as a lord or time lord: as the lord of a particular Ascendant, or as the lord of a profected Ascendant, a mundane distribution, or simply transiting through a sign. Thus if Saturn rules an Ascendant, or a profected Ascendant, a distribution, or transits through some sign, Book V considers each planet in combination with every sign. Obviously, this must be wholly general, but Abū Ma'shar does consider certain planetary conditions. For instance, Saturn has general indications by himself, as well as in certain classes of signs (such as watery signs), in particular signs (such as Aries), and in certain situations such as being northern or southern in latitude, easternizing or westernizing, being direct or retrograde, or being under the rays. The general idea seems to be that if a planet is a time lord, it will affect the class of beings/events of those signs in accordance with its planetary nature. However, in many cases it is difficult to determine clear-cut principles: for instance, why does Saturn retrograde in Taurus mean "the death of a mighty man," or if western, "an abundance of confusions" among the people? Abū Ma'shar is probably simply copying from some other predecessor, and some of the interpretations may be based on actual charts and events which they do not tell us.

*Book VI: Planets' transits over each other, in all signs.* Here we advance beyond planets-in-signs (Book V) by considering [1] each planet transiting all other planets in every sign, and [2] which planet is "higher" and so dominates the transit.

In traditional astrology, [1] a "transit" occurs where a planet actually is, and is primarily concerned with conjunctions. Today we commonly speak of, say, Jupiter's "transiting square to Venus," but this is not how it was primarily understood. Suppose Venus is in Aries, and Jupiter in Capricorn: it would be more accurate to say that Jupiter is transiting *in* Capricorn, and casts a square to Venus. Or, suppose Venus was in Aries in a natal chart, and later on Jupiter transits in Capricorn: it is more accurate to say that *natal Venus squares* Capricorn, and Jupiter is transiting *her square in Capricorn*. This may sound picky, but it could change how we interpret who is doing what in a transit, and it underscores that planets technically only make transits where they actually are. Thus in Book VI, Abū Ma'shar is mainly speaking of two planets conjoining rather than making aspects to each other, which he says are "less in manifestation and weaker in effect."[14]

When speaking of these transits, traditional astrologers wanted to know [2] who was transiting "over" the other, because its effect will dominate.[15] You might think that this simply means "which planet is higher up in the heavens," just as Saturn's sphere is always higher than Jupiter's. But this is not so: let me describe it in a simplified way. To be transiting "over" another planet, means that one planet is proportionately higher up *in its own planetary system* than the other one is. Suppose that there is a Venus-Saturn conjunction: if Venus's position is closer to the top of her deferent circle than Saturn is to his, then Venus is proportionately higher and she will be transiting "over" him despite being actually closer to the earth.

The measurement that is used to determine this, is called the "equation of the center." This is a technical bit of jargon in Ptolemy's astrology, but is very similar to the difference between the mean position of a planet and its true position, as I described above for Saturn-Jupiter conjunctions. Basically, it means this. If we ignore the movement of a planet *around* its epicycle and just focus on where the *center* of the epicycle is, that is the planet's mean position (as we already know). But this center can be viewed from two perspectives: from the equant point (which is part of the planet's system, and where we track its mean motion), and from the earthly or true perspective. Determining this is part of calculating the exact position of the planet itself, and we don't need to go into that any further. If the mean position or center of the epicycle is somewhere ahead of where it is from our perspective, then the planet is descending downwards in its circle. But if the mean position lags behind the true earthly perspective, then it is ascending in it. So, we need to know both values and to compare them; Abū Ma'shar gives an approximation of *pi* (22/7) to give some exactness to this, so we know precisely where a planet is ascending or descending in its circle.

Ascending—or ascending proportionately higher—is considered more powerful than descending, so if in our Venus-Saturn conjunction, Venus was ascending higher in her system and Saturn descending lower in his, then

---

[14] *BRD* VI.1, **13-14**.
[15] See *BRD* VI.1, **4-12**.

Venus would be transiting "over" Saturn, and her effect would be greater. We can see hints of the interpretive meaning of this, if we compare Abū Ma'shar's interpretations. In VI.1 he considers planets in Aries: if Saturn transits "over" Venus, it indicates middling rains because Saturn is a drier planet (**21**); but if she transits "over" him, it indicates more moisture or water because she is a moist planet (**28**). For several of the transits of Saturn over others in Aries, Abū Ma'shar says there will be an establishing of a new king: this is probably because Saturn indicates kingship and Aries is a royal sign, and so if he is higher then it shows this; but other planets transiting over him do not indicate a new king.

I can't say that I understand all of his interpretations, and some baffle me. In some cases it's not clear whether the transit shows a limited and precise effect by itself, or whether it simply highlights events that will be prominent *because* it is a conjunction. For example, Jupiter transiting over Mars in Cancer[16] indicates the death of the king's enemies—as though Jupiter exalted in Cancer somehow indicates royal power—or maybe a state of peace—and Mars in fall there indicates the downfall of hostile elements. That makes some sense. But then he says it *also* indicates "an abundance of robbers" (Mars). Does Mars being involved in a conjunction mean that robbers will be an important topic by itself, even if they and other hostile agents are also suppressed due to Jupiter's being above him? I'm not sure.

*Book VII: Profected or ingress Ascendants, if they activate prior charts' places, conjunctions, or directions and planets.* This is a somewhat confusing chapter, which is described differently in different places. In some ways it reflects the complexity of natal predictive techniques: revolutionary Ascendants and profected Ascendants will activate features of a prior natal chart, and they may have planets in them in the nativity and the revolution. Abū Ma'shar emphasizes three situations: [1] when a profected or ingress Ascendant is on (and so activates) the place of a prior chart; [2] if an ingress planet is transiting in that place of the prior chart; [3] if an ingress planet is in that place of the ingress. See my diagram and footnote at *BRD* VII.3, **2**.

---

[16] *BRD* VI.4, **17**.

Let us look at two chapters to help shine light on this. In VII.1, Abū Ma'shar considers Ascendants themselves. So, suppose that some Saturn-Jupiter conjunction was in Sagittarius, and the Ascendant of that ingress chart was Taurus. Over the next 20 years or so, if that profected Ascendant or an ingress Ascendant was Sagittarius or Taurus, or in a sign where a superior planet was at the conjunction, or a superior planet was transiting in that profected or ingress Ascendant, it will have 1st-place indications: the people's interests and initiatives. Then one looks at the lord of the sign, and interprets it according to its place and condition. This is just like in natal predictive techniques, but it gets complicated because we are comparing two different charts. If the conjunction was in that sign, then because conjunctions show complicated social changes, that year shows complicated changes and often problems. If a planet was transiting in it, then it further describes what the people's experience is like. It also seems that if a *superior* planet was transiting in it, it will especially describe what is happening with government—in line with the Persian theory of the superiors, as I have already described. But suppose the profected Ascendant or ingress Ascendant comes to Gemini, which was the 2nd place of the conjunction chart (or, planets were transiting in the 2nd of the revolution):[17] then the focus of the year will be on trade and people's lifestyles, and planets transiting in it will further describe what is happening with trade and lifestyles.

One possible kink in this otherwise smooth and straightforward approach, is the statement above that planets are transiting in the 2nd of the revolution. For the *Ascendant* is supposed to be activating the features of the previous chart: if the Ascendant is in the 2nd of the chart, *that* is why the *year itself* should be about trade, etc. But perhaps Abū Ma'shar means this: that if the profected or ingress Ascendant is the 2nd of the previous chart, it does mean that; but if planets *are also* transiting in the 2nd of the *ingress*, it simply *reinforces* the fact that trade is a key topic of the year. There is something also ambiguous about the conjunction being in "it," which might be solved in the same way: if the Ascendant was the 2nd of a previous chart, and the *conjunction* is in the 2nd of the *revolution*, it shows great changes in trade.

---

[17] *BRD* VII.2.

Unfortunately, Abū Ma'shar is not so clear and may have been too focused on his cookbook approach to notice that he was creating ambiguities.

*Book VIII: A general guide to disasters, wars, key historical charts, and fardārs.* This Book is a kind of grab-bag of general rules. The first part deals with some handy rules for predicting disasters and wars, and VIII.2 contains some foundational charts for understanding the first few centuries of Islamic rule as well as how to use the "lesser" *fardārs* (see §10.7 below).

The three foundational Islamic charts used by Abū Ma'shar are as follows: [1] the alleged Scorpio conjunction heralding Islam (571 AD), [2] the 'Abbāsid revolution (749 AD), and [3] the triplicity shift to fire which included the civil war between al-Amīn and al-Ma'mūn (809 AD).

### §8: Prophets (Chs. I.3-I.4)

Chapters I.3-I.4 are on the topic of predicting and describing "prophets." This may seem to be an odd topic for an Islamic culture, since Muhammad was said to be the "seal of" (i.e., the last of) the prophets. If so, then it would seem that such a question would be merely historical, concerning prophets prior to the 7th Century, or legitimizing Muhammad's own career astrologically. But in late antiquity, material on the native's "religion" also included the question of whether the native had the power of prophecy itself. And in BRD I.3, **40-47**, Abū Ma'shar applies certain mundane techniques to describe the career of a would-be prophet and leader, 'Alī b. Muhammad "the 'Alawite," who led a large-scale rebellion of primarily black African or "Zanj" laborers in southern Iraq from about 868-883 AD. So the question here is not just about "legitimate" prophets, but others who claimed such a role. The topics discussed include if and when a prophet will appear, what are the astrological proofs of his career, where he will appear, and so on.

For Abū Ma'shar, the primary indication of a future prophet is judged from the triplicity shift: if a superior planet (but especially Saturn) is in the third or ninth division of the chart. The use of superior planets is because they show the most powerful and longest civilizational trends. The mention of quadrant divisions is due to Abū Ma'shar's own preference for these over whole-sign places, which he showed in *PN4*. From such a chart, one then uses the quadruplicity of the Ascendant, the ninth, or the Moon, along with annual profections, to determine when the prophet is born. For example, one might profect from the Ascendant of the shift to the sign of the conjunction to identify the year. Or, if the places just mentioned were in double-bodied signs, the birth might be upon the *second* profection to the conjunction, or in the second conjunction of the triplicity itself: see I.3, **2-3** for his basic rules and an illustrative diagram.

Again, this does not mean that every triplicity shift will show a new prophet.[18]

From there, Abū Ma'shar turns to astrological proofs of a particular candidate's role as a prophet. For instance, certain Lots and signs indicate special physical marks on his body (I.3, **6-23**), or what kinds of revelations they may provide (**24-29**), in what year they will appear (**30-34**), in what city (**35-36**), the length of their careers (**37**), and what calamities they suffer (**38**). Thus for instance, in the case of the aforementioned 'Alī b. Muhammad the 'Alawite, the conjunction was in Sagittarius (indicating Baghdad), and the Ascendant of the triplicity shift to fire in 809 was Scorpio (indicating Basrah). So, he departed Baghdad and his deeds appeared in Basrah. Chapter I.4 goes further into understanding their reforming, religious message (**2-9**), the social effect (**10-32**), and their dress and riding animals (**33-50**). This last part may seem strange, but remember that in the Christian tradition, Jesus entered Jerusalem on a donkey.

## §9: Kings & dynasties (Book II)

Book II is devoted to the vicissitudes of kings and dynasties. Not surprisingly, this is also tied closely to triplicity shifts, but without the specifically religious use of the third and ninth places we find for prophets. Here, we want to know whether and when there will be changes of both dynasties and individual kings, as well as identifying who the likely candidates for kingship

---

[18] *BRD* I.4, **21**. This suggests that a shift which does *not* show a new religion or prophet may simply show a *change* in the religious community. So, a change in religion or prophets requires a shift, but not all shifts have the right indications for one.

are. This is harder to apply to the modern era, when so many countries have regular elections. But—and this is merely my own speculation—we might think of this in terms of long-term national and international policy. For example, perhaps we could think of the "globalist" or internationalist "liberal consensus" or "rules-based international order" which has driven much of Western policy since the fall of the Soviet Union, and which is lately coming under question. Or, the changes in British government and decision-making power initiated by Tony Blair's "New Labor" in the late 1990s. Or, the expanding role of the EU in Europe, over and above national legislatures. Or, the vicissitudes of Chinese Communism since 1949.

According to Abū Ma'shar, not every triplicity shift shows an abrupt change in religious communities, cultures, and dynasties.[19] Some of the indicators of change are as follows:

- *The shift*, for the nativities of future kings (*BRD* II.4).
- *Aversion between Ascendants*. If the Ascendant of a previous shift (say, to water) is in aversion to the Ascendant of the next shift (to fire), it suggests a sharper and more decisive change in dynasties during the new shift. In *BRD*, Abū Ma'shar ties this a bit too close to the singular event of Islam, because he supposes that a change of dynasties *also* occurs near the end of a Turn (viz., 580 AD).[20] And Mūsā also complicates this by speaking of the Ascendant of the "cycle," which could be any cycle at all.[21] However, in one of his own examples, Mūsā specifies that the Ascendants of the shifts to water (571) and fire (809) are in aversion, *as well as* the signs of the conjunctions themselves (Scorpio and Sagittarius respectively).[22] So, his use of "cycle" may be misleading.
- *The Sixties*. If a triplicity shift did show a change, then it may happen when the conjunction returns to the same sign in one of the Sixties; or even if it did not show a change, there might be a great disruption or challenge at these times.

---

[19] *BRD* I.1, **72**; II.1, **25**.
[20] *BRD* II.1, **4**.
[21] For Mūsā's statements, see *Fulfilment* Ch. 4, **4, 9-12, 15, 25, 27, 47, 72, 89**.
[22] *Fulfilment* Ch. 25, **9**.

- *Saturn-Mars conjunctions in Cancer.* This is a theory of al-Kindī,[23] who says that the greatest indication for "innovation"(حدوث) in the world (which he specifies is a change of dynasties and the length of kings' lifespans) is revealed by Saturn-Mars conjunctions in Cancer. He says that the presence of benefics in the sign of the conjunction (viz. Cancer) shows goodness (and probably, continuity); but infortunes in it [which would be true by definition] or squaring or opposing it, show a change of rule and bloodshed.

### §10: *Predictive techniques*

In this section I will delve more deeply into the techniques used by Abū Ma'shar, assisted by the discussions in Mūsā. In some ways, many of these are simple, and reflect Abū Ma'shar's own predictive practices for nativities. This will be obvious for people who understand Abū Ma'shar's admirable approach in his *PN4*, which I teach in my natal astrology course. But in mundane astrology there are some complications due to their historical beliefs and use of sidereal years, which can create frustrations for the modern student. (This is apart from the obvious fact that we have to switch to mundane thinking about countries and cultures, instead of natal thinking about individual lives.)

### §10.1: *General approach to mundane prediction*

Abū Ma'shar's general approach to natal predictive theory has three stages. We begin with [1] a root chart, namely the nativity: it contains information about the native's whole life, but in a state of potential because the chart itself remains unchanged. Then we apply [2] time lord techniques to the nativity: ordering mechanisms that tell us which of those rooted signs and planets will be "activated" at which time, for how long, and in what order. Two important techniques are annual profections of the natal Ascendant, and the distribution by primary directions of the natal Ascendant

---

[23] *Arab Rule*, p. 529 (in **BY**).

through the bounds. Finally, we [3] assess the activated time lords in "real time" during the years which were symbolically identified: this is normally done through solar revolutions (SRs)[24] or transits. For example, suppose that by profection we know that someone's natal Mars will be activated at Age 37: we would then cast the native's solar revolution for Age 37, and assess the condition and position of Mars to see exactly how the *generic* natal promise is actually expressed and modified in *that* year. Since profections occur in cycles and will activate that natal Mars again at some later date, the exact details of his expression will change somewhat in every iteration: hence the need to pair time lords with real-time SRs.

It is similar in mundane astrology. We begin with [1] some root chart (normally a conjunction), which gives us a baseline set of meanings that will last for a number of years (such as, until the next conjunction). We likewise [2] apply mundane time lord techniques like profections and distributions to that chart for the period in which it is in effect, and [3] generate annual ingress charts as the mundane version of natal SRs, to evaluate the manifestation of what is promised in the root. For the most part, all mundane charts are generated for the annual Aries ingress; sometimes they are also generated at quarterly or monthly ingresses.

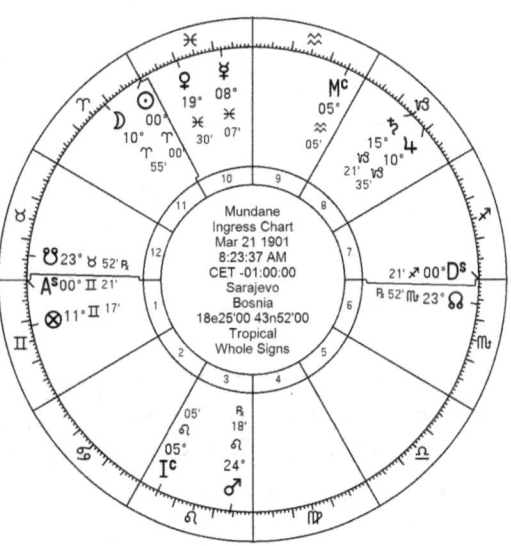

**Figure 12: 1901 conjunction**

Thus for instance, there was a mean Saturn-Jupiter conjunction on July 20, 1901, at 15° Capricorn; the 1901 Aries ingress chart became the root

---

[24] The annual solar revolution occurs when the Sun returns to the zodiacal position he held in a nativity. In mundane astrology, this occurs every year when the Sun returns to 0° Aries.

chart, because the conjunction occurred during that seasonal year.[25] We can see that the Ascendant at Sarajevo was Gemini, and Mars was in Leo, the 3rd place. These give some general indications for the 20 or so years governed by this conjunction until the next one.

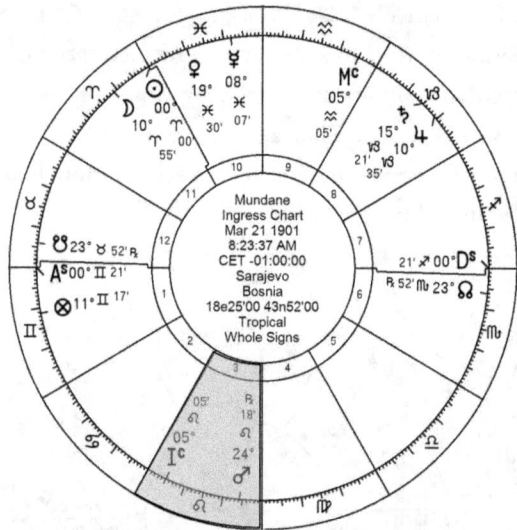

**Figure 13: Profection to 1903**

In Figure 13 we have applied mundane profections to the Ascendant of the conjunction (Gemini): it terminated at the Mars of the conjunction in 1903. This means that the sign which is the profected Ascendant for this year is Leo, and its lord the Sun is in the conjunctional 11th. Thus the promise of the conjunctional Mars and Leo (the 3rd place) will be especially active in this year.[26] Since annual profections go around a chart in 12-year cycles, this profection will be repeated in 1915. However, we do not yet know what real-time modifications and details will differentiate the effects of Mars and Leo in 1915, from their effects in 1903.

Both Abū Ma'shar and Mūsā also apply mundane profections to the sign of the conjunction. As an example, if we begin in Capricorn in 1901, we come to Aquarius in 1914 (the year in which World War I started). The lord of Aquarius (Saturn) is in the 8th, and Aquarius is opposed by Mars, indicating danger and violence, consistent with the occurrence of war.

---

[25] The ingress chart that is typically used, is the Aries ingress which immediately preceded the day of the conjunction. Thus, even if the mean conjunction were in January 1902, it would still fall under the seasonal year which began the previous spring, in March 1901.

[26] In this year, the king was assassinated by a cabal which included government ministers (the 11th, in many schemes).

Finally, we have the Aries ingress for the year 1903. We can see that in real time, the Ascendant is Libra: this means that not only will Libra-type effects manifest, but since Libra at the *conjunction* was the 5th, the general promise of the conjunctional 5th place will be "arising" or manifesting this year. Moreover, the conjunction Ascendant which governs these 20 years (Gemini) has now

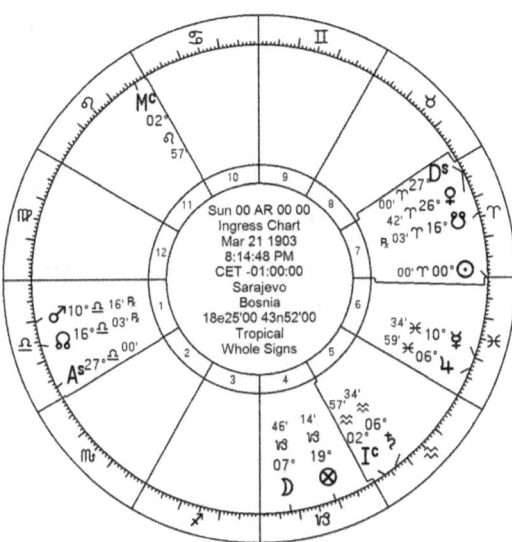

Figure 14: 1903 ingress

become the 9th, so that 9th-place matters will be highlighted. Again, the profection of the Ascendant had come to Leo, and we see the sign of the year Leo in the 11th, focusing the attention of the year especially on 11th-place topics. Finally, Mars in this year is in detriment and retrograde in Libra the Ascendant, meaning that his general effects which were promised in the conjunction, will manifest in and through things like the general public and the public's mood.

This is the general approach to mundane prediction as applied to a simple hierarchy of charts and techniques. In §7 above I outlined which parts of *BRD* can be used to interpret these various Ascendants and planets.

### §10.2: The red herring of the Flood

The main complication in traditional mundane astrology is that certain sets of time lords were based on astrological theories of when the Biblical Flood occurred. *These theories were wrong.* As I have discussed in my earlier books, astrologers assumed that the Flood happened at certain specific dates, and at certain conjunctions of planets. But since this didn't actually happen, they ended up associating historical events and interpretations with certain complicated but irrelevant lists of time lords. So, one big message I have to convey is this: *most of these time lords should be ignored*. That is, we can stick to conjunctions, profections, certain distributions, and transits, because we know when they occurred. But many time lords are based on a Flood which did not happen, or certainly not at the times they say.

I want to explain this point a bit further, because one of the major time lords mentioned by both Abū Ma'shar and Mūsā is associated with the Flood (the "Turn" or the "360"). This will be the subject of the next section, but now is a good time to understand how the different Floods were used by the Arabic-speaking astrologers.

Abū Ma'shar's version is the best known, so let's begin with him. Drawing upon some Indian theories as well as the Biblical Flood, he believed in a "world-year" of 360,000 sidereal years. This world-year begins with a conjunction of all of the planets at 0° Aries, to be ended with an identical conjunction at the end of that time. But in the middle, at exactly 180,000 years, he claimed another similar conjunction at 0° Aries, which was the date of the Biblical Flood, on February 18, 3102 BC. Thus, a Saturn-Jupiter conjunction in Aries coincided with the Flood.

Now it so happens that while their knowledge of cycles was very good, such a conjunction did not happen at this time. Moreover, Abū Ma'shar did something disappointing: when he calculated where the Indian theory would put Saturn and Jupiter at 180,000 years, he found that they did not actually meet at 0° Aries. For example, Saturn (in this Indian theory) would have been behind by about three signs (1/4 of the zodiac). So, Abū Ma'shar got rid of this fraction and rounded out the speed of Saturn so that he *would* conjoin with Jupiter on that day: in other words, he altered the data to match his theory! Now, 180,000 years is a long time, and spread over time that only alters Saturn's annual motion by the tiniest amount. But it means that his time lords, which were calculated for that Flood date, are simply wrong. Thus the cycles and time lords which depend on that date, are likewise wrong.

| Abū Ma'shar's Flood conjunction | Māshā'allāh's "indicator" conjunction |
|---|---|
| February 18, 3102 BC | September 21, 3381 BC |

**Figure 15: Two Flood conjunctions**

On the other hand was a theory of Māshā'allāh, which was taken from other Indian astrologers. According to this theory, there was a Flood conjunction on September 21, 3381 BC. It was *not* based on a notion of being in the middle of a world-year as Abū Ma'shar's was. Now, this Māshā'allāh date is 279 years earlier than the Abū Ma'shar Flood conjunction, so we have competing dates. In order not to have to choose between them, Abū Ma'shar appropriated Māshā'allāh's conjunction as merely "indicating," ahead of time, Abū Ma'shar's own Flood date. In this way, Māshā'allāh's has come to be known in the scholarly literature as an "indicator" conjunction,[27] and both were used together despite Abū Ma'shar's Flood being taken as the only valid one. Frankly, the only other reason for keeping Māshā'allāh's date was that it made a major change of time lords (namely, in the Turn or the 360s) in 580 AD just before the advent of Islam: so by harmonizing with those political and religious events, Māshā'allāh's indicator conjunction served the purpose of corroborating and explaining the rise of Islam. Let's turn to that now.

### §10.3: The Turn (or 360s) & the Quarters (BRD I.1, 71-91)

One of the most important sets of time lords used by Abū Ma'shar and Mūsā, is what I called the "Turn" (دور) in my previous books. But after translating Mūsā and seeing his more elaborate sets of cycles (دور) , I have adopted his vocabulary and will refer to this as the "360." In *BRD* though, I will still call it the Turn because Abū Ma'shar seems only to refer to his own version.

The 360 is a way of pairing signs and planets for periods of 360 sidereal years, by moving through the signs in zodiacal order, and through the planets in descending Chaldean order. The first 360 years are ruled by Aries-Saturn, then Taurus-Jupiter, Gemini-Mars, and so on. (These long periods are then subdivided into Quarters, annual rotations, and even directions through the degrees of the circle.) Whenever one reaches the end of the signs, one starts again with Aries; with the planets, one rotates back to Sat-

---

[27] Abū Ma'shar refers to it as such in *BRD* I.1, **72**.

urn. Changes from one cycle of 360 years to the next are supposed to correlate with historical periods and events.

But in his *Periods*,[28] Mūsā makes it clear that there were two ways of assigning the 360s: that of Abū Ma'shar, and that of Māshā'allāh. Mūsā follows Abū Ma'shar. According to this view, the Aries-Saturn 360 starts at the beginning of the world-year of 360,000 years, at the conjunction of all planets in 0° Aries. Since each cycle is 360 years, this means that the world will go through 1,000 of these cycles, the last one being Cancer-Mercury. But exactly in the middle is Abū Ma'shar's Flood conjunction at 180,000 years, again at 0° Aries: at that time the Sagittarius-Sun cycle begins. His Flood, this conjunction, and the Sagittarius-Sun 360, all begin on February 18, 3102 BC.

Māshā'allāh's theory of cycles[29] was embedded in older Indian and Zoroastrian theories, which had nothing to do with a Flood or Abū Ma'shar's 360,000 years. But since Māshā'allāh did believe in a Flood, he had to locate it somewhere: he or his predecessors calculated it for a Saturn-Jupiter conjunction on September 21, 3381 BC (his indicator conjunction), and *this* Flood occurred in the *middle* of a cycle of 360 in *his* series, namely Cancer-Saturn. So, the Māshā'allāh series does not correspond to the cycles in the Abū Ma'shar series.

Mūsā seems to reject the Māshā'allāh theory, and indeed it is rarely mentioned in the literature. So what was the point of referring to it, even by astrologers who rejected it? Because if we keep rotating through Māshā'allāh's 360s, his cycles change to Gemini-Venus in 580 AD, about 10 years after the triplicity shift which indicated Islam (usually, 571 AD). No such change occurs at that time in Abū Ma'shar's system. Since they were interested in correlating planetary conjunctions and cycles with major shifts and events in civilizations and religion, it was convenient to treat Māshā'allāh's series as indicating Islam as well. In this way one could appear to preserve both sets of cycles, even though Abū Ma'shar's system eventually became the mainstream view. Mūsā gives the Māshā'allāh series the special name "the cycle which was before the Flood," in order to distinguish it from Abū Ma'shar's, which he calls "following the mighty."

---

[28] *Periods* Ch. 2, **33-34** and **38-44**.
[29] *Periods* Ch. 2, **39-41**.

I mentioned above that astrologers also rotated the pairs of signs and planets annually, so that year 1 of any 360 was Aries-Saturn, year 2 of that same 360 was Taurus-Gemini, and so on. In this way, by the time one reaches the end of the 360 the final year would be Pisces (since 360 is divisible by 12), but the paired planet would be Mars. This annual rotation could then continue with Aries-*Sun*, then Taurus-*Venus*, and so on.

Finally, there is a method of "Quarters," which I follow Burnett and Yamamoto in capitalizing in order to distinguish it from quarterly ingresses. Here, according to some method I do not fully understand,[30] every 90 years of a 360 is governed by some planet. Both Abū Ma'shar[31] and Mūsā[32] describe methods for determining the lord of the Quarter, but it does not make sense. As an example, Mūsā says the lord or "manager" of the Quarter for 938 AD is the Sun, for 939 AD Jupiter, and for 944-46 AD Mercury:[33] but no annual rotation in Chaldean order could give us that result.

On the other hand, in II.7, **30-33**, Abū Ma'shar does apply the notion of the 360s and Quarters to the "direction" of degrees around the whole chart for 360 years. Here he associates major political changes within the 360 to sets of 90°.

### §10.4: Sets of 10 Saturn cycles (II.8, **146-57**)

An interesting approach which draws on the association of Saturn with prophets, lawgivers, and kings, is the set of (approximately) 10 tropical cycles of Saturn.[34] After 10 cycles (or sometimes 9 or 11, depending on some other factors), there should be a major civilizational change and the appearance of major historical figures.[35] Abū Ma'shar does not seem to be fully sold on the technique, and the way he orders his series of historical figures is wholly incorrect. But it is easy to rearrange his chronology and see that his events do, in fact, coincide quite well with Saturn's ingresses into Aries.

---

[30] Neither did **BY**, as they note.
[31] *BRD* Ch. I.1, **72-75**.
[32] *Periods* Ch. 2, **82-89**.
[33] See *Fulfilment* Chs. 48, 52, 72, 76, and 80.
[34] See II.8, **146-57** and **174-75**.
[35] II.8, **151**.

| | Saturn ingresses into Aries | |
|---|---|---|
| #1 | 331-330 BC – 301-300 BC | • Alexander the Great: conquests and reigns (336-323)<br>• Fall of Achaemenid Persians (330) |
| #2-#11 | 301-300 BC – 6 BC | |
| #1 | 6-4 BC – 24-26 AD | • Life of Jesus (ca. 0 – 33 AD) |
| #2-#8 | 24-26 AD – 230-32 AD | |
| #9 | 230-232 AD – 260-262 AD | • Ardashīr I founds Sasanian Persian Empire (225 AD)<br>• Manī appears in Persia to preach (242) |
| #1 | 260-262 AD – 289-291 AD | • Manī's further preaching, death (274) |
| #2-#10 | 289-291 AD – 554-557 AD | |
| #1 | 554-557 AD – 584-586 AD | • Birth of Muhammad (570) |

**Figure 16: Sets of 10 Saturn cycles**

The mean tropical period of Saturn (i.e., one circuit through the zodiac) is 29.42 years; 10 full cycles is therefore 294.2 years. Figure 16 shows the events which Abū Ma'shar identifies. Starting with the Saturn ingress into Aries in 331-330 BC, that cycle coincides with Alexander the Great's conquests and the fall of the Achaemenid Persians. After the 11th cycle, Jesus appears, and at the end of 9 cycles Ardashīr I and Manī. At the beginning of the next cycle we have Manī's death (and the ascendancy of the Sasanian Persians). After 10 cycles, we have the birth of Muhammad. Figure 17 shows the amount of years which one may use to calculate further cycles.

| Ingress | Lasts from | Lasts to |
|---|---|---|
| 1 | 0 | 29.42 |
| 2 | 29.42 | 58.84 |
| 3 | 58.84 | 88.26 |
| 4 | 88.26 | 117.68 |
| 5 | 117.68 | 147.10 |
| 6 | 147.10 | 176.52 |
| 7 | 176.52 | 205.94 |
| 8 | 205.94 | 235.36 |
| 9 | 235.36 | 264.78 |
| 10 | 264.78 | 294.20 |

**Figure 17: Sets of 10 Saturn cycles**

*§10.5: The Sixties (BRD II.8, **139-45**)*

Returning to the subject of Saturn-Jupiter conjunctions, we have the concept of what Mūsā calls the Sixties. By definition, any conjunction in some sign (let it be Scorpio) will count as conjunction #1. The conjunctions will return to the same sign approximately 60 years later, repeating and reinforcing the message of the shift. As I already explained, the Sixties are conjunctions #4, #7, and #10. It is part of Abū Ma'shar's theory (and detailed much more elaborately in Mūsā)[36] that the message of the shift—and its political changes—will usually manifest during the conjunction of a Sixty. Thus in BRD, the triplicity shift indicating Islam and its new culture occurred in 570-71. Successive Sixties which were also in Scorpio, show different stages in the battle for power and the establishment of its dynasties. In the Sixties listed here, we have the establishment of the Caliphate (630), the attempted takeover by al-Zubayr (690), and then the transfer of power to the 'Abbāsids (749). The actual events did not take place in these individual years, but in the 20 years of their period. (The dates can be seen in the table.)

---

[36] See especially his *Periods* Ch. 7, **133ff**.

|  | Year of Sixty | Event |
|---|---|---|
| Shift to ♏ | 570/571 | (*Conjunction indicating Islam and new religion*)[37] |
| Sixty #1 | 630 | Death of Muḥammad, accession of Abū Bakr (632) |
| Sixty #2 | 690 | Destruction of Ka'aba, death of al-Zubayr (692) |
| Sixty #3 | 749 | Emergence of Abū Muslim (747), transfer of power to 'Abbāsids (749-50), his death (755). |

Figure 18: The Sixties in early Islam (*BRD*)

### §10.6: Annual & quarterly ingresses

According to our usual way of thinking, annual ingresses should comprise the "meat" of mundane astrology: the year-to-year process of events and political struggles which face us in everyday life. This is somewhat true (apart from eclipses, which have their own timing method). But in such a low-level chart it may be difficult to distinguish temporary matters from the manifestation of large-scale developments which are presaged in a conjunction chart. Unfortunately, in Abū Ma'shar we have only a skeletal framework for interpreting annual ingresses—nothing like what we see in, say, Sahl's mundane book or Mūsā's *Fulfilment*.

However, let us remember that annual ingresses act as the "real-time" charts which express conjunctions and their annual profections from the Ascendant or the sign of the conjunction. In the example of the conjunction chart for Sarajevo above, I profected the Ascendant to Leo for 1903, with the conjunctional Mars in it. In the ingress chart for 1903, we see that Mars is now in the revolutionary Ascendant, affecting the general public, and the original sign of the year Leo (with the earlier Mars in it) occupies the revolu-

---

[37] As I have indicated elsewhere, this "shift" to Scorpio is a fiction, as it was said to happen at 4° Scorpio, which is impossible in any scheme of mean conjunctions. But the other conjunctions which recur in Scorpio are accurate.

tionary 11th. At a very crude level this could mean that the violence suggested in the conjunction for 1903, is now reflected in and through the topic of government ministers (one signification of the 11th), and affects the people (the Ascendant). This is the kind of thing that one would do with natal profections and revolutions, and the same applies here.

Finally, I should note some rules which can be found in standard sources like Abū Ma'shar's own *Flowers*, and here in VIII.1, **70-73**. If an annual ingress's Ascendant is a fixed sign, then it can stand as the chart for the whole seasonal year until the next Aries ingress. If double-bodied, then it partly stands for the whole year, but especially for the first six months: the last six months are governed in partnership with the Libra ingress. If it is convertible or cardinal, then we need all four seasonal ingresses (Aries, Cancer, Libra, Capricorn).

## §10.7: Fardārs (BRD VIII.2, **40-65**)

Another kind of time lord is the *fardār*, often called the *"firdaria."* It may come from the Greek for "period" (*periodos*). There are several types discussed in Mūsā's *Periods* Ch. 5, and only one is mentioned in *BRD*: the "lesser" *fardār* on the right of the table here. (But in VIII.2, **44**, Abū Ma'shar mentions three *fardār*s of the Sun, which means that he may be including others such as the "middle" *fardār*, and simply neglects to list them all.)

Although some *fardār*s begin their sequence from things like the Flood, in *BRD* VIII.2 Abū Ma'shar begins his lesser *fardār* from the year of the Hijrah or the beginning of the Islamic calendar, in 632 AD. This is a nice bit of information, because if the *fardār*s are valid, we can say that new sequences begin at the beginning of new eras or epochs, and do not have to derive from the Flood.

However, there is something puzzling about Abū Ma'shar's instructions. The order of the lesser and middle *fardār*s is based on the order of exaltations, starting with Aries: Sun (Aries), Moon (Taurus), Head (Gemini),[38] Jupiter (Cancer), and so on. But in VIII.2, **41** Abū Ma'shar explicitly says to

---

[38] This is according to the Persian theory; likewise the Tail being exalted in Sagittarius.

begin the counting (i.e., from the Hijrah) from Saturn, not the Sun. And in VIII.2, **35**, Abū Ma'shar seems to suggest that a *fardār* has an actual Ascendant, which he oddly links to the twelfth-parts. (One would think that it means one casts a chart for the moment in which a new *fardār* begins, but the passage is somewhat convoluted.)

| Greater | | Middle | | Lesser and its sublords | | |
|---|---|---|---|---|---|---|
| Sign | Years | Planet | Years | Planet | Years | Sublord |
| ♈ | 12 | ☉ | 75 | ☉ | 10 | 1/7 |
| ♉ | 11 | ☽ | 75 | ☽ | 9 | 1/7 |
| ♊ | 10 | ☊ | 75 | ☊ | 3 | |
| ♋ | 9 | ♃ | 75 | ♃ | 12 | 1/7 |
| ♌ | 8 | ☿ | 75 | ☿ | 13 | 1/7 |
| ♍ | 7 | ♄ | 75 | ♄ | 11 | 1/7 |
| ♎ | 6 | ☋ | 75 | ☋ | 2 | |
| ♏ | 5 | ♂ | 75 | ♂ | 7 | 1/7 |
| ♐ | 4 | ♀ | 75 | ♀ | 13 | 1/7 |
| ♑ | 3 | | 675 | | 75 | |
| ♒ | 2 | | | | | |
| ♓ | 1 | | | | | |
| | 78 | | | | | |

Figure 19: Mundane *fardārs* in Mūsā (Ch. 5)

I do note that many of the interpretations of the *fardārs* in VIII.2 deal almost entirely with "Babylon." Does this reflect a pre-Islamic source, namely a Sasanian Persian interest in basing the interpretations on the center of Sasanian power and their empire? Probably.

## §10.8: Mundane profections

I have already discussed profections several times, from Abū Ma'shar's schematic approach and my discussion of the Sarajevo chart (§10.2). In I.1, 92ff, he characterizes a number of profections in terms of what they mean, based on where they begin from.

| Chart | Profection from | Indication |
|---|---|---|
| Aries ♂ | ASC | Floods, earthquakes, epidemic |
| | ♂ | Short dynasties, their qualities |
| ♂ of religion | ASC | What occurs in religions |
| | ♂ | |
| ♂ of dynasty | ASC | What occurs in dynasties |
| | ♂ | |
| ♂ of triplicity shift | ASC | What occurs in dynasties (esp. kings of religious community) |
| | ♂ | |
| Lesser ♂ | ASC | What befalls important people |
| | ♂ | |

**Figure 20: General indications for mundane profections (*BRD* I.1)**

I am currently agnostic as to how well this holds up in practice, but it is nice to see an attempt to associate the meaning of various profections with the kind of chart they take place in. Throughout *BRD*, Abū Ma'shar gives extra clues as to how to use them, although he is not always clear. Here, though, are two examples.

- If, in a conjunction chart, the conjunction is in the whole-sign angles of the infortunes, Abū Ma'shar seems to say that the conjunctional period will contain some war. Thus, profections of the conjunction's Ascendant *to* the conjunction or those whole-sign angles, will trigger a war in the relevant year (VIII.1, **35**). Perhaps we should rather say that it *could* trigger a war, *if* the ingress of that year confirms it by replicating themes of conflict and violence.
- When a conjunction is activated by a profection coming to it, or by an ingress Ascendant falling on it, it shows hardship, disruption,

and changes (VII.1). This makes sense if we remember that the whole point of conjunctions is to mark important changes and alterations in politics and society—and traditionally, those changes tend to happen through conflict. Now, the 'Abbāsid empire was an international empire which contained many nationalities and regions which were not always happy with the administration: this means that *domestic* politics were simultaneously *international* politics, so we might expect wars to be more common. But in, say, a modern liberal democracy such wars and overlaps between domestic and international politics are not so common, so perhaps we should be looking more at changes in policy, in party politics, or national "controversies" which sometimes have wide-ranging effects apart from war.

### §10.9: Saturn-Mars conjunctions in Cancer (BRD II.8, **1**, 4-30, 174-75)

A secondary kind of conjunction described in *BRD* II.8, is that of Saturn and Mars in Cancer about every 30 years. Abū Ma'shar's account (II.8, **3-30**) is mainly from al-Kindī's essay on how long the Arabs would be in power, and the doctrine might well have originated with al-Kindī. Mūsā ignores it. In reality he seems to prefer true sidereal conjunctions in Cancer, and I have corrected his years and added footnotes below. The charts are cast for the Aries ingress.

As we consider the events below, it is clear that the Saturn-Mars conjunctions in Cancer are meant to be disruptive, destructive, indicating rebellion, disunity, and even assassination.[39] If Jupiter sees Cancer (this must mean at the revolution, but perhaps even on the day of the true conjunction), this is a mitigating factor: it could turn a potential shift of power to another dynasty, into a mere rebellion which is quashed. Abū Ma'shar mentions some other situations in his examples. The Moon is used in the timing of the events by converting the distance in degrees between her and the conjunction, into

---

[39] But Abū Ma'shar himself says that the indications are less widespread and deep than they are for the changes indicated by Saturn-Jupiter conjunctions (II.8, **1**).

months. Thus 74° would equal 74 months, or a little over 6 years, for the manifesting of the troubles. Perhaps one should bring in profections?

When thinking about these conjunctions, it is certainly true that both Saturn and Mars are in a poor condition in Cancer: one in detriment, the other in fall. However, the events which are delineated below all take place roughly in the region of Iraq. Here we come upon a different kind of chorography based on the bounds. For Abū Ma'shar follows al-Kindī's line that both Jupiter and Cancer—and especially the bound of Jupiter *in* Cancer—specifically designates Iraq. (See §14 below on chorography.) So, does the Saturn-Mars conjunction in Cancer always mean some disruptive change for the world as a whole due to their conditions in Cancer itself, or is this something only specific to the politics of the time—namely since much of the action in the Islamic empire was in or about *Iraq*? If we start assigning signs and bounds to different areas of the world, then Saturn-Mars conjunctions would happen more often, and they might show disruptions in different countries, depending on how we arranged our chorography. Indeed, II.8, **32ff** does offer brief delineations of their conjunction in other signs, but with little interest in cataloguing any events associated with them.

The table below lists the years of the Saturn-Mars conjunctions in Cancer as listed in Abū Ma'shar, with some key events stated either by him or al-Kindī (who is the source of the list). For a fuller table of both tropical and sidereal conjunctions, see *AW2* Appendix B.

| BRD's dates and events | Further details (Dykes) |
|---|---|
| 622 AD / AH 1 (**8**): The Hijrah (622) Khusrau II killed (628) Battle of Nihāvand (642) | Rome won a long war with the Sasanians (628), at which time Khusrau II was killed by his son (who was leading a coup), resulting in a devastating civil war (628-32). In 642 the Muslims destroyed the Persians at the Battle of Nihāvand, after which the last Shāh Yazdijird III had to flee and his power broken. |

| | |
|---|---|
| 652 AD / AH 31 (**19**): Death of 'Uthmān b. 'Affān (656) | Caliph 'Uthmān was killed in 656; due to his membership in the 'Umayya branch of Muhammad's family, power shifted westwards to Mu'āwīyah as governor of Syria. |
| 680 AD / 61 AH (**20**):[40] Civil unrest of al-Zubayr (683-92). | 'Abd Allāh b. al-Zubayr b. al-Awwām, from a famous family, led a rival Caliphate to the 'Umayyads, governed from Mecca, from 683-692. He was eventually killed in 692. |
| 710 AD / 91 AH (**21**): Civil unrest of ibn al-Muhallab (720)[41] | Yazīd b. al-Muhallab was an 'Umayyad governor who led widespread rebellions against the 'Umayyads in 720, and was killed in the same year. |
| 738 AD / 121 AH (**22**):[42] Breakdown of the 'Umayyad dynasty and shift to 'Abbāsid power in Iraq (744-750 AD) | After a period of widespread dissatisfaction, Caliph al-Walīd II was killed in 744. A quick succession of other Caliphs followed. The chief 'Abbāsid propagandist and general, Abū Muslim, arose in 745-747 and paved the way for the 'Abbāsid takeover in 749-750. |

---

[40] Abū Ma'shar makes this 681.
[41] Al-Kindī makes it seem that he was killed after 10 years (in 722), and Abū Ma'shar after 20 years (732).
[42] Abū Ma'shar makes this 739. The mean conjunction was in 740, with true conjunctions in both 738 and 740.

| | |
|---|---|
| 768 AD / 151 AH (**24**): The civil unrest of Muhammad b. ʿAbd Allāh b. al-Hasan al-ʿAlawī, and his brother Ibrāhīm b. ʿAbd Allāh (762-768). | Brothers Muhammad and ʾIbrāhīm were ʿAlīd rebels. Muhammad rose up against Caliph al-Manṣūr and was killed in 762; Ibrahim was killed in 763.[43] |
| 798 AD / 181 AH (**25**): The civil unrest of Muhammad b. al-Zubaydah, the rising of rebels, and the shift of power to east (809-approx. 819). | Caliph al-Amīn was born Muhammad b. al-Zubaydah (his mother's name). He ruled from Baghdad upon the death of his father (809), but there shortly followed the civil war in which his brother, al-Maʾmūn, eventually won and took the throne (813). There followed some power struggles for a few years afterwards.[44] |
| 826 AD / 212 AH (**26**):[45] Turks' strength, taking over management of the dynasty, and transferring the rulership to another place. | Caliph al-Muʿtasim had been putting together his own army of Turkish troops for many years; their influence was greatly resented. He eventually moved them to a new capital in nearby Samarra in 836. |

---

[43] But in his *History*, al-Tabarī mentions their deaths in the year 151 AH (i.e., 768, the year of this conjunction) as though it is a recent event. Unfortunately, the way al-Tabarī constructs his history can make it difficult to tell when an event actually happens. Surely something else must have happened after the date of this conjunction.

[44] Abū Maʾshar's (and al-Kindī's) descriptions of these events are highly political—and for good reason. Abū Maʾshar was well connected to the court of al-Maʾmun, and knew the Caliph personally. In order to make sense of the providential success of his master and/or patron, he here depicts *al-Amīn* as the rebel and upstart, when in fact al-Maʾmūn had only been given governorship over Khurāsān by their father, not the Caliph's seat in Baghdad. By the time the civil war between the brothers was really underway, I suppose that each side was depicting the other as the rebel aggressor.

[45] This was actually in 211 AH.

| | |
|---|---|
| 857 AD / 242 AH (**27**): Civil unrest of al-Mustaʾīn, wars, the shedding of blood (861-70).<br><br>Appearance of man claiming divinity, but who lasts only 15 years. | The "Anarchy at Samarra" occurred under Caliph al-Mustaʾīn, who had been installed by Turkish troops in place of the intended successors. Many revolts and riots followed until he abdicated (865).<br><br>The man claiming divinity was ʿAlī b. Muhammad the ʿAlawite, described in Ch. I.3, **40-47** above. |
| **The dates below are after Abū Maʾshar's time:** ||
| 887 AD / 272 AH (**28**): Formidable, mighty affairs, the death of kings and leaders. | Perhaps: two Caliphs died between the 5th and 16th years of the 5th fiery conjunction (of 888): al-Muʾtamid and al-Muʾtadid. See Mūsā's *Fulfilment* Ch. 27.<br><br>Perhaps: the attack on the Hajj by Zikrawayh b. Mihrawayh (905 AD)? See Mūsā's *Fulfilment* Ch. 28. |
| 916 AD / 303 AH (**29**): Corruption and rebellion in the region of the west. | Perhaps: the Qarmatian rebellions of 906-928? Baghdad attacked in 927-28. See Mūsā, *Fulfilment* Ch. 30. |
| 945 AD / 333 AH (**30**): Civil unrest and many wars, and triumph of Muslims. | Perhaps: the rise of the Buyid confederation, a Shīʿa dynasty led by ʿAlī b. Buya. In 945 they captured Baghdad. |

Figure 21: Saturn-Mars conjunctions in Cancer

## §11: Special victors

In profections, the "lord of the year" means the lord of the sign of the terminal point—that is, where the profection comes to. Thus if the profection comes to Gemini, the lord of the year is Mercury. However, in mundane astrology the lord of the year also refers to a special planet in an ingress chart which is meant to sum up the general meaning of the year. This is a kind of "victor" (in Latin called an *almuten*, from the Ar. *al-mubtazz*, "victor"), a planet whose strength and position allows it to predominate over other planets' significations. The same thing occurs in natal astrology, when we try to find a victor or predominator over the natal chart as a whole (sometimes called a "chart ruler"). Two other special victors are the "indicator of the king" and the "indicator of the subjects." *BRD* either does not mention or does not emphasize these three victors, perhaps because Abū Ma'shar is concerned with dynasties and religions, not low-level annual ingresses. His references to the "indicator of the king" seems to be due to his lifting passages from Māshā'allāh.

More relevant to *BRD* is a fourth victor, the "indicator of the acceder": this is used to determine the qualities and even lifespan of the acceder to the throne. In some places, this indicator is a general significator, such as Saturn (as a significator of a king or authority)[46] or his lord,[47] or the Sun (ditto).[48] But in two places Abū Ma'shar makes it more specific. First, it could be the lord of the sign which a profection reaches (from some earlier root or time lord period), in the year of a conjunction which shows the beginning of a new religious community or dynasty.[49] Thus, Abū Ma'shar seems to follow al-Kindī in saying that at the Scorpio conjunction for Islam in 571, the profection from an earlier chart had reached Gemini: this makes Muhammad be signified by Mercury, its lord. But a second indicator which looks more like a normal victor, is one which is taken at an Aries ingress from the

---

[46] *BRD* II.4, **71**; II.5 (*passim*).
[47] *BRD* II.4, **30-31**.
[48] *BRD* II.7 (*passim*).
[49] *BRD* II.4, **97-100**.

best and strongest of the following: (1) the sect light, (2) the Hermetic Lot of victory,[50] and (3) the lord of the bound of the MC.[51]

## §12: Mundane Lots

As in nativities, some traditional mundane astrology employs a number of special Lots. The table below is a list of those mentioned in *BRD*. (Mūsā uses only the Lot of Fortune, in passages he has copied from *BRD*.) Some are actually natal or horary Lots which have been repurposed for mundane use. Abū Ma'shar does not always say whether they are reversed by night, nor what his sources are. You can also see that many mentions of his Lots of rulership are left undefined or unidentified (see middle of table).

It is interesting to me that mundane authors rarely focus on the Lot of Fortune, although Sahl does seem to make some special use of it. If we consider the meaning of Fortune—as a complicated web of causal influences that present or hinder opportunities and benefits, a web which is not totally under one's control but appears more as good or bad luck—one would expect mundane astrology to emphasize it. For the broad systems of events that are at play here, such as economics, domestic and international politics, dynastic and cultural shifts, weather, agriculture, and so on, should be just the things that are described by the Lot in a mundane chart. Understanding the role of Fortune in mundane charts would be a worthwhile research project.

| Lot | From | To | Project | (R)? |
|---|---|---|---|---|
| **Fortune** I.3, **6-20**; II.4, **16, 18, 65**; VIII.1, **23, 28** | Sun | Moon | ASC | Y |
| **Body marks** I.3, **23** | Lord hour | Sun | SR ASC | ? |

---

[50] This is a Spirit-Jupiter Lot; Abū Ma'shar calls it here the Lot of elevation (II.7, **61-67**), and in *Gr. Intr.* the Lot of prosperity and aid (VIII.3, **40**), which is not the same as the Lot of exaltation (measured from the sect light to the degree of its exaltation).
[51] *BRD* II.7, **61-63**.

| Rulership & authority I.4, **18-28**[52] | Mars | Moon | ASC, esp. shift | Y |
|---|---|---|---|---|
| Rulership I.4, **30** | ASC of ♂ | ♂ | SR ASC | ? |
| Authority I.4, **31** | Sun | SR MC | Jupiter | N |
| Rulership II.2, **2-6**; II.2, **7-9** | One of the I.4 Lots | | | |
| Rulership II.3, **1-4**; II.3, **11-15**; II.3, **16-18**; II.4, **28-29**; II.4, **51-52**; II.4, **86-89**; II.7, **79-80** | Undefined | | | |
| Lot of king's involvements II.4, **90-98** | ☉ (day) or ☽ (night) of accession | 15° ♌ (day) or 15° ♋ (night) | ☽ (day) or ☉ (night) | N |
| Lifespan II.5, **81-90**[53] | Jupiter | Saturn | SR ASC of accession | Y |
| Lifespan A II.5, **91-96** | Eastern | Profection from ASC of religion | SR ASC | ? |
| Lifespan B II.5, **91-96** | Western | Profection from ASC of lesser ♂ | SR ASC | ? |
| Lifespan II.5, **97-100** | Sun | Saturn | ♂ of shift | ? |
| Lifespan II.5, **97-100** | Jupiter | Saturn | ♂ of shift | ? |

---

[52] See also VIII.4, **281-83**.
[53] More conditions are added to this calculation in the text.

| | | | | |
|---|---|---|---|---|
| Elevation, victory, prosperity<br>II.7, **61-67** | Spirit | Jupiter | ASC | Y |
| Prosperity<br>VIII.1, **44, 46-47** | Sun | DESC | ASC | ? |
| Battle<br>VIII.1, **45-46** | Mars | Moon | Sun | ? |

**Figure 22: Mundane Lots in *BRD***

### §13: *Mundane indications of the places & planets*

In this section I'd like to address the mundane indications of the places and planets. *BRD* contains many of these in Books V and VII (and by aspect combination in Book III), and Mūsā in his *Periods* Ch. 1.1. However, our sources are not always helpful in their official lists. For instance, we might learn that the third place means "brothers," a straightforward application of natal meanings. Well, how does that help us in a mundane chart, unless we are restricting the third place to the ruling family alone (such as the sibling of a king)? If however we consider the Persian model of political astrology and look around at other things, like aspect interpretations in *BRD* III or VII, we can start to enrich our vocabulary. In what follows I give some basic indications from *BRD* and Mūsā, along with some of my own ideas. I also include things like basic transit meanings of the planets.[54] Remember too that there will still be some crossover from natal astrology: for instance, Saturn on the IC in a revolution chart could be interpreted not as agriculture or land management for an individual, but as a "national building project," such as a large construction effort in roads, railways, and bridges. In a mundane seminar I once gave to Chinese students, they immediately identified such a Saturn as referring to the Chinese "Belt and Road initiative"; one might also point to there being a real estate crisis in China. This serves to show that in mundane astrology one often needs to know what is actually going on in a particular country before understanding what a planetary placement will indicate.

---

[54] This is from a prose version of Dorotheus, in Schmidt's *Teachings on Transits*.

In my Mūsā volume I will expand on these indications based on how Mūsā actually interprets chart positions, and I will also include William Ramesey's mundane significations for planets in all of the places, from Book IV of his *Astrologie Restored* (1653).

| | Planets: Mundane Significations |
|---|---|
| ♄ | BRD III: The king (maybe: state of the kingdom), the pious, monks, poor; fraud, falseness, secrets; prisons; tribulation; villages, estates, digging, building.<br>BRD V: The administration.<br>BRD VIII: Fear, war, death.<br>Mūsā Ch. 1.1: Laws, ordinances, prophets; distresses.<br>Transits: Hinders, tamps down, fines, or damages things; or dangers from authorities. |
| ♃ | BRD III: Religion, science, jurisprudence, modesty, morality.<br>BRD V: The status of kings.<br>BRD VIII: Victory, respect, civilization, prosperity.<br>Mūsā Ch. 1.1: Safety, jurisprudence; justice, truth-telling.<br>Transits: Alleviates, adds favor and honor and victory. |
| ♂ | BRD III: Fraud, robbery, resentment and rebellion, riots and wars, *jihād*, propagandists, lawsuits; disgrace.<br>BRD V: Transgression.<br>BRD VIII: War, and respect from winning.<br>Mūsā Ch. 1.1: Swearing false oaths, injustice, hardness of heart.<br>Transits: Harms good things (or can make them base, if by day), adds irregularities and enmities; but adds energy and resolve to Saturn.<br>Dykes suggests: "Laying down the law." |
| ☉ | BRD III: By assembly, he annuls or destroys the other planet's indications; by good aspect, publicity; by bad aspect, oppression and arbitrary power.<br>BRD V: Power and authority for planets he is associated with.<br>BRD VIII: Obedience from others; prosperity.<br>Mūsā Ch. 1.1: Respectable families, authority.<br>Dykes suggests: The principle of authority itself. |

| | |
|---|---|
| ♀ | *BRD* III: Condition of women, children and childbirth, entertainment, sex, feminine-type occupations, art.<br>*BRD* V: Community harmony, reverence in religion.<br>*BRD* VIII: Prosperity, safety.<br>Mūsā Ch. 1.1: Cultivation and planting.<br>Transits: Makes things more cheerful, fine, and pleasurable; but can be excessive and bring censure and trouble. |
| ☿ | *BRD* III: Secretaries, books, forgery, disputation and lawsuits, technical arts, rumors; violence and upset due to falseness; partnerships and business; the reporting or revealing of things to the public.<br>*BRD* V: Unrest, disparagement of leaders.<br>*BRD* VIII: *Too mixed to be certain.*<br>Mūsā Ch. 1.1: Businessmen, handling property, eloquence, debate, knowledge.<br>Transits: Adds stimulation, inventiveness, order, organization.<br>Dykes suggests: The media (both in good sense of reporting, and bad sense of sensationalism and propaganda). |
| ☽ | *BRD* III: The people, mass behaviors, divinity, prophethood, illumination/channeling.<br>*BRD* V: Social disruption, disagreement between rulers and ruled.<br>*BRD* VIII: Prosperity (good condition), but disorder in the administration.<br>Mūsā Ch. 1.1: Public, postal system, reports; inceptions of matters. |
| ☊ | *BRD* VIII: Expansion of rule, victory, good obedience from others. |
| ☋ | *BRD* VIII: Abjectness, debauchery. |

Figure 23: **Mundane significations of the planets**

| | Places: Mundane Significations |
|---|---|
| 1st | What the common people are interested in, are doing, or embrace.[55] |
| 2nd | Productivity<br>*Dykes:* "Consumer confidence"? Standard of living, cost of goods. |
| 3rd | Community feeling; social harmony.[56]<br>*Dykes:* Political parties, as a proxy for communal moral feeling and standards. Community organizations, activists. |
| 4th | Real estate, building, feelings towards ancestors<br>*Dykes:* Engineering, agricultural policy, real estate on a larger scale, natural disasters. |
| 5th | Military spending?[57] Good fortune generally for planets in it.<br>*Dykes:* Children (viz. big events involving children),[58] or people viewed as under protection; patronage or countries which are protectorates of other, powerful ones. |
| 6th | Underclass, illegal immigrants, crime, civil unrest.[59] |
| 7th | Sudden ups and downs among people of status.[60]<br>*Dykes:* The national "challenge" or obstacles to be dealt with; dissidents; special prosecutors. |
| 8th | Supply chain, consumer confidence, debt.[61]<br>*Dykes:* Taxes. |
| 9th | Intelligence, reports, the sciences.<br>*Dykes:* International outreach and foreign aid; foreign policy and international opinion. |
| 10th | Famous people, surprising public events.[62] Maybe: style and attitude of leaders? The vigor, authority, and stability of the regime.[63] |

---

[55] *BRD* III.1, **2-3**.
[56] *BRD* VII.3, **2**.
[57] *BRD* II.8, **135**; see also the 11th.
[58] We might think of events involving children or young people which become national news stories, like Greta Thunberg's activism, or the "Covington Kids" hoax of 2019 in the USA.
[59] *BRD* VII.6, **2**
[60] *BRD* VII.7, **2**.
[61] *BRD* VII.8, **2**.

| | |
|---|---|
| 11th | Fulfilment of hopes;[64] good fortune for the class of people whose planet is in it. |
| 12th | Fear, wrong, confusion, imprisonment.[65] *Dykes*: Scandals? |

Figure 24: **Mundane significations of the places**

## §14: *Chorography & peoples*

Chorography assigns planets and zodiacal signs to regions of the earth, and by extension to national peoples or even religious communities and civilizations. Possibly the most well-known of these schemes is that of Abū Ma'shar's *Gr. Intr.* VI.9, which Mūsā relies on in his books. There are others in my *AW2*. Because of the *pastiche* nature of *BRD*, its chorography is confusing and inconsistent. Most of the useful passages may be found in II.4, 17;[66] II.8, **32-59, 159-162**; VIII.2, **44-56**. Book IV is unhelpful as it describes indications for Babylon practically regardless of what sign is involved.

However, something new emerges from *BRD*[67] (and one sentence in Sahl),[68] which is further explained by al-Kindī. Many readers may know that Venus is sometimes assigned to Islam, and Scorpio to the Arabs. The association of Scorpio with the desert is well known, and I have conjectured that the use of Venus for Islam is related to the daily purification rituals performed before prayer (Venus being associated with purification and cleanliness). And that may indeed be how the association was originally formed. But al-Kindī explains in his *Arab Rule* that the pairing of planets and signs actually refers to the *bounds within* those signs:

---

[62] *BRD* VII.10, **2**.

[63] *BRD* II.4, **81-85**. That is, not the king or leader as a *person*, but the principle of authority itself.

[64] *BRD* VII.11, **2**. This doesn't necessarily mean that the hopes are well-founded or good: perhaps the people desire some action from a government which is actually tyrannical. (One could argue that most people prefer strong authorities.)

[65] *BRD* VII.12, **2**.

[66] This is from al-Kindī.

[67] *BRD* II.8, **3-4** and **13**; see also II.4, **17**.

[68] *Revolutions* Ch. 18, **32**.

| Bounds | People/regions |
|---|---|
| Saturn-Libra (0°-6°) | Rūm (Anatolia) |
| Jupiter-Cancer (19°-26°) | Iraq |
| Mars-Leo (24°-30°) | Turks |
| Venus-Scorpio (7°-11°) | Arabs |
| Mercury-Capricorn (0°-7°) | India |
| Sun-Aquarius (*no degrees*) | Boundary of Rūm |
| Moon-Virgo (*no degrees*) | Boundary of Turks |
| Sahl: Venus-Taurus,[69] | San'ā' |

**Figure 25: Bounds assigned to people and regions**

This scheme assigns each of the five major regional powers of the time, to a particular planet (based on its nature) and then its bound in some sign, with the exception of the luminaries which have no bounds but here instead govern frontiers. Note that the Arabs are not assigned to the fertile areas of Iraq (Cancer) but to the desert areas (Scorpio). This suggests to me that the scheme was invented after the 'Abbāsid revolution, when Persian elements were in control of Iraq. If it had been invented before Islam, the Persians would be assigned to Iraq; if under the 'Umayyads, the Arabs would likely have gotten it.

Sahl's attribution of Venus-Taurus to San'ā' may represent an attempt to expand the chorography, because the obvious use of all planets and the five regional powers in the al-Kindī scheme seems already complete and deliberate.

For the reader's interest, here are some further attributions of the planets to religious communities and practices:

---

[69] Sahl's text has from 0°–6°, but there are actually 8° in her bound, so this may be a scribal error.

|   | BRD I.4, 4-17<br>Religions | BRD I.4, 22-28<br>Objects of worship | BRD I.4, 35-41<br>Clothing |
|---|---|---|---|
| ♄ | Judaism; exclusive religions | Images of iron, brass | Black, coarse, dirty |
| ♃ |  | Gold | Wool, ascetic |
| ♂ | Fire worship; Mazdaism | Fire | Red and yellow |
| ☉ | Planetary worship, idols, wonders | Wood | Silk, raw silk |
| ♀ | Islam, revealed monotheism | Silver | (Expensive and female) fabric from Quhistān and Merv |
| ☿ | Christianity; futile, doubtful, hard religions | Churches | Embroidery, silk |
| ☽ | Doubtful, confusing, deviating religions; skepticism | Moon images | Crude, white |

Figure 26: Religious indications of the planets

*A note on Fārs vs. Persia.* In this text there is some ambiguity between "Persia" and "Fārs," which are the same word in Arabic. The term "Persia" in English generally refers to the many Persian empires which were hostile to Greek and Roman powers from early antiquity through the 600s AD. But after Islam, Fārs was considered more a particular province in the 'Abbāsid empire rather than a general term. I have sometimes read the Arabic as Fārs when it seems to be one of the provinces, but Persia when it seems to be a regional power. But because we do not currently know all of Abū Ma'shar's sources, these choices are still provisional.

## §15: Colors of the signs & places

*BRD* also includes a scheme of colors attributed to the signs and places, which is supposed to show what the people indicated by them will have preferences for in their clothing. For the places, one can see that the 7th forms the center, with a blackish color, then flanked by black, white, and so on, until reaching the Ascendant with a dusty color. I cannot account for colors like green, but there must be some atmospheric considerations involved in the rest.

| Signs: Book IV | | Places: Book VII | |
|---|---|---|---|
| ♈ | Red | 1 | Dusty, dark |
| ♉ | White | 2 | Green |
| ♊ | Green | 3 | Yellow |
| ♋ | Smoke | 4 | Red |
| ♌ | Dark shades | 5 | White |
| ♍ | Green, multi | 6 | Black |
| ♎ | Black | 7 | Black inmixed |
| ♏ | Black | 8 | Black |
| ♐ | Smoke | 9 | White |
| ♑ | Black | 10 | Red |
| ♒ | ? | 11 | Yellow |
| ♓ | White | 12 | Green |

Figure 27: Colors of the signs and places

## §16: Abū Ma'shar's charts

*BRD* contains five historical charts, four of them explicitly included in the manuscripts, and one implied through a verbal description but easy to calculate. Several of them are also presented by Mūsā (*Fulfilment*) and Māshā'allāh (*Conjunctions*), albeit with different values. In the Figure below they are listed in order of appearance, but can also be organized this way:

- Three "foundational" charts for doing mundane astrology in the middle ʿAbbāsid Caliphate: [#4] the triplicity shift to water of 571, indicating the coming of Islam; [#5] the Aries ingress for 749, the ʿAbbāsid revolution which eventually replaced the ʿUmayyads; [#1] the triplicity shift to fire of 809, which also indicated the civil war that put Caliph al-Maʾmūn on the throne.
- The Aries ingress of 622, the year in which the Hijrah took place. Since this was the beginning of the Islamic Hijrah calendar, it makes sense to include it here.
- The solar eclipse of 841, which—without naming him—Abū Maʿshar must be relating to the death of Caliph al-Muʿtasim (in 842). This is the implied chart which was only verbally described.

| #1: Triplicity shift of 809, al-Maʾmūn, birth of al-ʿAlawi | | |
|---|---|---|
| **BRD I.3, 40; VIII.2, 20** | ***Fulfilment* Ch. 25, 8** | ***Conjunctions* Ch. 11, 1-2** |
| ASC: 7° 27' ♌ (better: 27° 27') | ASC Baghdad: 29° ♊ <br> ASC middle earth: 2° ♋ <br> ASC middle 4th clime: 1° 44' ♋ | ASC: 3° ♋ |
| ☽: 16° 30' ♈ | ☽: 5° 04' ♈ | ☽: 16° 39' ♈ |
| (#2): Solar eclipse of 841, death of al-Muʿtasim | | |
| **BRD II.7, 58** | | |
| #3: Ingress of 622, year of the Hijrah | | |
| **BRD II.8, 9** | | |
| ASC: 3° ♋ | | |
| ☽: 6° 31' ♉ | | |
| #4: Triplicity shift of 571, to water and Islam | | |
| **BRD VIII.2, 9** | ***Fulfilment* Ch. 16, 16** | ***Conjunctions* Ch. 7, 4-6** |
| ASC: 27° 54' ♎ | ASC middle earth: 27° ♐ <br> ASC middle 4th clime 11° 20' ♐ | ASC: 22° ♎ |
| ☽: 1° 09' ♋ | ☽: 21° 09' ♊ | ☽: 1° 10' ♋ |

| #5: The Sixty of 749, the 'Abbāsid revolution ||| 
|---|---|---|
| BRD VIII.2, 15 | Fulfilment Ch. 24, 19 | Conjunctions Ch. 10, 1-3 |
| ASC: 27° ♍ | ASC middle earth: 27° 28' ♐ ASC middle 4th clime: 11° 32' ♐ | ASC: 25° ♏ |
| ☽: 25° 48' ♒ | ☽: 15° 09' ♒ | ☽: 23° 05' ♒ |

**Figure 28: Five charts in *BRD***

In this translation of *BRD* I make some comments about the charts themselves; moreover, **BY** explain that the manuscripts include more than one version of the charts, in both Arabic and Latin (they usually follow MS **B**).

In my Figure I have included only the Ascendant and Moons because those move quickly and give a better sense of the time frame identified by the calculations. Abū Ma'shar and Māshā'allāh have virtually the same Moons, but their Ascendants diverge somewhat; especially odd is chart #5, in which the degrees are almost the same but in two different signs; I suspect there might be a clerical error stemming from one of their source charts.

Mūsā's charts stand out as the most different. As I will explain in his volume, Mūsā normally used a sidereal year of 365.2584375 days, which is a little shorter than Abū Ma'shar's (365.259) and Māshā'allāh's (365.2590278). This is only a tiny difference over 1 year, but the difference between 622 AD and 809 AD adds up to several hours, thus shifting the Ascendant a couple of signs; plus, we do not know exactly where Māshā'allāh and Abū Ma'shar always cast their charts for. Moreover, when the value of Mūsā's Moon is about 10° off from the others', it even suggests that the dates of the charts might differ by 1 day.

# The Book of Religions & Dynasties
## by
## Abū Ja'far b. Muhammad al-Balkhī

## [Introduction]

*In the name of God the Compassionate, the Merciful, and in Him we seek help.*

**1** This book is on the whole of the indications of upper bodies for lower events coming to be in the world of generation and corruption, with respect to their positions in[1] the Ascendants of conjunctional and other Beginnings. **2** It is in Eight Books and 63 Chapters, authored by Abū Ma'shar Ja'far b. Muhammad, and is called *The Book of Religions and Dynasties*.

**3 Book I:** On how to look from conjunctions for the appearance of prophets and conquerors, and what attaches to them; and it is in 4 Chapters.

**4 Book II:** On the whole of the affairs of dynasties and their shifting, and the conditions of kings and what attaches to them; and it is in 8 Chapters.

**5 Book III:** On how to know the indications of the connections of the planets and their combinations with each other in the revolutions of years; and it is in 6 Chapters.

**6 Book IV:** On how to know the indications of the signs if they were the Ascendants of the Beginnings which we mentioned before, or the years' terminating at [the signs][2] from one of the Ascendants of the preceding Beginnings or from the positions of the conjunctions; and it is in 12 Chapters.

**7 Book V:** On how to know the special property of the planets' indications individually if they had victorship over the Ascendants of one of the Beginnings, or they had lord-of-the-yearship, or distributorship, or upon their being parallel with (or the parallelism of the two crossing-points of the

---

[1] عند.

[2] That is, by annual profection.

north and south, or the tailed stars, with) the rest of the signs, in the sense of mixture; and it is in 7 Chapters.

**8 Book VI**: On how to know the lower events from the influences of the upper bodies in the revolutions of years, from the transits of one over the other; and it is in 12 Chapters.

**9 Book VII**: On how to know the indications for lower events of [1] the sign of the terminal point, or [2] one of the annual revolutionary Ascendants, when one of the two coincides with a house relative to one of the foundational Ascendants of the preceding Beginnings or the conjunctions, or [3] the direction or [4] one of the upper bodies was in it or in the revolutionary divisions); and it is in 12 Chapters.

**10 Book VIII**: On the sum of how to know the indications of upper bodies for lower events, from the terminal points of the years and conjunctions, and what attaches to them; and it is in two Chapters.

# Book I: [Principles & Prophets]

**On how to look with respect to conjunctions for the appearance of prophets and conquerors, & what attaches to them**

*And it is in 4 Chapters:*

**1** Chapter I.1: On setting forth the universal Beginnings which are of great usefulness.

**2** Chapter I.2: On knowing the strongest of the conjunctional signs of the triplicities, and the appearance of their indications in the regions attributed to them.

**3** Chapter I.3: On how to know the conjunctions indicative of the nativities of prophets and conquerors, their morals and character, the marks coming to be on them, the tokens of their prophethood, the timing of their appearance, the locating of each one of them, and the span of their years.

**4** Chapter I.4: On knowing their customs and laws, their dress, and transport.

BOOK I: PRINCIPLES & PROPHETS 73

## Chapter I.1: On setting forth the universal Beginnings which are of great usefulness

**1** Discovering the knowledge of the indications of heavenly bodies for lower events is sought from natural motions, since they[1] are the closest to [human] perception among the indications of the upper bodies. **2** Whereas natural motions do not exceed three classes, [when] looking at the arrangement of the layers of the spheres of upper planets, and the difference of their cyclical movements, they too are divided into three classes. **3** One of them is the superior planets arranged above the greater luminary; the second class is the greater luminary; and the third class is the inferior planets arranged below the greater luminary. **4** So, each of the classes of the upper bodies is related to each of the natural motions due to their strong analogy to[2] them, and the succession of their influences in the world of generation and corruption.

| Motion | Planet | Time period | Stages | Indications |
|---|---|---|---|---|
| Around center | ♄ | Long | Beginning | Religions, dynasties |
| | ♃ | | Completion | Laws |
| | ♂ | | Breakdown | War, struggle |
| From center | ☉ | Medium | | Kings, overlords |
| Towards center | ♀ | Short | Beginning | Marriage, garments |
| | ☿ | | Completion | Writing, calculation |
| | ☽ | | Breakdown | Migration, travel |

**Figure 29: General theory of mundane astrology**

**5** And since the first of the natural motions moves about the center, and the second motion moves away from the center, and the third motion moves

---

[1] That is, natural motions: see **2**.
[2] Or, their "relationship" to them (مناسبة). See also **15**.

towards the center,[3] the first class (of the superior planets and their influences)[4] is associated with the first natural motion[5] which is about the center, due to their height, and their closeness to [the first motion],[6] and their distance from the third natural motion (which is towards the center). **6** So, from this perspective they come to have the indication for things over prolonged terms and periods, due to their analogy with the first motion and the languor[7] of their course. **7** And so the indication for affairs [which produce new] beginnings[8] like religious communities, dynasties, and whatever is over prolonged periods is attributed to the farthest of the superior planets from the world of generation and corruption (which is Saturn), since he is like a beginning for the rest of the heavenly bodies in [terms of] elevation. **8** And the indication for revealed laws[9] and what resembles them (which are what bring to completeness[10] the rest of the preceding and inceptional affairs) is attributed to the planet succedent to him in rank (which is Jupiter). **9** And the indication for wars, struggles, and what resembles those (which are like a declining of the culmination of matters and their ending, because the ending of affairs are indicative of the breakdown of their arrangements after their completeness, and the corruption of their structure) is attributed to the third planet among them in rank (which is Mars).

**10** And upon the breakdown of these things there will be a destruction of the borders, struggles [for supremacy], uprisings requiring wars,[11] and compulsions, necessitating the [mutual] adjustment[12] of these three conditions and their being linked with one another. **11** And it is that when one of them is deficient, the reduction affects the perfection of the other two states, in accordance with what the natural affairs necessitate among the three condi-

---

[3] See Aristotle's *De Caelo* I.2, 268b11-27, and the discussion in my Introduction.

[4] Namely, the superior planets Saturn, Jupiter, and Mars.

[5] That is, the primary motion of the rotation of the universe.

[6] Namely the primary or diurnal motion of the universe about the earth: that is, they are closest to the outer edge of the universe.

[7] تراخ. Perhaps a better word would be "leisureliness."

[8] Lit., "inceptional affairs." See also **8**.

[9] نوامس.

[10] Lit., "the culminations of completeness."

[11] والمخارجات المحوجة إلى الحروب.

[12] انتظام.

tions (which are the beginning, culmination, and decline): for wars do not come to be in most cases except by reason of laws, and laws do not come to be except by reason of religious communities and dynasties. **12** And if these situations are arranged in reverse, the matter once again forces their linking and ordering. **13** Because religious communities and dynasties do not come to be except through laws, and for the most part laws do not come to be except through wars: for changes become widespread through religious communities, dynasties, and laws, because of which there occur an abundance of disagreements; and if the differences multiply, disparity occurs; and when disparity occurs, wars take place. **14** For this reason then, these three states are associated with the superior planets, and they are like the principal [beginnings] for the secondary indications which follow them.[13]

**15** The greater luminary and his effects are associated with the second, natural, middle motion (which is *from* the center) due to the closeness of his analogy to it (since he stands in the middle of the heavenly bodies in rank, and the conditions attributed to him occupy the middle between the first motion and the third motion), and due to the moderation of his motion. **16** So, he comes to have an indication for kings and overlords since they are distinguished more firmly by the conditions of the first and second classes,[14] in accordance with what we will explain about others.

**17** Then, the inferior planets and their effects are associated with the third natural, lower motion (which is *towards* the center) due to their closeness to the third motion and their distance from the first natural motion (which is *around* the center). **18** So, in this respect they come to have the indication for the occurrence of things of shortened terms and periods, due to their analogy with the third motion, and the quickness of their motion. **19** The classes of the three inferior planets are as though subsequent to the three first classes[15] in indication due to the firmness of the first classes' need for them,[16] and their connection to them. **20** Thus to the highest of the infe-

---

[13] This is a major claim for why we look at these planets' conjunctions, and treat them as important general significators in charts.
[14] That is, the significations of Saturn and Jupiter.
[15] That is, the significations of Saturn, Jupiter, and Mars.
[16] That is, the higher classes of states and conditions need more material, mundane states to manifest them.

rior planets (which is Venus) is attributed the indication for marriages,[17] garments, and what resembles that since they are analogous to the first class indicative of beginnings.[18] **21** And to the planet succeding her in rank (which is Mercury) is attributed the indication for writing, calculation, and what resembles that since he is analogous to the second class indicative of culminations.[19] **22** And to the planet succeding her third in rank (which is the Moon) is attributed the indication for movement, migration, travels, and what resembles that since she is analogous to the third class indicative of decline.[20]

**23** And these indications are attributed to these three planets due to [1] the necessity of the people of religious communities and dynasties' needing marriages[21] and garments (since nature incites them to that),[22] and due to [2] the need of the laws (which are contracts and ordinances) for writing and calculation (since the whole of them are completed through writing, and the arrangements of the people of their time are put in order[23] by means of calculation), and [3] wars' need for travels and transportation (since this business is accomplished by movement). **24** So, for this reason these three states of affairs are attributed to the inferior planets, since they are as though secondary (due to their connection with the first states of affairs[24] and the need of the first ones for them).

---

[17] المناكح, which by its root is closely related to marriage but really refers to sexual relationships. **BY** understandably translate it as "marriage" and I follow them but Lane is clear that it literally means "women."

[18] She is therefore similar to Saturn.

[19] He is therefore similar to Jupiter.

[20] She is therefore similar to Mars.

[21] See footnote to **20**.

[22] This accounts for Venus; the next two points refer to Mercury and the Moon.

[23] Or perhaps, "entered into" (تنتظم).

[24] That is, those of the superiors.

BOOK I: PRINCIPLES & PROPHETS    77

*[First four types of mundane chart]*

**25** And whereas the matters from which one seeks foreknowledge about occurrences belonging to universal [matters] (and their particular [manifestations]) in repeated[25] [future] periods is discovered from six components:

**26** The first of them is from the positions of the upper bodies in the Ascendants of the revolutions of years in which occurs the uniting of the two superior planets[26] in the spring convertible sign, [which] comes to be every 960 solar years.

**27** The second is from the positions of the upper bodies in the Ascendants of the revolutions of years in which their[27] uniting comes to be, at their shift from triplicity to triplicity, occurring every 240 solar years.

**28** The third is from the positions of the upper bodies in the Ascendants of the revolutions of years in which the uniting of the two infortunes happens in Cancer, and from the time of their uniting in it [which] occurs every 30 years.

**29** The fourth is from the positions of the upper bodies in the Ascendants of the revolutions of years in which their[28] conjunction occurs in every sign, [which] come to be every 20 years.[29]

| 1 | ♄☌♃ in ♈ | 960 years | Universal events, floods, dynasties |
|---|---|---|---|
| 2 | ♄☌♃ in a triplicity shift | 240 years | |
| 3 | ♄☌♂ in ♋ | 30 years | Elevated people and nobility |
| 4 | ♄☌♃ in any sign | 20 years | |
| 5 | Lunation before ♈ ingress ♈ ingress charts | Annual | General public, weather, prices |
| 6 | Lunation before all other ingresses All other ingress charts | Monthly | |

**Figure 30: Six types of mundane chart**

---

[25] Lit. "renewed" (المستأنفة). **BY** translate this as simply "future" times or periods.
[26] That is, Saturn and Jupiter.
[27] Saturn and Jupiter.
[28] Saturn and Jupiter.
[29] For the fifth component, see sentence **64** below.

## [Interlude on distances and timing of conjunctions]

**30** And of course the [total] years of their uniting at the beginning of Aries, the triplicities, and in each sign may increase and decrease, and that is because when Saturn and Jupiter unite by mean [motion] at the beginning of a sign of a triplicity, their uniting after that will be at the end of an arc whose amount is 242° 25' 17" 10''' 06'''', and indeed in each sign in which they unite they add (based on where they united in the first sign) 2° 25' 17" 10''' 06''''. **31** Thus their uniting in the signs of a triplicity may in this way be 13 conjunctions, and that is a period greater than the amount which we determined,[30] especially if their uniting at the beginning of one of the signs of the triplicity to which they shift was less than 56':[31] for then they will unite 13 times in that triplicity. **32** And if their uniting at the beginning of one of the signs of the triplicity was at more than 56' 33" 18''' 48'''', then their uniting in that triplicity will be 12 times. **33** And if they unite 12 times in one triplicity and 13 times in [another] triplicity, their uniting in two triplicities will be 25 times, so their uniting in the rest of the triplicities will be 50 times.

**34** And[32] between one conjunction and [another] conjunction is 19 years, 314 days, 14 hours, 23 minutes, 37 seconds, 18 thirds, 6 fourths, and 48 fifths in years of the mean Sun (which is 365 days without the addition of one-fourth to that). **35** Now when you multiply these 50 conjunctions by the period between one conjunction and another (and its fractions), that comes to 996 years. **36** This exceeds the amount of the period we set forth before as coming to be from the time of their uniting at the beginning of Aries up to the time of their return to it.[33] **37** And when they unite 12 times in a triplicity, their conjunction comes to 29° 03' 26" 01''' 12'''' and what re-

---

[30] See **27**: 12 conjunctions every 20 years is 240 years; but if there were 13, it would be 260 years.

[31] Reading more correctly for "54'": see the value in **32**.

[32] As I mention in my Introduction, this sentence gives the conjunctional period as measured in a year of 365 days, which is irrelevant.

[33] See **26**, which gives a standardized 960 years. Just as he pointed out in **31** (and my footnote to it), if there are sometimes 13 conjunctions in a triplicity, that will add more years to the standard 960.

mains, up to the completion of 30°. **38** And if they conjoined in less than that they need 13 conjunctions.

**39** And an example of that is that a conjunction was in the first fifth[34] of Cancer. **40** When what is between one conjunction and [another] in degrees (and its fractions) was added on top of that, according to what we set out before, their [next] conjunction occurred in 2° 25' 17" 10'" 06"" of Pisces.

**41** And when what is between two conjunctions in degrees (and their fractions), was added on top of these portions, their [next] uniting occurred in 4° 50' 34" 20'" 12"" of Scorpio.

**42** And when what is between two conjunctions was added on top of these portions, their [next] uniting occurred in 7° 15' 51" 30'" 18"" of Cancer.

**43** And when what is between two conjunctions in degrees (and their fractions) was added on top of that, their [next] uniting occurred in 9° 41' 08" 40'" 24"" of Pisces.

**44** And when what is between two conjunctions was added on top of these portions, their [next] uniting occurred in 12° 06' 25" 50'" 30"" of Scorpio.

**45** And when what is between two conjunctions was added on top of these portions, their [next] uniting occurred in 14° 31' 43" 00'" 36"" of Cancer.

**46** And when what is between two con-

| Conjunctional distance: 2.42143565° ||
|---|---|
| Fire (1) | 0.00000000° |
| 2 | 2.42143565° |
| 3 | 4.84287130° |
| 4 | 7.26430694° |
| 5 | 9.68574259° |
| 6 | 12.10717824° |
| 7 | 14.52861389° |
| 8 | 16.95004954° |
| 9 | 19.37148518° |
| 10 | 21.79292083° |
| 11 | 24.21435648° |
| 12 | 26.63579213° |
| 13 | 29.05722778° |
| *Triplicity Shift* ||
| Earth (1) | 1.47866342° |
| 2 | 3.90009907° |
| 3 | 6.32153472° |
| 4 | 8.74297037° |
| 5 | 11.16440602° |
| 6 | 13.58584166° |
| 7 | 16.00727731° |
| 8 | 18.42871296° |
| 9 | 20.85014861° |
| 10 | 23.27158426° |
| 11 | 25.69301990° |
| 12 | 28.11445555° |

**Figure 31: Abū Ma'shar's triplicity shifts**

---

[34] That is, 0° 00' 00" 00'" 00"" 01""'". This is about the tiniest amount in the sign where one could place the conjunction.

junctions was added on top of these portions, their [next] uniting occurred in 16° 57' 00" 10'" 42"" of Pisces.

**47** And when what is between two conjunctions was added on top of these portions, their [next] uniting occurred in 19° 22' 17"[35] 20'" 48"" of Scorpio.

**48** And when what is between two conjunctions was added on top of these portions, their [next] uniting occurred in 21° 47' 34" 30'" 54"" of Cancer.

**49** And when what is between two conjunction was added on top of these portions, their [next] uniting occurred in 24° 12' 51" 41'" 00"" of Pisces.

**50** And when what is between two conjunctions was added on top of these portions, their [next] uniting occurred in 26° 38' 08" 51'" 06"" of Scorpio.

**51** And when what is between two conjunctions was added on top of these portions, their [next] uniting occurred in 29° 03' 26" 01'" 12"" of Cancer.

**52** And that completes 12 conjunctions even though the full sign is not finished. **53** And that indicates that they have a 13th conjunction in this triplicity, for if what is between two conjunctions is added on top of these portions, their [next] uniting will occur in 1° 28' 43" 11'" 18"" of Aries.[36] **54** So, their uniting will occur in the portions of the tenth sign from which they began,[37] and their shift will be from the watery [triplicity] to the fiery one; and of course it is necessary that the [next] conjunction will shift to Leo. **55** So, when it is necessary that they have 13 conjunctions, they will shift to the tenth sign [from the beginning sign], which is of the fiery triplicity.

---

[35] Reading for the text's erroneous "19".
[36] This explanation is somewhat misleading. The conjunction at virtually 0° Cancer (**39**) is the *first* conjunction in that triplicity. This means that the conjunction at 29° is the *thirteenth* conjunction, even though Abū Ma'shar says that it "completes 12 conjunctions."
[37] Namely, from Cancer.

**56** Now if what they travel through in 12 conjunctions is added on top of that (and it is 29° 03' 26" 01'" 12""), they will shift to Taurus (which follows upon Aries), and their [next] conjunction[38] will be in [00°] 32' 09" 12'" 30"" of it. **57** And if they unite in 13 conjunctions in the triplicity, they will unite in the tenth sign from where they [had] united [first]. **58** And if they unite in 12 conjunctions in the

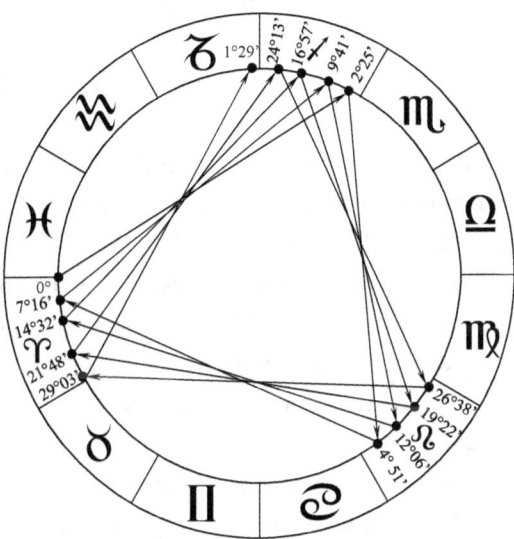

Figure 32: Abū Ma'shar's triplicity shift after 13 conjunctions

triplicity, they will unite in the second [sign] from where they [had] united [first].

**59** As for knowing how many days there are between two conjunctions, one looks at the amount of Saturn's cycles in terms of degrees in 360,000 solar years (and it is 12,214 cycles), and at Jupiter's cycles in that [time] (and it is 30,352 cycles). **60** One subtracts the lesser of the two cycles from the greater of them, and there remain 18,138. **61** One divides into that the days in 360,000 years (and that is one hundred thirty-one million, four hundred ninety-three thousand, two hundred and forty days, [or] in the Indian manner, '131,493,240').[39] **62** The result of that is the period which is between two conjunctions. **63** The days of the conjunction and its portions are multiplied by what Saturn cycles through in 360,000 years, and are divided by the days in 360,000 years, and what comes out from that are the degrees of the arc (and its fractions) which come to be between two conjunctions: and that is, as we set out before, 242° 25' 17" 10'" 06"".

---

[38] Or rather, the next triplicity shift.
[39] 131,493,240 days divided by 360,000 years, equals a solar year of 365.259 days.

## [5ᵗʰ and 6ᵗʰ types of mundane charts]

**64** As for the fifth [component], it is from the positions of the upper bodies in the Ascendants of the times in which [1] the conjunctional and full-[Moon] Beginnings arrive, which precede the parallelism of the greater luminary with the point of the beginnings of the convertible signs, and at [2] the time of his parallelism with them.[40]

**65** The sixth is from the positions of the upper bodies in[41] the Ascendants of the times in which [1] the conjunction or full-[Moon] Beginnings arrive, which precede the parallelism of the greater luminary with the beginnings of [all other] signs, and [2] at the time of his parallelism with the point of their beginnings.[42]

**66** At the presence of one of these times which we have determined, one makes an examination of the Ascendants of those periods, and the location of the upper bodies in them, and the rest of their natural and incidental conditions in themselves and relative to the Sun and the circle,[43] and one discovers [1] what their indications are from the victors over the principal positions, and [2] when [they will be], in accordance with what the indicators point out about that.

## [How the six types of charts differ]

**67** Then[44] one looks at the indication of these six principles:

**68** For if they are divided into three classes, one of them[45] is peculiar to universal states, such as the special jurisdiction of the indicators of the great

---

[40] That is, at [1] the lunation which immediately precedes each quarterly ingress, and [2] at the time of each quarterly ingress itself.

[41] عند, here and elsewhere.

[42] That is, at [1] the lunation which immediately precedes every other sign ingress, and [2] at the time of all of those other ingresses.

[43] That is, things like retrogradation, being under the rays, and in good and bad places of the circle.

[44] **BY** put this sentence at the end of the previous paragraph, but that seems redundant because we have just been told to look at all of those charts. Abū Ma'shar is now about to tell us some of the categories of what to look for in them, so I have moved the sentence to the beginning of this new subsection.

Beginnings indicative of universal affairs like floods, dynasties, religions, and what resembles that, at the uniting of the two superiors in Aries, and at their uniting at the time of their shifting from triplicity to triplicity.

**69** The second[46] is peculiar to the sum of the portions of those universal things, like the special jurisdiction of the indicators of the uniting of the two infortunes in Cancer, and the uniting of the two superiors in the rest of the signs, for the condition of elevated people among leaders and the nobility, in that transit.

**70** And the third[47] is divided into many classes in which all of the indicators collaborate in the parts of sum[48] of the portions of universal things,[49] such as the collaboration of the indicators of the years, quarters, and months in the conditions of the people and the air, and the rest of the upper occurrences, and fertility and sterility, and what resembles that.

## [The Turn]

**71** And the lord of the Turn also collaborates with these indicators. **72** And it is that one looks at the shifting of the conjunction from triplicity to triplicity: for if it was indicative of a shift of religious communities and dynasties, that time is made the beginning of the periods whose amount is like the amount of the degrees of the sphere,[50] and the lord of the Turn is made to be the planet at which the counting arrives[51] from the lord of the Turn of

---

[45] This refers to chart types [1] and [2], in **26-27** above. See throughout the rest of Books I-II.

[46] This refers to chart types [3] and [4], in **28-29** above. Descriptions and delineations of these are found in Chs. II.8, **1-30** (Saturn-Mars conjunctions in Cancer), and in I.2 (general statements about the Saturn-Jupiter conjunctions).

[47] This refers to chart types [5] and [6], in **64-65** above. Since these refer generally to annual revolutions and the pre-ingress lunations, they can be found throughout, but see especially Ch. VIII.1.

[48] الجمل.

[49] Abū Ma'shar's use of "parts/portions," "sums," and so on, are more opaque than in earlier works like the *Gr. Intr.* Here he seems to be speaking about how all manner of individual significators and multiple charts may play a role in determining some effect. See especially Ch. VIII.1.

[50] That is, 360.

[51] See **82-83**.

the conjunction indicative of the Flood[52] (or the conjunction which comes to be at the beginning of Aries),[53] and it is made to have the beginning in the management of those periods. **73** Then one divides those periods into Quarters like[54] the amount of the quarters of a year, and each one of its Quarters is made the beginning of what belongs to the explanation of what will occur from the changes at the termination of every Quarter, in religious communities, dynasties, and kings, [or] such as the change of the conditions of the air, and the difference in its qualities at the shifting of the greater luminary from quarter to quarter. **74** And the lord of the Turn is made an indicator over the first Quarter (which is 90 years), and to the second quarter belongs the planet which the Turn reaches from the lord of the first Quarter, along with the partnership[55] of the lord of the first Quarter with it. **75** And the matter in the indicators of the Quarters is used in this way until their completion.

**76** And an example of that is that the conjunction [of 3,381 BC] indicative of the Flood was prior to the conjunction indicative of the religious community of the Arabs by 3,950 years.[56] **77** And the ruler of the Turn at that time[57] was Saturn along with the sign of Cancer, while the Flood was after that by 279 years.[58] **78** So between the first day of the year of the Flood

---

[52] That is, Māshā'allāh's "indicator" conjunction of 3381 BC, in Scorpio. See §§10.2-10.3 in my Introduction.

[53] See **81**. That is, Abū Ma'shar's own theory.

[54] Lit., "of."

[55] متشارك, but reading as the verbal noun تشارك.

[56] The year of the conjunction for Islam (570 AD) – 3,950 years = 3,381 BC, Māshā'allāh's indicator conjunction.

[57] That is, at the indicator conjunction of 3,381 BC.

[58] Reading more correctly for 287. Abū Ma'shar is being slightly deceptive here, because like other astrologers he is trying to combine his version of time lords and the Flood, with Māshā'allāh's. Māshā'allāh's indicator conjunction was in 3,381 BC, but Abū Ma'shar did not claim to have an indicator conjunction preceding his own Flood, which was 279 years later (3,102 BC). It was *Māshā'allāh* who began the Cancer-Saturn Turn in 3,381 BC, and it just so happens that that the 360 years of the Turn encompasses both the Māshā'allāh Flood and the Abū Ma'shar Flood. Thus Abū Ma'shar is adopting a time lord system which he does not otherwise follow. Mūsā is correct (in his Ch. 2, **45**) that the Abū Ma'shar theory of a Flood at the middle of a world-year of 360,000 years requires that the Turn be at Sagittarius-Sun, not Cancer-Saturn.

[in 3,102 BC] and the first day of the year in which was the conjunction indicative of the religious community of the Arabs, there were 3,671 years.

**79** And Abthnūs[59] and others have stated that between the beginning of the creation of Adam (the blessings of God be upon him) and the night of Friday in which the Flood was, was 2,226 years, 1 month, 23 days, and 4 hours. **80** So, in this way what is between the creation of Adam (peace be upon him) and the first day of the year in which was the conjunction indicative of the religious community of the Arabs, was 5,897 years, 1 month, 23 days, and 4 hours.

| Māshā'allāh's Turns | | Year | Turn | Years of Thousand | Mūsā / Abū Ma'shar Turns | |
|---|---|---|---|---|---|---|
| ♊ | ☽ | -3740 | #500 | 180,000 | ♏ | ♂ |
| ♋ | ♄ | -3380 | #501 | 180,360 | ♐ | ☉ |
| ♌ | ♃ | -3020 | #502 | 180,720 | ♑ | ♀ |
| ♍ | ♂ | -2660 | #503 | 181,080 | ♒ | ☿ |
| ♎ | ☉ | -2300 | #504 | 181,440 | ♓ | ☽ |
| ♏ | ♀ | -1940 | #505 | 181,800 | ♈ | ♄ |
| ♐ | ☿ | -1580 | #506 | 182,160 | ♉ | ♃ |
| ♑ | ☽ | -1220 | #507 | 182,520 | ♊ | ♂ |
| ♒ | ♄ | -860 | #508 | 182,880 | ♋ | ☉ |
| ♓ | ♃ | -500 | #509 | 183,240 | ♌ | ♀ |
| ♈ | ♂ | -140 | #510 | 183,600 | ♍ | ☿ |
| ♉ | ☉ | 220 | #511 | 183,960 | ♎ | ☽ |
| ♊ | ♀ | 580 | #512 | 184,320 | ♏ | ♄ |
| ♋ | ☿ | 940 | #513 | 184,680 | ♐ | ♃ |

Figure 33: Flood and Islam Turns of Māshā'allāh and Abū Ma'shar

---

[59] أبثنوس, an unknown astrologer whose name is spelled differently in various manuscripts.

| 82-83 | Turn (in 580): Gemini-Venus |
| --- | --- |
| 81 | Profection from ♈, in 570: Pisces |
| 84 | Direction in 570: 20° Pisces |
| 85 | Lord of Quarter 1: Mars |
| 86 | Lord of Quarter 2: Sun |
| 86 | Lord of Quarter 3: Mercury |
| 86 | Lord of Quarter 4: Saturn |

**Figure 34: Key planets and positions for early Islam**

**81** If we divide the years which are between the conjunction [indicative] of the Flood and the conjunction indicative of the religious community of the Arabs[60] by 360, and take a year for every sign, and we begin projecting from Aries, the year reaches Pisces.[61]

**82** If we divide those years by 360 and for every Turn we take a sign, and we begin casting out from the managing sign (which belonged to the Turn in that time indicative of the Flood, which is Cancer), the Turn terminates at the conjunction indicative of the religious community, at Gemini.[62] **83** And if we grant one of the cycles to each planet and we begin casting out from the planet which belongs to the Turn in the conjunction indicative of the religious community, the counting terminates at Venus.[63]

---

[60] Again, 3,950 (see **76**).

[61] Unless I am misunderstanding him, Abū Ma'shar is being misleading or careless here, as he seems to be equating the exact years up to 570 AD, with the actual date of the Turn in 580 (see **82** and the instructions in **72**); moreover, he is not really taking one year per sign, but one sign per Turn. If we assign Aries to the Turn of the indicator conjunction (Cancer-Saturn) and then each subsequent sign to the other Turns, then the Islam conjunction/Turn of 570/580 (Gemini-Venus) will be Pisces.

[62] See the Figure above. Abū Ma'shar is not exactly right: the Turn changed to Gemini-Venus in 580 AD, not 570. In the Mūsā version of the Turns which Abū Ma'shar ought to be using, the Turn in 580 was Scorpio-Saturn.

[63] See the Figure above.

**84** And if we cast out from the Ascendant of the conjunction which was at the beginning of Aries, a year for every degree, it terminates in the conjunction indicative of the religious community at 20° of Pisces.[64]

**85** And the victor over the Turn, the lord of the Ascendant, and the lord of the sign of the conjunction is Mars:[65] so the management [of Mars] belongs to the first Quarter, which was 90 years from the beginning of the conjunction indicative of the dynasty of the Arabs. **86** The second Quarter belongs to the Sun, the third Quarter to Mercury, and the fourth Quarter to Saturn: that is in accordance with the victorships of the planets over the[66] Turn, and over the Ascendant and the sign of the conjunction, and their[67] partnership with the first lord of the Turn (which was Venus).[68]

**87** And one may also look at the conjunction coming to be at the end of each of the Quarters which we described in the preceding (and one does not pay attention to the Quarter preceding nor following it), and one makes [it be] one of the principles which we mentioned.[69]

---

[64] This is unnecessarily complicated. Since the direction begins at 0° Aries at the beginning of every Turn, we don't need to go as far back as the Aries conjunction to count this. It is enough to know that the direction began again at 0° Aries at the beginning of the Taurus-Sun Turn; since the Islam conjunction of 570 is 10 years before its end (and the beginning of the Gemini-Venus Turn in 580), the direction obviously terminates at 20° Pisces, which is 10° before the end of the zodiac.

[65] **BY** conjecture the following (see also **86**): in the assumed chart for the Islam conjunction, the conjunction was in Scorpio (ruled by Mars), Mars was in Gemini (the sign of the coming Turn), and he was sextiling Venus, the lord of the Ascendant (Libra). See VIII.2, **9**. If so, then the Sun, Mercury, and Saturn are victors over the Quarters because of their roles in *those* charts cast 90, 180, and 270 years later. See an alternative in **88** below, which assigns the lords (or victors) of the stakes of the revolution chart to each of the Quarters. Note that Mūsā (Ch. 2, **89**) mentions this approach, but says the chart is that of each 360 or Turn, not of the conjunction.

[66] Omitting "lord of the," as indicated by **BY**.

[67] Reading the plural with MSS **BN**, for the dual.

[68] The Turn belongs to Venus-Gemini. But the reason for these other planets is unclear to me. See also **91**, which suggests that the ingress chart every 90 years could be used to find the lord of that Quarter.

[69] This seems to mean that we should pay attention to important conjunction (e.g., indicating a shift in religions or dynasties) which occur very close to a division near Quarters, and not just the change of Turns. If so, then we can start counting 360 years from it.

**88** And one also makes the lord of the Ascendant of the year in which the conjunction indicative of the occurrence of religious communities and dynasties is, be an indicator over the first Quarter (which is 90 years), and the lord of [its] tenth an indicator for the second Quarter, the lord of the seventh an indicator for the third Quarter, and the lord of the fourth an indicator for the fourth Quarter, contrary to the usual practice in the first division.[70]

**89** And one makes the sign at which the year terminates at the shifting of the dynasty to be indicative of the nature of the people of that dynasty, as well as of their clothing, form, and allies.[71]

**90** And the lord of the sign of [that] terminal point [is made] an indicator over their periods of time and their strength, while the lord of the fourth Turn[72] collaborates with it.

**91** In addition, the lord of the Ascendant of each one of the Quarters (which is 90 years) is made to be the lord of that Quarter.

### [Mundane profections]

**92** Now[73] as for the terminal points from [1] the Ascendants of these times,[74] and from [2] the positions of the conjunctions, for each one of them there appear many indications for types [of things] peculiar to itself and not others:

**93** Such as [1a] the indication of the sign of the terminal point from the Ascendant of the conjunction coming to be in Aries, for general, comprehensive affairs, floods, earthquakes, infectious disease, and what resembles that. **94** And such as [1b] the sign of the terminal point from the position of

---

[70] That is, as opposed to **73-75** above. See **85-86**, which almost follows the instructions here.

[71] Perhaps the rules for prophets in I.4 could be adapted to dynasties. For example, the color of the 'Abbāsid banners was black, and that of the 'Umayyads green.

[72] **BY** plausibly read this as "the fourth lord of the Turn."

[73] For the application of the following to specific signs in Abū Ma'shar's time, see VIII.2, **28ff**.

[74] الأزمان.

the conjunction (and its lord)[75] coming to be in Aries, for what occurs in the rest of short[76] dynasties in those periods, and in the amount of their people's esteem, and what among them is more inclined towards universal affairs.

95 And such as [2a] the sign of the terminal point from the Ascendant of the conjunction of the religious community and from [2b] the sign of the conjunction of the religious community (and the lords of both)[77] for what occurs in religious communities.

96 And such as [3a] the sign of the terminal point from the Ascendant of the dynasty and from [3b] the sign of the conjunction of the dynasty (and the lords of both) for what occurs in dynasties.

| Chart | Profection from | Indication |
|---|---|---|
| Aries ♂ | ASC | Floods, earthquakes, epidemic |
| | ♂ | Short dynasties, their qualities |
| ♂ of religion | ASC | What occurs in religions |
| | ♂ | |
| ♂ of dynasty | ASC | What occurs in dynasties |
| | ♂ | |
| ♂ of triplicity shift | ASC | What occurs in dynasties (esp. kings of religious community) |
| | ♂ | |
| Lesser ♂ | ASC | What befalls important people |
| | ♂ | |

Figure 35: General indications for mundane profections

97 And such as [4a] the sign of the terminal point from the Ascendant of the shifting of the triplicity (and its lord) for what occurs in the dynasties of the kings of the religious community, and such as [4b] the sign of the terminal point from the sign of the conjunction of the triplicity (and its lord) for what occurs in the nature[78] of the dynasties as well.

---

[75] I doubt this use of profections from the lord of the conjunction. In later Books, Abū Ma'shar is only interested in the sign of the conjunction itself, which makes more sense.

[76] Lit., "shortened" (المختصرة).

[77] See my footnote above.

[78] نفس, lit. "soul, self."

**98** And such as the [5a] sign of the terminal point from the Ascendant of the conjunction coming to be in[79] the annual revolutions, and from [5b] the sign of the conjunction (and the lord of both) for what occurs in the people of the elevated, noble houses in that conjunction.

**99** So when these signs are illuminated by the fortunes, or their lords were fortunes or made fortunate, they indicate good fortune in all of the types [of things] one seeks information about. **100** If they were easternizing they indicate the appearance of their indication and the quickness of its occurrence, and if they were pivotal[80] they indicate their power and safety. **101** And if they were middling in condition, they indicate what is middling in that. **102** But if they were in the antithesis of what we have mentioned (in good fortune, easternization, being pivotal, and power), they indicate the badness of those types and their obscurity, the slowness of their occurrence, their weakness, abasement, and troubles.

**103** And if those times[81] were of the periods indicative of the disappearance of one of the types,[82] what we have described will be among the strongest warnings of the cutting-off of its period of time and its ruin.

**104** And in the rest of the years one applies the lords of the Turns and of the terminal points, in accordance with directions from the Ascendants of the Beginnings, and from the positions of the conjunctions, a year for every sign in the succession of signs.

*[Mundane directions]*

**105** And of course you should also direct from the portion of the Ascendant of the shift of the triplicity, a year for every degree, and you should look also at the lord of that bound in which the distribution is, so that you make it the distributor. **106** And you look at the rays of the fortunes and the infortunes existing in the degrees of the distribution: so you judge in accordance with that.

---

[79] Lit., "in it in."

[80] That is, on or near the axial degree or stake, lit., "stake-y" (وتدية).

[81] الأوقات.

[82] See generally Book II.

**107** And of course one looks at the sign at which the year of the world terminates from the Ascendant of the religious community: it is divided into twelve divisions,[83] and one seeks information from the first division in accordance with the nature of [that] sign [itself] and the lord of its indication. **108** And the second division [is] for the sign following it (and its lord), and one applies this management up to the endpoint at the end of the signs.

**109** And when the direction from one of the positions which we have determined has reached the rays of a planet (of the rays which are in a conjunctional year),[84] that indicates the occurrence of what the year of the conjunction indicated. **110** And if that was at the time of the shift of the transit, that is an indicator of the fulfilment of what the year of the transit promised, through that planet whose ray it reached. **111** And likewise, if the ray which it reached was of the rays of the beginning of the religious community, it fulfils what that planet promised, whose ray it was at the start of the religious community.

**112** Now as for how to know the signs of the terminal points [which come] from the positions we mentioned before in the rest of the years, we will provide that in more appropriate places, if God (be He exalted!) wills.[85]

**113** Since we have completed what we wanted to explain, let us conclude Chapter I.1, with the help of God.

---

[83] I.e., the twelfth-parts.
[84] This simply seems to mean that the mundane distribution reaches some planet's rays *in* the same year of a conjunction.
[85] See VIII.2, **28-31**.

## Chapter I.2: On knowing the strongest of the conjunctional signs of the triplicities, & the appearance of their indications in the regions attributed to them

**1** In this chapter let us get to know thoroughly the strongest of the signs of the triplicities indicative of the greatness of the periods and their shortness,[86] since they are like the supports for what we are seeking to gain in knowing the quality of the things we made mention of before.

*[Strength and timing of events from triplicities]*

**2** We say that if the conjunction occurs in the fiery triplicity, that indicates the strength of the people of the east; the strongest of its signs is Sagittarius, its middling one Leo, and its weakest Aries. **3** If that was in the earthy triplicity, that indicates the strength of the people of the west; the strongest of its signs is Capricorn, its middling one Virgo, and its weakest Taurus. **4** If that was in the airy triplicity, that indicates the strength of the people of the northern region; the strongest of its signs is Aquarius, its middling one Libra, and its weakest Gemini. **5** And if that was in the watery triplicity, that indicates the strength of the people of the southern region; the strongest of its signs is Pisces, its middling one Scorpio, and its weakest Cancer. **6** And that is due to the power of their lords.[87]

| Strongest | Middle | Weakest | Direction | Mūsā |
|---|---|---|---|---|
| ♐ | ♌ | ♈ | E | E |
| ♑ | ♍ | ♉ | W | S |
| ♒ | ♎ | ♊ | N | W |
| ♓ | ♏ | ♋ | S | N |

Figure 36: Strength and direction of signs

---

[86] كثرة...قصرها. This is a strange phrase because "abundance" or "greatness" is not the contrary of "shortness." I would have expected him to say their "length" (طول) and shortness.

[87] Abū Ma'shar's assignment of cardinal directions to the triplicities makes no astrological sense except for the fiery signs (east). Mūsā gives the more obvious one, which I include here.

BOOK I: PRINCIPLES & PROPHETS

**7** Now as for the timing of the appearance of the indication of the fiery triplicity, that indicates three conjunctions *after the return* of the conjunction to the sign of the triplicity which the shift of the conjunction came to.[88] **8** In the airy triplicity and the earthy one, four conjunctions. **9** And in the watery triplicity, two conjunctions. **10** But it is possible that there will be a difference in the times of the indications of the shift to the fiery triplicity in this arrangement: after nine conjunctions from the time of the shift; and in the airy and earthy one, after eight conjunctions; and in the watery triplicity, after six conjunctions.[89]

|  | ♂ after return to shift | Or ♂ after shift: |
|---|---|---|
| Fire | 3 | 9 |
| Air | 4 | 8 |
| Earth | 4 | 8 |
| Water | 2 | 6 |

**Figure 37: Effects in which conjunction**

*[Lifespan of kings from triplicities and planetary periods]*

**11** Now as for the triplicities in which the conjunction indicative of the [long] length of the kings' lifespan occurs, [they are] the triplicities in which Saturn has testimony.

**12** And one also seeks information about the power of the people of the regions (at the time of the shift of the conjunction from triplicity to triplicity), from the rotations[90] of the planets about the Ascendants of the conjunctions and their positions. **13** For if that rotation[91] belonged to Saturn, that indicates the strength of the people of the first clime, then the rest

---

[88] This must be something like, "the *most powerful timing*," since in II.8, **139-45** every return of the conjunction to the sign of the triplicity shift will show changes and developments.

[89] **BY** say that the second column (9-8-8-6) is more likely 9-12-12-6, so that the numbers in the first column would all be multiplied by 3. But there may be some other reason for the 9-8-8-6 values.

[90] استدارات. Meaning unclear.

[91] استدار.

of the planets following Saturn in the order of spheres, and the first clime [again] in the order of numbers until one comes to the last of them.

**14** Now as for the amount of their lifespans in the fiery triplicity, they are shortened periods, unless the conjunction is in Sagittarius: for that is an indicator of the long length of their periods. **15** And as for the two conjunctions of Aries and Leo, their periods of time in them will be in accordance with the duration of one conjunction; and in the conjunction of Sagittarius it is indicative of the duration of two conjunctions, apart from what falls to Jupiter in that (in terms of increase).[92]

**16** As for the earthy triplicity, their lifespans in it are long, and the best of that is Capricorn. **17** And when the acceder accedes in the year of the conjunction of Capricorn, and that[93] is in the aspect of Saturn and Jupiter, it indicates periods of the span of two conjunctions, except for what falls to Saturn and Jupiter in that (in terms of increase). **18** And if the conjunction was in Taurus at his accession, it indicates the span of one conjunction; but if that was when the Moon and Venus are in excellent positions, it adds to those periods. **19** And if the conjunction was in Virgo, and Saturn and Jupiter witnessed, that indicates the span of one conjunction.[94]

**20** If the conjunction was in the airy triplicity, it indicates the long length of their periods, especially if Saturn and Jupiter had testimony by their both alighting in the stakes (or one of them did, and the one of them handing over was in a stake): for if it was like that, the matter indicates the span of one-and-a-half conjunctions. **21** If his accession was in the year of the conjunction of Gemini, that indicates the span of two conjunctions apart from what falls to Saturn and Jupiter in terms of increase above those periods, due to their testimony. **22** But if the conjunction was in Libra, it indicates that the amount of those periods will be in accordance with what is between Venus and Saturn in numbers, or according to the years of both. **23** And if his accession was in the revolution of the year of the conjunction of Aquarius, and

---

[92] This seems to refer to adding, e.g., 12 years for the lesser years of Jupiter.

[93] This may be an Ascendant; it would not make sense for this to be the sign of the conjunction, since Saturn and Jupiter would already be in it.

[94] The fact that Virgo needs help to even complete one conjunction, suggests that Mūsā is right about Taurus being in the middle and Virgo weakest (*Periods* Ch. 3, **13-14**).

Saturn had testimony in [the year],⁹⁵ that indicates a span of three conjunctions. **24** And if the conjunction returned to Aquarius and Saturn had testimony in it like his testimony in the first time, that indicates a span of six conjunctions, and the matter in that will be according to what we stated up to the time of the corruption of the testimony of Saturn and Jupiter.

**25** (And one should certainly have fear at the completion of every conjunction, until there has passed by (in terms of years) the amount of what is between the place of the conjunction up to its Ascendant, a year for every sign:⁹⁶ for if that did pass by, it fulfills the conjunction. **26** And it is necessary that one use this management in every year whose span is greater than one conjunction.)⁹⁷

**27** Now if the conjunction occurred in this triplicity⁹⁸ and Saturn and Jupiter bore witness, that indicates the long length of the time, unless the conjunction was in Libra: for that is an indicator of the quickness of the shift as well as ruin (and the indication at the uniting in Capricorn is like that).

**28** And if the conjunction was in Cancer and its triplicity, it will be below what we stated before in terms of the length of the periods, except that the best of the signs of the watery triplicity are Pisces and Scorpio, because they are two houses belonging to two superior planets, since the signs of the superior planets are more indicative of the long length of the periods than the signs of the inferior planets.

**29** And of course one may also seek information about the size of the amounts of the lifespans of the people of the dynasty from the years of the lord of the Turn, and the years of the lord of the sign at which the profection⁹⁹ has terminated at the shift of the Quarters, just as we have made clear in the first Chapter.¹⁰⁰

---

⁹⁵ The feminine ending on فيها means that it is "the year" and not "the revolution," although this is the same thing if we are only looking at revolutions and not profections.

⁹⁶ For other examples of profections between the Ascendant of a conjunction and the conjunction, see I.3, **31-33**.

⁹⁷ **BY** are not sure what this means; I think it means that this method should be used for all of the above, where they say that the span will be more than one conjunction.

⁹⁸ The airy triplicity.

⁹⁹ الدور.

¹⁰⁰ See I.1, **92-104**.

**30** As for knowing the quality of the sum of indications of the triplicities, if the shift is in the fiery triplicity or the airy one, that indicates the appearance of kings and leaders, nobles, the mighty, scholars, and the elevation of the people of this class. **31** And if the shift was to the watery or earthy one, that is an indicator of the superiority of the common people, people in the middle, and their equivalence to the leaders in rank.

**32** Since we have completed what we wanted to describe, let us break off Chapter I.2.

BOOK I: PRINCIPLES & PROPHETS                    97

**Chapter I.3: On knowing the conjunctions indicative of the nativities of prophets & conquerors, their morals & character, the marks coming to be on them, the tokens of their prophethood, the timing of their appearance, the locating of each one of them, & the extent of the quantity of their years**

1 Since we have set forth in Chapter I.2 what was necessary to state first in terms of how to know the strongest signs of the triplicities, and the timing of the appearance of their indication, in this chapter let us state the shifts of the conjunctions indicative of the nativities of prophets and conquerors, and all of their conditions.

*[Conjunctions indicating prophets]*

2 We say that when the conjunctions shift from triplicity to triplicity, and one of the three superior planets (and especially Saturn) is in the ninth or third from the Ascendant of that conjunction indicative of their appearance,[101] that is an indicator of the nativities of prophets. 3 Now if the divisions[102] of the Ascendant or the ninth, and[103] the Moon, are in embodied signs, it indi-

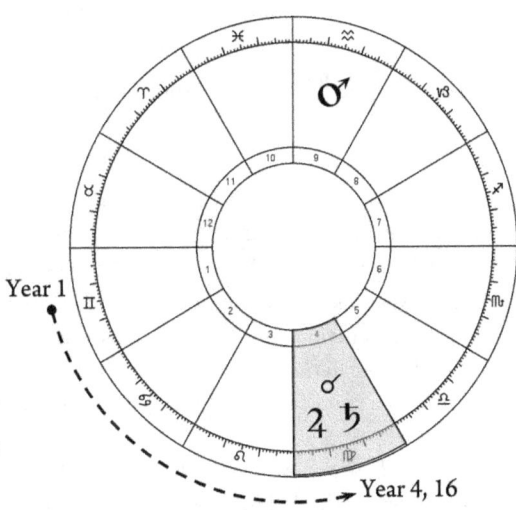

Figure 38: Second rotation of profection to conjunction (I.3, 3)

---

[101] This is ambiguous. It probably just emphasizes that the superiors' presence in the third or ninth at a shift *is* what indicates a prophet. The Islam chart in VIII.2, **9** does have a superior in its ninth (Mars). But perhaps there are other criteria for charts showing the appearance of prophets? See also **30** below.

[102] أقسام. This sounds like quadrant divisions.

[103] This probably means "or."

cates that their nativities will be [either] in the second conjunction from that conjunction,[104] or at the terminating of the second rotation [by profection] from the Ascendant of the conjunction at the position of the conjunction.[105]

### [Their morals and character]

**4** As for their morals and character, discovering the knowledge of that will be with respect to the place of the Moon in the revolution of the year indicative of their nativities.[106] **5** If that was in her *halb* or *hayyiz*, that will be an indicator of the goodness of their morals and character; and if she was in the antithesis of that, it indicates the contrary of it.

### [The marks on their bodies]

**6** As for the marks existing on their bodies (of birthmarks, moles, and what resembles that), the knowledge of that is derived from the place of the Lot of Fortune.[107] **7** For if in the year indicative of their nativities it was in the

---

[104] I take this to mean the conjunction 20 years later. But in the example below (**43**), Abū Ma'shar takes this to mean that while the new prophet was born sometime in the first conjunction, his *appearance* was when the conjunction occurred in Sagittarius *for the second time*, namely during the Sixty. So the "second conjunction" might mean "the next one" (in 20 years) or "the next time the conjunction happens in *this* sign" (the Sixty).

[105] Let this figure show the revolution chart for a triplicity shift into the earthy signs (starting with Virgo). The superior in the ninth suggests the birth of a prophet (**2**). Moreover, the Ascendant of the chart is double-bodied. This means that either the prophet will be born in the next conjunction in Taurus 20 years later (**3**), or when the annual profection from the Ascendant of this revolution reaches the sign of the conjunction for the second time. If the year of the conjunction is Year 1, it will reach the conjunction in Year 4, and then again 12 years later, in Year 16.

[106] That is, *not* (necessarily) in the first conjunction chart itself, but in the later revolutionary chart already identified by the above methods. For example (as I understand it), in the case above it could be at the revolution for Year 16. (See footnote to **3**.)

[107] Again, in the year of their actual nativity as mentioned in **4**.

right division[108] from the Ascendant, it indicates that those marks exist on their right side; and if it was in the left division, then on the left side.

**8** And indeed one may look at [the Lot's] position among the houses of the circle: for if it alighted in the degrees of the Ascendant above the earth, it indicates that that mark is on the right side of their foreheads; and if its alighting was in the degrees existing below the earth, then on the left side. **9** And if it was in the second, then on their mouths, lips, and faces. **10** If it was in the third, on their left upper arms. **11** If it was in the fourth, on their left sides. **12** If it was in the fifth, in the region of their left upper thighs.[109] **13** If it was in the sixth, on their left legs and feet. **14** If it was in the seventh, in the degrees which are above the earth, it indicates that that mark exists on the right side. **15** If it was in the degrees which are below the earth, then on their left side. **16** If it was in the eighth, on their sides which border on their right upper thighs. **17** If it was in the ninth, on their right sides, their chests, or between their shoulders. **18** If it was in the tenth, also on their right sides. **19** If it was in the eleventh, in the region of their right upper thighs. **20** And if it was in the twelfth, on their right legs and feet.

**21** And we may also seek information about the positions of the marks existing on them in another way, and it is by looking at the Ascendant of the conjunction indicative of their nativities. **22** For if it was masculine, the marks on them will be in the region on the right, and the quality of their color will incline towards the red and white; but if it was feminine, the marks on them will be on their back[110] in the region of the left, and the quality of their color will incline to the black and green.

**23** And one may also derive the place of the marks on their bodies from the Lot taken from the lord of the hour to the Sun,[111] with the degrees of the Ascendant added to it, [and] cast out from it: and where it ends in the signs, is the mark on the limb of that sign in which the Lot alights, in the order of the indications of the signs for the limbs.

---

[108] That is, "side." If we fact east, the right side of the Ascendant is the upper or diurnal hemisphere to the south, and the left is the lower or nocturnal hemisphere to the north. See also **8** below.

[109] Or, "hips" (أوراكهم).

[110] Reading uncertainly with **BY** for في مؤاخرهم.

[111] I am supposing this is in the revolutionary chart for the year of their birth.

## [Tokens of their prophethood]

**24** Now as for the tokens of their prophethood, discovering the knowledge of that will be from the victor over the Ascendants of their nativities. **25** For if the victor over that was Saturn, it indicates that their revelation will be in miraculous[112] and wondrous things. **26** And if it was Jupiter,[113] it indicates that their revelation will be in renunciation, and commanding the people to practice that, and their warring over that. **27** <And if it was Mars, it indicates their application of renunciation, and commanding the people to that, their warring over it, fighting enemies, and clashing with them.>[114] **28** And if it was one of the luminaries and it was in a praiseworthy position from the Ascendant, it indicates the revelation of what they accomplish and its being made conspicuous, and the honoring of the tokens and their triumph.[115] **29** And if their positions were suitable it is more powerful for that, and especially if the indicator of that was the Moon at the time of her separation from the Node of the meeting:[116] for that is an indicator of the confirmation of what we described, and they will be of those who adore wisdom in their youth. **30** And likewise too if the Moon was separating from the Node of the meeting and connected with a planet receiving her: it indicates that in addition their speech will be received.

---

[112] معجزة, which despite having connotations specifically for prophets, comes from a verb having to do with old and decrepit (i.e., Saturnian) things.

[113] Here Abū Ma'shar seems to have blended the indications for Jupiter and Mars (notice the reference to "warring" at the end of the sentence). Musā has both, but also seems to do some blending: "And if it was Mars, it indicates their application of renunciation, and commanding the people to that, their warring over it, fighting enemies, and clashing with them."

[114] Adding with Mūsā's *Periods* Ch. 4, **151**.

[115] Tentatively reading with **BY** (ظهور), although this verbal noun normally refers to "appearance" and "manifestation."

[116] That is, the pre-chart conjunction.

## [Timing of their appearance]

**31** And[117] as for how to know the time at which they will appear,[118] it is derived from [1] the Ascendant of the conjunction and [2] the position of the conjunction which are indicative of their coming forth.

**32** For if [1] the Ascendant was one of the houses of the superior planets, or the exaltation of Jupiter and the house of the Moon,[119] and Saturn was in a stake by counting or by equation,[120] then the direction[121] will be from the [1] Ascendant of the conjunction to [2] the position of the conjunction, a year for every sign.

**33** But if [1] the Ascendant was not one of what we described, then the direction[122] will be from [2] the conjunction to [1] the Ascendant of the conjunction, a year for every sign—except that if the sign[123] was embodied, that is an indicator that the time of his birth will be at the time when the rotation[124] from [1] the Ascendant returns[125] to [2] the position of the conjunction, or from [2] the position of the conjunction to [1] the position of the Ascendant, and their appearance will be the time of the return of the conjunction to the sign in which the conjunction was at their nativities. **34** (And sometimes it is in the conjunction following that conjunction, as we have mentioned previously.)[126]

**35** And the amount of his years is the same as the period which is between the time of their childbirth up to the time of their appearance.

---

[117] For **31-34**, cf. Mūsā Ch. 4, **193-97**, which attributes this to Māshā'allāh but reads slightly differently (and more awkwardly).

[118] But see below, where Abū Ma'shar uses these rules to determine their *birth*, and the return of the conjunction to the same sign for their *appearance*.

[119] Namely, Cancer.

[120] That is, by whole sign or quadrant division.

[121] Or rather, the profection.

[122] Again, the profection.

[123] Of the conjunction: see **39** and **41**.

[124] الدّور. That is, profection.

[125] That is, for the second time: see **2-3** above.

[126] See **3**.

| BRD I.3, 31-34 | Musā Ch. 4, 193-97 | Profection |
|---|---|---|
| ASC a house of superiors or ♋, and ♄ in stake [of ASC] | [ASC is house or exaltation of ♄, or ♋], and ♄ or ☽ not in stakes of ASC | ASC → ♂ |
| ASC a different sign [and ♄ not in a stake?] | ASC is house or exaltation of ♄ or ♋, and ♄ and ☽ not in stakes of ASC | ♂ → ASC |
| Sign of ♂ double-bodied | | Birth is at 2nd profection of above, and appearance at return of conjunction to that of their birth (or the one after their birth) |
| | Sign of ♂ double-bodied | Accession is at 2nd profection of above |

Figure 39: Time of appearance (of prophet [*BRD*] or acceder [*Musā*])

*[Where they will appear and act]*

**36** And their coming forth is from the cities of the sign in which the conjunction occurs.

**37** Their deeds will be in the cities of the signs square to the Ascendant of the conjunction.

*[Their term and calamities]*

**38** The days of their terms in authority will be according to the lesser years of the lord of the sign of the city in which their deeds appear.

**39** And their calamity will be upon the corruption of the lord of the sign by means of burning or other things, and especially if that was in one of the stakes of the signs in which their activities appear.[127]

---

[127] See **45**.

[*Example: 'Alī b. Muhammad the 'Alawite and the Zanj rebellion*]

| | | | |
|---|---|---|---|
| 40 ♍︎ / ♎︎ | \<ASC\> ♌︎ 7° 27' | ☊ 21° 37' ♋︎ | ♊︎ |
| ♏︎ 26° 40' | | | ♉︎ 26° 40' |
| ♄ 3° 22' ♐︎ / ♃ 0° 12' ♑︎ / ☋ 21° 37' | ♒︎ | ♂ 24° 02' | ♈︎ 0° 01' / ♓︎ ☽ 16° 30' / ☿ 16° 00' / ♀ 12° 08' |

Figure 40: Triplicity shift to fire (809 AD) and appearance of al-'Alawī al-Basrī[128]

**41** And an example of that[129] is that when the conjunction shifted from the watery triplicity to the fiery triplicity, the time of the birth of al-'Alawī al-Basrī[130] was in the 17th year from the time of the conjunction, and that was because the Ascendant of the conjunction was Leo, and the conjunction was in Sagittarius, in an embodied sign.[131]

**42** And if it had not been embodied, his birth would have been in accordance with what was be-

---

[128] This is the chart as found in VIII.2, **20**. As I explain in my footnote there, the values for the Ascendant and Midheaven cannot be correct; a more likely Ascendant is 27° 27'.

[129] Notice that in this example of a triplicity shift there is *not* a superior in either the ninth or third, as was required (**2**), although the luminaries are there. Are they enough? Are there other criteria for finding prophets?

[130] See al-Tabarī's *History*, Vol. 36, pp. 29ff. 'Alī b. Muhammad "the 'Alawite from Basrah" claimed descent from the fourth Rashidūn Caliph 'Alī (hence "'Alawite") and for that reason claimed to be the true Caliph. Born near Rayy, he appeared in Basrah in 869, declared himself Caliph, and led a long-lived rebellion among the black ("Zanj") laborers, and others, in southern Iraq. The Zanj rebellion lasted from about 868 to 883, when he was killed in August 883. According to al-Tabarī, the people of Bahrain considered him a prophet (from about 864), and he claimed some prophetic skills, including having heard a voice telling him to go to Basrah.

[131] See **3**: because it was embodied, one method is to profect from the Ascendant of the revolution to the place of the conjunction, twice. If the revolution was in 809, then the Ascendant would profect to the conjunction in Sagittarius in 813. But because we must do it twice, that adds 12 more years, or 825 AD.

tween the Ascendant of the conjunction and [the conjunction's] position by counting,[132] and that is 5 years.[133] **43** But given that it was embodied, a second rotation was turned for it, and that came to 17 years.[134]

**44** And when the conjunction returned to Sagittarius and remained in the triplicity, this native appeared and was a son of 43 years: 3 of them in the completion of the conjunction of Sagittarius, 20 years belonging to the conjunction in Leo, and 20 years for the conjunction in the sign of Aries.[135]

**45** When the conjunction returned to Sagittarius,[136] he went out of the City of Peace (of which Sagittarius was the indicator, which was the sign of the conjunction), and the appearance of his deeds was in the countries of the sign squaring the Ascendant (which was Scorpio),[137] and it was Basrah.

**46** His term [in authority][138] was the same as the amount of the lesser years of the lord of the sign of the city he was placed in (which belonged to Mars), and it is 15 years.[139]

**47** And his calamity[140] was at the burning of the lord of the sign (which was Mars) in Leo, which was one of the stakes of the sign of the city in which his activity appeared.[141]

**48** Since we have completed what we wanted to explain, let us break off the discussion.

---

[132] That is, a profection by whole signs.

[133] In other words, in 813 AD.

[134] So according to this method, al-ʻAlawī was born in roughly 825 AD.

[135] The conjunction in Sagittarius happened again in November 868 AD, after that year's ingress. Thus if he was born in 825, he would have been 43 at the return of the conjunction to Sagittarius.

[136] Again, in 868.

[137] See **36**.

[138] See **37**.

[139] The term from 868 to his death in 883 equals 15 years.

[140] See **38**.

[141] See al-Tabarī's *History* Vol. 37, p. 139. After the 15 years elapsed, ʻAlī b. Muhammad was killed on August 11, 883, when Mars was burned by the Sun by a conjunction within 1° in Leo.

## Chapter I.4: On knowing their customs & ordinances, their dress, & transport

**1** In this chapter let us report their customs and ordinances, their dress and transport, and the revelations of the people of the religion to which the dynasty shifts.

*[Jupiter and his combinations]*

**2** We say that since Jupiter by character is an indicator of religion, and the differences in religions in the periods, religious communities, and dynasties, are from his combining with Saturn and the combinations of the rest of the planets with [Jupiter], it is necessary for one to look at Jupiter. **3** For if he was in the position of religion[142] relative to the Ascendant of the conjunction indicative of the shift, and the victor over the position of religion was combining with him, the statement about that will be in accordance with [that planet].

**4** So if he was combining with Saturn, that indicates that the religions of the people of that religious community are Jewish, resembling the essence of Saturn (since the planets connect with him, and he does not connect with any [other] planet among them), and likewise the people of all the religions affirm the Jewish one while it does not affirm them,[143] and most of their practice will belong to what resembles this religion or is like it. **5** And if the one combining with [Jupiter] was Mars, it indicates the worship of fire and the religion of Mazdaism.[144] **6** And if the one combining with him was the Sun, it indicates the worship of the planets,[145] idols, and wonders. **7** And if the one combining with him was Venus, that indicates the revealed[146] religion and

---

[142] That is, the ninth. But perhaps also the third?
[143] Judaism had a respected status among many ancients due to its historically recorded history and legends about the power of Hebrew magic and mysteries (such as: the skills of Solomon).
[144] That is, the Magi.
[145] This reminiscent of Firmicus Maternus's hymn to the planetary gods (*Mathesis* I.10, 30-38), and his II.30, **5** and **26**.
[146] ظاهرة. But one could also read this as "triumphing" or "manifest," meaning the existing Islamic religion.

monotheism, such as Islam and what is like that. **8** And if the one combining with him was Mercury, it indicates Christianity, and every religion in which there is futility, doubt, and hardship. **9** And if the one combining with him was the Moon, it indicates doubts, confusion, discontinuity, deviation,[147] and skepticism in religion: and that is due to the quickness of the Moon's change and her motion, and due to her scant lingering in the signs.

*[Lord of the Ascendant of the conjunction]*

**10** And the knowledge of that is also derived from the character of the lord of the Ascendant of the conjunction. **11** For if it was Saturn, it indicates the suffering of the people of that religion. **12** If it was Jupiter, they will be companions of unity and piety. **13** If it was Mars, then companions of travels, bloodshed, a scarcity of obedience, and disagreement between some of them and others. **14** If it was the Sun, then companions of beauty and garments. **15** If it was Venus, then companions of entertainment and comfort. **16** If it was Mercury, companions of the sciences and lawsuits. **17** And if it was the Moon, then they will be in accordance with the planet which the Moon combines with.

*[Three Lots of authority and rulership]*

**18** And information about that is also sought from the location of the Lot of rulership and authority,[148] taken from Mars to the Moon, with there being added to it the degrees of the Ascendant of the transit indicative of the shift (and cast out from it), so that where it terminates, there is the Lot. **19** If the location of this Lot was in the ninth or tenth relative to the Ascendant of the conjunction, that is an indicator of their worship of God in truth. **20** But if it was in the eleventh or twelfth, it indicates that they will speak that and not act on it.

**21** And one should also look at the location of the Lot in the houses of the planets when it is *not* the shift indicating the ordinances, but does indicate the corruption of the religion and its shifting. **22** For if it was in the

---

[147] Or, "apostasy" (الإحاد).
[148] See *Gr. Intr.* VIII.4, **281-83**.

houses of Saturn it indicates that their worship will be of images of iron and brass. **23** If it was in the houses of Jupiter, then of images of gold. **24** If it was in the houses of Mars, then [those] of fire. **25** If it was in the house of the Sun, then of images of wood. **26** If it was in the houses of Venus, then of images of silver. **27** If it was in the houses of the Scribe (and it is Mercury), then of churches. **28** And if it was in the house of the Moon, then of the Moon.

**29** (And of course it is necessary for you to draw out these indicators which we have described, in several ways, and that one judge the strongest of them in indication, and the most evident in testimony.)

**30** And the Lot of rulership may also be extracted in another way, and it is that it is taken from the degree of the Ascendant of the conjunction to the degree of the conjunction, and the degrees of the Ascendant of the revolution are added on top of it, and it is cast out from it: so where it terminates, there is the Lot of rulership.

**31** And indeed the Lot of authority may also be extracted by being taken from the degree of the Sun[149] to the Midheaven of the revolution by [both] night and day, and the degrees of Jupiter are added on top of it, and it is cast out from him: so where it terminates, there is the Lot of authority.

**32** And these three Lots may be used in the rest of the conjunctional revolutions, and one judges them in accordance with their location relative to the foundations[150] of the sphere, and from the fortunes' and infortunes' inspection of them, and one speaks in accordance with what emerges from that.

### [Their dress: planets in or ruling tenth places]

**33** Now as for the knowledge of their dress, it is derived from the planet alighting in the tenth from the lord of the Ascendant at the shift of the conjunction. **34** But if there was not a planet in its tenth, then [use] the lord of

---

[149] Reading with al-Qabīsī V.17, for the text's "from the degree of *the Midheaven of* the Sun."

[150] أوضاع. These are probably the foundational charts which one uses, such as in VIII.2: the chart of the triplicity shift showing a new religion, the chart of the conjunction showing a dynasty change, and any other triplicity shift.

the tenth of the Ascendant. **35** So, if the indicator of that was Saturn, it indicates that the majority of the clothing of the people of that religious community is black, of hair cloth, and coarse cotton fabric, and dirty clothes. **36** And if it was Jupiter, then the clothes of ascetics, like wool and what resembles that. **37** And if it was Mars, then clothes tinted with red and yellow. **38** And if it was the Sun, then silk and raw silk. **39** And if it was Venus, then clothes from Quhistān and Merv, and what is similar to that among the clothes of women. **40** And if it was Mercury, then embroidery and silk. **41** And if it was the Moon, then crude[151] clothes, white garments, and what resembles that.

### [Their transport: planets in or ruling fourth places]

**42** As for the knowledge of their transport, that is derived from the planet alighting in the fourth from the lord of the Ascendant at the shift of the conjunction. **43** But if there was not a planet in its fourth, then [use] the lord of the fourth from the Ascendant. **44** So, if the indicator of that was Saturn, it indicates that the majority of the riding animals of the people of that religious community will be mules. **45** If the indicator was Jupiter, then elephants. **46** If it was Mars, then work horses. **47** If it was the Sun, then horses. **48** If it was Venus, then camels. **49** If it was Mercury, then donkeys. **50** And if it was the Moon, then cattle.

**51** Since we have completed what we wanted to explain, let us break off Chapter I.4, and conclude Book I, if God wills.

---

[151] Or, "rough, rugged" (الغلاظ).

# Book II: [Dynasties & Kings]

## On the whole of the affairs of dynasties & their shifts, & the conditions of kings & what attaches to them

*And it is in 8 Chapters:*

**1** Chapter II.1: On how to know the shift of the dynasty from nation to nation, and to which nation it passes.

**2** Chapter II.2: On how to know to which of the regions the dynasty shifts, and the locations of the cities of its kings.

**3** Chapter II.3: On how to know the length of the duration of rulership among the people of the religious community to whom it has shifted, their strength and weakness, the number of their kings, and what the people of the kingdom to which it has shifted will do to the people of the kingdom from which it has shifted.

**4** Chapter II.4: On knowing the nativities of the kings of the people of that religious community in accordance with the alighting of the [planetary] bodies and their combination in the divisions of the sphere in the Ascendants of the shift of the conjunction in the triplicities, and how to know that in terms of their own nativities, and when that is, and what their ages are at their accession, and the whole of what their character is like, from the alighting of any of the bodies and their combination in the divisions of the sphere as well as from the two Lots indicative of that (and apart from [these] two).

**5** Chapter II.5: On how to know the length of their terms.

**6** Chapter II.6: On [knowing] what their ailments are, indicating their disasters.

**7** Chapter II.7: On knowing the manner of their disasters, and the day on which that will be, and to whom the rulership will pass after them.

**8** Chapter II.8: On the indication of the uniting of the two infortunes in all of the signs, and their alighting in the triplicities, for the lower events coming to be from their influences, and what resembles that, if God wills.

## Chapter II.1: On how to know the shift of the dynasty from nation to nation, & to which nation it passes

**1** Since we have set forth in Book I what is necessary to explain about how to know the affairs of prophets, their ordinances, and what resembles that, in this Book II let us state how to know the affairs of dynasties and kings. **2** And in this chapter let us begin with how to know the shift of the dynasty from nation to nation, and to which nation it passes, since the rank of kings follows the rank of prophets.

*[When dynasty shifts happen]*

**3** We say that one needs to derive the knowledge of that just as we have already made clear in Chapter I.1: knowing the Ascendants of the beginnings of the transits in which the beginning of the dynasty is, and knowing the Ascendants of the conjunctions occurring in them, and the Ascendants of the years and the quarters, and that one should direct for each thing from its own position; and a statement is made in accordance with their mixture.

**4** And where the shift of the dynasty from nation to nation is at the termination of the Turn,[1] if the Ascendant of the first religious community falls away from[2] a trine of the Ascendant of the conjunction in which the Ascendant of the shift from triplicity to triplicity is (or from its sextile, or from one of its stakes), then if the matter was like that in the way we described, it indicates a shift of dynasties and the appearance of people of the adherents which the shift of the transit indicated, and the passing of the dynasty to them and in them.

*[What kind of people the dynasty changes to]*

**5** Now if the Turn was exhausted and indicated a shift of the dynasty, then one looks at which sign the year has terminated upon the shifting of the

---

[1] دور. This was the case for Islam, in which the triplicity shift occurred in in 570 AD, and the new Turn (Venus-Gemini) occurred 10 years later in 580. See I.1, **82-83**.

[2] That is, in aversion to. See also **15-16** below. For more comments on continuity versus change, see my Introduction §9.

# BOOK II: DYNASTIES & KINGS

conjunction from triplicity to triplicity,³ and at the sign in which [Saturn and Jupiter] unite: for it is an indicator of the people and region to which the dynasty shifts.

### [The reason for the change]

**6** And the sign at which the year terminates from the Ascendant of the new conjunction is an indicator of the reason for which the dynasty shifts.⁴ **7** So, if its termination was at the ninth or third, then that will be because of religion, especially if the lord of the house of the conjunction is in that sign; and [if] it terminated at positions other than these two, then the matter in that will be in accordance with the indication of the place.

### [Their helpers]

**8** And their helpers⁵ will be from the region in which Mars is alighting, relative to the Sun: if he was eastern, then it is the people of the east or south; and if he was western, then the people of the west or north. **9** And if in addition Mars was in the stakes, facing opposite the conjunction,⁶ it hastens the matter which he indicated and speeds it up; but if he was withdrawing, his indication is delayed. **10** And if he was in the sixth, it indicates that their helpers will be from among the slaves and the underclass. **11** If he was in the triplicity of the sign of the conjunction, they will be from among the people of the house of the acceder.

---

³ But from which point? According to VIII.2, **10**, the profection from the Ascendant of the Flood reached Libra, but from the conjunction itself at Sagittarius. But see also **15-16** below, which says that the lord of the conjunction indicates the new people and their dynasty.

⁴ What this seems to mean is that we profect from the Ascendant of the triplicity shift *until* the dynasty actually changes. See also **15-16**.

⁵ That is, the people who help put the new dynasty into power, especially through military action (hence, Mars).

⁶ قابلًا للقران. Or perhaps, "receiving" the conjunction, but positions like conjunctions are not normally understood to be "received."

**12** And if Mars was falling,[7] it indicates that they will be base people, [but] then gain rulership. **13** But if he was in a stake, it indicates that they will be people of rank and authority, and that they will gain the rulership through force.[8]

**14** Now if he had looked at the conjunction from a square, that does violence to the soldiers of the king and his allies, and the area of his kingdom; and its harm will be in accordance with the position of the aspect and its strength, especially if Mars was in the fourth from the conjunction.

## [Continuity with the religious community]

**15** And you ought to know the terminal point of the year upon the shift of the conjunction from triplicity to triplicity.[9] **16** For if the year terminated at one of the stakes of the Ascendant of the religious community, and the Ascendant of the year is fixed,[10] it indicates the fixity of the dynasty up to the time of the completion of the Turn,[11] especially if the year terminated at the house of the planet governing the matter of the people (which is the lord of the house of the conjunction)[12] and the indicator of their dynasty, kingdom, and religious community—except that sometimes an expansion will take place in the kingdom from the time of the shift of the conjunction from tri-

---

[7] Probably this means "dynamically withdrawing," and not cadent or falling by sign.
[8] Or, "power" (قُوَّة).
[9] See **23**: perhaps we are tracking the profections from the religion.
[10] I.e., in the revolution of the year when the profection from the Ascendant of the shift reaches its own stakes. This seems to mean the following: the Ascendant of the shift for Islam was commonly taken to be Libra. If, then, in a year when the profection of the Ascendant reached the other convertible signs, the Ascendant of *that* year's revolution was fixed, then it shows stability for the dynasty. But perhaps it would also be true if the profection reached the whole-sign angles of the *conjunction*, then a fixed Ascendant in that year's revolution would also show it.
[11] دور.
[12] **BY** extend their parentheses to include "religious community," as though the lord of the house of the conjunction is also the indicator of the dynasty, etc. It is hard to know which is the right answer. But the scenario here seems to be that the profection from the Libra Ascendant of the shift reaches Aries (a convertible sign), ruled by Mars (the lord of the Scorpio conjunction). See **23** below, which seems to refer to this and is probably tied closely to Islamic history.

plicity to triplicity, and gaining mastery over the frontiers will increase, and the fading of their favor at the conjunction indicating the general public of the triplicity, according to what we set forth before.[13]

**17** And if Saturn at the time of the conjunction was transiting over Jupiter, it indicates that the changes which come to be in that time will be by the sword and injustice. **18** But if Jupiter was transiting over Saturn, it indicates that those changes will be with fairness and justice.

**19** And if the lord of the bound of the meeting or fullness which comes to be before entering the year of the conjunction, and before the revolution of one of the years (or one of the quarters), is an infortune, that is an indicator of the attack of rebels upon kings, and the opponents they[14] have in future periods.

**20** And if the conjunction [of Saturn and Jupiter] was in the convertible signs, it indicates universal changes. **21** If that was in the fixed ones, it indicates the fixity of the situation, and what changes there are will turn towards what is suitable. **22** But if it was in the embodied ones, the matter in that will be middling, and upon their uniting it indicates that most of the suitability will be in the countries of Jupiter, and the corruption in the countries of Saturn.[15]

**23** Now[16] if the year terminated at the seventh from the Ascendant of the religious community, and the lord of the seventh was an infortune, that is also an indicator of contention. **24** And if the infortune was the indicator of the people and there was contention and separation between them, they will be corruptive for their dynasty and those contending in it; then the matter in that will be put in order.

**25** Now if there was a shift of the transit in one of the years, but it was not of the years indicative of a shift of religious communities,[17] then one must keep watch over the Ascendant of the shift of the transit in which the religious community was, along with [this] second shift. **26** But if the shift of the transit *was* indicative of a shift in the dynasty, then one can make do with

---

[13] Reference uncertain.
[14] This seems to mean the king's opponents.
[15] But the delineations in Book VII suggest that conjunctions are always disruptive.
[16] See my footnote to **16** above.
[17] See I.3, **2-3**.

its Ascendant without the Ascendant of the first transit, because the second shift will become the beginning of it.

**27** And as for the shift of the dynasty and the rulership within a single community from the people of one house to the people of another house, that will be when one of the inferior planets is in charge of the Turn,[18] and the shift will be when the Turn[19] reaches one of the Quarters.[20]

*[When the change will happen]*

**28** And if the conjunction indicated a shift and it was in an embodied sign, and the Ascendant likewise, it is an indicator that the change[21] will be upon the year's reaching the position of the conjunction by direction.[22] **29** But if it was not at that time, then in the second conjunction.

**30** And when the conjunction is in the beginning of the sign, the change will be in the third conjunction; if it was in its middle, that will be in the second conjunction; and if it was at its end, that will be in the first conjunction.

**31** And one should also look at the Lot of rulership. **32** For if it occurred in the first parts of signs, it indicates the people of that religious community's fighting one another; but if it occurred in their middles, it indicates the duration of their rulership; and if it occurred in their last parts, it indicates an attack upon them by people not of their religious community, who seek the rulership.

---

[18] دور.

[19] دور.

[20] Thus the shift proclaiming religion was just before Māshā'allāh's new Turn in 580, ruled by Venus (an inferior planet) and Gemini, and after 90 years or so (around 670) the dynasty changed to the 'Umayyads in Damascus. But I do not see a clear change in the following increments of 90 years (760 and 850). The year 760 was 10 years after the 'Abbāsid revolution, and 850 was years before the Anarchy at Samarra or the Zanj rebellion.

[21] الأنقلة.

[22] Or more likely, profection (see I.3, **33**).

*[The quality of the people of the new dynasty]*

**33** And if one wants knowledge of the quality of the people to whom the dynasty shifts, one should look at the Lot of rulership:[23] to which planet does it hand over its management?[24] **34** For that rulership will shift over to the people whose indicator is the planet handed over to.

**35** Since we have completed what we wanted to explain, let us break off Chapter II.1.

---

[23] Probably from I.4: note that there are variations on this Lot.
[24] Lots do not hand over management. But perhaps Abū Ma'shar is referring to its lord?

## Chapter II.2: On how to know to which of the regions the dynasty shifts, & the locations of the cities of its kings

**1** Since we have set forth in Chapter II.1 the reason necessitating the shift of the dynasty to the people of another religious community,[25] and its shift from one nation to [another] nation from among the people of [that same] religious community,[26] let us report the regions to which the dynasty shifts, and the locations of the cities in it.

### [The region of the new dynasty]

**2** As for the way of knowing the derivation of that, one should look at the Lot of rulership, mention of which we set forth in Chapter I.4.[27] **3** For if it was in the region of the east, the shift will be towards that region; if it was in the region of the west, then to that. **4** And if it was in the stake of the earth, the shift will be to the region of the north and the furthermost regions of the earth, and the barbarous countries. **5** And if it was in the Midheaven the shift will be to the region of the south along with the support of a nation from among the people of the religious community. **6** And if it was between these stakes, the shift is attributed to the direction which is closer to that one of the two stakes, than the other.

### [The location of their cities]

**7** Now if one wants the way of knowing the positions of their cities, one should look at the place of the lord of the Lot of rulership in the sphere. **8** For if it was in the Midheaven, it is in the middle of the climes; and if it was withdrawing, their cities will be withdrawn from that boundary, and their cities in that direction will be in accordance with their position relative to the east, south, west, north, or what is between them. **9** But if it was a watery sign their cities will be on the coasts and mighty rivers.

---

[25] See II.1, **6-7**.
[26] Perhaps II.1, **27**.
[27] See I.4, **18** and **30-31**.

**10** And of course it is necessary that one examine the revolutions of years in which it is possible for one of the planets to be in the [very] minute of its own exaltation, and the Moon adheres bodily to it: for if the matter was like that, it indicates the appearance of that planet's nature in the rest of the world, especially if it governed the year. **11** And sometimes the residences of kings change to the climes of which it is the indicator.

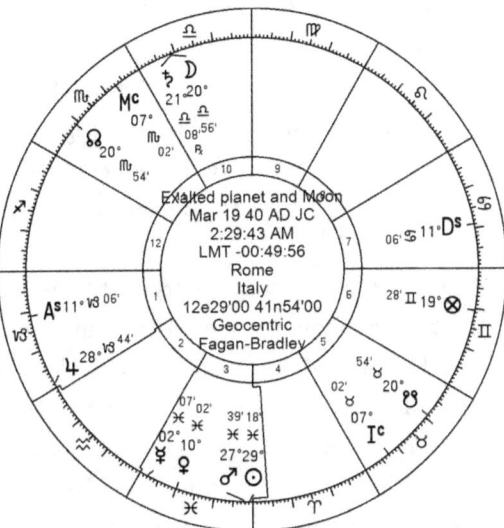

Figure 41: Approximation of II.2, 10, in the Fagan-Bradley sidereal zodiac

**12** Since we have completed what we wanted to explain, let us break off the Chapter.

## Chapter II.3: On how to know the length of the duration of rulership among the people of the religious community to whom it has shifted, their strength & weakness, the number of their kings, & what the people of the kingdom to which it has shifted will do to the people of the kingdom from which it has withdrawn

**1** Since it is most necessary that knowledge of the length of duration of the rulership among them follows upon what we set forth in Chapter II.2 (on the knowledge of the regions to which the dynasty shifts, and the positions of their cities in them), we say that the way of knowing that is that one looks at the position of the Lot of rulership relative to the Ascendant of the shift of the conjunction indicative of their dynasty. **2** For if it was in a stake and its lord in a stake, it indicates that their period will be of the amount of the duration of the greatest cycle, which is 960 solar years. **3** And if the Lot was withdrawing from the stake and its lord in a stake, it indicates that their period will be of the amount of the duration of the middle cycle, which is 240 solar years. **4** And if they were both falling away from the stakes, not looking at the Ascendant, that indicates that their period is of the amount of the duration of the smallest cycle, which is 20 solar years.

**5** And sometimes their term increases beyond these three periods or decreases from them, in accordance with what the shift of the conjunction from triplicity to triplicity necessitates, of the fixity of the dynasty and its disappearance.[28]

**6** And knowing the duration of the amount of their period is derived in another way, and that is that one looks at the conjunction and the positions of the victors among the planets, and especially the Moon. **7** For if they were alighting in the stakes, it is an indicator that the duration of the amount of their period will also be of the amount of the greatest category;[29] and if they were in what follows the stakes, they indicate the middle category; if they were withdrawing from the stakes, they indicate the lesser one.

---

[28] See perhaps II.1, **15-16**.
[29] This sounds like the cycles in **2-4** above, not the planetary years.

**8** And the knowledge of that is also derived by way of the place of the conjunction and its lord, relative to the spherical divisions. **9** For if the conjunction indicative of their dynasty, and its lord, were in the stakes and free of misfortunes, in an excellent place in the circle, not made unfortunate, that is an indicator of the strength of the people of that dynasty, their victory, the [successful] conclusion of their affairs and their increase, and the long length of the duration of their term. **10** But if the conjunction and its lord were in the stakes of the infortunes or in the stakes of retrograde, falling planets, that is an indicator of the shortness of their term, the fading of their dynasty, their ruin, and the majority of the manifestation of these indications will be in countries whose indicator is the sign of that conjunction.

### [The number of their kings]

**11** Now as for how to know the number of their kings, the amount of that will be in accordance with the number which is between the Lot of rulership and its lord,[30] along with the planets which come to be between them. **12** (And if any of the planets was in an embodied sign, it doubles that number.)

**13** And the amount of that number may be understood from the ascensions of the sign of the Lot, or from the years set down for the lord of the Lot: and the amount of that will be according to what the Lot and its lord necessitate for the long length of the period of their terms, as well as their middle or shortened [periods].

**14** As for how to know that from the Lot, that is derived from the lesser period;[31] as for [knowing it] from the ascensions of the sign, it is from the middle period;[32] and as for the years set down for the planets, from the greater period[33] **15** And on top of what is put down for the planets (of the greater years established for them), there may be added what they have for

---

[30] This is probably counting by sign.
[31] دور. **BY** understand this to be the lesser planetary years. But the exact method and its variants in the rest of the sentence, are not clear to me.
[32] دور.
[33] دور.

their lesser period,[34] if the lord of the Turn[35] and the lord of the sign of the terminal point require it.

### [How they will be treated]

**16** Now as for knowing the kind of thing which the people of the religious community to which it shifts, will do to the people of the religious community it has withdrawn from, that is derived from the lord of the Lot of rulership. **17** For if it was inspecting the indicator of the first religious community from a praiseworthy figure (like the trine and sextile), they will be safe from their adversities. **18** But if it was inspecting it from a figure not praiseworthy (like the square and opposition), it indicates that wars and bloodshed will occur between them, especially if Mars had strength there in one of the stakes: for it indicates the strength of the matter in that, and its harshness.

**19** Since we have completed what we wanted to explain, let us break off the discussion.

---

[34] دور.

[35] دور. **BY** understand this to be the Turn.

## Chapter II.4: On how to know the nativities of the kings of the people of that religious community in accordance with the alighting of the [planetary] bodies in the Ascendants of the shift of the conjunction in the triplicities

*And how to know that in terms of their own nativities, & when that is, & what their ages are at their accession, & the whole of what their character is like from the alighting of any of the bodies & their combination in the divisions of the sphere as well as from the two Lots indicative of that (& apart from [these] two)*

**1** In this Chapter let us state how to know the nativities of the kings of the people of the house of the religious community, from the alighting of the upper bodies coming to be in the Ascendants of the shift of the conjunction in the triplicities, and from their own nativities, when that is, and the rest of what we will enumerate in this chapter.

*[Whose nativities will show rulership]*

**2** We say that when the portion[36] of the Ascendant of someone born (of the people to whom the rulership has shifted) is the same as [1] the portion of the Ascendant of the shift of the transit, or [2] the two portions of their luminaries, and especially the one which has the turn[37] [by sect], or [3] the portions of Saturn and Jupiter, or his Ascendant was [4] one of the stakes of the position of the indicator,[38] or [5] one of the two indicators, and two planets collaborate in the indication, that indicates his becoming king, his bearing and aptitude, and that will be in accordance with the sign and its lord at the shift of the triplicity.

**3** Now if his Ascendant was the sign of the Midheaven [of the shift], and its lord strong, eastern, in a sign in which it has a claim, it indicates that he

---

[36] That is, "degree."
[37] النَّوبة. That is, the sect light: the Sun by day or the Moon by night.
[38] What is this indicator, or the "two indicators" in the next clause?

will be a king having fame, respect, capability, overpowering enemies, hostile to them, overcoming many of their countries and their authority.³⁹

**4** But if the matter was to the contrary of that, the matter will be in accordance with what occurs from the sign which is his Ascendant in the root, or the downfall⁴⁰ of its lord: and the statement in that will be in accordance with the strength of the sign, and its lord and its strength (or its weakness), and the planets in the root looking at it.

### [Comparing multiple nativities and the triplicity shift]

**5** Now if you wanted the way of knowing that from their own nativities, then one should look at the Ascendants of the nativities which are of the family of the house of the kingdom.

**6** Now if they had the Sun in his own house, exaltation, the Midheaven, or one of the stakes, and the lords of the Ascendants connected with him from praiseworthy positions, and he is received (and especially from one of the stakes), they will rule.

**7** But if the Sun was not in this condition and he is weak, then one should look at Saturn. **8** For if he was in the condition I described for that Sun, they also will rule. **9** But if he was weak and there was not a connection between the lords of the Ascendants and the Sun, then one should look at the lords of the Midheaven.⁴¹ **10** For if they were in the condition which we described for the lords of the Ascendants (concerning their connecting with the Sun or Saturn), they will rule.

### [Other indications of rulership and eminence]

**11** And if the Moon by night was in the portion of her exaltation, it indicates the nativities of kings, and especially if she was in the Midheaven.

---

³⁹ Or, "government" (سلطانهم).

⁴⁰ سقوط. To me this suggests that even if he does come to rule, his level of respect will be in accordance with the nature and condition of the sign and of the *particular* meaning of its lord when in a bad condition. For instance, if the lord of the sign was Venus, then his reputation and influence will suffer the problems of a bad Venus.

⁴¹ Or especially, the Midheavens (plural) among the charts one is comparing.

**12** And if the Moon separated from the Node and connected with an eastern planet in the Midheaven or in the degree of its[42] own exaltation, it indicates the nativities of kings.

**13** And if the Moon was in the exaltation of a planet, and that planet in the exaltation of the Moon, and the Moon connected with it, it indicates the nativities of kings.

**14** And[43] if the fixed stars having first and second magnitude were in the degree of the Ascendant or the degree of the Midheaven, they indicate the nativities of kings.

**15** And if the two luminaries were in the spear-bearing of the planets, they indicate the nativities of kings.

**16** And if the two fortunes were in the degrees of their exaltations and they were in the Midheaven of the Lot of Fortune,[44] and the Lot of Fortune in the Midheaven of the Ascendant, and especially if one of [the fortunes] was the lord of the Lot of Fortune, it indicates the nativities of kings.

**17** And if the planet of the clime (such as Saturn for India, Jupiter for Babylon, Mars for the Turks, the Sun for Rūm, Venus for the Arabs, Mercury for Egypt, and the Moon for China) was the lord of the Midheaven in the Ascendants of nativities, and it connected with the lord of the Ascendant, and they were both in their own exaltations, eastern, that is an indicator that that native will rule that clime.

**18** And if the lord of the Midheaven, the Moon, and the Lot of Fortune are praiseworthy, and their lords in their *halb*, it indicates the most powerful authority.

**19** And if the greater luminary was in the minute of the Ascendant, in Leo or Aries, or the Moon was in the minute of the Ascendant, in Taurus or Cancer, it indicates the nativities of kings.

**20** And if the two luminaries in the nativities were in the degrees of their exaltations, and the Moon was in her *halb*, it indicates the nativities of kings.

---

[42] Grammatically this could also be the Moon's exaltation, but I take it to mean the planet she connects with.

[43] This is a standard rule for fixed stars and eminence: see Sahl's *Nativities* Ch. 2.2, **1**, and Ch. 10.2, **3**.

[44] That is, in the Lot of Fortune tenth (by sign). But it would be even more powerful if they corresponded to its degree in that place.

## [When they will rule, during their lives]

**21** Now if you wanted knowledge of when that is (after the appearance of the indication due to which he will attain rulership), one should look at the lords of the Ascendants. **22** For if they connected with the three things which we mentioned (and they are the Sun, Saturn, and the lord of the Midheaven), and their connections are close, then they will rule at the beginning of their lifespans; and to the extent that the connection is closer, the sooner will be the rulership. **23** But if the lords of the Ascendants connected with planets not of the three which we mentioned, and *those* planets were not connecting with the Sun, Saturn, nor the lord of the Midheaven, that will be in the middle of their lifespans—and especially if there was a single planet between the two.[45] **24** But if there were two planets between the two and Saturn, it will be at the end of their lifespans.

**25** And when the direction[46] of one of them from the Ascendant of his nativity reaches one of the signs indicative of that, and especially the sign of the Midheaven (and it is possible that it reaches from the Ascendant of the religious community to that sign), it indicates that the command will pass to the native in that time, if he had already reached the age at which he can accede to it.

**26** Now if one learned that the owners of several nativities will rule, so you wanted knowledge of which of them would rule before his associate, the one whose lord of the Ascendant is closer by connection,[47] and the first of them to connect, is the one who will rule first; then the [next] closest is the [next] closest in connecting.

**27** And when one of them is confirmed,[48] and the Ascendant of the confirmation which binds [him] is *not* one of the stakes of the dynasty indicative of their rule, that confirmation will not be completed for him.

---

[45] Meaning unclear; likewise with the next sentence.

[46] Or perhaps, profection.

[47] Probably with the Sun, Saturn, or the lord of the Midheaven (**6-9**), and probably in their own respective nativities.

[48] عقد لأحدهم. This connotes taking on an obligation, which in context here seems to mean that he is designated to rule but does not actually accede. Or, perhaps he takes the oath of office but cannot complete the term?

# BOOK II: DYNASTIES & KINGS 125

**28** Now if one wanted knowledge of when the year of his accession will be, one should look at the lord of the Lot of rulership. **29** For if it was assembling with the Lot of rulership, that indicates the youngness of his age; if it was in its trine, that indicates his adulthood; and if it was in its square, it indicates his middle age; and if it was in its opposition, it indicates his seniority and old age.

## [The king's condition and character, from the lord of Saturn]

**30** And[49] if one wanted knowledge of the manner of his condition and character from the alighting of any of the bodies and their combination in the spherical divisions, one should look at the lord of the first Arrow (which is Saturn).[50] **31** For if [Saturn's lord] was received, free of the infortunes, and it is looking at him, that is an indicator of the fine condition of the acceder, his uprightness and fairness, along with the suitable condition of the subjects, and the goodness of their obedience towards him. **32** (And likewise, if Saturn was in a praiseworthy place.) **33** But if it was not received, or in a place not appropriate for it, that indicates his crudeness, injustice, and corruption. **34** And if his lord was corrupted, it indicates the corruption of his subjects, their hatred towards him, and his burden upon them.

**35** And if his lord was assembling with an infortune at the revolution indicative of his accession, that is an indicator of the suitability of his situations at the beginnings of his affairs, but the badness of his outcomes and the corruption of his end.

**36** And if it was enclosed[51] between a fortune and infortune, and the fortune was [zodiacally] in front of it and the infortune behind it, that is an indicator of the badness of his situations at the beginnings of his affairs, and the suitability of his outcomes. **37** But if the infortune was in front of him

---

[49] The following rules seem to refer to the revolution of the year of the accession: see the rule for Jupiter in **58**, and the Head in **66**. But it may also refer to the chart of the accession itself: see **67**. See also Ch. II.5.

[50] That is, look at the lord of Saturn. See also the footnote to II.5, **102** below.

[51] That is, "besieged."

and the fortune behind him, it is an indicator that the corruption will be at the ends of his affairs, and the suitability at their beginnings.[52]

**38** And if the lord of his house was connecting with him from something other than an opposition, it indicates the fine obedience of the subjects towards him. **39** But if it was separating from him, it indicates his preference for the good, and his reputation for it, and his might in it, but his scant fidelity to it. **40** And if its separation from him was from the opposition, that indicates the scant benefit that his subjects have from him.

**41** And if the lord of the house of Saturn was assembling with him, it indicates his mastery over his subjects and his victory over enemies. **42** And if it was separating from him, it indicates his weakness and the strength of his enemies over him.

**43** And[53] if it was with him in a sign, and its connection was [first] with another [planet] from another sign, [and] then it connected with Saturn before it[54] went out from its sign, it indicates an abundance of rebels attacking from among the people of his own house, and his encountering hardship from that, and his victory over them. **44** But if it does not connect with Saturn before it leaves its sign, it will be weaker for that and the departure of the rulership will be feared for him.

*[The king's enemies, from the lord of Saturn's seventh]*

**45** Now if the lord of the seventh from Saturn handed over its management to a planet under the rays, it indicates the ruin of his enemies at the hands of someone else. **46** But if the planet being handed over to was going out of the rays, it is stronger for the enemy [but] with their scarcity[55]—unless that planet is connecting with an eastern planet in a good position: for

---

[52] In the MSS this sentence erroneously switched "beginnings" and "ends" around, giving it the same interpretation as in **36**. I have changed them to be in their proper place.

[53] See a similar situation in **72** below.

[54] Here and in **44**, the "it" could refer grammatically to either Saturn or his lord, but I believe Abū Ma'shar means Saturn: this refers to the planetary configuration of "escape" (*Gr. Intr.* VII.5, **119**).

[55] This is because a planet leaving the rays is considered strong (or gaining strength) but still immature and "new" in its manifestation.

if the matter was like that it indicates their abundance, and that the beginning of their command and meeting together will be from the region of the east.[56]

**47** And if the lord of the seventh from Saturn handed over the management to him from a sextile or trine, it indicates the scarcity of his enemies, his protection from wars, his enemies' need for him, and their concluding truces with him.

**48** And if the lord of the seventh from Saturn was in a strong position, and planets handed over the management to it, it indicates an abundance of rebels attacking him, those contending with him, and defeating him, along with their abundant gathering together, and their winning over most of the acceder's allies, and ruin will be feared for him for that reason.

**49** And if the lord of the seventh from Saturn (or the lord of the tenth)[57] was one of the luminaries, it indicates that those rising up against the acceder, and the combatants he has, are people of the family of his own house.

**50** Now if Saturn in diurnal revolutions was in his exaltation, in the view of Jupiter, it indicates his settlement[58] of countries and the subjugation of his enemies.

**51** And one also seeks information about that from the lord of the Lot of rulership: for if it was in the trine of Saturn or in his sextile, or one of them was receiving its associate, it indicates the love of the subjects for him in that time. **52** And if it was in his square, the matter will be in the middle. **53** And if it was in his opposition, that indicates their battling against him.

**54** And one also seeks information about that from the locations of the planets: and that is if Jupiter was looking down upon[59] the Sun, Moon, or Ascendant from a royal sign (and especially if it was convertible)[60] in the revolution indicative of his accession, that indicates his collecting of assets and his love for them. **55** But if that was from [signs] having bodies, it is firmer for that and greater for his eagerness for them or for their collection.

---

[56] Because the planet is "easternizing" out of the rays.
[57] The text actually puts this "or the lord of the tenth" after the phrase "one of the luminaries," but it seems better here even though it might identify a different planet.
[58] Or, "colonization, building" (عمارة).
[59] That is, overcoming from the superior square.
[60] Namely, Aries.

**56** And if it was from the fixed ones, it indicates his fixity and the long length of his term, and the long reach of his reputation, and his grasp on his government, and his power over that.

### [Jupiter]

**57** And if Jupiter was falling away from the inspection of the luminaries and the Ascendant, that [power] will not be immense, along with the shortness of his term.

**58** And if Jupiter was under the rays in the revolution of the year in which the acceder acceded, it indicates his love for collecting assets. **59** But if Mars or the Sun connected with him, along with his collecting assets he will disperse them,[61] and especially if he was in the seventh.

**60** And if Jupiter was withdrawing and Mars connects with him, it is an indicator of his dispersing the assets both rightly and pointlessly, with their scarce value for him. **61** And if in addition Jupiter was in his house, it indicates his sending out assets in ways [by which] their suitability will accrue to the subjects.

**62** And if Jupiter was in a house appropriate to himself, in a strong position relative to the Ascendant, free of the infortunes, it indicates his collecting assets as well as seeking them; but if it was to the contrary of that, it indicates his scattering them.

### [Mars]

**63** And if Mars was in an excellent, praiseworthy position, and he is in a house of Jupiter, and Jupiter in his[62] house, that is an indicator of his sharpness, and the obedience of the people of his kingdom towards him, and his grasp on it, along with the long reach of his reputation and his mastery over his enemies and their countries, especially if the revolution was by day or the Sun looking at them from a stake or from one of the praiseworthy places.

---

[61] مفرّقًا لها.

[62] I believe this means, "Jupiter is *also* in *his* own house," not that Jupiter is in a house of Mars. But I could see it either way.

**64** And likewise if Mars by night was in his house, or in the house of his exaltation, or in a house of Jupiter, in the view of Jupiter, that is an indicator of his respect, the long reach of his reputation, and the abundance of his benefit.

**65** But if Mars was assembling with the Lot of Fortune, it is an indicator of his exhaustion in shedding blood and killing his peers, along with the intensity of his love for weapons and journeys.

### [The Head]

**66** And if the Head was assembling with the fortunes in the Ascendant of the revolution of the year indicative of his accession, that indicates his strength, and his mastery over the rest of the leaders and subjects.

### [The Sun]

**67** And when the Sun connects with Mars at the accession of the acceder, and [Mars] is empty in course, not inspecting Saturn, it indicates the soldiers' falling upon him, and the harshness of their despoiling, and their mocking of him, along with an abundance of rebels, the diminishment[63] of his borders, and the intensity of his distress. **68** But if Mars *was* connecting with Saturn, it indicates the calmness of the soldiers, and their fine obedience towards him, the weakness of the rebels and their scant remaining, especially if Saturn was cleansed and he is in his own house.

**69** Now if the Sun connected with Jupiter without the view of Saturn, it indicates an abundance of those attacking him, especially from among his subjects and the people of his house, and distresses will come to him for that reason. **70** But if Jupiter *did* look at Saturn, it indicates the stilling of that, and his calmness, the harmony of his affairs, the weakness of the rebels and victory over them, and especially if Saturn was cleansed, in his own house.

**71** But if the Sun connected with Saturn it indicates the safety of the acceder, his victory and strength, and more firmly for that if Saturn was free of misfortunes.

---

[63] Or, "weakening" (انتقاص).

72 Now if the Sun separated from Jupiter and connected with Mars, [and] then [the Sun] connected with Saturn before [the Sun] went out from the place [the Sun] was alighting in, he indicates the rising up of one attacking [the acceder], from among the people of his own house or one who is of his rank, and distresses will affect him for that reason—[but] then he will have victory over him. 73 And if Saturn was made fortunate in his own house, then if the Sun does not connect with Saturn before [the Sun] goes out from the position he was alighting in, he indicates the strength of the rebels, and the harshness of what he will encounter from them, and fear for his rule.

### [The Persian theory]

74 Now if Mars separated from Jupiter and connected with Saturn, a propagandist from among the people of prophecy will come out against him. 75 But if Jupiter was connecting with Saturn, they will submit after that and obey him.

76 Now if Mars separated from Saturn and connected with Jupiter, it indicates his changing over[64] to one of the people of his house, and his going out against him for that reason, and his disobedience to him. 77 But if Jupiter connected with Saturn he will have victory over him, and especially if he is in his own house, cleansed. 78 And if Jupiter was empty in course and was safe from the infortunes, in his own light, the rebel will be strong and his command stern.

### [Planets in and ruling other stakes]

79 And[65] if one of the planets was in the seventh from the Ascendant, in its own exaltation, it indicates the harshness of the king towards his subjects, and the badness of their condition in his time. 80 But if it was in its fall in the seventh, it indicates his weakness and the fine condition of the subjects.

81 And of course one also ought to look at the tenth from the Ascendant, or the tenth from the Sun. 82 For if it was in the fixed signs and the fortunes

---

[64] تغييره.

[65] For **79-80**, these rules seem backwards.

are alighting in them, that indicates his good fortune, the abundance of his superiority, and his long length [of time].[66] **83** And if there were planets in these two places, in their own exaltations, or they were eastern or in their *hayyiz*, or they were northern in latitude, adding in motion, it will be more excellent for that.

**84** And if the lord of the fourth or seventh was in the Ascendant or in the Midheaven, that indicates the submission of his enemies to him. **85** And if the lord of the Ascendant or the lord of the Midheaven was in the fourth or seventh, it indicates his submission to his enemies.

### [Several Lots]

**86** And one should look at the Lot of rulership. **87** For it was in the bound of a fortune, it indicates his application of fairness; and if it was in the bound of an infortune it indicates his application of wrong. **88** And if the lord of the Lot of rulership was separating from the lord of the house of assets, it indicates his squandering of assets; but if its lord was connecting with it, it indicates his collecting [them]. **89** And if it was not inspecting [it], it indicates that assets will have no value or worth for him.

**90** As for how to know his nature from the two Lots[67] indicative of that [when] they occur in the two houses of a planet, the way of knowing their place is that it is taken at the time of his accession from the Sun to 15° of Leo, and cast out from the position of the Moon, and where it terminates, there is the first Lot. **91** Then it is taken from the Moon to 15° of Cancer and cast out from the Sun, and where it terminates, there is the second Lot. **92** Now if they occurred in the houses of Saturn, that indicates his use of building, digging canals and rivers, cultivation, and what resembles that. **93** And if they occurred in the houses of Jupiter, that indicates his use of piety, uprightness, virtue, and what resembles that. **94** But if they occurred in the houses of Mars, that indicates his attention to the matter of soldiers and his use of war and weapons. **95** And if they occurred in the houses of Venus, that indicates his use of Venusian matters like songs, entertainment, perfume, enjoyment,

---

[66] طول. Or perhaps, "patience."
[67] Let us call these the "Lots of the king's involvements."

and what resembles that. **96** And if they occurred in the houses of Mercury, that indicates his attending to the land-tax, calculation, the sciences, writing, and what is similar to that.

| Caliphs | Years | Planet |
|---|---|---|
| Muhammad (Prophet) | 622-632 | ☿ |
| Abū Bakr | 632-634 | ☽ |
| ʿUmar I | 634-644 | ♄ |
| ʿUthmān | 644-656 | ♃ |
| ʿAlī | 656-661 | ♂ |
| Muʿāwiya I | 661-680 | ☉ |
| Yazīd I | 680-683 | ♀ |
| *Muʿāwiya II* | *683-684* | |
| *Marwān I* | *684-685* | |
| ʿAbd al-Malik | 685-705 | ☿ |
| Al-Walīd I | 705-715 | ☽ |
| Sulaymān | 715-717 | ♄ |
| ʿUmar II | 717-720 | ♃ |
| Yazīd II | 720-724 | ♂ |
| Hishām | 724-743 | ☉ |
| Al-Walīd II | 743-744 | ♀ |
| Yazīd III | 744-744 | ☿ |
| *Marwān II* | *744-750* | |
| Al-Saffāh (ʿAbbāsid) | 750-754 | ☽ |

**Figure 42: Planetary indicators of Caliphs**

**97** And it is necessary that one join the indication of the indicator of the acceder to the indication of the two Lots: and that is that one looks at the conjunction indicative of the new religious community or dynasty, and at the lord of the sign at which the year terminated,[68] and assign the first indicator to the acceder who accedes to that command, and you assign the one which follows it in the sphere as the indicator of the second acceder—in the order of the lords of the hours. **98** Then the indication of the planet indicating the acceder partners with the indication of the two Lots, and you speak in accordance with that. **99** And an example of that is that the year in which there was the conjunction indicative of the religious community, terminated at Gemini,[69] and the indi-

---

[68] This is ambiguous. Abū Maʿshar doesn't mean to look at the conjunction of the new religion *separately* from the lord of the profection, but to find the conjunction and then identify the lord of the profection in that year. See below.

[69] This may derive from al-Kindī. As I explained in *AW1* Section I.1, al-Kindī believed that the profection reached Gemini in 571 (the year used for the revolution of the triplicity shift for Islam). If we count back in years (ignoring calendrical differences in counting), the profection from the Flood of 3102 BC was also Gemini. So, I

cator of the Prophet (peace be upon him) was Mercury, the lord of the sign of the terminal point (which was Gemini), and the indicator of Abū Bakr was the Moon (which follows upon Mercury in order). **100** And in this way the management in that was up until it arrived at Abū al-'Abbās [al-Saffāh], so that his indicator was the Moon: then one does like that into future [times] in this way.⁷⁰

**101** Since we have completed what we wanted to explain, let us break off Chapter II.4, if God wills.

---

conjecture that when Abū Ma'shar says the profection "terminated at Gemini" in 571, he is using a measurement from al-Kindī. See VIII.2, **10**, which says that the profection from the Ascendant of the Flood conjunction reached Libra, but that "from the terminal point of the *dawr* [profection? Turn?] it had reached Gemini. So Abū Ma'shar may be relying on more than one system here without mentioning it explicitly.

⁷⁰ One can see from this list (derived from Māshā'allāh) that some 'Umayyad caliphs are missing.

## Chapter II.5: On how to know the length of their terms

**1** Deriving the knowledge of the length of their terms is distinguished by looking at it in two classes: one of them is [1] from the revolutions of the years of the world and the conjunctions,[71] and the second is [2] from their accession.[72]

*[The length of the term from revolutions and conjunctions]*

**2** Now as for looking from [1] the revolutions of the years of the world and the conjunctions, it is that one looks at the revolution of the year of the world in which the acceder accedes. **3** Then one looks at Saturn, for if he was in his own house, the knowledge of the length of the acceder's lifespan is derived from five positions:

**4** One of them is [a] what is between Saturn and the Ascendant by the amount of degrees, a year for every 30°.
**5** The second is [b] what is between the Ascendant and his house, in the amount of degrees.
**6** The third is [c] what is between [his] position up to the position of the conjunction, in the amount of degrees.
**7** The fourth is [d] what is between the Ascendant of the conjunction up to the position of the conjunction, in the amount of degrees.
**8** The fifth is [e] up to[73] the completion of that conjunction.

**9** Now if Saturn was in one of his two houses and has already passed beyond 5° up to the completion of 25°, fearing for him will be at two times: one of them is the year in which the conjunction is, and the second time is the amount of what is between the Ascendant of the conjunction up to the posi-

---

[71] See **2-39** below.
[72] See **38** below, and **103ff.**
[73] **BY** add, "<from the number of degrees> up to...". But what would the "completion of the conjunction" be, in terms of degrees or otherwise? It may simply mean, "until the next conjunction occurs, namely about in about 20 years. See **23**, which seems to confirm this.

tion of the conjunction,⁷⁴ a year for every sign. **10** And he also has two [other] times: one of them is his reaching the years of the conjunction (which is 20 years), and the second is his reaching the lifespan of the religious community, which is 25 years.⁷⁵ **11** And it is known that that will be from the terminal point of the turning,⁷⁶ a year for every sign, up to the stakes of the conjunction, or the trine, or the turning's reaching the infortunes or their stakes.

**12** And if Saturn was as we mentioned (in one of his houses), and he was from 1' up to the completion of 5°, or from 25° up to the completion of 30°, then that is an indicator of the shortness of the acceder's term. **13** And knowledge of *that* time is derived from the amount he has moved in his sign, and the amount of what remains to him: so one assigns a year to each degree, and a month to every 5', and a day to every 12". **14** And one turns for help with that to the turning⁷⁷ from the year of the conjunction terminating at the stakes of the infortunes, a year for every sign.

### [Saturn and his lord]

**15** Now,⁷⁸ one should look: for if Saturn was alighting in the houses of the superior planets,⁷⁹ and he and the lord of his house are in one of the stakes, then one should count from the lord of his house up to him by degrees of equality,⁸⁰ a year for every 30°, and a month for every 2.5°, and a day for every 5': and what is brought together from that is the extent of the lifespan.⁸¹ **16** But if Saturn and his lord are in what follows the stakes, then let it be taken from the lord of his house up to him, and one does just like the first

---

⁷⁴ This is like [4] above, but using signs instead of degrees.
⁷⁵ The reason for this number is unclear.
⁷⁶ دور. That is, by profection, here and later in the sentence.
⁷⁷ دور. Again by profection.
⁷⁸ From here up to **24**, compare with **78-80** below.
⁷⁹ For the inferior planets, see **20** below.
⁸⁰ Degrees of equality are zodiacal degrees. However, **BY** take this to be degrees of right ascensions. I can understand both possibilities as a method.
⁸¹ Note that if we give 1 year for every 30°, the maximum years in the whole zodiac would be 12. Something seems wrong here, but Abū Ma'shar affirms this in **31** below.

method. **17** And if one of them is in a stake or what follows a stake, and the other is withdrawing, then one should count from the one in the stake or what follows the stake, up to the one withdrawing from the stake: and that [time] is established according to what we set forth before.

**18** Now if there were less than 300° between Saturn and his lord,[82] then one should appoint a month for every degree, and a day for every 2', for the amount of time will be in accordance with that. **19** But if there were more than 300° between them up to 360°, then one should subtract that from 360, and one should assign a month for every degree which remains after the subtraction, and a day for every 2': and what there is, is the amount of time.

**20** Now if Saturn was alighting in one of the houses of the inferior planets or [that of] the Moon, and they are looking at him, then one should operate in that just like the first method: and it is that one takes from the planet which is in the stake up to the planet which is in what follows the stake, or from the planet which is in what follows that stake up to the planet withdrawing from the stake, and grant a year for every 30°, in accordance with what we set forth in the first situation.

**21** But if they were *not* looking at Saturn, then one casts out one-half of the degrees which are between them, and let there be taken a year for every 30° of [that] half; and let us begin the counting from the weaker of the two in position up to the stronger of the two in position. **22** But if they were equal in positional strength, one should count up to that one of them which is in [its] "goodliness."[83] **23** Now if his lord was receiving him one should not cut it [short], and the amount of time will be up to the time of the conjunction.

**24** And he has another time, and it is that one assigns a month to every degree between them both, and one operates just like the first method (after one-half has been cast out from that, if they were not looking at him).

---

[82] This is probably if one or both are withdrawing and therefore weak.
[83] الحلّيّة. **BY** say that MS **T** reads *halb*.

## [Saturn and the Sun]

**25** And if Saturn was in the *hayyiz* of the greater luminary[84] and the revolution was by day, what is between the greater luminary and Saturn should be taken,[85] and one operates with it just like the first method. **26** And he has another time, and it is that one assigns a month for every degree which is between them both, if there were less than 300° between them. **27** And if there was more than 300°, one should subtract that from 360 and operate with it just like the first method.[86] **28** If the revolution was by night, then let it be taken from Saturn up to the greater luminary and one operates with it just like the first method, and what there is will be the amount of time.

**29** And if in these situations Saturn was received and he is in a sign having two bodies, then one should double what comes out in terms of the years, months, and days.

**30** And when Saturn is burned in the revolution of the year in which the acceder accedes, the acceder will not complete one year.

## [Jupiter and his lord]

**31** And this is also employed with Jupiter and his lord, but one assigns a month for every sign between the two, contrary to what one assigns to Saturn (a year for every sign).[87] **32** And it is joined to what comes out of the number that is between Saturn and his lord,[88] and especially if Saturn and Jupiter are in the stakes; except that if Saturn is in a house of an inferior planet and his lord is not looking at him, one does not seek information from Jupiter and his lord for any increase in the time.

**33** And one looks too at Jupiter at the time of the revolution: for if he was inspecting Saturn and he[89] is in a stake or in what follows a stake, in a bad

---

[84] This probably means that Saturn is in the same hemisphere as the Sun (and by day, in the upper one).
[85] This seems to mean, *from* the Sun *to* Saturn; by night it is the converse, as in **28**.
[86] See **19**.
[87] See **15**.
[88] Omitting an extra "and between him/it."
[89] This must be Jupiter.

condition, one adds 12 months to the amount of time (or 12 days or 12 hours).

### [Other rules]

**34** And when one of the two infortunes is in the tenth in the revolution of the year, one should take care <to convert> what comes out in years into months and days. **35** But if one of them is in the eleventh it is longer for the term, and this indication is strong in the triplicity of Cancer. **36** As for the rest of the remaining triplicities, if the beginning of a revealed law or rulership is in them, sometimes the planets indicate months (of the amount of time), in accordance with the degrees between the two indicators, [even] when there are 360° between them.[90] **37** And sometimes the planets indicate their years for the amount of the term.

### [The length of the term from the accession]

**38** As for [2] the amount of their terms from their accession,[91] it is derived from the distance which comes to be between Mars and his lord in the revolutions of the years in which they accede, in the amount which is used for Saturn[92] and Jupiter[93] (a month or year for every sign between them), in accordance with his strength and weakness.

### [More rules for revolutions and shifts]

**39** And as for the kings of civil unrest and who among them accedes at the shift of the transit from triplicity to triplicity, one should not look at the amount of their lifespans from the perspective of Saturn and his lord, and Jupiter and his lord. **40** What is most dependable for deriving knowledge of the amount of their lifespans in that, is from the distance which comes to be

---

[90] This seems to mean Saturn and his lord, as in **15-19**.
[91] That is, the chart of the accession itself, not the revolution for that year. See also **103**, where Abū Ma'shar returns to this.
[92] In **15-24**.
[93] In **31-33**.

BOOK II: DYNASTIES & KINGS

between the Ascendant of the conjunction and the sign of the conjunction, a year for every sign. **41** And if it went beyond that, then [look] at the opposition of the conjunction; except that if the direction's[94] arrival at the opposition is closer to it than the sign of the conjunction, the timing is according to that, if God wills.

**42** If the feared distribution is completed, then one should look at the sign at which the year terminated: for if it was corrupted by the square of Mars or Saturn at the revolution of the year, along with the greater luminary, then one should judge cutting. **43** But if it was safe, then one should turn for another cycle,[95] and judge cutting for him when the turning[96] terminates at the square of the infortunes, or upon the corruption of the sign at which the year terminated by the greater luminary, or Saturn. **44** But if one of them was corrupted and the other suitable, then one should judge illness and what resembles that.

**45** Now if the year terminated at the sign which was the Ascendant of the conjunction, or at the position of the conjunction, or at its opposition by direction,[97] or one of its triplicities,[98] then it is feared for the acceder in that year. **46** And if a fortune showed up in that place, it neutralizes that fear until an infortune shows up in that position at the conversion[99] of years. **47** And as for the misfortune, it will come to be at the square of the infortunes in the revolution of the year, and the [profection] terminating at their square in the root of the religious community, or the conjunction, or at the square of the conjunction itself. **48** And if Saturn was in his houses, one should turn[100] from his position just as the Sun is turned.[101]

---

[94] One would expect this to be a profection, but **42** confirms that Abū Ma'shar seems to mean a primary direction that measures 30° increments on the celestial equator. (Or is he using both directions and profections?)

[95] This is certainly a profection.

[96] الدّور.

[97] See **41-42**.

[98] That is, "trines," or the signs which are a member of the conjunction's triplicity.

[99] That is, "revolution."

[100] فليدر. Again, a profection, here and later in the sentence.

[101] تدار.

**49** And[102] one may know that in another way, and it is that one looks at the Ascendant of the revolution of the year of the conjunction: for if it is one of the two houses of Saturn, or his exaltation, or the house of the Moon, then one should count from the Ascendant to the position of the conjunction, a year for every sign—if Saturn and the Moon by counting[103] or by equation[104] were in a stake. **50** But if the Ascendant was one of these signs (or others) and neither Saturn nor the Moon were in the stakes, then one should count from the position of the conjunction to the Ascendant.

**51** Now if the conjunction was in the houses of the inferior planets and it was in the third or ninth, one should count from the position of the conjunction to the Ascendant.

**52** And if the Ascendant of the year of the conjunction was one of the houses of the superior planets, and it was in the third or ninth, and especially if it was in Aquarius, it is that one should not fear for the acceder when the year reaches it.

**53** And if Saturn was in his house, the amount of the lifespan of the acceder is one conjunction. **54** But if he was in a house of Jupiter or Mars, one should count from the position of Saturn to the position of his lord, and make it be a year for every 12°.

**55** And one should also look at what is between the portion of the Ascendant at the revolution of the year when the acceder accedes, and the portion of the lesser conjunction, and make it be a year for every 30°. **56** But if [the acceder] passes beyond that, then his disaster will be at the terminating of the direction[105] at the position of Mars or the opposition of his degree, a year for every sign.

**57** And one employs that in another way, and it is that one looks at Saturn: for if he was in the tenth or eleventh from the Sun, that indicates that the amount of their lifespans will be in the amount of the lesser years of the Sun. **58** But if there was 35°[106] between Saturn and [the Sun], that indicates

---

[102] According to Musā Ch. 4, **194-95**, this is the view of Māshā'allāh.
[103] That is, by whole sign.
[104] That is, by quadrant division.
[105] Or rather, profection.
[106] **BY** note that the Māshā'allāh version in their Appendix IV (*On the Accession of the Caliphs*) gives 15°.

one-fourth of [the Sun's] years; and to the extent that the arc which is between [the Sun] and Saturn is reduced by degree, a year is subtracted up to the completion of 30°. **59** And if there were 66° between [the Sun] and [Saturn], that indicates one-fourth of [the Sun's] years; and to the extent that one subtracts a degree from that, a year is subtracted, up to 60°. **60** But if it increased beyond that, one does not operate according to the amount of their lifespans using this method.

**61** But[107] if Saturn was in the tenth or eleventh from the Sun, that is an indicator that sometimes their lifespans are prolonged until the two superiors are united in a single degree.[108]

**62** Now if Saturn was in a stake of the revolution of the year in which the acceder acceded, in his own house,[109] and he wants to shift [to another sign] or is not firmly established in it (and it is that he is at its beginning, in less than 5°, and at its end, passing beyond 25°), that is an indicator that the remainder of the acceder's period will be in accordance with what remains to Saturn in his sign, in the form we have explained (a year for every degree),[110] and especially if it was Capricorn or Aquarius.[111] **63** But if [the acceder] went beyond that, one should cast out the degrees of Saturn from 30,[112] and what remains after that is the amount of time of the lifespan.

**64** Now if Saturn was in the seventh from the Sun, in the first face of the sign, that is an indicator that the amount of their lifespans will be one-half the years of the Sun. **65** And if Saturn was in [the Sun's] right trine, and Jupiter in the eleventh from [the Sun], it indicates three-fifths of [the Sun's] years. **66** But if Saturn was in the sixth from [the Sun] and Mars with [the Sun], it indicates [the Sun's] lesser years. **67** And if he was in [the Sun's] left

---

[107] Sentences **61-68** are very close to, but not identical with, the version of Māshā'allāh (in **BY**'s Appendix IV, p. 547).

[108] Compare with **57**.

[109] This might include Libra (his exaltation): see footnote at the end of this sentence.

[110] See **12-13**.

[111] Since Capricorn and Aquarius *are* the houses of Saturn, Abū Ma'shar might be thinking that Libra is also an option.

[112] This probably means 30 years minus the degrees which he has just completed. Thus if Saturn were in 24° of the sign, then if the king is still alive after 6 years (the remaining degrees in the sign), he will live for 24 more (30 - 6 = 24).

trine, that indicates that the amount of their lifespans will be like the amount of one-half of [the Sun's] years.

**68** And if the Sun was connecting with Jupiter and [Jupiter] is in the tenth from [the Sun] or in the eleventh [from him], received, that indicates the amount of the years of Jupiter or in accordance with counting what is between the Sun and the infortune.

**69** And for every acceder whose positions of the planets are *not* found to be as we described in the revolution of the year of his accession, let the time of his disasters be appointed in accordance with what is between the Sun and Saturn or Mars, a year for every sign. **70** But if he was safe from that, let it be increased for him in this manner,[113] for the cutting will be at that [point].

### [Other rules]

**71** And knowledge of that may be derived in another way, and it is that one looks in the year in which the acceder acceded or from the time of his accession, and count from the stronger of the two planets, or the easternizing one of them (I mean, Saturn and Jupiter), up to the greater luminary, and from the greater luminary to the weaker of them, and the westernizing one, a year for every sign. **72** Then one brings the two numbers together, and what there is, is the term of the acceder. **73** And the truest for that is if the greater luminary was sextiling the two planets, or trining them: for the judgment about that is true, and he will complete the two numbers which we described.[114]

**74** And their lifespans become long from the method of the conjunctions in some of the signs of the triplicities: and that is that it is possible for the amount of the term of the lifespan to be 40 years and more than that, and especially in the *fardārs* of the superior planets, because when the Sun indicates the lifespans by the periods[115] of the planets with which he has partnership in the matter of kings, it lengthens the term and it will go beyond his lesser years to the middle or greater ones.

---

[113] In the Māshā'allāh version, this means to count to the next infortune.
[114] See **71-72**.
[115] أدوار.

**75** Now as for the periods[116] of Venus, Mercury, and the Moon, they do not indicate more than their lesser years in their periods;[117] and sometimes they add one-third or one-fourth until an infortune encounters [the Sun]. **76** For if an infortune encountered him or connected with him, the cutting will be in that time because the inferior planets do not have a partnership with him in the matter of kings like his collaboration with the superior planets in their[118] greater years; and every planet looking at him increases them in accordance with its own lesser years: so the lifespan becomes long in this way. **77** And as for the *fardārs* of the inferior planets, they do not indicate that, due to what we set out before.[119]

**78** And[120] if Saturn was in the houses of the superior planets, received, and the planets looked at him (or they do not look), that is an indicator of the long length of the acceder's lifespan. **79** And if he was in the houses of the inferior planets and they were looking at him and he is received, it indicates the long length of their lifespans. **80** But if they are not looking at him and he is not received, it is an indicator of the shortness of their lifespans.

### [Lot of lifespan]

**81** And knowledge of the amount of their lifespans may also be derived from the Lot of lifespan, taken from Jupiter to Saturn by day (and the contrary by night), and cast out from the Ascendant of the revolution of the year in which the acceder accedes;[121] where it terminates, there is the Lot. **82** And if Jupiter was in an embodied sign and the revolution by day, and he is falling away from the stakes, then let it be taken from Saturn to [Jupiter], and one should add one sign to the calculation and cast out from the Ascendant; where it terminates, there is the Lot. **83** And if the calculation was by night and Jupiter is in a stake, let it be taken from him to Saturn and cast out from

---

[116] أدوار.
[117] أدوار.
[118] Or perhaps, "his."
[119] See **76**.
[120] Compare with **15** and **20** above.
[121] This is the "Lot of livelihood" from *Carmen* I.29, **29**, which Abū Ma'shar counts as his Lot of life (Lot #8) in *Gr. Intr.* VIII.4, **16-21**.

the Ascendant; where it terminates, there is the Lot. **84** And if Saturn and Jupiter were opposed and they were falling away from the Ascendant,[122] then let what comes out between them be halved and cast from the Ascendant. **85** And if Jupiter was in his exaltation and the revolution was by night, then let it be calculated from him to Saturn, and cast out from the Ascendant.

**86** Then one should look at the time of the Sun's terminating at the position of the Lot, and the amount of what is between the Sun and the Lot (in terms of signs) is taken, and a year is assigned to every sign up to the time of the disaster.

**87** Now if Saturn and Jupiter are opposing the position of the Lot, then one should look at the two luminaries: for when the greater luminary is corrupted by Saturn and the lesser luminary by Mars, it will be the time of the disaster.

**88** And one should also look at the Sun's entrance into the sign of the terminal point. **89** For[123] if that was more indicative of the disaster than the Lot is (when the Sun reaches a time), [then] one should also fear the year [when] the Moon is revolved in its Ascendant or its Midheaven, upon the Sun's reaching the second sign from the Ascendant—except that if the Moon was in a house of Saturn, in a praiseworthy place from the Ascendant, and [she and] her lord both free of burning and misfortune—the disaster will go beyond the amount of 6 months, and the disaster will be upon the Sun's reaching the second from the Ascendant.

**90** And along with that, the Lot and the misfortune of the portion of the meeting employ their[124] ascensions, and it is stated in accordance with that.

---

[122] That is, in aversion to the Ascendant. **BY** bracket this as incorrect and to be deleted as an error, namely so that Saturn and Jupiter only need to be cadent or dynamically withdrawing (in which case they would be falling from the *stakes*, as in 82). If they are right, it would make these sentences more symmetrical.

[123] From here until "except that if," the reading of this sentence is uncertain, particularly the meaning of the clause, "when the Sun reaches a time." I am tempted to read the phrase "for if that" (فإن كان ذلك) as "For, *that* is more indicative," as though the فإن is missing the *shadda* (فإنّ), but that would be ungrammatical because a verb should not intervene between it and the word "that" without adding an attached pronoun (فإنّه).

[124] This should be in the dual, not the plural, so something may be wrong here.

## [Two other Lots of lifespan]

**91** And of course the extent of the amount of their lifespans may also be derived from the place of two Lots at the revolution of the year in which they accede: and the way of knowing their operation is that one looks at the sign at which that year terminates from the Ascendant of the religious community, and at the sign at which the year terminates from the lesser conjunction. **92** Then it is taken from the eastern planet (of Saturn and Jupiter) to the position of the degree of the religious community's termination point from its Ascendant, and on top of it are added the degrees of the Ascendant of the revolution, and it is cast out from it, so where it ends, there is the first Lot. **93** Then it is taken from the western one of the two, up to the degree of the terminal point from the Ascendant of the lesser conjunction, and on top of it is added the degrees of the Ascendant of the revolution, and it is cast out from it, so where it ends, there is the second Lot. **94** Now if Saturn and Jupiter were both eastern or western, one should begin the first Lot from Saturn and the second from Jupiter.

**95** Then,[125] one counts what is between the eastern planet and the Sun (in degrees and minutes), and multiply that by 12, and divide by what the eastern planet has traveled in its own sign (in degrees and minutes): and what comes out is the size of the acceder's term, a year for every 30°. **96** But if you wanted knowledge of that from the second Lot, then multiply what is between the Sun and the western planet (in degrees and minutes) by 12, and divide by what the western planet has traveled in its own sign (in degrees and minutes), and on top of it are added the degrees of the Ascendant, and it is cast out from the Ascendant, and where it ends, one should count from that degree up to the portion of the eastern one of the two, and what there is, is the lifespan of the acceder, the same amount of one year for every 30°.

## [Variation on the two Lots of lifespan]

**97** And these two Lots may be used in another way, and it is closer to the affairs indicative of the conditions of kings due to the collaboration of the

---

[125] **95-96** seem to be an alternative method to **92-94**.

two Lots in it. **98** And it is that it is taken from the portion of the greater luminary up to the degree of Saturn, and on top of it is added the portion of their[126] union at their shifting from triplicity to triplicity, and it is cast out from that sign, and where it ends, here is the first Lot. **99** And as for the second Lot, it is taken from the degree of Jupiter to the degree of Saturn, and on top of it are added the degrees of their union which comes to be in that time, and it is cast out from that sign, and where it ends, there is the second Lot. **100** Then one sees how much there is from each one of the two Lots to its lord, or from its lord to it, or from each one of them both to Mars, or from Mars to them: and make it be one year for every 30° of it.

**101** Now as for investigating knowledge of the amount of what the two Lots indicate, it is found in *The Book of the Two Lots*,[127] a restatement of which would be a kind of reduplication, since our intention [here] is to summarize.

**102** Now[128] as for what the astrologers used to believe in the matter of the "two Lots" (and they rejected[129] judging it for the lifespans of kings), they

---

[126] That is, Jupiter and Saturn. Thus the first Lot is a Sun-Saturn Lot, and the second one a Jupiter-Saturn Lot (**99**).

[127] This book has not yet been identified. Since Abū Ma'shar apparently wrote it, it must use these two lifespan Lots. However, Māshā'allāh is also attributed a *Book of the Two Lots*, and we see in **102** that Abū Ma'shar does not understand how Saturn and Jupiter are also called the two "Arrows," it's possible that this is a *Book of the Two Arrows* and might refer to the Persian theory of these planets as the Arrows and Mars as the Sword, something else might be going on here. See my Introduction and the footnote below.

[128] This sentence is ambiguous and contains an implicit criticism. As I have said in the Introduction, the usual word for "Lot" in Arabic is سهم (*sahm*), which actually means an "arrow." So when we read in some authors that Saturn is the "first *sahm*" and Jupiter the second *sahm*," at first we think something is wrong because they are not Lots. But when we see in the full context of the Persian theory of superior planets and war that they are each a *sahm* while Mars is the "Sword," it becomes clear that Saturn is the first *Arrow* and Jupiter the second *Arrow*, making each of the superiors a weapon of war. It could be that Abū Ma'shar does not have this fuller text as we find in Sahl's *Revolutions*, even though he has quoted parts of it above. Thus he seems to imply, when referring to the superiors as "Lots" (sc. Arrows), that astrologers had some idiosyncratic and false idea of what a *sahm* was, when in fact they *did* know what it meant.

used to think that the first Lot is Saturn and the second one is Jupiter:[130] and in judging it they used to operate in accordance with how one does it with the two Lots whose account we have set forth.[131]

### [More on lifespan from the accession]

**103** Now as for knowing the amount of their lifespans from the perspective of the second class (and it is from the time of their accession), one looks for that from the Ascendant and Midheaven, and extracts a releaser and house-master for him just as one does in nativities. **104** Then one directs the degree of the Ascendant for his body, and the Midheaven for his authority, and one makes turnings[132] from them both together.

**105** So if the direction and turning from them both together terminate at misfortune, it judges cutting.[133] **106** And if the corruption was of [just] one of them [and] not the other, then one should judge the corruption of that one. **107** And if the degree of the Ascendant terminated at the infortunes and the misfortune was harsh, one should judge cutting for him; but if [the misfortune] was less than that, one should judge illness for him, *if* the direction from the degree of the Midheaven was suitable. **108** And if there was corruption from the direction of [the Midheaven's degree] apart from[134] the Ascendant, it judges corruption for [his] authority. **109** But if there was corruption from them both, it judges cutting.

**110** And for that one may call upon the Ascendant of the religious community, and the Ascendant of the conjunction, and the terminating of the

---

[129] يدفعون. **BY** read this as "apply," as though the astrologers applied Saturn and Jupiter for this method. But Abū Ma'shar proceeds to say they did *not* use Saturn and Jupiter for the lifespans.

[130] Again, the older astrologers were right in calling these the Arrows and Mars the Sword, because they used different techniques for them apart from the lifespan of rulers.

[131] Nevertheless I do not find evidence in Sahl of their using them directly for lifespan.

[132] الأدوار. That is, profections.

[133] That is, the cutting-off of the life force or lifespan.

[134] دون.

directions and turnings[135] at the square of the infortunes in those positions. **111** And sometimes the event which the year indicates will occur when the direction from the sign of the terminal point or from the Ascendant reaches the square of that indicator, or the position of the indicator, or the amount of the degrees between them.[136] **112** And in the year in which the acceder accedes, one should look at which sign the year terminates, and where the distribution terminates (by bound and degree), and whether there is the ray of a planet in that bound in the root, or in the conjunction which was in the year in which the beginning of the dynasty was, and whether that corresponds to one of the Quarters or not.

**113** Then one looks at the lord of the terminal point in that year, and lord of the first division,[137] and at the degree[138] of the direction, to see how much is between them both and the ray of the infortunes, and one judges in accordance with that.

**114** Since we have completed what we wanted to explain, let us break off the chapter, if God wills.

---

[135] الأدوار. That is, profections.

[136] This last clause seems to mean, "profect for as many years as there are degrees between the two." Such a profection would not, therefore, guarantee coming to the indicator or its square.

[137] القسم. Unclear. According to **BY**, the Latin glossator indicates that this is the first category in **1** above, namely the determination from the revolutions and conjunction. But that does not make sense to me.

[138] Or more likely "arc," namely the arc of direction between each of these two planets and the infortunes.

## Chapter II.6: On what their ailments are, indicating their disasters

**1** Since we have set forth in Chapter II.4[139] how to know their character, let us state in this chapter what their ailments are, indicating their disasters.

**2** We say that if one wants knowledge of that, one looks at the Ascendant of the year indicative of their accession.

**3** Now if that was in the houses of Saturn, that indicates that the ailments feared for him will be due to coldnesses and wetness, bowel movements[140] and tuberculosis, especially if it was in Capricorn; and if it was in Aquarius, then because of coldness and winds.

**4** And if it was in the houses of Jupiter, it indicates that their fate will be a praiseworthy death. **5** If it was in Sagittarius, then because of hotness and winds; and if it was in Pisces, then because of windiness, like swelling in the belly and what resembles that.

**6** And if it was in the houses of Mars, then because of hotness. **7** If it was in Aries, the majority of the illnesses will be what is their heads; and if it was in Scorpio, it will be wetness along with the hotness, and the ailments will be in their lower parts.

**8** And if they were in the house of the Sun it indicates that their ailments will be because of hotness and dryness, and it is harsher for that if the Sun was made unfortunate by Mars.

**9** Now if it was in the houses of Venus, that will be because of remedies and poisons, and what there is of it will be quick-[acting]. **10** If it was in Taurus, then because of coldness and dryness, and because of riding animals; and if it was in Libra, then because of hotness and wetness, and from pains in the throat, especially if Venus was in Aries.

**11** And if it was in the houses of Mercury, and especially Gemini, that will be because of hotness and wetness, and pains of the liver, inflammation of the lung, and what resembles that, and the disappearance of reason. **12** And if it was in Virgo, then because of a corruption of the liver, the gall-bladder, and the intestines.

---

[139] Reading more accurately for the "fifth" chapter.
[140] **BY**: "diarrhea."

**13** And if it was in the house of the Moon, then because of coldness and wetness. **14** And the planets looking at her ought also to be mixed in, and the statement made in accordance with that: for if the planets looking at her are similar to what we described, it will be more truthful for the indication. **15** But if they are not similar, then one should mix the character of the planets looking at *them*, and the statement made according to that.

**16** Since we have completed what we wanted to explain, let us break off the chapter, with the good fortune of God and His aid.

## Chapter II.7: On knowing the manner of their disasters, & the day on which that will be, & to whom the rulership will pass after them

**1** Since we have set forth in Chapter II.6 the knowledge of what their ailments are, in this Chapter let us state the manner of their disasters, and the day on which that will be, to whom the rulership will pass after them, and the civil unrest occurring for those reasons.

*[Types of disasters, and some timing]*

**2** Now if one wanted knowledge of it, one should look, in the Ascendant of the revolution of the year in which the acceder acceded, at the position of Saturn and Mars relative to him. **3** For if Mars was assembling with Saturn or[141] connecting with him from the square or opposition, or looking at him from one of the aspectual figures, it indicates his killing, especially if Saturn was not receiving Mars and Saturn is weak in his position. **4** But if Saturn was received in a strong place, and Mars in a weak place, not in one of his shares, it indicates that [his killing] is wanted, but he will be protected from it, and civil unrest will take place for those reasons.

**5** And if Saturn was under the rays, burned, and the Sun handing over to him, that is an indicator of their being killed.[142]

**6** And if Mars was separating from Saturn from a square or opposition, and the Moon is transferring between them with no planet's light cutting her off, and Saturn is falling away from the Ascendant, and Mars in an excellent position, it indicates his being killed. **7** And likewise if the Moon transferred between them,[143] it indicates the same thing.

**8** And when Saturn was falling away from the stakes and Mars strong in his place (or in a stake), and they connected from a sextile without the light of a planetary fortune (or another) cutting between them, it indicates the shortness of his remaining, and that his disaster will be by iron; and some-

---

[141] Reading for "and."
[142] See also **20** below.
[143] This is redundant, and something might be missing.

times that will affect him on journeys, and especially if he was looking at him from a sextile in the year of the shift of the transit from triplicity to triplicity.

**9** And if Jupiter was the lord of the house of Saturn, and he is corrupted by the assembly of Mars (or his square or opposition) without the fortunes looking at him, it indicates his being killed.

**10** And if Mars assembled with Jupiter in the fall of Mars, or in his unhealthiness,[144] or at the end of the sign without a planet cutting off their light before their connection is completed, it indicates the same thing.

**11** And if Mars was with the Sun or in the second sign from him,[145] and [the Sun] is raised up above him,[146] or <Mars is> in the eleventh or twelfth from [the Sun] and [Mars] is raised up above [the Sun], it is an indicator of his being killed, and after him there will be civil unrest in his land.[147] **12** But if there was 30° between them, his remaining will be for 30 months, and the civil unrest after him will last for 15 months, in accordance with the years of Mars as months. **13** And if there was more than 30° between them (up to 15 [more]),[148] that is an indicator that his term will be in the amount of double those degrees, and after that the civil unrest will last in accordance with what we set forth, except that [the civil unrest] will be easier than when the extent of the distance between them is 30°.

**14** Now if the situation of the Sun relative to Mars was not as we described at the time of the revolution of the year in which he accedes, one should see what is between the Sun and Saturn, and assign a year for every sign. **15** But if Mars cuts off between them by his inspection of them, one should assign a half-year for every sign.

**16** And one also ought to look, in the year of the conjunction or in the year in which the year terminates at it from the Ascendant of the conjunc-

---

[144] That is, in his detriment.

[145] Reading منها for منه ("from [Mars]").

[146] منصّبة عليه. Meaning unclear. This is not the usual term for overcoming by a superior aspect. The Māshā'allāh version (in **BY** Appendix IV) says virtually the same thing (تنصب عليه). Perhaps it simply means "in an earlier degree or sign."

[147] دار, which can also mean "home or house," but metaphorically refers to a land or region.

[148] That is, up to a total of 45°.

tion, at the position of the conjunction or at one of its triplicities:[149] for if there happens to be an infortune in that place, the fear will be disruptive.[150] **17** And if it was a fortune instead of the infortune, the fear will fade away. **18** But if it is an infortune and the conjunction was in the first quarter [of the year],[151] it will be feared for the acceder at the beginning of that year; and likewise if it was in the rest of the quarters, one judges the fear in the rest of the quarters of the year in that way.

**19** And if a shift from triplicity to triplicity occurred, and the conjunction was in a house of Jupiter (or his exaltation), that indicates an abundance of travels, and his being killed.

**20** And if Saturn was burned, bodily with the portion of the Sun, a year will not be completed for him, and that will be a warning of his being killed.

**21** And if the lord of the Midheaven was in the sign at which the matter of the years terminated, that indicates his death; and if Mars makes it unfortunate, it indicates his being killed.

**22** And if the acceder acceded in the year of the conjunction of the triplicity,[152] and Mars looked at the position of the conjunction from the rest of the figures without an aspect from the fortunes, that is an indicator of killing. **23** But if he does not see it, it indicates[153] death; and sometimes it indicates his fleeing.

**24** Now if the acceder acceded in some year, and Saturn was not in view of Jupiter at the time of the revolution, it indicates the absence of rebels during the length of his term. **25** And if Mars does not look, it indicates the absence of wars during the length of his term. **26** Now if Mars did see Saturn and he is received in the year of his accession, the wars will be weak during the length of his term. **27** But if Saturn received him that will be a firmer confirmation of the weakness. **28** And if he opposed him at the time of the

---

[149] That is, the signs of its triplicity, which form trines with it. What Abū Ma'shar may also have wanted to include was the opposition, as he emphasizes in II.5, **41-42** and **45**.
[150] Lit., "cutting, a cutter" (قاطعًا).
[151] Adding tentatively, instead of treating it as a Quarter.
[152] That is, at the triplicity shift.
[153] Surely this should read, "it *does not* indicate death."

revolution and there was not reception between them both, that indicates the abundance of wars and civil unrest.

**29** And if in addition to that Saturn and Jupiter were the master of that clime, it is an indicator of the general public pouncing upon him, and his being killed, and the occurrence of civil unrest after it (and the majority of what occurs is civil unrest), and especially in the dynasty of the Arabs before the occurrence of the Quarters (or after them), in the amount of 7 years, more or less.

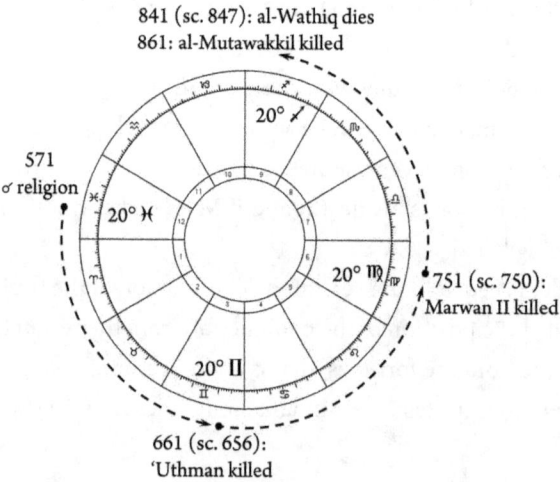

Figure 43: Zodiacal directions of 90°

**30** And example of that is that the direction in the year of the religious community terminated at degree 21 of Pisces. **31** When the direction terminated at 20° of Gemini, 'Uthmān b. 'Affān (may God be pleased with him) was killed:[154] and that was in the year 81 from the revolution of the year of the shift of the triplicity. **32** And when the direction terminated at 20° of Virgo, at the beginning of the 90th year from the killing of 'Uthmān b. 'Affān, Marwān b. Muhammad b. Marwān b. al-Hakam was killed. **33** And when the direction terminated at 20° of the sign of Sagittarius, and that is at the end of Caliphate of al-Wāthiq, al-Mutawakkil was killed after the completion of the Quarter, and civil unrest occurred and disagreements multiplied.

**34** Now if the lord of the sign of the Sun was made unfortunate and the Moon in an embodied sign,[155] it indicates the death of two acceders in that

---

[154] It would have been better for Abū Ma'shar to have said that Caliph 'Alī died, since he was indeed killed in 661; but perhaps for political reasons he preferred to mention 'Uthmān.

[155] This could also be read as, "if the lord of the sign of the Sun and Moon was made unfortunate in an embodied sign."

conjunction. **35** But if it was made unfortunate in the sign of the Midheaven, it indicates the death of the acceder.

**36** And if the lord of the Midheaven was burned, and corresponds to the degrees of the Sun, it indicates his death. **37** But if it had already gone past [the Sun's] degrees, he will not die but distress will enter upon him and he will be sad; then it will go away. **38** Now if the lord of the Midheaven was in an embodied sign, two rulerships[156] will have disasters in that conjunction, unless the planet was an infortune: for it indicates the long length of the duration of that, and its harshness, and it is feared that his disaster will be in accordance with the essence of the sign in which the infortune is, among the quadrants of the circle. **39** If it was in the sign of illness, then illness; and if it was in the sign of death, death. **40** But if the fortunes looked at it, he will escape.

**41** And one should also look for that from the meeting of the indicator with the infortune, and the statement made in accordance with that. **42** And if the infortune was looking at the indicator of the acceder from the assembly, square, or opposition, death will be feared for him. **43** And if that was in a stake, and its lord[157] going into burning, and an infortune corresponded[158] to it in the position of the indicator, the Midheaven, or the Ascendant, it will be feared for him unless a fortune partners with it in the aspect, and the infortune was a helper to it in essence.

**44** And if Mars was retrograde in Taurus[159] or Scorpio at the revolution of the year of the acceder, death will be feared for him in that year. **45** And if he was retrograde in one of the two [signs] after the [Sun's] entry into the year, it will also be feared for him, even if the first [situation] is more confirmed than the second.

---

[156] Or, "two kings" (ملكان).
[157] This must be the lord of the indicator of the acceder.
[158] ووافقه. Or perhaps, "coincides" with it?
[159] Mars cannot be retrograde in Taurus at an Aries ingress. But see Mūsā's *Fulfillment* Ch. 37, **14**, where he tracks Mars and notes that he went retrograde and stationed in Taurus *later* in the year. Abū Ma'shar might also really mean that Mars is there in some subsequent revolution cast for the annual *time of* the original accession.

**46** And when Mars wavers[160] in the sign of the religious community of a people or their dynasty, or in its opposition, and that year is close to the completion of the acceder's term, his ruin will be in [that year].

**47** And if Saturn assembled with the lord of his house, and the lord of his house connected with Mars,[161] and Mercury is with Mars or inspecting him or inspecting Saturn and his lord, that is an indicator that the acceder will wail due to poisons, and be killed.

**48** And one should also look at the planet from which one seeks information about the condition of the acceder, and at its reception of light, and handing it [over], and know thoroughly what will be concerning his condition, and what will befall him day by day in terms of harshness and comfort, good and evil, what the subjects will have from him, and what he will have from them.

**49** And when the direction of the degree of the Ascendant or the portion of the Midheaven (or its lord) terminates at an infortune, it is also feared for the acceder, as well as the occurrence of wars and rebellion. **50** And if the infortune doing violence to the year was retrograde, it indicates that same as that.

**51** And one may derive knowledge of that (I mean, the affairs because of which there is killing) in another way too, and especially for kings of uprightness: because that is made possible at the corruption of the distribution in the house of Mercury or Mars by the rays of Mars or Saturn happening to be [there], or at the year in which they acceded terminating at Mercury, and the distribution at Saturn, and one of the two was corrupted by its lord in the year of the conjunction without the rays of Jupiter being in the bound in which they are (or the sign). **53** And their accession will be in the year in which the turning[162] terminates at Mars, and the distribution belongs to Mercury or Mars, in the house of Saturn (and especially in Aquarius), and the connection of the direction with the rays of Mars or the body of Saturn, in the house of Mars, and that ray and body of the infortune is in the root of

---

[160] **BY** understand this to mean "stationing." Wavering is indeed a valid meaning for this. See the reference to Mūsā in the previous footnote.
[161] The Persian name for Mars is used in this sentence (*Bahrām*).
[162] That is, profection (دور).

the dynasty or the Quarter, or in the current conjunction. **53** But if it occurs in the image[163] and does not reach the bound, that is also made possible.

**54** And as for the kings completing a chapter[164] [of time], if the direction connected with the rays of Mars in the root of the religious community, and he also has rays in the current conjunction, it indicates his being killed, and especially of the connection was in the houses of Mercury or his bounds. **55** And all of these signals are indicative of what we described.

**56** And among the worst of matters as well in cutting off their lifespans, is if the principles we have set forth warn of that: such as the eclipse of the Sun in Leo or Aries, for it indicates the ruin of the acceder. **57** And if that was at the conjunction and [the Sun's] eclipse was with the Head, it also indicates his ruin.

**58** And if the Sun was eclipsed in Libra while Saturn is in Capricorn and Mars in Cancer, it indicates that he will be killed, poisoned, or betrayed, and that will be at the assembling of the Sun with Saturn in Capricorn, and Mars in Cancer.[165]

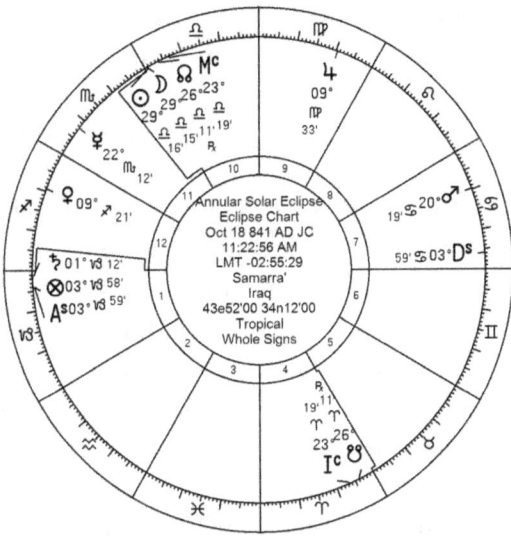

Figure 44: Solar eclipse, 841 AD: death of al-Mu'tasim?

---

[163] That is, the face or decan.

[164] انقضاء الفصل. **BY** read this as "rendering judgment," but the sense of this phrase is to complete something; note that the instructions have to do with showing when such a king will be killed. Nevertheless I feel like the phrasing could be clearer.

[165] This description is so specific I feel it must refer to an actual chart: and indeed, there was a solar eclipse just like this in 841 AD, a year before the Caliph al-Mu'tasim died. Al-Ṭabarī does not mention any kind of plot against al-Mu'tasim, who died after a short illness; but the editors do report that his current doctor changed his usual medical regimen, with lethal results (*History* Vol. 36, pp. 207-08).

**59** Now if any of the planets eclipsed the greater luminary and an infortune appeared,[166] that indicates the disaster of the acceder at the time of its[167] reaching the last portion of the sign of the triplicity in which the eclipse occurred, and [it will last] until [the Sun][168] arrives from the following sign at the last of the signs of the triplicity, in the same degree of that sign of the triplicity as it occurred for the eclipse.

**60** And if the Moon was eclipsed in Aries, with Saturn in Cancer and Mars in the opposition of Saturn, it indicates the ruin of the acceder upon the Sun's reaching the sign of Aries in that year.[169]

*[A method for upcoming disasters]*

**61** And if the term in which it is feared for the acceder draws near, you ought to revolve the years for him so you may know his condition is in them, by your looking in diurnal revolutions at [1] the Sun, [2] the Lot of elevation, victory, and prosperity (taken by day from the degree of the Lot of the Absent[170] to Jupiter, and by night the contrary, and cast out from the Ascendant), and [3] the lord of the bound of the Midheaven. **62** And if it was by night, then [look] at [1] the Moon, [2] the Lot of elevation, and [3] the lord of the bound of the Midheaven. **63** For whichever of these was in a stake or in a praiseworthy place, strong, is the indicator of the acceder in that year. **64** So, if it was safe from misfortune and harm, and especially from the lord of its[171] fourth, sixth, seventh,[172] eighth, and twelfth, that indicates his safety in that year. **65** But if it was made unfortunate by one of them and the one making it unfortunate was the lord of the fourth (and especially if it was

---

[166] Another planet eclipsing the Sun would occur if they were conjoined both by latitude and longitude, but I am not sure what Abū Ma'shar means by an infortune "appearing." Another possibility would be that the Moon eclipses the Sun, and as the sky darkens at the totality, Saturn or Mars appears close to them.

[167] Perhaps the infortune?

[168] Reading tentatively, but the feminine singular seems to confirm the Sun.

[169] This also sounds like an actual chart example, but I cannot find a plausible one.

[170] That is, the Lot of Spirit.

[171] This probably refers to the chart, but it's possible Abū Ma'shar is speaking of these derived places from the indicator of the acceder.

[172] Not all MSS include the seventh.

Mars), that is an indicator that his disaster will be by being killed in [official] meetings. **66** And if it was the lord of the sixth, ailments will find him from abscesses, pustules, and what is like that. **67** And one should judge for each house by the situation of the infortune according to what every nature resembles.

**68** And one looks also at the twelve houses: for whichever house has an infortune alighting in it, his enemies will be from that region, and it stirs up fighting against him from people[173] in accordance with the nature of the infortune. **69** And wherever there were fortunes, benefit and delight will come to him from that direction, in accordance with the character of that fortune. **70** And if the infortunes were falling, especially under the earth, his enemies' command will convert to weakness and insignificance. **71** And one should work like that too if the lord of the Ascendant and the lord of the Midheaven were in a stake.[174]

**72** And if the year terminated at a sign in [any] single year,[175] that is an indicator of the strength of the people of the country of that sign at which the year terminates; and it indicates their victory and conquering those who make an enemy of them, and the scant power of the acceder over them.

## [The time of the disaster]

**73** Now as for how to know the day on which their disaster will be, it is derived from the position of the Moon at the revolution of the year in which the acceder accedes, and her location in the signs: for wherever she was in them, he will be afflicted on the day[176] of the lord of that sign in which she is. **74** Now if she had a mixture[177] with the lord of her house, that is more con-

---

[173] Lit., "peoples" (أقوام).

[174] Abū Ma'shar seems to mean that if these last two planets are advancing in a stake, then the acceder will be stronger (and thus the enemies weaker).

[175] Lit., "in units of years" (في آحاد السنين).

[176] This seems to mean "the day of the week," so that if she were in a sign of Mars, the disaster will come on a Tuesday.

[177] I.e., a configuration of some kind.

firmed for her indication, and more truthful for it, and especially if she was in the house of a planet congruent[178] with her.

## [Who will come after]

**75** And as for how to know the one who takes charge after him, it is derived from the planet which the indicator of the king[179] hands over to. **76** For if it was handing over to a planet[180] in a sign consistent with its essence, then the command will pass to someone of the people of his house. **77** And if it was of the planets having two signs, then one should look at which of the two is more excellent by aspect, for it is the sign to seek information from. **78** And if it was handing the management over to a planet in a sign not consistent with the essence of its sign, it is an indicator that the rulership will pass over to someone not of the people of his house, and it will go out from nation to nation.

**79** Now if the indicator of the king was not handing over the management to a planet, then the rulership will pass to one in whose sign the Lot of rulership occurs. **80** And if the sign in which it occurs was consistent with the essentiality of the indicator of the king, what passes to him will be from the people of his house; but if it was not that, then to others besides them.

**81** And if, of what we have set forth, it appeared that the rulership is passing to the people of his house, and one wants to know to whom among them it will pass, one should look at the planet to which the Sun hands over at the revolution. **82** For if he was handing over to the lord of the fifth, then it will pass to his son. **83** And if it was the lord of the third, then to his brother—and let us speak likewise in accordance with the indication of the house in terms of the places of the circle.

**84** Now if the indicator of that was the lord of the house of children and one wants to know which of them it is, then one should look at the lords of the triplicities of the house of children: which of them is more numerous in shares in the house of children? **85** For it is the one who will take charge of

---

[178] Or perhaps, "agreeing" (الموافق), which does not add much clarity.
[179] Perhaps, the indicator of the acceder in **61-63** above? See also **80** below.
[180] Omitting "bad" (رديء). **BY** point out that the Latin version does not contain it, and indeed it does not make sense.

the command after him. **83** If it was the first [triplicity lord], then from among the eldest; if it was the second, then from among the middle ones; and if it was the third, then from among the youngest.

**87** And in short, if the Ascendant of his [own] birth[181] was the house of children,[182] he is the one taking charge of that command; and let us speak likewise about the brothers and others.

**88** Since we have completed what we wanted to explain, let us break off Chapter II.7, with the aid of God.

---

[181] That is, the birth of the person just identified by the triplicity lords.

[182] This probably means, "if his natal Ascendant was the same sign as the house of children in the *revolution*" which we just used to identify him.

## Chapter II.8: On the indications of the uniting of the two infortunes in all of the signs, & their alighting in the triplicities, for the lower events coming to be from their influences, & what resembles that

**1** Since we have provided the sum of the conditions of the uniting of Saturn and Jupiter in the triplicities,[183] and Mars is one of the superior planets, and he has a strong indication for kings and dynasties upon his assembling with Saturn, and even though his assembling with Saturn does not have power over changes like the power of the assembly of Jupiter and Saturn, still his indication is one of the things needed when attesting to what the assembly of Jupiter with Saturn indicates.

**2** And since the matter is like that, let us single out their[184] indication in this chapter, because it is one of the important things to have prior knowledge of for the conditions of dynasties and religious communities from the method of conjunctions, by the grace[185] of God.

*[II.8.1: Saturn-Mars conjunctions in Cancer]*

**3** We[186] say that the most evident of the indications coming to be from the influence of the uniting of Saturn and Mars is in the sign of Cancer, since this sign is the unhealthiness of Saturn and the fall of Mars, and since this sign along with Jupiter has the indication for Iraq, Scorpio with Venus for the Arabs, Libra with Saturn for Rūm, Capricorn with Mercury for India, Leo with Mars for the Turks, the Sun with Aquarius for the borders of Rūm,

---

[183] This probably refers to I.1-I.2.
[184] Saturn and Mars.
[185] Lit., "good fortune" (بيمن).
[186] This entire section (**3-30**) is virtually verbatim from al-Kindī's *Arab Rule* (see Appendix III in **BY**). For **3-4**, al-Kindī explains that the pairing of sign-planet for these regions mainly means the *bounds* of those planets in those signs (see **4** and **13** below). The Sun and Moon, which do not have proper bounds of their own, indicate the boundaries or frontiers of countries. Note also that al-Kindī is also roughly dividing the entire region into five major powers and districts (Rūm, Iraq, the Arabs, Turks, and India), he is not trying to identify all possible attributions of the bounds in each sign. For more on chorography, see §14 of my Introduction.

and Virgo with the Moon for the borders of the Turks (just as we have already made clear in Chapter II.4[187] of this Book).[188]

**4** And each sign has an indication for one of the regions, because sometimes a city is attributed to one of the signs and the victor over them,[189] apart from the lord of that sign, such as the indication of Cancer with Jupiter for Iraq: because Jupiter is the victor over the sign indicative of Iraq (and that is from 19° to 26° of it, because this amount of degrees in the sign of Cancer is the bound of Jupiter, indicative of Iraq). **5** So when the fortunes alight in this place or look at it from the trine or sextile, that indicates in accordance with the condition of the people of Iraq, the strength of their king,[190] and the fertility of their country. **6** And the alighting of the infortunes in it, and their looking at it from the square or opposition indicates evil, the shift of rulership, and the shedding of blood, if the triplicity to which the conjunction shifted had necessitated that, and especially if the two infortunes met without the inspection of the fortunes.

**7** [Our] predecessors[191] disagreed about the foundations of the components from which are derived the extent of the duration of dynasties, and they operated accordingly. **8** For among them were people[192] who used an example of the uniting of the infortunes, and they said that whereas the Hijrah of the Prophet (peace be upon him!) was on Wednesday when 18 nights of Rabī' I had elapsed of Year 1,[193] and the revolution of the year of the world was on Sunday when 3 nights of the month of Ramadan had elapsed, at the end of the fifth hour of the day[194] (and that was before the year of the

---

[187] Reading for **5**. See II.4, **17**.
[188] This parenthetical remark is Abū Ma'shar's, but do not be misled by the "just as": for in II.4, **17** Abū Ma'shar provides a slightly different system for these regions.
[189] That is, the signs (although this should be in the singular).
[190] Or, "rule" (ملك).
[191] This includes al-Kindī, as sentence **7** is by Abū Ma'shar. See other groups of these at **146-57** and **158-62**.
[192] This must at least include al-Kindī, since the following is taken from him.
[193] According to **BY**, this date corresponds to Wednesday, September 29, 622. But elsewhere the Hijrah is taken to be on July 15, 622: See *AW2*, my Introduction p. 44, and *Thousands* p. 34.
[194] That is, March 21, 622. The Hijrah is taken to have been on July 15, 622. Thus the revolution is prior to the Hijrah by 3 months, 27 days, as is stated next. (That is,

Hijrah by 3 months, 27 days), and they had a conjunction in this year, and its Ascendant and stars were as in this image:[195]

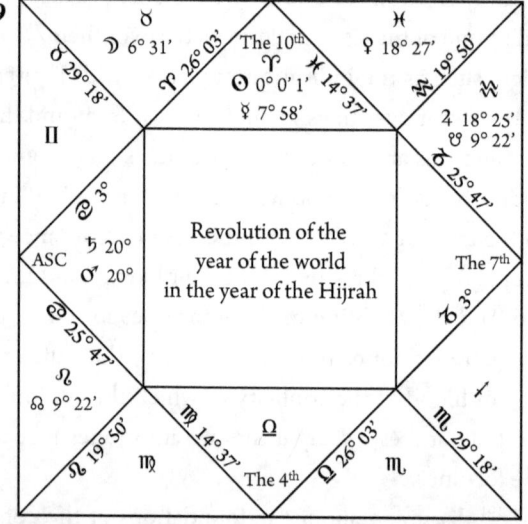

Figure 45: Ingress of year of Hijrah (622 AD)

**10** So since the two infortunes had a conjunction at this time, in the position of Cancer indicating Iraq, and the planetary victor over Iraq (who is Jupiter) was falling away from their inspection, that indicates the corruption of the rulership of Persia, and the appearance of the Arabs.[196] **11** And the victor over the house of the Moon aiding the dynasty was Venus, because she is the lord of the house of the Moon: so the Moon transferred the rulership and handed it over to Venus, for [the Moon] was in [Venus's] shares, and was connecting to her from where [Venus] received [the Moon].[197] **12** And Jupiter was not in-

---

three months of 30 days, plus 27 days, if we count the day of the ingress as the first day.)

[195] I treat the chart itself as sentence **9**.

[196] What Abū Ma'shar means is that because the Sasanian Persians ruled Iraq (indicated by the bound of Jupiter in Cancer), this conjunction harms their rule; the new power happened to be the Arabs. The bound does not *directly* indicate Persia nor the Arabs.

[197] The logic here seems to be this: the conjunction harms Iraq directly, but Cancer more broadly. The lord of Cancer is the Moon. But she is applying to her own lord (and victor), Venus. (Applying to one's own lord is a kind of reception, called "handing over nature" by Abū Ma'shar in *Gr. Intr.* VII.5, **95**). This means that Venus has some management power over the matter.

specting the position of the mixture,[198] but if he had looked, he would have reduced their evil.

**13** And Venus was in the sign of her exaltation,[199] in the ninth place, indicating religion; and she is the indicator of the Arabs by [her] character, so she granted them the rulership and transferred it to them and to their land because of her victorship over the place indicating the Arabs in the sign of Scorpio (and that is from 7° to 11° of it), because the extent of these degrees of the sign of Scorpio is the bound of Venus.[200] **14** And because she was in the ninth place indicating religion, she indicated that their appearance would be for reasons of religion.

**15** And what remains to Venus in her sign in which she is alighting, is 11° 33': that was an indicator that the rulership would remain with her[201] in the amount of what remains to Venus in her sign in terms of degrees and minutes, a year for every minute (the sum of that is 693 years).[202]

---

[198] Jupiter in Aquarius is in aversion to Cancer, where the Saturn-Mars conjunction is.

[199] The reference to her exaltation might not be merely incidental: it might mean that the people she indicates (Arabs) will rise and be victorious.

[200] Remember **3-4** above. Since the special pairing of Venus is to Scorpio and the Arabs, her taking over management of the matter from the Moon means that the Arabs will be involved.

[201] And therefore with the Arabs (or, the Muslims, although the leadership was more Persian under the 'Abbāsids).

[202] Al-Kindī derives this number through a kind of numerology using Arabic letters. But it is also true that if 11° 33' remains for her in Pisces, that equals 693'.

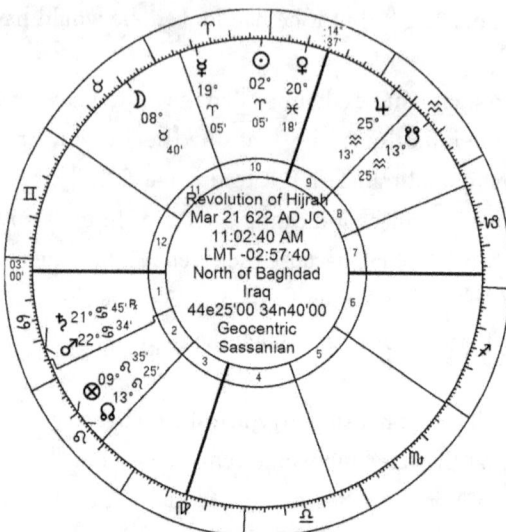

Figure 46: Modern approximation of BRD's Hijrah[203]

**16** And the killing of the king of Persia[204] was at the end of 74 months, and it was that the Moon was in 6 portions of Taurus, and the uniting of the infortunes was in 20 portions of Cancer, and the extent of the arc which is between them was 74 portions. **17** And because the direction was from a fixed sign to a convertible sign, it made a month for every portion.[205]

**18** And the ruin of the king of the people of Persia was after that by 20 years, because the conjunction was in 20 portions of Cancer and they were both in one of the stakes of the Ascendant: so it indicated years.[206]

---

[203] Note that this revolution occurred nearly on the day of the third true Saturn-Mars conjunction (since Mars is separating from Saturn for the last time). Their mean conjunction was on January 2, 622. By comparing these luminaries here with those of al-Kindī above, we can see that he is using a sidereal zodiac which is about 3° off from the tropical zodiac.

[204] Yazdijird III. For more on these events and in the charts below, see the section on Saturn-Mars conjunctions in the Introduction (§10.9).

[205] Converting the ecliptical distance between two significators into units of time is method #1 in Sahl's *On Times* (Ch. 3, **9**). The reason for using the Moon is presumably because she rules the sign being harmed (Cancer), so the distance shows the time until some disaster strikes.

[206] This refers to the Battle of Nihāvand (642), in which Yazdijird III was defeated by Arab Muslim armies and had to flee until his death in 651.

**19** And in the cycle[207] of year 31 they met in Cancer in 29°, and the Moon was in Gemini in 6 portions, and between them was 53 portions: so ʿUthmān b. ʿAffān (may God be pleased by him!) was killed at the end of 53 months, and the rulership transferred to the west due to the Moon's handing over to Mercury (who was the lord of the house indicating the region of the west).[208]

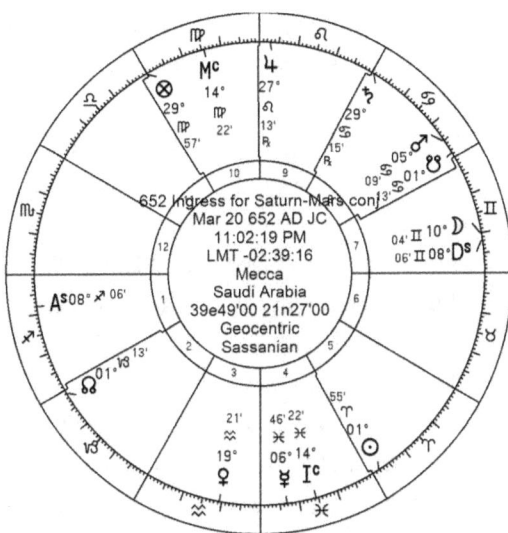

Figure 47: Modern approximation of 652 AD revolution for Saturn-Mars conjunction

**20** And in the cycle of year 61 they met in Cancer, and Jupiter did look at them, so there was not a change of rulership except that there was the civil unrest of ibn al-Zubayr.

**21** And in the cycle of 91 they met in Cancer, and there was the civil unrest of ibn al-Muhallab after 10[209] years.

**22** And in the cycle of 121 they met in Cancer, and Jupiter was not looking at them, but the Moon was in Sagittarius, handing over the management to the lord of her house (who was Jupiter), and he received her: and there was civil unrest after that by 5 years, and the rulership transferred to Iraq. **23** And in that time there was the killing of al-Walīd b. Yazīd, and the rising up of Abū Muslim after his killing by 2 years, and the ruin of the sons of ʿUmayya,[210] and the dynasty transferred to the people of the Sawād.

---

[207] دور, from here up to **30**.
[208] The figure here is my approximation of the 652 AD revolution. I have put Gemini on the Descendant because of the statement in **19** that Mercury ruled the house indicating the west. If we forgive a 1°-2° in the position of Mercury, the Moon hands over to him.
[209] Reading with al-Kindī for Abū Maʾshar's 20. See my Introduction.
[210] That is, the ʿUmayyads.

**24** And in the cycle of 151 they met in Cancer, and Jupiter was in Pisces, in their trine, so the rulership did not change—but they did indicate wars and fighting.

**25** And in the cycle of 182[211] they met in Cancer, and Jupiter was falling away from them, and the Moon was in Pisces: so the rulership was not corrupted, but they did indicate that the rulership would shift at the end of the cycle from place to place after that, by 10 years: so there was the civil unrest of ibn Zubaydah, and the rising up of rebels, and a shift of the rulership to the region of the east.

**26** And in the cycle of 212[212] they met in Cancer, and indicated the strength of the affairs of the Turks, and their taking over the management of the dynasty, and the transfer of the rulership from place to place.

**27** And in the cycle of 242 they met in Cancer, and indicated the civil unrest of al-Musta'īn, wars, the shedding of blood, and the appearance of a man whom everyone who asserts divinity and inspiration (and what resembles that) follows, and his command would not be complete, and his abiding was in accordance with the lesser period[213] of Mars.

**28** And in the cycle of 272 they will meet in Cancer, and they will indicate formidable, mighty affairs, and the death of kings and leaders.

**29** And in the cycle of 303 they will meet in Cancer, and indicate corruption and rebellion[214] which will be in the region of the west.

**30** And in the cycle of 333 they will meet in Cancer, and indicate civil unrest and many wars, and that Islam will triumph over the majority of the religions.

**31** Since we have completed what we wanted to explain—the completion of our statement of their indication when considering their assembling in the sign of Cancer—let us provide a statement of the indication of their assembling in the rest of the signs in order, with the combination of some of the planets with them.

---

[211] Reading with al-Kindī for Abū Ma'shar's 181. See my Introduction.
[212] This was actually in AH 211 (826 AD).
[213] دور.
[214] Or, "breakdown" (انتقاض).

## [II.8.2: Saturn-Mars conjunctions in other signs]

**32** We say that if Saturn and Mars united in Aries, that indicates the existence of civil unrest and wars that will be between Rūm and the Arabs. **33** But if Jupiter and the Moon were witnessing them, that indicates drought, the appearance of fairness and the people's returning to it, and the appearance of a portent occurring in the atmosphere at the end of the day or the end of the night.

**34** And if it was in Taurus, it indicates the occurrence of civil unrest between the people of Jibāl and the Arabs. **35** And if Jupiter was with them it indicates the death of the acceder, and travel made ready for kings, with illnesses befalling them and the rest of the nobility and the general public, and an abundance of death in women, and a bitter stomach[215] overcoming them. **36** But if that was with the witnessing of the luminaries, Jupiter, and Venus, that indicates an abundance of lying and deception among the people, false rumors, the increase of waters, the disaster of the exalted among kings, the humiliation of the underclass, and a group of the people of Jibāl attacking kings, with the long length of their term (then they will be killed after that). **37** And [it indicates] the insolence of women towards men, an abundance of fornication, the perishing of riding animals, an abundance of blood, and a decrease in trees and vegetation, along with much blowing of the winds.

**38** Now if that was in Gemini, it indicates the occurrence of civil unrest among the people of the west. **39** And if that was with the viewing of the luminaries, Venus, and Mercury, that also indicates disasters befalling writers, calculators, and soldiers stirring up riots against kings, the corruption of birds (and their scarcity), and the cheapness of prices.

**40** And if that was in Cancer, it indicates the occurrence of wars between the people of Armenia and the Arabs. **41** And if that was with the luminaries and Jupiter witnessing them, that indicates drought in all areas.

**41** And if that was in Leo, it indicates the occurrence of evil between the Turks and the Arabs, and the intensity of the people's fear of the authorities, and some of them fearing others, and an incident befalling them because of

---

[215] Reading somewhat uncertainly for المرار. **BY** read "cholera," following the medieval Latin translation.

heavenly portents and earthquakes, with corruption affecting the produce and animals. **42** And if the Moon was with them both, that indicates kings' killing one another, and harm affecting the people from predatory animals, with an excess of heat and clouds.

**43** And if that was in Virgo, that indicates civil unrest happening between the Copts, the Nubians, and the Arabs. **44** Now if Mercury was witnessing them, that indicates troubles occurring in the sowing. **45** But if the two luminaries were witnessing then, that is an indicator of the corruption of the crops, and the haughtiness of kings towards the people with respect to their assets, with corruption appearing in women.

**46** And if that was in Libra, it indicates civil unrest occurring between Rūm and the Arabs again. **47** And if Jupiter was witnessing them it indicates a bad condition befalling the people of nobility, amusement, and comfort, and redness taking place in the atmosphere in that year.

**48** And if that was in Scorpio, it indicates wars befalling the Arabs concerning what is between themselves. **49** Now if Jupiter and the Moon were with them, that is an indicator of the abundance of rains in the majority of places, and the agitation of the seas. **50** And if Venus was with [the infortunes] it indicates venomous animals stinging some of the kings, and their sons' conflict with them,[216] and the appearance of wrong (and its abundance). **51** And if Mercury was with them, it indicates the occurrence of illnesses in the people of Babylon, and a disaster coming to the king of Persia.

**52** And if that was in Sagittarius, it indicates wars occurring between the Turks and the Arabs again. **53** Now if that was with the witnessing of Jupiter, Mercury, and the Moon, that indicates an abundance of wars, the confusion of kings, and the elevation of the nobles, writers, and people of the sciences, sorcery, and spells, and what resembles that.

**54** And if that was in Capricorn, it indicates wars occurring between Ethiopia, the Zanj, India, and the Berbers, and the people of those regions. **55** Now if the Sun and Mercury were witnessing them, that indicates illnesses ruinous to kings, and that abscesses will affect them, and cutting and

---

[216] That is, the sons of kings will have conflict with their own fathers, the kings.

cauterization because of them, with an abundance of winds, lightning, fog, and fire, a scarcity of vegetation, and an abundance of robbers.

**56** And if that was in Aquarius, it indicates civil unrest taking place between the people of the Sawād and Kūfa. **57** Now if the Moon was witnessing them, that indicates a scarcity of the rains and an abundance of fog and clouds, the death of women for approximately 40 nights, and highway robbery against travelers.

**58** And if that was in Pisces, it indicates wars happening between the people of China, the people of the seas, and the Arabs. **59** And if Jupiter witnessed them, it indicates the death of the nobles and the mighty. **60** But if the Sun was made unfortunate by Mars,[217] that indicates the killing of kings. **61** And if he was made unfortunate by assembly, that indicates a scarcity of moistures, and an abundance of marine animals and locusts.

*[II.8.3: Saturn-Mars in the exaltation signs]*

**62** And one should look at their uniting in the rest of the signs having an exaltation. **63** Now if it happened that that was in the degree of a planet's exaltation,[218] that is an indicator that evil, fighting, and corruption will find the people of the clime whose indicator that planet is, especially if the lord of the exaltation looked at them. **64** Now if its looking at them was from a fixed sign, that indicates the long length of that evil, and its fixity. **65** If it was embodied, it indicates the middling of the matter in that. **66** And if it was convertible, it indicates the quickness of its termination and its scant fixity.

**67** But if it is not looking at that degree but a planet reflected [the infortunes'] light to it, that indicates that difficulty and corruption will come to the people of its clime, because of unknown people taking refuge with them, or because of peoples not from their climes and cities. **68** Now if it was not looking at them and a planet did not reflect their light to it, it introduces distresses upon the people of that clime; then that will be removed from them without something detestable finding them.

---

[217] The text uses the Persian name for Mars.
[218] For more on planets' exaltations, see Sahl's *Revolutions* Ch. 6.

## [II.8.4: Saturn-Mars in the triplicities]

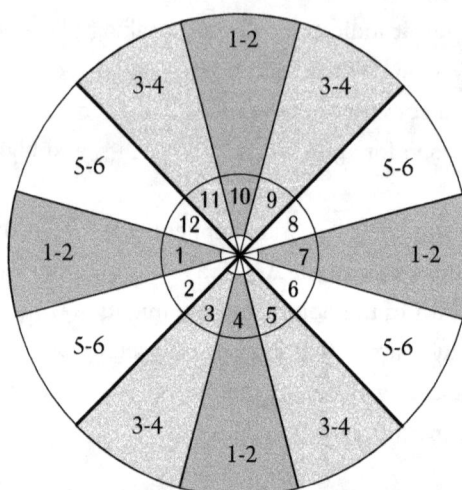

**Figure 48: Six configurations of infortunes in the triplicities**

**69** And the way of knowing the indication of the two infortunes for lower events may be derived from their alighting in all of the triplicities, because when one of them is in the stakes (or not the stakes), there manifests for it a special property of the indication for some situation, and that will be with intensity, weakness, and distinctiveness in one of the classes, in accordance with their positions, and their directness in their motion or their retrogradation.[219]

## [Saturn in the triplicity of Aries]

**70** So when Saturn is parallel with Aries or one of its triplicities at the revolutionary beginnings, and he is the victor,[220] [1] direct in motion, in a stake, it indicates diminishment happening in the clime of Babylon, an abundance of rains, a scarcity of cold, and disputes between kings. **71** And if

---

[219] In the figure here, the infortunes have three broad positions they may be in, and may either be direct or retrograde. In configurations [1]-[2], they are in the whole-sign angles and thereby see or aspect the rising sign. In [3]-[4], they are in other places besides the angles, but are still configured to the rising sign. These two positions exhaust the traditional "good places" of the chart. In [5]-[6], they are in the "bad" places: those in aversion to the rising sign. In whole signs, this fills out all places in an easy pattern. But if we were to use quadrant divisions, awkward or impossible situations would arise. For example, let the MC be in the eleventh sign, and Mars in the twelfth: in quadrant divisions, that would put him in an angle or stake that does *not* see the Ascendant, whether by sign or a degree-based aspect.

[220] This seems to mean, "lord of the year": see **78**.

Mars was handing his power over to him, that indicates the subjects' contending with kings, and more forcefully for that if he[221] was in the Midheaven. 72 Now if Saturn was [2] retrograde it is weaker for that, but harsher for it in the region of Khurāsān and the Turks, along with the bad condition of the people, and distresses and evil befalling them.

73 But if he was [4] not in the stakes and he is looking at the Ascendant <but is retrograde>,[222] it indicates the corruption of the houses of assets and their devastation, and harsher for that if he accepted the management of the Moon and Mars: because if the matter was like that it indicates the harshness of the cold [which is] destructive to livestock, along with the harshness of the wars and civil unrest. 74 And if he was [3] not in the stakes and is looking at the Ascendant, being direct in motion, it indicates hardships coming to the people of the nobility.

75 And if he was [5] falling, not looking at the Ascendant, and he is direct in motion, and Mars falling away from him, it indicates the occurrence of intense cold destructive to livestock. 76 And if he was [6] retrograde and Mars looking at him, there will be contention among the subjects because of fanaticism. 77 And if Mars was falling away from him, it is below that.

### [Mars in the triplicity of Aries]

78 And if Mars was in this triplicity and he is the lord of the year,[223] [1] direct in motion, in a stake, it indicates heating, drying illnesses befalling the people, and the contention of some kings against others, and an abundance of disputes in the majority of the climes. 79 And if he was [2] retrograde it is stronger for that, and indicates an abundance of Kurds, robbers, and the underclass, and there will be contention in the clime of Babylon, and harm coming to livestock, and it is harsher for that in those having fur, and troubles befalling predatory animals, with the endurance of the heat and its intensity until he shifts from his position.[224]

---

[221] I take this to be Saturn.
[222] Adding with Sahl's *Revolutions* Ch. 1.2.
[223] See §11 of my Introduction.
[224] That is, "until he enters a different sign."

**80** And if he was [3] not in a stake and he is looking at the Ascendant, direct in motion, it indicates the people's doing wrong to each other, and harm will find the country of the sign in which he is (and its square and opposition) in accordance with what we have set forth. **81** And if he was [4] retrograde it is harsher for that.

**82** And if he [5] fell away from the inspection of the Ascendant and he is direct in course, it indicates an abundance of heat. **83** And if he was [6] retrograde, it indicates its intensity, and damaging the people of the country of the signs which he looks at from the square and opposition, in accordance with the essence of the sign and its nature.

### [Saturn in the triplicity of Taurus]

**84** And if Saturn was in Taurus and its triplicity, and he is the lord of the year, [1] in a stake, direct in motion, that indicates contention, wars, and the death of sheep and cattle in the countries in whose sign he is. **85** And if he was [2] retrograde it indicates the corruption of the seeds and the scant growth of the vegetation, the existence of wars in other places,[225] the death of boys and youths, and it is harsher for that and more universal if he was in the Midheaven.

**86** But if he was [3] not in the stakes except that he was looking at the Ascendant, and he is direct in motion, then that is an indicator of the scarce corruption which will befall the vegetation. **87** And if the Moon was in the third sign from him it indicates the death of the king if the direction bore witness to that. **88** And if he was [4] retrograde it indicates the corruption of the vegetation, a scarcity of seeds, and the death of youths.

**89** And if he was [5] not looking at the Ascendant and he is direct in motion, and Mars falling away from him, it indicates the weakness of the evil and its people, and the appearance of the good. **90** And if he was [6] retrograde and is in view of Mars, it indicates the corruption of seeds and an abundance of death, especially in the lands in whose sign he is, and in its square and opposition.

---

[225] في غير ما مكان.

## [Mars in the triplicity of Taurus]

**91** And if Mars was in this triplicity and he is the lord of the year, and he is [1] direct in motion, in a stake, that indicates the corruption of the produce, the death of livestock, and contention and fighting will befall the people. **92** And if he looked at the lord <of the Ascendant>[226] of the year, that will pervade the people. **93** And if he looked at the indicator of the king,[227] that will be particular to the king. **94** And if he was connecting with Saturn, it will be harsher and more prolonged for that even if Mars was [2] retrograde, because he already indicates the hostility of enemies towards the king, along with an abundance of damage, contention, and the shedding of blood for that reason.

**95** And if he was [3] not in a stake and was looking at the Ascendant, and he is direct in motion, falling away from Saturn, it indicates a decrease in everything we have explained, except that harm will come to the lands whose sign he is parallel with, and the lands of the signs squaring him, and the lands of the planets looking at him. **96** But if he was [4] retrograde, that indicates the harshness of what befalls the people of the land of his sign and its square, from robbers and the perishing of riding animals, the corruption of the seeds, and harsher for that if he was handing over the management to Saturn: for it indicates the loss of vegetation.

**97** And if he was [5] not looking at the Ascendant and he is direct in motion, falling away from Saturn, that is an indicator of safety from most of what we have described. **98** And if he was [6] retrograde, it indicates a decrease in the conditions of the lands whose sign he is in (and the square), and it is harsher for that if he handed his management over to Saturn.

## [Saturn in the triplicity of Gemini]

**99** And if Saturn was parallel with the sign of Gemini or its triplicity, and he is the lord of the year, [1] in a stake, direct in motion, it indicates the blowing of the winds of the north, and their raging, and the intensity of the cold, a scarcity of rains, and illnesses of Saturn befalling the people, along

---

[226] Adding with Sahl's *Revolutions* Ch. 1.2, **64**.
[227] See §11 of my Introduction.

with an abundance of contention, wars, and the shedding of blood. **100** And if he was [2] retrograde, it indicates the contending of kings against one another, their disasters, and the occurrence of earthquakes (and it is harsher for that if he was in the fourth stake). **101** Now if he was not the lord of the year but was in the fourth stake, accepting the management of the lord of the Ascendant, many of the people will die by reason of earthquakes. **102** And if he accepted the management of the lord of the Midheaven, it indicates contention, wars, and civil unrest because of the king and his demands.

**103** And if he was [3] not in a stake and was looking at the Ascendant, and he is direct in motion, it indicates the abundant blowing of the east and west winds, the abundant intensity of the cold of winter, and the occurrence of earthquakes. **104** Now if he was [4] retrograde, it indicates illnesses befalling the people from winds and moisture, and the occurrence of earthquakes.

**105** And[228] if he was [5] not looking at the Ascendant and he is direct in motion, it indicates the blowing of the winds, their gentleness, and the intensity of the cold in countries of the sign which he parallels. **106** And[229] if he was [6] retrograde, it indicates the successive blowing of the south winds, and their raging, and illnesses and upheaval coming to the people of the countries of the sign parallel with him, as well as fanaticism, and that will be general among those having a low [status] and the underclass.

### [Mars in the triplicity of Gemini]

**107** And if Mars was in this triplicity and he is the lord of the year, [1] direct in motion, in a stake, that indicates contention, fighting, wars, civil unrest, and the shedding of blood, and that will be by reason of justice and the seeking of truth. **108** And if he was [2] retrograde, it indicates that those wars will be because of wrong, aggression, and seeking what is not necessary.

**109** Now if he was [3] not in the stakes but was looking at the Ascendant, direct in motion, that indicates that illnesses from winds and blood will befall

---

[228] Sahl (*Revolutions* Ch. 1.2, **127**) reads this sentence as his own [6], where Saturn is retrograde.

[229] Sahl (*Revolutions* Ch. 1.2, **128**) reads this sentence as his own [5], where Saturn is direct.

the people, and it is harsher for that in the countries whose sign he is in parallel with, and in its square and opposition. **110** But if he was [4] retrograde, that is an indicator of epidemics.

**111** And if he was [5] not looking at the Ascendant and he is direct in motion, it indicates an abundance of burning and damage from fires, ailments befalling the people from blood, and the corruption of the vegetation because of the raging of the winds. **112** And if he was [6] retrograde, it indicates disasters befalling the people for the reasons we set forth.

## [Saturn in the triplicity of Cancer]

**113** And if Saturn was in Cancer and its triplicity, and he is the lord of the year, [1] in a stake, direct in motion, and Mars fell away from him, that indicates the intensity of the cold and illnesses befalling the people of the countries of the sign he is parallel with (and in its square and opposition), and an abundance of locusts. **114** And if he was [2] retrograde, it indicates an abundance of death. **115** But if Mars looked at him[230] and the fortunes fell away from him, that indicates the occurrence of mighty civil unrest, and sweeping death befalling the people along with an abundance of hardships.

**116** And if he was [3] not in a stake and he is looking at the Ascendant, direct in motion, it indicates an abundance of rains, waters, and cold. **117** But if the fortunes connected with him, it will take away from that evil. **118** And if Saturn was in the eleventh from the Ascendant of the revolution, and the Moon in the Ascendant, connecting with him, it will be feared for the king at that [time]. **119** And if he was [4] retrograde and Mars inspecting him, that is an indicator of ruin and corruption happening in the people of the countries of the sign he is parallel with (and its square and opposition), and an abundance of locusts.

**120** Now if he was [5] falling away from the inspection of the Ascendant and he is direct in motion, and Mars falling away from him, that is an indicator of the appearance of good, a scarcity of evil, and an abundance of safety. **121** And likewise if he was already passing beyond one-half of the sign he is parallel with—except that along with that illnesses will befall the people of

---

[230] ناظره, which might also mean looking from the opposition.

the countries of the sign he is parallel with, and they will be healed of them. **122** And if he was [6] retrograde and he is looked at by Mars, and the fortunes falling away from him, that indicates that the nobles will encounter hardship and tribulation from the underclass, the cold will intensify, and waters and locusts will become abundant.

### [Mars in the triplicity of Cancer]

**123** And if Mars was in this triplicity and he is the lord of the year, [1] in a stake, direct in motion, not handing over to Saturn, that is an indicator of contention occurring in the land of the Arabs, and the appearance of the injustice of the government in the land of Tabaristān and Daylam. **124** And if he was [2] retrograde and he is handing over to Saturn, it indicates fighting occurring in the land of the Arabs, the shedding of blood, the occurrence of epidemics, an abundance of death, and it will be feared for the king in that revolution, if[231] the mother of years[232] already testified to that.

**125** And if he was [3] not in the stakes and he is looking at the Ascendant, direct in motion, free of Saturn, that indicates the movement of the Turks, wars befalling the majority of the people of the outer provinces, the disappearance of evil from most of the people of the climes, and their tranquility. **126** And if he was [4] retrograde, harm, fighting, and evil from kings will come to the people of the countries of the sign he is in parallel with (and its square and opposition), especially if he was in the eleventh.

**127** Now if he was [5] not looking at the Ascendant and he is direct in motion, free of Saturn, it indicates the weakness of the evil and its people, except that benign ailments will befall the countries which belong to the sign he is parallel with. **128** And if he was [6] retrograde and he is handing over to Saturn, and Saturn is in a stake, that is an indicator of the occurrence of evil happening among the people, and the beginning of that will be for weak reasons; then it will intensify and much blood will be shed, and intense illnesses will occur, and incidental death. **129** And if Saturn was falling away from him, illnesses from hotness and wetness (like measles and smallpox)

---

[231] وإن, which usually means "even if."
[232] Reading أمّ for أمر ("matter"), with **T** and against **BY**. As we know from Sahl (*Revolutions* Ch. 1.2, **79**), the mother of years is the most recent triplicity shift.

will occur in the countries of the sign which he is parallel with, along with illnesses resembling the essence of that sign.

### [II.8.5: Saturn-Mars in the divisions or places]

**130** Since we have completed the summary of the indications of the uniting of the infortunes in the signs and triplicities, let us report their indication at their uniting in the rest of the spherical divisions at the time of the revolution.

**131** So, we say that when Saturn and Mars unite in the Ascendant, that indicates a general harm spreading among the subjects.

**132** And if that was in the second or eighth, it indicates the corruption of assets, the undistinguished reputation of the rich, the appearance of need and poverty, and weakness in the general public.

**133** And if it was in the third or in the ninth, it indicates the appearance of disease in the mosques and houses of worship, and detestable illnesses along with mishaps in building and worship.

**134** And if that was in the fourth and tenth, it indicates that demolition will befall buildings in the cities.

**135** And if that was in the fifth or eleventh, it indicates the corruption of those who are born and an abundance of soldiers and weapons.

**136** And if that was in the sixth or twelfth, it indicates an abundance of gazelles, riding animals, and their being taken, and sometimes trouble will occur in these two categories.

**137** And if that was in the seventh, it indicates the emergence of enemies and people doing damage to most of the regions.

**138** And if that was in the Midheaven, it indicates the death of the mightiest kings in the climes, especially kings of the countries which the sign they are united in, indicates.

## [II.8.6: The Sixties]

**139** And of course the uniting of the infortunes comes to be every 30 years, and despite the weakness of these 30 years in which they unite,[233] one also seeks information about the affairs of dynasties in accordance with what we have set forth: and that is from the returning of the conjunction[234] to the sign to which it shifted from the first triplicity, because whenever a dynasty takes place due to the shift of the conjunction from triplicity to triplicity, and then the conjunction returns to the sign to which the shift was, it indicates a shift from the people of that dynasty to other people. **140** (But if there was not a shift [in the dynasty], there will be disturbance among the people of that dynasty.)

**141** And that is like the indication of the shift of the conjunction from Libra to Scorpio and its triplicity at the birth of the Prophet (peace be upon him).

**142** For when the conjunction returned to Scorpio after 60 years, it indicated his demise (may God bless him and grant him salvation), and his demise was in the third year from the time of the return of the conjunction to the sign which it had shifted to.

**143** Then the conjunction returned to Scorpio after 120 years, and in that year was the demolishing of the Ka'aba and the killing of 'Abd Allāh b. Zubayr.

**144** Then the conjunction returned to Scorpio after 180 years and there was the emergence of Abū Muslim and the shift of the rulership to the Sawād.

**145** Then the conjunction shifted over to Sagittarius after 238 years from the year of the conjunction signifying the religious community: and whenever the conjunction returned to Sagittarius, it indicated a matter taking place.

---

[233] See **1** above.

[234] That is, the Saturn-Jupiter conjunction. See §5 and §10.5 of my Introduction.

BOOK II: DYNASTIES & KINGS

|  | Year of Sixty | Event |
|---|---|---|
| Shift to ♏ | 570/571 | *(Conjunction indicating Islam and new religion)*[235] |
| Sixty #1 | 630 | Death of Muhammad, accession of Abū Bakr (632) |
| Sixty #2 | 690 | Destruction of Ka'aba, death of al-Zubayr (692) |
| Sixty #3 | 749 | Emergence of Abū Muslim (747), transfer of power to 'Abbāsids (749-50), his death (755). |

**Figure 49: The Sixties in early Islam**

[II.8.7: *Sets of 10 Saturn cycles*]

**146** Another category of [our predecessors][236] stated that the amount of the period of the dynasty's remaining in every one of the religious communities will be in accordance with the amount of 10 Saturnian cycles, and for that they offered an example, and that is close to the periods which we stated before about the cycle[237] in terms of conjunctions in Chapter I.1.[238]

**147** And they said that the shift will be upon the completion of 10 Saturnian cycles, and especially if that corresponds to the shift of Saturn to the convertible signs, and the Ascendants of those periods are convertible signs, for it hastens the shift. **148** And sometimes in these times in which it shifts, there occur higher and lower portents, like star showers, earthquakes, and what resembles that, and especially if Jupiter fell away from [Saturn]: for he changes the conditions, and sometimes the rulership shifts from man to man. **149** So, one should look at the year in which Saturn shifts to the con-

---

[235] As I have indicated elsewhere, this "shift" to Scorpio is a fiction, as it was said to happen at 4° Scorpio, which is impossible in any scheme of mean conjunctions. But the other conjunctions which recur in Scorpio are accurate.

[236] See **7** above, and §10.4 of my *Introduction*.

[237] دور.

[238] This seems to refer to how a triplicity with more than 12 conjunctions will increase the number of years for a triplicity shift, such as 260 years instead of 240. See I.1, **31ff**.

vertible signs: for if Jupiter was looking at him or was with him in that sign, much of the evil is extinguished. **150** But if Jupiter fell away from him and was weak, and Mars is strong by his alighting in the stakes of the Ascendant, it indicates the shift of most of the conditions, and their collapse; and indeed his[239] alighting in the beginnings of the convertible signs will be every 7 ½ years. **151** And at his completing 10 of his cycles there will occur many conditions and changes: in the appearance of prophethood, the shifting of dynasties and religious communities, and customs in accordance with what I will describe.[240]

**152** Let an example be taken from the earliest periods: and it is that when 10 cycles were completed for Saturn in the days of Darius son of Darius, there was the appearance of Alexander son of Philip, and the disappearance of the dynasty of the Persians.

**153** And when there was completed for him another 10 cycles, there appeared Ardashīr b. Bābikān, and the dynasty of the Persians returned, and he established their affairs [again].

**154** And when another 10 cycles were completed for him, there appeared Jesus son of Mary (peace be upon him), with a change of the religious community.

**155** And when another 10 cycles were completed for him, there appeared Manī, and he produced a religion which is between Mazdaism and Christianity.

**156** And when another 10 cycles were completed for him, the Prophet (peace be upon him) brought forth the religion of revealed Islam.

**157** And sometimes the incidents are set forth before the completion of 10 cycles, so that it takes place in the ninth cycle, and sometimes they lag behind the 10 cycles so that the event is in the eleventh cycle, and that is in accordance with what the preceding conjunctions necessitate for that, in terms of the long length of the term or its shortness.

---

[239] This must be Saturn.
[240] Nevertheless these cycles do not really make sense as Abū Ma'shar reports them: for instance, Jesus (**154**) appeared long before Ardashīr, the founder of the Sasanian dynasty (**153**). I have put these in their proper order in the Introduction.

## [II.8.8: Dynasties by the planets' greatest years]

|   | Lesser | Middle | Greater | Mighty |
|---|---|---|---|---|
| ♄ | 30 | 43 ½ | 57 | 265 |
| ♃ | 12 | 45 ½ | 79 | 427 |
| ♂ | 15 | 40 ½ | 66 | 284 |
| ☉ | 19 | 39 ½ | 120 | 1461 |
| ♀ | 8 | 45 | 82 | 1151 |
| ☿ | 20 | 48 | 76 | 480 |
| ☽ | 25 | 39 ½ | 108 | 520 |

**Figure 50: Planetary years**

**158** And another category of [our predecessors][241] stated that the amount of the duration of their dynasty will be in accordance with the size of the periods established for the planets indicative of the people of the dynasty, and they produced an example for that. **159** They said that since Saturn has the indication for Caliphs, the duration of the dynasty among them is 265 years (which is approximately the <greatest> period[242] of Saturn).

**160** Since Jupiter has the indication for Persia, the duration of the dynasty among them is 427 years. **161** And by the same token it is necessary that the term of the dynasty of Rūm be in accordance with what belongs to its planet (which is the greater luminary), indicating for it from among the established periods, and that is 1,461[243] years. **162** And according to this it is necessary that the term of the dynasty of the Arabs be in accordance with what belongs to their planet (which is Venus), indicating for them from among the established periods, which is 584 years—and that is close to what we stated.[244]

---

[241] See **7**.
[242] دور.
[243] Reading for 1,460.
[244] See **15** above. But there he uses the number 693, which does not seem close to me. This number 693 was gotten independently by some gematric numerology in *Arab Rule* (Appendix III in **BY**).

## [II.8.9: Trepidation theory][245]

**163** And the masters of talismans stated that the sphere has a movement of 8° in which it advances and retreats, and that its advancement and retreating in each degree is every 80 years; and that when a degree in its advancement or retreat is completed, and that is at the shifting of Saturn from sign to sign, and especially to the convertible signs—when it is like that, it indicates shooting[246] stars and a change of dynasties. **164** And likewise, whenever Saturn has shifted from sign to sign it indicates the generation of events in the world, and heavenly and terrestrial portents, and a transfer of religious communities, the shifting of sovereignty from people to people, the occurrence of wars and emaciation, and the generation of earthquakes in the climes. **165** And it is more true for that if it was at the time of the completion of 80 years, at the advancement of the sphere by one full degree, or at its retreating by the same amount.

**166** And also, the greatest universal change will be at the completion of the motion of the sphere, whether it be by 8° advancing or retreating: and that will occur every 640 years.

**167** Now[247] if one wants knowledge of its advancing or retreating, [namely] in which of the periods that is, and the amount of the advancing or retreating degrees, one should add 789 years to the whole years of Yazdijird, and divide what is gathered together by 640, and see what comes out from the division, and cast it out one by one (and one begins with the retreating of the sphere, then its advancement), and see where it terminates. **168** For if its termination was at the advancement, then the sphere is advancing; and if its termination was at the retreat, then the sphere is retreating. **169** Then one looks at what remains of the number (of what is not divided), and divide it by 80, and what comes out from the division is degrees, and what remains by less than 80 is portions of a degree.

---

[245] **BY** refer here to Theon, and to their p. 580. I have also touched on trepidation in my comments and footnotes to *Leopold*, Ch. I.1.
[246] القضاضات.
[247] For this, see **BY**'s p. 155 and 580.

**170** At the beginning of the year 265 of Yazdijird, the termination of the sphere by advancement was at 5° 09'[248] 45". **171** And there is added the amount of degrees which comes out from the motion of the sphere to the positions of the wandering stars, the crossing [points] of the north and south, and the fixed stars, if the sphere was advancing. **172** And if it was retreating, then subtract what comes out from the degrees and minutes of its retreating from 8°, and add what remains to the positions of the planets so as to correct their positions exactly, according to what appears by observation. **173** And what pertains to the planets in increase in this our time, is the amount of degrees which the motion of the sphere stopped at in the time we determined it by the *Canon*, or close to it.

**174** And[249] with respect to the disagreement in their statements (about the elements of deriving the periods of dynasties),[250] what is in agreement with what we set forth is due to what the conjunctions indicate: because the statements which do agree with that in giving information, happened due to the agreement of [their] coincidental indications with the indications of the conjunctions in those periods they set down. **175** For, they adopted those coincidences as foundations without regard to the foundation for which the indication for that was: so disagreement happened among them, and they held fast to their own beliefs in that respect.

**176** Since we have completed what we wanted to explain, let us break off Chapter II.8, since it is at its end; and success is through God.

**177** Book II has come to an end, and Book III follows it, if God wills (and He is the one called upon for help).

---

[248] Reading with **BY** for 15.
[249] This is a difficult paragraph. What Abū Ma'shar seems to be saying is that *for dynasties*, it is Saturn-Jupiter conjunctions which matter the most: not Saturn-Mars (**8-30**), nor sets of 10 Saturn cycles (**146-57**), nor the greatest years (**158-62**). These do denote years which are close to those of Saturn-Jupiter conjunctions, but the similarity is at least somewhat coincidental, and they erred by assuming that these other methods were the basis of prediction, rather than being supplemental.
[250] Namely, Saturn-Mars conjunctions, Saturn cycles, and greatest planetary years.

# BOOK III: [MUTUAL ASPECTS OF ALL PLANETS][1]

## On knowing the quality of the connections of the planets & their combinations with each other in the revolutions of years[2]

### And it is in 6 Chapters:

1 Chapter III.1: On the combinations of the planets with Saturn.
2 Chapter III.2: On their combinations with Jupiter.
3 Chapter III.3: On their combinations with Mars.
4 Chapter III.4: On their combinations with the Sun.
5 Chapter III.5: On their combinations with Venus.
6 Chapter III.6: On the combinations of the Moon with Mercury.

---

[1] Original text: "Book III of *The Book of Conjunctions*, written by Abū Ma'shar."
[2] Omitting the prior pious statement: *"In the name of God the Merciful, the Compassionate."*

## Chapter III.1: On the combinations of the planets with Saturn

**1** Since we have set forth the sum of the indications of the conditions of kings from the method of the shifting of conjunctions in the triplicities, and the conjunction of the two superior planets in them, and the assembling of the two infortunes in all of the signs,[3] <know that>[4] all of the planets have conditions upon their combining in the Ascendants of the years of the shifts of the conjunctions. **2** And one will come to recognize [these conditions] within the people of religious communities and dynasties by means of their blending, because when one of them is placed with another in some figure at the time of the shifting of the conjunction from triplicity to triplicity, it indicates that the people of that religious community will mainly engage in things resembling those indications. **3** Now if that was at the time of the revolution of some [other] year or quarter, that indicates their engaging in those same things attributed to those indications in that time as well.[5]

**4** However,[6] since the indications of the inferior planets are of a shorter duration than the indications of the superior planets,[7] the indications of the superior planets are more evident in action at the time of [1] the Ascendants of the shifts of the conjunctions in the triplicities, and [2] the terminal points of the direction[8] from the Ascendants of the conjunctions of transits existing in the Quarters (in accordance with what we have explained), than [the inferiors] are at the revolutions of the [annual] quarters.

**5** So if the inferior planets belong [more] to the indications of the revolutions of years and [their] quarters due to the shortness of the duration of their indications, the indications of the superiors are stronger and more evident in action in the extended periods, and more lasting in effect than the inferiors.

---

[3] See II.8, especially **32-61**.
[4] Reading for "and."
[5] This also suggests that "lesser" conjunctions (the Twenties) would also have less of a definitive and lasting effect.
[6] Lit., "except that." The following few sentences comprise one long convoluted one in Arabic, and I feel obliged to divide it up into more digestible parts.
[7] See I.1, **5-6** and **17-18**.
[8] I could see this as being either profections or primary directions.

**6** Nevertheless,[9] even though the inferiors indicate events coming to be in short periods, their indications do also manifest at the *end* of the extended periods from time to time, since their connections differ in location in all periods, and the indications in all of them can be continuous, successive, and cyclical.[10]

**7** [So] it is most necessary that one produce their indications for events at the time of the revolutions of the periods which we described, in terms of the location of the place of one of them relative to the other according to the rest of the types of figure,[11] so that it may be one of the aids in explaining the effects of the higher bodies in lower events, in accordance with what we have set forth.

**8** So, in this Book let us also state the indications of the planets combining with each other in their indications.[12]

❧ ❧ ❧

**9** We say that when there is a conjunction of the two superior planets necessitating some matter in the shifts of religious communities and dynasties, and the shifts of ordinances and customs, the occurrence of mighty matters, the shift of a kingdom, the death of kings, the occurrence of prophets, revelation, and marvels in religious communities and dynasties (just as we have set forth), the combination of all of the planets [by conjunction] and their connections with each other in the rest of the figures have many indications for the affairs manifesting at the end of the complete[13]

---

[9] Again, reading for "except that," and adding a sentence break.

[10] I am not sure what Abū Ma'shar's point about "location" is supposed to convey, but the general idea seems to be that the inferiors' significations are more intermittent, and may take a long time to have an effect, whereas the superiors' significations are broader and more enduring, usually from the start.

[11] Namely, aspects or configurations.

[12] Note that these only involve *aspects*, and looser *assembling* in the same sign. Proper, exact conjunctions by transit are in Book VI.

[13] الكلية. I think this refers to the statements in **6** above: that due to the relevance of a chart like the triplicity shift for many years, the indications may not appear to later, and when the period is complete. For example, that the last king of a dynasty may be killed, followed by a change to another dynasty at some later conjunction or shift.

years indicative of religious communities and dynasties (in terms of the actions of kings and the subjects).

**10** Now as for all of the connections of Jupiter with Saturn and the planets in all of the figures, we will state that in this chapter. **11** We say that if Jupiter connected with Saturn from a sextile or trine, that indicates the appearance of guardians, kings, nobles, prophethood, revelation, and secrets. **12** And if that was from a square and it was from the fourth, that indicates the concealment of the guardians and those seeking rulership, and the changing of many things among matters of rulership and religion. **13** And if that was from the seventh, it indicates an abundance of lawsuits among the people of the kingdom and the nations, and an abundance of terrors. **14** And if that was from the tenth, it indicates an abundance of lawsuits between kings, authorities, and judges.

♄♂ **15** Now since we have set forth in Chapter II.8 the indications of the uniting of Mars and Saturn in all of the signs, and it has the characteristic property of the excessive occurrence of smallpox, pustules, and eruptions, as well as cunning, deception, and astonishing statements, and new rulership for a man in the land of that sign in which they unite, along with what we specified about that in each one of the signs individually—in this chapter let us state the indications of the rest of his connections with him, and the assembling of the planets with Saturn and their connections with him.

**16** We say that if Mars connected with Saturn from a trine or sextile, that indicates fraud entering into the affairs of pious people and kings, and confusions occurring in what is among the people because of the matters of religions. **17** But if it was from a square and it was from the fourth, it indicates an abundance of stealing, robbers, and the concealing of most of that.[14] **18** And if it was from the seventh, that indicates the people's opposition to each other, their estrangement, mutual hostility, and mutual contention. **19** And if it was from the tenth, that indicates that the subjects will have hardship from the Sultan, and their obedience towards him will be burdensome.[15]

---

[14] This is similar to Mars overcoming Saturn.
[15] This is similar to Saturn overcoming Mars.

♄☉ **20** And if the Sun assembled with him, that indicates the annulling of evil and the disappearance of what is vain and fraud. **21** And if he connected with him from a sextile or trine, it indicates the kings' lacking their subjects, and their need for them. **22** And if it was from a square and it was from the fourth, that indicates the kings' announcing of many of [their] secrets and affairs.[16] **23** And if it was from the seventh, that indicates the kings' contending with people from among the subjects, like monks, the poor, and what resembles that. **24** And if that was from the tenth, that indicates hardships, fear, and terror coming to kings from their subjects, along with their abundant use of prisons and their tools, like shackles, handcuffs, and what is like that.[17]

♄♀ **25** And if Venus assembled with him, it indicates the corruption of the conditions of women, the intensity of lewdness in men, an abundance of children, false rumors and anxieties among the people, and the year will be hard for the people of the coasts as well as Egypt, and emigration will multiply among them along with the cheapness of watery gems like pearls and what resembles that, and difficulty and hardships coming to the general public. **26** But if she connected with him from a trine or sextile, that indicates corruption befalling children and fetuses, and the difficulty of childbirth for women. **27** And if it was from a square and it was from the fourth, that indicates women's falling into confusions due to their relatives and husbands, and the corruption of [women's] situations for these reasons.[18] **28** And if it was from the seventh, it indicates the abundance of women's quarreling with their husbands. **29** And if it was from the tenth, that indicates that lawsuits will befall women, because of which they will appeal to the authorities, and they will be exposed in that, and Venusian affairs will be corrupted, such as perfume and what resembles that.[19]

♄☿ **30** And if Mercury assembled with him, that indicates the people's use of spells and sorcery, and disasters befalling writers, and their replacement, troubles befalling household managers, and that death and hunger will befall the people, and the occurrence of mighty affairs. **31** Now if he

---

[16] This is similar to the Sun overcoming Saturn.
[17] This is similar to Saturn overcoming the Sun.
[18] This is similar to Saturn overcoming Venus.
[19] This is similar to Venus overcoming Saturn.

connected with him from a trine or sextile, that indicates an abundance of examining the books of religious communities and what resembles them. **32** And if it was from the square and it was from the fourth, that indicates the appearance of the secrets of knowledge, sorcery, spells, and what resembles that. **33** And if that was from the seventh, that indicates the people's contrivance of extraordinary statements, and forgeries in the creation of books, and what resembles that. **34** And if it was from the tenth, that indicates the revelation of books, the use of sorcery and spells, like snake-charming and what resembles that.

♄☽ **35** And if the Moon assembled with him, that indicates infeasibility in affairs and their difficulty, and harm coming to the people because of prisons, fetters, troubles, tribulation, the destruction of villages and cities, and the emigration of their people, and the scarcity of the water of springs and rivers. **36** And if she connected with him from a trine or sextile, that indicates the people's use of false oaths, forgery, fetters, prisons, beating with whips, injustice, and distress because of that, the stirring up of black bile and an abundance of illnesses for that reason, the appearance of demolition in most of the countries, miscarriage in pregnant women from an abundance of snows (and the ruin of people because of them and their being buried in them), involvement in planting and vegetation, the digging of enclosures and buildings with stones and adobe, an abundance of buildings and their strengthening, an abundance of the people's devotion to [visiting] cemeteries, prisons, and what resembles that. **37** And if it was from a square and it was from the fourth, it indicates an abundance of the people's dreams and their fear in their sleep, and an abundance of fearsome delusions enflaming them.[20] **38** And if it was from the seventh, it indicates lawsuits, and worry and anxiety because of them, and the some of the people's falling into what is detestable, and what is like that. **39** And if it was from the tenth, that indicates lawsuits occurring between kings and their subjects, and their wrong towards them, and their deceit towards them, and the abundance of their fear of them and because of them.[21]

**40** Since we have completed what we wanted to explain, let us break off Chapter III.1, with the aid of God and His support.

---

[20] This is similar to the Moon overcoming Saturn.
[21] This is similar to Saturn overcoming the Moon.

## Chapter III.2: On the combinations of the planets with Jupiter

**1** Since we have set forth in Chapter III.1 the connections of the planets with Saturn, in this chapter let us state their connections with Jupiter.

♃♂ **2** We say that if Mars assembled with Jupiter, that indicates most of the people's involvements being in raids and wars, and an abundance of Khārijites and Exchangers,[22] an abundance of lawsuits, the occurrence of epidemics in some of the climes, the perishing of some of the riding animals, and dreadful things occurring in the atmosphere, along with fertility at the beginning of that period and drought at its end, and the death of a king in that revolution. **3** But if he connected with him from a trine or sextile, that indicates an abundance of *jihād* and raids because of religion. **4** Now if that was from a square and it was from the fourth, it indicates an abundance of propagandists, fighting, triumphing, robbers, and their practice of that will be in mystery and secretly.[23] **5** And if it was from the seventh, that indicates the occurrence of lawsuits and an abundance of the people's accusing each other of robbery. **6** And if it was from the tenth, it indicates that tribulation, alarm, and hardship will affect the people from the Sultan.[24]

♃☉ **7** And if the Sun assembled with him, it indicates the ruin of fair people and judges, and the corruption of some of the religion and its ambiguity.[25] **8** And if he connected with him from a sextile or trine, that indicates the appearance of religion, science, and jurisprudence. **9** And if it was from a square and that was from the fourth, it indicates the appearance

---

[22] These are two names for a schismatic movement in early Islam. Certain groups of Muslims got up and "left" (Khārijites) the discussions about choosing a new rightful ruler (as they thought one was not needed), and thereby separated themselves from the mainstream. The name "Exchanger" is related to Qur. 2:207, and means that these same types of people wanted to exchange the merely worldly (and political) life for a higher one with God. Generically, the Arabic word for Khārijites also means simply "rebels." See also VII.4, **11**.

[23] This is similar to Mars overcoming Jupiter.

[24] This is similar to Jupiter overcoming Mars.

[25] غموه, which also means "concealment" (as presumably Jupiter would be concealed by the Sun or under the rays. But because of the pairing with corruption, I take it that something about the religion is not "evident" (another way to talk about unconcealment), and so is ambiguous.

of the power of judges and their use of fraud.²⁶ **10** Now if that was from the seventh, that indicates an abundance of lawsuits and propagandists [calling] for wrongdoing, and its appearance. **11** But if it was from the tenth, it indicates the strength of those who pass judgment, their showing fairness, and their use of justice.²⁷

♃♀ **12** And if Venus assembled with him, that indicates the modesty of women and their self-restraint, the goodness of their condition, the expensiveness of perfume and pearls, and that good and fertility will come to the countries of the sign in which they are united, and women will be sincere towards their husbands, and virtuousness will be shown by them in the majority of the climes, and comforts will come to them, and the goodness of the way of life. **13** And if she connected with him from a sextile or trine, it indicates the adornment of women, their asceticism, and their constancy in their conviction and religion. **14** And if it was from a square and it was from the fourth, it indicates the fineness of [women's] conduct and their constancy.²⁸ **15** And if it was from the seventh, it indicates that women will multiply in [their] lawsuits because of religions, and they will proclaim that, and that what is between them and their husbands will be suitable.²⁹ **16** And if it was from the tenth, it indicates that the women of kings will be involved in charitable things and perfume, and their seeking of perfume, types of good-smelling things, oils, and what is like that will multiply.³⁰

♃☿ **17** And if Mercury assembled with him, that indicates the people's seeking knowledge, writing, wisdom, and the learning of jurisprudence, religion, and secrets, as well as epidemics and the intensity of the heat in the air. **18** And if he connected with him from a sextile or trine, it indicates the abundance of the people's lawsuits in religions, and their use of disputation. **19** And if it was from the square and it was from the fourth, it indicates the quarreling of experts in jurisprudence,³¹ and the appearance of

---

²⁶ This is similar to the Sun overcoming Jupiter.
²⁷ This is similar to Jupiter overcoming the Sun.
²⁸ This is similar to Jupiter overcoming Venus.
²⁹ Or, "will be reconciled" (يصلح).
³⁰ This is similar to Venus overcoming Jupiter.
³¹ In the modern world, perhaps this means that certain important legal questions are being decided, or that there are cultural debates between public intellectuals.

many secrets.³² **20** And if it was from the seventh, it indicates the occurrence of lawsuits because of purchases, business relationships, and contracts in use among the people, and what is like that. **21** But if it was from the tenth, it indicates the abundance of the people's seeking profit, along with an abundance of kings' seeking the sciences and books, arts, and deeds.³³

☽ **22** And if the Moon assembled with him, it indicates the abundance of people's applying uprightness and stories,³⁴ and populating the mosques, and seeking religions and jurisprudence, praising [God], and invoking His name. **23** But if she connected with him from a sextile or trine, that indicates the appearance of the affairs of divinity, religion, prophethood, and wisdom. **24** And if it was from the square and it was from the fourth, it indicates the concealment of secrets and religions. **25** And if it was from the seventh, that indicates a lawsuit in the religions and jurisprudence, and examining that, and what is like that. **26** But if that was from the tenth, it indicates the elevation of judges and worshippers, and exertion in the building of mosques and houses of worship, and what is like that.

**27** Since we have completed what we wanted to explain, let us break off the discussion with the help of God and His support.

---

³² This is similar to Mercury overcoming Jupiter.
³³ This is similar to Jupiter overcoming Mercury.
³⁴ القصص. Probably pious and moral stories and principles. **BY** read this as "sermons."

## Chapter III.3: On the combinations of the planets with Mars

**1** Since we have set forth in Chapter III.2 the connections of the planets with Jupiter, in this chapter let us state their connections with Mars.

♂☉ **2** We say that if the Sun assembles with Mars, that indicates an abundance of killing among the people of theft and robbery. **3** And if he connects with him from a trine or sextile, that indicates kings providing ordinances and revelations. **4** And if it was from a square and it was from the fourth, that indicates a scarcity of lawsuits and disputation, and the concealment of what comes from that.[35] **5** And if it was from the seventh, it indicates an abundance of wars and fighting, and what is like that. **6** And if it was from the tenth, that indicates an abundance of wrongdoing and oppression by the authorities, the appearance of fire, and what is like that.[36]

♂♀ **7** And if Venus assembled with him, that indicates an abundance of adultery and debauchery, and evil in women, and the ruin of the king of Rūm, and disasters and tribulation finding them. **8** And if she connected with him from a sextile or trine, that indicates an abundance of children and the ease of childbirth for women. **9** And if it was from a square and it was from the fourth, it indicates an abundance of adultery and debauchery, forming friendships [with women], and the concealment of that.[37] **10** And if it was from the seventh, that indicates hardship coming to the people. **11** And if it was from the tenth, that indicates an abundance of women's being disgraced by the authorities, and [women] will encounter tribulation and detestable things from them.[38]

♂☿ **12** And if Mercury assembled with him, that indicates an abundance of the people's use of minting dirhams and small copper coins, alchemy and what resembles that, and the occurrence of fear and alarm among businessmen and the people of culture. **13** And if he connected with him from the trine or sextile, that indicates the people's seeking of alchemy and the arts which use fire. **14** And if it was from a square and was from the fourth, that indicates the abundance of the people's use of alchemy,

---

[35] This is similar to the Sun overcoming Mars.
[36] This is similar to Mars overcoming the Sun.
[37] This is similar to Venus overcoming Mars.
[38] This is similar to Mars overcoming Venus.

arms, and their concealing that.³⁹ **15** And if it was from the seventh, that indicates an abundance of lawsuits, deception, and fraud, astonishing things in medical treatments and works, and killing, cunning, thievery, and what resembles that. **16** And if it was from the tenth, that indicates the authorities' use of the people of the arts, alchemy, gemstones, and weapons.⁴⁰

♂☽ **17** And if the Moon assembled with him, that indicates the people's use of lies and the shedding of blood, along with an abundance of people making demands, and adornment. **18** But if she connected with him from a trine or sextile, that indicates the scarce consideration for the people of the religions, and the use of ignorance, along with an abundance of slaughters [of animals] at festivals and banquets. **19** And if that was from a square and it was from the fourth, that indicates the opposition of the Sultan to the subjects, with injustice and wrongdoing. **20** And if that was from the seventh, that indicates an abundance of wars, fighting, contentions, and division due to falsehood. **21** And if it was from the tenth, that indicates the engagement in wars, injustice, and wrongdoing by the authorities, administrators, and the leaders of armies.

**22** Since we have completed what we wanted to explain, let us break off the chapter.

---

³⁹ This is similar to Mercury overcoming Mars.
⁴⁰ This is similar to Mars overcoming Mercury.

## Chapter III.4: On the combinations of the planets with the Sun

**1** Since we have set forth in Chapter III.3 the statement about the combinations of the planets and their connections with Mars, in this chapter let us state the indications of their connections with the Sun.

☉♀ **2** We say that if Venus assembled with the Sun, that indicates harm coming to pregnant women, with an abundance of lawsuits between [pregnant women]. **3** And if she connected with him from a sextile, that indicates the elevation of women.

☉☿ **4** And if Mercury assembled with him, that indicates the concealment of matters and their secrets, the hiddenness of knowledge and wisdom, and the burial[41] of books and reports.

☉☽ **5** And if the Moon assembled with him, that indicates an abundance of secret matters and their concealment, an abundance of evil between the authorities and the general public,[42] an abundance of fugitives among slaves and others, and the easiness of the work of alchemy for the people. **6** Now if she connected with him from a trine or sextile, that indicates the revealing of secrets and their being spread about. **7** And if it was from a square and it was from the fourth, that indicates severe deceit in matters and actions, and their slowness. **8** And if it was from the seventh, it indicates an abundance of antagonisms and lawsuits, and the refutability of adversaries in their relating of evidence. **9** And if it was from the tenth, that indicates the revealing of secrets and announcing them, and spreading about the reports of kings.

**10** Since we have completed what we wanted to explain, let us break off the chapter.

---

[41] دفن. Or by analogy, "concealment, hiding."
[42] Here the Moon seems to be the people, and the Sun indicates the authorities and the use of arbitrary power.

## Chapter III.5: On the combinations of the planets with Venus

**1** Since we have set forth in Chapter III.4 their connections with the Sun, in this chapter let us state the indications of their connections with Venus.

**2** We say what if Mercury assembled with Venus, it indicates the revealing of reports and books, the people's involvement in repugnant and ugly matters, and their disgrace for those reasons, along with an abundance of their delighting in women, and amusement with them, an abundance of false rumors with the shedding of blood, and mighty conquests coming to be in the world. **3** And if he connected with her from a sextile, that indicates the appearance of befriending and corresponding with women, and what resembles that.

**4** Now if the Moon assembled with Venus, that indicates an abundance of the people's involvement in singing, melodies, entertainments, enjoying women, and using good-smelling things. **5** But if she connected with her from a trine or sextile, that indicates the people's involvement in musical things like dancing, the *zamr*,[43] singing, and going out to promenades, gardens, and what resembles that. **6** But if that was from a square and was from the fourth, that indicates an abundance of the people's getting involved in marrying, [sexual] pleasure, and their concealment of that. **7** And if it was from the seventh, it indicates the lawsuits of women against their husbands, and the frequency of [women's] abandoning [them] and their contributing to confusing [men], and what resembles that. **8** And if it was from the tenth, it indicates the appearance of debauchery and an abundance of fornication, and announcing that.

**9** Since we have completed what we wanted to explain, let us break off the chapter, if God wills.

---

[43] A wind instrument.

## Chapter III.6: On the combinations of the Moon with Mercury

**1** Since we have set forth in Chapter III.5 the statement of the indications of the planets' combinations with Venus, in this chapter let us state the combinations of the Moon with Mercury, so that what we have made clear about that may be complete, with the aid of God.

 **2** We say that if the Moon assembled with Mercury, that indicates the seeking of knowledge and books, spells and sorcery, astrology, and everything secret and concealed. **3** And if she connected with him from a sextile or trine, and she is made fortunate, that indicates investigating the sciences, seeking them, and the ready support for everything one seeks of that, and its acceptance. **4** But if she was made unfortunate, it indicates the antithesis of that. **5** And if it was from the square and was from the fourth, that indicates a scarcity of false rumors and the investigation of the sciences.[44] **6** And if it was from the seventh and she was made fortunate, that indicates quarrels and lawsuits while seeking the truth and justice.[45] **7** But if she was made unfortunate it indicates the seeking of conflicting things, the practice of overstepping [boundaries] when addressing [people], and injustice in judgment. **8** And if it was from the tenth and she is made fortunate, it indicates the ready market for the books of religions. **9** And if she was made unfortunate, it indicates books of sophistry and allegory, and what is like that.

※ ※ ※

**10** And when, for any one of these planets, there is none of the [applying] connections from these figures in the periods which we have determined, but one of them is *separating* from another, that indicates the people's scant engagement in the indications of those two planets (of those types [described]), and their rejection of them. **11** So, they will be involved in what the connection of one to the other necessitates, but neglect things whose

---

[44] It is hard to know whether the "scarcity" refers both to false rumors and investigating the sciences, or just to the false rumors. **BY** believe it refers to both.
[45] Or even, "vengeance" (انتصاف).

fading away occurs because of the separation of the two indicators indicating existing things.

**12** And when they are made fortunate, they indicate an increase in what they indicate (of the matters of good fortune) and a decrease in matters of bad fortune. **13** But if they are to the contrary of that, they indicate the antithesis of what we have described.

**14** Since we have completed what we wanted to explain, let us break off the chapter with the aid of God and His support. **15** Book III is completed, and praise be to God greatly!

# BOOK IV: [EACH SIGN AS AN ASCENDANT, PROFECTED ASCENDANT, OR PROFECTION FROM A CONJUNCTION]

On how to know the indications of the signs if they were the Ascendants of the Beginnings which we mentioned before, or the years terminated at them[1] from one of the Ascendants of the preceding Beginnings, or from the positions of the conjunctions

*And it is in 12 Chapters:*

**1** Chapter IV.1: On the indications of Aries for lower events if it was the Ascendant of one of the revolutionary periods, or the years terminated at it from one of the Ascendants of the preceding Beginnings, or from the positions of the conjunctions.

**2** Chapter IV.2: On the indications of Taurus in the same way.
**3** Chapter IV.3: On the indications of Gemini in the same way.
**4** Chapter IV.4: On the indications of Cancer in the same way.
**5** Chapter IV.5: On the indications of Leo in the same way.
**6** Chapter IV.6: On the indications of Virgo in the same way.
**7** <Chapter> IV.7: On the indications of Libra in the same way.
**8** <Chapter> IV.8: On the indications of Scorpio in the same way.
**9** <Chapter> IV.9: On the indications of Sagittarius in the same way.
**10** <Chapter> IV.10: On the indications of Capricorn in the same way.
**11** <Chapter> IV.11: On the indications of Aquarius in the same way.
**12** <Chapter> IV.12: On the indications of Pisces in the same way.

---

[1] That is, by annual profection.

## Chapter IV.1: On the indications of Aries for lower events if it was the Ascendant of one of the revolutionary periods, or the years terminated at it from one of the Ascendants of the preceding Beginnings, or from the positions of the conjunctions

**1** Since we have already set forth in Book III the connections of the planets and their combinations with each other, in this Book let us provide a statement of the indications of the signs individually if they were the Ascendants of the periods we stated before, or the years had terminated at them from the Ascendants of the preceding Beginnings, or from the positions of the conjunctions.

**2** We say that if the Ascendant of one of the revolutionary periods was Aries, or the years terminated at it from one of the positions which we stated before,[2] that indicates that in the cities it governs there will appear tyrannical and authoritative kings, along with their people's use of iron tools, weapons, and what resembles that, as well as killing, fighting, burning with fire, exemplary punishment among the people,[3] fickleness in exploits, quickness in shifting from condition to condition; and disunion, emigration, and travels will be abundant in their people, and pain in the eyes and headache, and death will spread among them, and the abundant death of riding animals along with the blowing of the east and west winds, the calm composition[4] of the air of the spring quarter, and the goodness of the air of summer (and the autumn will be similar to it in quality), the harshness of the cold of winter and the occurrence of snows (and especially with the Sun's coming to the sign of Libra), an abundance of grasses and pastures for livestock, the mediocrity of the crops and a decrease in [their] growth,[5] along with the harsh demand upon the people because of the land-tax, and corruption will come to food because of moisture, and sandy-[soil] crops will be scarce along with

---

[2] Namely, a previous Ascendant or previous conjunction.

[3] والمثلة بالنّاس.

[4] تماسك. BY: "firmness."

[5] Tentatively reading الارتفاع for الإرفاع (the verbal noun of an unattested Form 4).

the fine harvest[6] of the rest of the crops. **3** And [it indicates] that in terms of colors red clothing will predominate among them.

**4** And in addition it indicates travel will happen for the king of Babylon, his victory over his enemies, and ailments will come to him in accordance with the lesser period of the Sun, and some of his women who reverence him will die,[7] and the people of his country will have joy and tranquility.

**5** And it indicates the death of the king of India and the appointment of his son as successor to the [royal] power after him.

**6** And the people of Fārs and the people of the east will have troubles, along with death among them, the perishing of cattle, a scarcity of food, and the swelling of rivers.

**7** And there will be drought and intense hunger in Armenia.

**8** And death will occur in the land of Rūm, along with concluding a truce with their enemies; and anxiety and intense sorrows will befall them.

**8** And wars between the Arabs will be prepared.[8]

**9** And[9] if the portions of the Ascendant were in the first third of it (or the direction was in it, or one of the victors, or the terminal point reached it), it indicates an abundance of thunder, lightning, and winds. **10** And if it was in the middle third of it, it indicates the mixture of the air. **11** And if it was in the last [third] of it, it indicates its hotness. **12** And if that was in its northern portions, it indicates the hotness of the air and its moisture. **13** If it was in the southern ones, it indicates its coldness.

**14** Since we have completed what we wanted to explain, let us break off the chapter.

---

[6] دنوّ, lit. the "nearness" of something, suggesting that the harvest is what draws near. (Following **BY**.) Nevertheless I feel something is wrong with this word.

[7] ويموت بعض من يكرم عليه نسائه. **BY** read this as though the women are revered, but the attached pronoun is singular masculine. Still, I could see **BY**'s reading as being what was intended.

[8] تتهيّأ, which can also mean "are possible."

[9] For this paragraph, see *Tet.* II.11 (Robbins p. 201).

## Chapter IV.2: On the indications of Taurus in the same way

**1** We say that if it had the indicators which we described, that indicates that in the cities which it governs there will appear troubles befalling the people, along with exemplary punishment[10] among them, and the stability of matters in a single condition, and pains of the throat, swelling, and languor will befall them, and the occurrence of epidemics, and an abundance of death and fear, and desire for women will multiply, and the enjoyment of them, and seeking everything having four feet (of what is eaten and used [by people]), along with a good trade in cattle, and the year will be middling, and sometimes drought will occur in it, and food, drink, and produce will be abundant. **2** And clothing of wool and hair will predominate among them, and of colors the white.

**3** And it indicates that in the land of Fārs there will be illnesses, and an abundance of the death of animals used [by people], the blowing of the winds, and the west and east wind, along with the harshness of the cold of the spring quarter, the fine mixture of the air of the autumn quarter, and the winter quarter will be warm. **4** And snows will be abundant in its middle, and the cold will intensify, and rains, thunder, and lightning will be scarce, along with the occurrence of corrupting cold and the abundant swelling of the seas.

**5** And the people of Babylon will have terrors, false rumors, and evil, and the leaders will envy each other, and they will plot against the king so as to kill him, but he will be victorious over them and for that reason will shed much blood.

**6** And[11] if the portions of the Ascendant were in the first third of it (or the direction was in it, or one of the victors, or the terminal point arrived at it), that indicates an abundance of tremors and the blowing of winds. **7** And if it was in the second third, that indicates an abundance of moistures and coldness. **8** But if it was in the last third of it, it indicates the intensity of the heat and an abundance of lightning and lightning bolts. **9** And if that was in its

---

[10] الملة.

[11] For this paragraph, see *Tet.* II.11 (Robbins pp. 201-03).

northern portions, it indicates the fine mixture of the air. **10** If it was in the southern ones, it indicates the alteration of the air and its shifting.

**11** Since we have completed what we wanted to explain, let us break off the chapter.

## Chapter IV.3: On the indications of Gemini in the same way

**1** We say that if it had the indications which we described, it indicates that in the cities which it governs there will appear the abundant investigation of the sciences which are above nature, like divinity and the heavenly and higher sciences, and the conditions of religions and philosophy, the stars, medicine, the composition of melodies and the rest of the mathematical [arts], and there will predominate among them fine images and the liberality of souls, working with skill, management, fickleness in works, and the shifting of things from one to another, and collaborating in them, using images and engravings, decoration and colors, and building famous cities, high and splendid castles and architecture. **2** And among them will appear illnesses and headaches, vomiting, hardship, and ruin, and death will spread in livestock along with an abundant blowing of winds in the spring quarter, with the blowing of *simooms* in the summer quarter, and the calm composition of the air in the autumn quarter, and an abundance of rain in the winter quarter. **3** And of the colors, clothes of green will be predominant.

**4** And it indicates that illness will come to the king of Babylon but then he will be safe from it, and he will estranged from his viziers[12] and be victorious over some of them.

**5** And there will be an appearance of rebels in Armenia, and some of them will fight against each other, and they will run away to cities other than their own, and their affairs will be changed, and their enemies will have power over them and be victorious over them.

**6** And troubles will come to Rūm, and death will occur among them from more than a single ailment, and their sorrows will multiply for those reasons, and rains will be abundant there.

**7** And it indicates troubles will befall the people of Isfahān from fighting and illnesses, and an abundance of thunder and lightning, and eastern winds corrupting the crops, and especially the region of the south.

**8** And seeds will be abundant in most of the climes, along with the miscarriage of pregnant women, the occurrence of death among children and

---

[12] ويتغيّر لوزرائه. Reading with **BY**, although this particular meaning (being "estranged from") is not listed in the lexicon.

youths, an abundance of wheat, barley, and dates, fertility, and the occurrence of mildew in vineyards, with the safety of trees.

**9** And[13] if the portions of the Ascendant were in the first third of it (or the direction was in it, or one of the victors, or the terminal point arrived at it), that indicates the moisture of the air. **10** And if it was in the middle third, it indicates the fineness of its mixture. **11** And if it was in the last third, it indicates its motley mixture[14] and change. **12** And if it was in its northern portions, it indicates tremors and winds. **13** And if it was in its southern portions, it indicates dryness and hotness.

**14** Since we have completed what we wanted to explain, let us break off the chapter.

---

[13] For this paragraph, see *Tet.* II.11 (Robbins p. 203).
[14] اختلاط.

## Chapter IV.4: On the indications of Cancer in the same way

**1** We say that if it had the indications which we described, it indicates that in the cities which it governs there will appear an abundance of sexual intercourse, procreation, travels and moving, upheaval in things from one condition to another, and that they will have hunger and poverty because of drought, their fear of their enemies will be abundant, and among them will occur epidemics and death. **2** And the year will not be financially abundant for the people due to the abundance of fighting which occurs among them, and an abundance of corrupting locusts, aquatic animals, and venomous animals, and predatory animals harming the people, the digging of rivers, the increase of waters along with the cold of the spring quarter, the middling quality of the air of the summer quarter, the abundant blowing of the western winds, floods, the harshness of the cold in the winter quarter, the evenness of the air of the autumn quarter, and the thriving of plantings and sown crops. **3** And the wearing of garments whose colors resemble that of smoke[15] will be predominant among them.

**4** And <it indicates> the hesitation of the king of Babylon, the scarcity of his movement and travels, enemies and rebels seeking access to most of his countries, and for those reasons many anxieties will come to him, and the shedding of blood (and the duration of that is four months).

**5** And the land of Rūm will be fertile, and pains of the eyes and throat will befall them, and perishing will occur among the horses and donkeys, and death in livestock, and food and drink will be abundant.

**6** And[16] if the portions of the Ascendant were in the first third of it (or the direction was in it, or one of the victors, or the terminal point arrived at it), it indicates tremors and the heat of the air. **7** And if it was in the middle third of it, it indicates the fine mixture of the air. **8** And if it was in the last third of it, it indicates the blowing of the winds. **9** And if it was in its northern portions, it indicates the harshness of the heat. **10** And if it was in the southern ones, it indicates the same thing.

**11** Since we have completed what we wanted to explain, let us break off the chapter.

---

[15] That is, brownish or brownish-grey.
[16] For this paragraph, see *Tet.* II.11 (Robbins p. 203).

## Chapter IV.5: On the indications of Leo in the same way

**1** We say that if it had the indications which we described, it indicates that in the cities which it governs there will appear abundant births to kings and authorities, their conspicuousness and management with strength, steadfastness, courage, force, awe, an abundance of anger, mighty ambition, a love of reputation, remoteness from danger,[17] stratagems, cunning, deception, griefs and anxieties, exemplary punishments among the people,[18] and a desire for gold, silver, and precious gems. **2** And illnesses will befall the people, and especially in [their] stomachs, mouths, and hearts, along with the occurrence of epidemics and the abundance of death, and the intensified hardship of childbirth for pregnant women, and predatory animals harmful to the people will be abundant, and the atmosphere will be dark from time to time, along with the middling quality of the air of the spring quarter and its inclination to cold, the intensity of the heat in the summer quarter, the successive blowing of the western winds and the harshness of their motion at its end, an abundance of rains, the harshness of cold in the winter quarter and the scarcity of the winds at its end, and what the trees bear will be scarce, and plantings will improve, and the waters of springs will decrease. **3** And clothes of a darkish color will predominate among them, among garments of various colors (like white, yellow, and red).

**4** And[19] if the portions of the Ascendant were in the first third of it (or the direction was in it, or one of the victors, or the terminal point arrived at it), it indicates the harshness of the heat, and distress. **5** And if it was in the middle third, it indicates the fine mixture of the air. **6** And if it was in the last third of it, it indicates moistures and dews. **7** And if that was in its northern portions, it indicates the changing of the air, and its warmth. **8** And if it was in the southern ones, it indicates the moisture of the atmosphere.

**9** Since we have completed what we wanted to explain, the chapter is done.

---

[17] بعد الغرر. **BY:** "spreading danger."

[18] والمثلة بالنّاس.

[19] For this paragraph, see *Tet.* II.11 (Robbins p. 203).

## Chapter IV.6: On the indications of Virgo in the same way

**1** We say that if it had the indications which we described, it indicates that in the cities which it governs there will appear kings with fine forms, having handsome looks, along with their engagement in sexual intercourse not in accordance with the Sharī'ah, and their engagement in the sciences which are above nature, eloquence in speech, fine moral character, a good soul, stratagems and cunning, shrewdness and skill, dexterity in matters, perfume and good-smelling things, involvement in amusements and idleness, building, sown crops and planting, and collaboration in things. **2** And in [these matters) hunger, illnesses, and killing will multiply (and that will last a long time), along with pains of the throat, and the majority of the children of that year will be females, and the majority of the offspring having four feet will also be female, along with the difficulty of childbirth for them. **3** And the air will be dark from time to time, and the spring quarter will have an abundance of rains and snow, with the successive blowing of the northern winds and their intensity, the air of the summer quarter will be good, the autumn quarter middling, the beginning of the winter quarter temperate and its end [having] intense cold, and in it will blow the northern winds along with the swelling of rivers and the flourishing of the crops (and especially the fruit of olive trees). **4** And among them green clothing and garments dyed many colors will predominate among them, like embroidered fabrics and what is like that.

**5** And ailments will befall the king of Babylon, and especially upon the Sun's being parallel with his own house (and that will be in accordance with the lesser period[20] of Jupiter), and locusts, food, and drink will be abundant in Babylon.

**6** Now[21] if the portions of the Ascendant were in the first third of it (or the direction was in it, or one of the victors, or the terminal point arrived at it), that indicates the hotness of the air. **7** And if it was in the middle third, it indicates the fineness of its mixture. **8** And if it was in the last third of it, it indicates the moisture of the atmosphere. **9** And if that was in its northern

---

[20] دور.

[21] For this paragraph, see *Tet.* II.11 (Robbins p. 203).

portions, it indicates the blowing of the winds. **10** But if it was in the southern ones, it indicates the fine mixture of the air.

**11** Since we have completed what we wanted to explain, let us break off the chapter, if God wills.

## Chapter IV.7: On the indications of Libra in the same way

**1** Since we have set forth in Chapter IV.6 the knowledge of the quality of Virgo's indications, in this chapter let us state the knowledge of the quality of the indications of Libra.

**2** We say that if it had the indications which we described, it indicates that among the people of the cities it governs, there will appear the practices of prophets and their ordinances, religions, and discussions in them, the building of mosques and houses of worship, their attendants and overseers, with a fine shape and beauty in them, generosity, justice, fairness, truthfulness in speech, clarity, truth, taking and giving, buying and selling, calculation and engineering, the various sciences among those composing melodies, entering into [temporary] marriage, amusement, delight, joy, and the people's delighting in each other. **3** And assets will be abundant in their hands, and they will build cities, castles, gardens, promenades, and habitations,[22] having variation in their conditions, the quick transformation of things from condition to condition, and partaking in them, and tribulation and hardships will affect [the people], along with the safety of pregnant women and their children. **4** And the air will become dark from time to time, and the blowing of winds will be abundant in the spring quarter, the blowing of *simooms* in the summer quarter, the temperateness of the autumn quarter, and the middling quality of the winter quarter. **5** And among colors, clothes of black will predominate among its people.

**6** And joy will come to the king of Babylon upon the greater luminary's paralleling all of the sign of Cancer, his soul will be pleased, he will see what he delights in, and movement and hunting will be abundant, and death will occur in his subjects.

**7** And[23] if the portions of the Ascendant were in the first third of it (or the direction was in it, or one of the victors, or the terminal point arrived at it), it indicates the fine mixture of the air. **8** And likewise the second third of it, and the third. **9** And if that was in its northern portions, it indicates the blowing

---

[22] Or, "cultivation" or things which manifest cultivation (عمارات).
[23] For this paragraph, see *Tet.* II.11 (Robbins p. 205).

of the winds. **10** But if it was in the southern ones, it indicates an abundance of moistures.

**11** Since we have completed what we wanted to explain, let us break off the chapter.

## Chapter IV.8: On the indications of Scorpio in the same way

**1** Since we have set forth in Chapter IV.7 the knowledge of the quality of the indications of Libra, in this chapter let us state the knowledge of the quality of the indications of Scorpio.

**2** We say that if it had the indication which we described, it indicates that in the cities which it governs there will appear kings of fine shape, generous, spending many assets, sexual intercourse, and doctors and those applying treatments and remedies will be abundant, while people's stratagems in the things they seek will be few; and civil unrest, wars, anger, violence, recklessness,[24] sorrow, confinements and the confined, anxieties, griefs, betrayal, slander, calumny, fighting, and illnesses will be abundant. **3** And darkness will occur in the air from time to time, rains will be abundant, the spring quarter will be hot (and clouds, rains, winds, and cold will be scarce in it), the summer and autumn will be temperate, and the cold of winter harsh (and in its middle will blow western winds, and in it rains and powerful floods will be abundant). **4** And it indicates an abundance of food and seeds, the corruption of pastures because of the snow damaging that, an abundance of aquatic beasts and its living things, things crawling on the earth and people being hurt by them. **5** And among them will predominate clothing of black.

**6** And it indicates an abundance of terror in most of the earth, but a scarcity of fighting, an abundance of death in children and women, the death of everything having four feet, an abundance of troubles in livestock, the appearance of various metals (of iron and others), and the year will be suitable for pregnant women.

**7** Now[25] if the portions of the Ascendant was in the first third of it (or the direction was in it, or one of the victors, or the terminal point arrived at it), it indicates an abundance of clouds. **8** And if it was in the second third of it, that indicates the fine mixture of the air. **9** And if it was in the third third, it indicates softness and hotness. **10** And if that was in its northern portions, it

---

[24] Or, "inconstancy," "fickleness" (الطَّيْش).

[25] For this paragraph, see *Tet.* II.11 (Robbins p. 205).

indicates the hotness of the atmosphere. **11** But if it was in the southern ones, it indicates the same thing.

**12** Since we have completed what we wanted to explain, let us break off the chapter.

## Chapter IV.9: On the indications of Sagittarius in the same way

**1** We say that if it had the indications which we described, it indicates that in the cities it governs there will appear the strength of kings and nobles, and their management will triumph over the management of others among the general public, an abundance of horsemanship, weapons, iron, the instruments of war, the administration of soldiers, cunning and stratagems, generosity, the collecting of assets and spending them, and cleanliness in food, drink, clothing, and the rest of things. **2** And illnesses and the disturbance of the blood will find the people, and the pain of pregnant women will intensify, and predatory animals and riding animals will be abundant. **3** And the spring quarter will have many clouds, rains, and winds, the autumn quarter will have temperate winds, and the winter quarter cold [and] moist. **4** And the good and food will be abundant, as well as insects, and sometimes it indicates the corruption of ears of grain. **5** And among colors, what will predominate among its people is the smoky.

**6** And the illness of fever and headache will find the king of Babylon, and that will last for 22 days.

**7** And enemies will roam around the countries of Rūm, and that will be rough for them.

**8** And good and evil will come to the land of Daylam, and sometimes a pain of the joints will find them, and that will disappear from them.

**9** And[26] if the portions of the Ascendant were in the first third of it (or the direction was in it, or one of the victors, or the terminal point arrived at it), it indicates the moisture of the air. **10** And if it was in the middle third, it indicates the fineness of its mixture. **11** And if it was in the last third, it indicates its hotness. **12** And if that was in its northern portions, it indicates the blowing of the winds. **13** But if it was in the southern ones, it indicates the moisture of the atmosphere and the quickness of its alteration.

**14** Since we have completed what we wanted to explain, let us break off the chapter.

---

[26] For this paragraph, see *Tet.* II.11 (Robbins p. 205).

**Chapter IV.10: On the indications of Capricorn in the same way**

1 Since we have set forth in Chapter IV.9 the indications of Sagittarius, in this chapter let us state the indications of Capricorn.

2 We say that if it had the indications which we described, it indicates that in the cities it governs there will appear an abundance of desire for women, passion, sexual intercourse, hunting, violence, recklessness,[27] anger, anxieties, lying, wrong, cunning, evil, highway robbery, along with the harsh violence of the people towards each other. 3 And sometimes epidemic will find them, and an abundance of rains in the spring quarter, the goodness of the air in the summer quarter (and the blowing of the eastern winds in it, along with the warmth of the autumn quarter and its gentleness, and middling cold in the beginning of the winter quarter, but its intensity at its end, and the corruption of fruits and vegetation. 4 And the year will be middling, and the increase of the water moderate. 5 And among colors, black clothing will predominate among its people.

6 And it will be feared for the king of Babylon due to some of his enemies, and misfortunes will happen in his city from terror, death, and false rumors, and among the people will occur rancor for about 40 days, then the king will make peace between them. 7 And blood will be shed around Babylon, and that will be upon the Sun's being parallel with the third face of Scorpio.

8 And[28] if the portions of the Ascendant were in the first third of it (or the direction was in it, or one of the victors, or the terminal point arrived at it), it indicates the hotness of the air. 9 And if it was in the middle third, it indicates the fineness of its mixture. 10 And if it was in the last third of it, it indicates the same thing. 11 And if it was in its northern portions, it indicates the moisture of the atmosphere. 12 But if it was in the southern ones, it indicates the same thing.

13 Since the chapter is complete, let us break it off.

---

[27] Or, "inconstancy," "fickleness" (الطَّيْش).
[28] For this paragraph, see *Tet.* II.11 (Robbins p. 205).

## Chapter IV.11: On the indications of Aquarius in the same way

**1** We say that if it had the indications which we described, it indicates that in the cities which it governs there will appear an involvement in building cities and lofty castles, and the digging of rivers, the planting of trees, thinking about the dead and the condition of ancestors, the use of glass and what resembles that among smooth[29] substances, and troubles will befall livestock. **2** And the spring quarter will be middling in cold, with an intensity of heat in the summer quarter, with the autumn quarter inclining to the hot, and in it lightning, thunder, and rains will be abundant, and the cold will intensify in the winter quarter, with an abundance of snows, the blowing of the eastern winds, and moistures will damage vineyards. **3** And the year will be fertile, and food [items] and dates will thrive, and the planting of trees, and locusts harming them will be abundant.

**4** And troubles like drought, illnesses, and what is like that will come to every land on the shores of seas or the banks of the Euphrates and Tigris.

**5** And good and joy will abound in the land of the Arabs, and Rūm's warring against their enemies.

**6** Now[30] if the portions of the Ascendant were in the first third of it (or the direction was in it, or one of the victors, or the terminal point arrived at it), it indicates the moisture of the atmosphere. **7** And if it was in the middle third, it indicates the mixture of the air. **8** And if it was in the last third, it indicates the continuous blowing of the winds. **9** And if it was in its northern portions, it indicates the blowing of the winds. **10** But if it was in the southern ones, it indicates an abundance of clouds.[31]

**11** Since we have completed what we wanted to explain, let us break off the chapter.

---

[29] Lit., "loose, soft" (الرّخوة).
[30] For this paragraph, see *Tet.* II.11 (Robbins p. 205).
[31] This would include fog and mist (الغيوم).

## Chapter IV.12: On the indications of Pisces in the same way

**1** Since we have already set forth what was needed, we say that if it had the indications which we described, it indicates that in the cities which it governs there will appear an examination of the subject of divinity, along with the use of cleanliness, studying jurisprudence in religions, fastidiousness in things, an abundance of using women [for sex], cheerfulness in the people, friendliness towards each other, trust, tranquility, devoutness, the soundness of associations among them in it, the abundant use of refinement, stratagems, and exemplary punishment among the people.[32] **2** And illnesses will find them, and the appearance of predatory animals of the land and sea will be abundant, rains and waters, the digging of rivers, and the planting of trees, with an abundance of watery gemstones like pearls. **3** And among colors, the white (and what resembles that) will predominate among them.

**4** And ailments will befall all of the countries of Aquarius (and especially the people of Kūfa) at the time of the spring quarter, while the year will be fertile.

**5** And food will be scarce in the land of Taurus, Libra, and Scorpio.

**6** And illnesses, ailments, and wounds will be widespread, and harms will come to pregnant women at the time of childbirth, along with an abundance of enemies in the majority of areas, and the year will be harsh, and war will come to the people in it so that they will move from their [current] places to others, and fighting will be abundant, and there will be death, alarm, and false rumors in the majority of the climes.

**7** And it indicates the abundant blowing of the western winds, and the existence of rains in the spring quarter, the intensity of the heat in the summer quarter, the middling quality of the air of the autumn quarter, and the intensity of the cold in the winter quarter.

**8** And the arable land will be suitable, and the produce and food will be abundant, with the scarce raising of [the price of] the crops.[33]

**9** And[34] if the portions of the Ascendant were in the first third of it (or if the direction was in it, or one of the victors, or the terminal point arrived at

---

[32] والمثلة بالناس.

[33] مع قلّة رفع الغلّات. **BY:** "a paucity in the harvest of crops."

[34] For this paragraph, see *Tet.* II.11 (Robbins p. 205).

it), it indicates the fine mixture of the air. **10** And if it was in the middle third, it indicates its moisture. **11** And if it was in the last third of it, it indicates the warmth of the atmosphere. **12** And if that was in its northern portions, it indicates the blowing of the winds. **13** But if it was in the southern ones, it indicates the moisture of the atmosphere.

**14** Since we have completed what we wanted to explain, let us break off the discussion. **15** Book IV is completed.

# BOOK V: [EACH PLANET AS A TIME LORD, IN ALL SIGNS]

**On how to know the special property of the planets' indications by themselves if they had victorship over the Ascendants of one of the Beginnings, or they had lord-of-the-yearship, or distributorship, or upon their being parallel with (or the parallelism of the two crossing-points of the north & south, or the tailed stars, with) all of the signs, in the sense of mixture[1]**

*And it is in 7 Chapters:*

**1** Chapter V.1: On knowing the quality of Saturn's indications by themselves if he had the victorship over the Ascendants of one of the Beginnings, or he had lord-of-the-yearship or distributorship, or upon his being parallel with all of the signs, in the sense of mixture.

**2** Chapter V.2: On how to know the indications of Jupiter in the same way.

**3** Chapter V.3: On the indications of Mars in the same way.

**4** Chapter V.4 On the indications of Venus in the same way.

**5** Chapter V.5: On the indications of Mercury in the same way.

**6** Chapter V.6: On the indications of the Moon in the same way.

**7** Chapter V.7: On the crossing-point of the north and south, and the tailed stars, upon their parallelism with the rest of the signs, in the sense of mixture.

---

[1] Omitting the pious opening prior to the Book title: *In the name of God the Merciful, the Compassionate, and the prayers of God be upon our master Muhammad and his family.*

## Chapter V.1: On knowing Saturn's indications by himself if he had the victorship over the Ascendants of one of the Beginnings, or he had lord-of-the-yearship or distributorship, or upon his being parallel with all of the signs, in the sense of mixture

**1** Since in Book IV we have offered how to know the indications of the signs individually when they are the Ascendants of one of the preceding Beginnings (which we set forth a statement of), or the years terminated at them from one of the Ascendants of the preceding Beginnings or from the positions of the conjunctions, in this Book let us state the knowledge of the special property of the quality of the planets' indications by themselves when they have the victorship over the Ascendants of one of the Beginnings, or they have the lord-of-the-yearship or the distributorship, or upon their being parallel with (or the parallelism of the crossing-point of the north and south,[2] or of the tailed stars[3] with) all of the signs, in the sense of mixture.

**2** We[4] say that if Saturn had the indications which we described and his indication was relevant to humankind, that is an indicator that long-lasting illnesses will befall them, tuberculosis, wasting, damage from moisture, an effusion of waste products, quartan fevers, fleeing, confusion, civil unrest, wars, death, and difficulty, especially for those advanced in years, and the killing of kings, and troubles befalling them because of predatory animals. **3** And an unpraiseworthy king will rule Babylon, and evil will be abundant in it, and searching for a livelihood and possessions will be made improbable, the wealthy will become poor, the poor will die, and the nobles will be unjust. **4** Now if that was in the class of animals which people use, it indicates that trouble will come to them, along with killing; and in whatever is the antithesis of that,[5] there will occur the corruption of their bodies, along with illnesses occurring to those using those animals (which will resemble those [animals'] ailments), and that will be the cause of their ruin. **5** And if his indication was for the airy element, that indicates the intensity of the cold, an abundance of freezing, and the corruption of things along with the congeal-

---

[2] That is, the Nodes.
[3] That is, comets.
[4] For this whole paragraph, see *Tet.* II.8 (Robbins pp. 179-81).
[5] That is, "animals which are *not* used by people."

ing of fog, unhealthy air, the bad mixture of the air, an abundance of clouds and vapors, thunderclaps, thunder, lightning, and intense floods of snows, along with what is generated from that air in terms of vermin harmful to the nature of people. **6** If his nature was indicative of the watery element, that indicates that an intensity of cold and submersion will happen in rivers and seas, along with the difficulty of sailing the seas, a scarcity of aquatic animals, an abundance of ebbing and flowing, and an extreme increase in the flow and ebb. **7** And if the indication was for produce, that indicates their corruption and lack, and especially those which incline toward the acidic, and that will be because of worms occurring in them, and locusts, or due to an abundance of rains and cold.

♄♈ **8** As for his indication by mixture with the sign of Aries during his parallelism with it, [it is for] the occurrence of death in youths, an abundance of captivity, fighting and civil unrest (and especially in the region of the south and east), with an abundance of robbers and highway bandits, the incidence of evil with an abundance of false rumors, agitation, and contempt for the rulers, with an abundance of poisonous animals on the ground, the blowing of the winds, the fine mixture of the air, and sometimes an intensity of heat and corruption will occur in the atmosphere, with a lack of food, drink, and oils. **9** Now if his latitude was northern, that indicates the intensity of the heat and a scarcity of good. **10** But if it was southern, it indicates an intensity of cold and an abundance of ice and fine rain. **11** And if he was easternizing, it indicates sorrows befalling kings because of false rumors. **12** But if he was westernizing, it indicates fighting occurring among the people because of ancestors, with pains and a hindering of rains, and scarce evenness in the mixture of the air. **13** And if he was retrograde, it indicates the existence of thunder, lightning, and lightning bolts. **14** Now if he appeared from under the rays in it, that indicates an abundance of wars and civil unrest in the region of the east, and an abundance of robbers, the corruption of the lands, with an abundance of insects, the occurrence of death in predatory animals, and a scarcity of food and drink in the region of the west.

♄♉ **15** And if he was parallel with the sign of Taurus, it indicates an abundance of fighting in the region of the east and west, the weakness of the aged among the people, the abundance of their illnesses, and the diversity of their conditions, with the abundant death of cattle, the appearance of venomous animals, the occurrence of snows, successive rains, the intensity of the cold, an abundance of foods, drinks, and oils, the spring will depart from its [usual] heat, and the corruption of the sowing (and sometimes the expensiveness of food because of that). **16** And if his latitude was northern, that indicates the fine mixture of the air. **17** But if it was southern, it indicates evil thoughts appearing in the people, with an abundance of infectious disease and the scarce temperateness of the air. **18** Now if he was eastern, that indicates the movement of rains, and an accident occurring in some places. **19** But if he was western, that indicates the bad conduct of kings, with an abundance of confusions occurring in the people, false rumors, shamelessness, robbery, and the appearance of smallpox. **20** And if he was retrograde, it indicates anxiety befalling kings and the death of a mighty man, especially in the region of the south, along with a decrease in the land-tax. **21** And if he appeared from under the rays in it, that indicates the intensity of the cold in the east and west, an abundance of rains and the blowing of winds, and the occurrence of death in camels and cattle, with the corruption of the produce, and a scarcity of food and drinks, especially in the region of the west.

♄Ⅱ **22** And if he was parallel with the sign of Gemini, that indicates an abundance of death happening in men, with their inability to do what they attempt, the slowness of movement in that, the moving of armies and their hostility (and their spoiling many lands for that reason), with the occurrence of snows (and the intensity of floods without them), the successive blowing of raging winds, a copious amount of rains, the fine mixture of the air, and the corruption of the tilling [of the land]. **22** And if his latitude was northern, it indicates the incidence of earthquakes and the raging of winds. **23** But if it was southern, it indicates the dryness of the air, the intensity of the heat, and the scarcity of the yield. **24** And if he was eastern, it indicates the illness of kings. **25** But if he was western, it indicates the thickness of the air and a scarcity of rains. **26** And if he was retrograde, it indicates kings' squandering of the assets in their treasuries. **27** Now if he appeared from under the rays in it, that indicates the intensity of the cold, the raging of winds, an abundance of waters, the corruption of food, the occurrence of infectious disease, and death in the region of the north.

♄♋ 28 And if he was parallel with the sign of Cancer, that indicates the appearance of illnesses befalling the people because of winds, and attacks of colds, coughing, and inflammation of the lung occurring [among them], the frequent emigration of the people from their homelands because of bad events [causing] confusions among them, with illnesses befalling the aged among the people due to an excess amount of blood in their bodies; and it indicates an abundance of ice, rains, and waters. **29** And if his latitude was northern, it indicates the confusion of affairs and their scarce evenness. **30** But if it was southern, it indicates a copious amount of rains. **31** And if he was eastern, it indicates a copious amount of rains and an increase in the waters of rivers. **32** But if he was western, it indicates pains befalling people in the eyes, colds, and an abundance of death occurring in women, with benefit coming to the people of war. **33** And if he was retrograde, it indicates death befalling the nobles. **34** And if he appeared from under the rays in it, that indicates illnesses befalling the people in their chests, with an intensity of coughing, and an abundance of rebels and incursions upon those who border them, with an abundance of wars and bloodshed, the stillness of winds, the occurrence of problems in food, and a scarcity of pressed juices and oil.

♄♌ **35** And if he was parallel with the sign of Leo, that indicates an abundance of illnesses befalling women (like measles, daily and tertian fever), and death occurring among them, an abundance of robbers, infectious disease, wars (and especially in the region of the east), and the successive blowing of *simooms*, a scarcity of rains, intense dryness (and that will also be in the region of the east), with the fine mixture of the air; and sometimes infectious disease will occur. **36** And if his latitude was northern, it indicates confusions in matters, and their scarce evenness. **37** But if it was southern, it indicates an abundance of rains. **38** And if he was eastern, it indicates an increase in rivers and their overflowing. **39** But if he was western, it indicates illness befalling women (especially the women of kings, along with their weakness because of that), and sometimes tertian fevers will come to [women]. **40** And if he was retrograde, it indicates the corruption of the air, the occurrence of infectious disease, and the intensity of heat and the *simooms*. **41** And if he appeared from under the rays in it, that indicates the occurrence of civil unrest and wars, an abundance of fevers, and death befalling the people, along with what happens to them from [other] troubles, poisons, and snakebites, with the intensity of the heat, the duration of the *simooms*, a scarcity of rains, and an abundance of thirst, with the raging of the winds. **42** And if Jupiter and the Moon were close to him, it will dissolve the death, illness, and infectious disease we explained. **43** If Mars and Venus were close to him, it indicates the intensity of fighting in the region of the east. **44** And if Mercury were close to him, it indicates the death of the mighty.

♄♍  **45** And if he was parallel with the sign of Virgo, that indicates corruption befalling the people, and many false rumors, and infectious disease will come to the nobles along with the incidence of epidemics befalling women (and especially the young ones of them), with the corruption of the air and middling rains (and sometimes they will be abundant). **46** And if his latitude was northern, it indicates the fine mixture of the air. **47** But if it was southern, it indicates the same thing. **48** And if he was eastern, it indicates an abundance of rains, thunder, and lightning, and an increase of the waters in rivers. **49** But if he was western, it indicates illnesses befalling kings because of pains in the eyes and colds, with a scarcity of rains. **50** And if he was retrograde, it indicates the citizens' abundant conflict with their rulers. **51** And if he appeared from under the rays in it, and with him was Venus, it indicates the occurrence of death in women (and especially the virgins among them), a scarcity of rains, the incidence of acute fevers, fighting happening between the west and the south, and portents occurring in the atmosphere. **52** But if Mars was there, wars will happen. **53** And if Mercury was there, the air will be disturbed and the winds will rage. **54** And if Jupiter was there, it indicates a scarcity of death and the occurrence of locusts in the crops, along with [other] troubles and harm appearing.

♄♎  **55** And if he was parallel with the sign of Libra, that indicates that pains of the head and belly will befall the people, and illnesses from moistures, an abundance of women's divorcing their husbands, and for those reasons harm and tribulation will come to [the women], with the successive blowing of the *simooms*, the fine mixture of the air, and a scarcity of food and drink. **56** And if his latitude was northern, that indicates the abundant blowing of winds, and their raging. **57** But if it was southern, it indicates the appearance of infectious disease in the people. **58** And if he was eastern, it indicates that illnesses will befall the people, and harmful confusions among them. **59** But he was western, it indicates the dryness of the air, a scarcity of rains, and the intensity of the cold. **60** And if he was retrograde, it indicates the incidence of chronic illnesses in the people, and especially in their mouths and ears, along with a scarcity of evenness in the mixture of their bodies. **61** And if his appearance was in it, it indicates the occurrence of wars. **62** And if Mars was there that will intensify, and fears and apprehension will befall the people. **63** And if Jupiter or the Moon was looking, the wars will cease, and that indicates the occurrence of infectious illness befalling the people as well as death, with an abundance of civil unrest, the darkness of the atmosphere, the disturbance of the air, the raging of the winds, the intensity of the heat, the separation of many men from their women, and a scarcity of food, pressed juices, and oil.

♄♏ **64** And if he was parallel with the sign of Scorpio, that indicates the scarce balance of the people's temperaments, and the occurrence of death in them (and especially in juveniles), and illnesses will become abundant in middle-aged people, with harm from enemies and the intensity of the cold of winter, along with an abundance of snows harmful to sown crops. **65** Now if his latitude was northern, that indicates the intensity of the heat and eye inflammation. **66** But if it was southern, that indicates an abundance of rains and moistures. **67** And if he was eastern, it indicates the contending of enemies with kings, and their distress for those reasons. **68** But if he was western, it indicates illness befalling kings and some of their women, along with the soldiers' seeking rest, the burdensomeness upon them of moving, and their scarce obedience for those reasons. **69** And if he was retrograde, it indicates the difficulty of matters, and the slowness of movement, an abundance of false rumors, and the dryness of the air and [its] agitation. **70** And if he appeared [from under the rays] in it, it indicates the shedding of blood in what is between the region of the north and west, and an abundance of death in old women,[6] with the death of children. **71** And if Jupiter and the Moon were close to him, that indicates a pain in the eyes, and the occurrence of stones in their bladders, an abundance of lightning and floods, the raging of the winds, the intensity of the cold, and the occurrence

---

[6] العجائز, which can however include the elderly generally.

of snows. 72 And if Mars was close to him, it indicates the corruption of the produce and seeds, and the scarce benefits of the lands. 73 And if Jupiter was close to him, it indicates a scarcity of infectious disease, the clarity of the air, and ailments occurring to people in their eyes.

♄♐ 74 And if he was parallel with Sagittarius, that indicates the incidence of epidemics befalling the people, and especially the nobles and their eminent people, with the harshness of pains to the eyes, and there will be fighting in the region of the east, with an abundance of anxieties befalling women, the descent of locusts, the occurrence of death in birds, and the fine mixture of the air. 75 And if his latitude was northern, that indicates the blowing of the winds. 76 But if it was southern, it indicates the scarce stability of affairs, and the quickness of their alteration. 77 And if he was eastern, it indicates an abundance of fevers befalling the people. 78 But if he was western, it indicates the occurrence of tribulation and sorrows among the people, and the humiliation among the aged of them due to slander, and disdain for them, with the difficulty of affairs for them, and the [affairs'] weakness, and the fine mixture of the air. 79 And if he was retrograde, it indicates the expensiveness of food. 80 And if he appeared [from under the rays] in it, it indicates the occurrence of death among the mighty, and the incidence of wars in the region of the west. 81 And if Mars and Venus were close to him, that indicates a scarcity of death, with an abundance of illnesses befalling the people from pains of the eyes, colds, infectious disease, lung inflammation, fevers, pains in the legs, the death of birds, and the spread of locusts, with scarce food, pressed juices, and oil.

♄♑ 82 And if he was parallel with the sign of Capricorn, it indicates the frequent weakening[7] of established matters, the occurrence of fear among the people, and false rumors, with an abundance of rains and the incidence of earthquakes, and the corruption of the plowing and the crops because of an abundance of waters and moistures. 83 And if his latitude was northern, it indicates the abundant occurrence of snows and ice, the intensity of the cold, and excess moistures. 84 But if it was southern, that indicates the same thing as before. 85 And if he was eastern, it indicates an abundance of death befalling women. 86 But if he was western, it indicates the emer-

---

[7] انتقاص, which can also include the notion of disparaging.

gence of enemies, the occurrence of agitation in the people, and the corruption of the livestock, with an abundance of difficulty in sailing the seas. **87** And if he was retrograde, it indicates an abundance of agitation and confusion, with the squandering of assets, and the abundant incidence of agreements between people. **88** And if he appeared [from under the rays] in it, it indicates the occurrence of cold, with the abundant intensity of the rains and the raging of winds. **89** And if Jupiter was close to him, it indicates the incidence of wars in the region of the east, an abundance of troubles happening in the lands, with the abundance of pressed juices and oil.

♄♒ **90** And if he was parallel with the sign of Aquarius, that indicates the occurrence of death in the people, false rumors, intense fear for that reason, the emigration of most of them from their homelands, an abundance of locusts, a copious amount of rains and floods harming the people, the successive blowing of raging winds, the occurrence of earthquakes, and sometimes a decrease will befall the produce, food, and drink in that year. **91** Now if his latitude was northern, that indicates the occurrence of corruption in the yield. **92** But if it was southern, that indicates an abundance of clouds and a copious amount of rains. **93** And if he was eastern, that indicates that sorrows and anxieties befall the king. **94** But if he was western, that indicates an abundance of hardships befalling the people, the incidence of death in those of them advanced in age, with the occurrence of moistures and the corruption of bodies. **95** And if he was retrograde, it indicates the occurrence of snows and the intensity of the cold. **96** And if his appearance [from under the rays] was in Aquarius, it indicates the occurrence of terrors in the people, an abundance of vapors in the world, an abundance of civil unrest and the conflict of some of the people of the claims against some of their kings and authorities, their[8] being driven from their countries, and the incidence of death and infectious disease in young women. **97** And if the luminaries were close to him, that indicates a scarcity of oil along with what will befall the people in terms of anxieties, false rumors, and pains happening in their limbs, with an assault of waters, a decrease in the yield, the propagation of locusts, and the corruption of pressed juices and oil.

---

[8] It is unclear whether this refers to the kings and authorities, or the people.

♄♓ **98** And if he was parallel with the sign of Pisces, it indicates that death will befall the people because of the occurrence of turmoil among them (and especially the nobles and leaders), with the intensity of the heat and cold in their own [proper] times, and the scarce rise [in price] in the crops. **99** And if his latitude was northern, that indicates the successive blowing of winds. **100** But if it was southern, it indicates an abundance of rains and the increase of rivers. **101** And if he was eastern, it indicates a scarcity of rains, the middling amount of wind, and an abundance of confusion. **102** But if he was western, it indicates that distresses and sorrows will befall kings because of the movement of enemies, and an abundance of illnesses occurring from colds. **103** And if he was retrograde, it indicates death befalling the nobles. **104** And if he appeared [from under the rays] in it, it indicates an abundance of waters and floods, the intensification of the cold, and the incidence of evil befalling the people. **105** And if Mars and Venus were close to him or in [his] opposition, or the Moon was opposing him, that is an indicator that pains of the eyes will befall the people, along with a scarcity of rains and food, the safety of the trees and their abundance, and especially olive trees.

**106** Since we have completed what we wanted to explain, let us break off the discussion.

## Chapter V.2: On how to know the indications of Jupiter in the same way

**1** Since we have already made clear in Chapter V.1 the knowledge of the special property of Saturn's individual indications when he has the victorship over the Ascendants of the Beginnings, or he has the lord-of-the-yearship or the distributorship, and during his parallelism with all of the signs in terms of mixture, in this chapter let us state how to know the special property of the indications of Jupiter in the same way.

**2** We[9] say that if he had the indications which we explained, and was relevant to the category of people, that indicates the might of the affairs of kings, the elevation of their matters, their abundant giving, the raising of their status, their suspicion of some of their associates and taking advantage of them for those reasons, along with the suitable condition of the king of Babylon and the Arabs. **3** And there will be powerful civil unrest in Rūm, and the ruin of a mighty man among them because of prisons, and the surpluses of the houses of assets, the easiness for the people of the countries in supplying the land-tax, the people's use of truth-telling in their speech, the appearance of the good and the soundness of bodies and souls, the suitable condition of businessmen, the excellence of income and profits, the abundant pregnancy of women (and especially male [babies]) and coming to full term.[10] **4** Now if that was for the category of beasts (and especially those which people use), that indicates their abundance and increase, while for what is of the antithesis of that, corruption and ruin will occur. **5** And if his indication was for the airy element, that indicates an abundance of rains, the blowing of winds, the moisture of the air, and its fine mixture. **6** And if his indication was for the earthy element, that indicates its cultivation along with an abundance of produce, the suitability of wheat and barley, and sometimes mildew will occur in the seed (so that it spoils it). **7** And if his indication was for the watery element, that indicates the safety of sailing the seas, the abundant swelling of rivers, and fish.

♃♈ **8** Now as for his indication in his mixture with the sign of Aries during his parallelism with it, it indicates the occurrence of battles

---

[9] For this whole paragraph, see *Tet.* II.8 (Robbins pp. 183). Ptolemy however does not provide any country-specific indications, only general ones.
[10] Lit., "coming to completed births."

and fear among the people of Khurāsān and Armenia, with the good health of the bodies of the people, and sometimes illnesses, headaches, and coughing will be abundant, and that will be harsher in the autumn quarter, and the intensity of heat at its beginning (and cold at its end), the intensity of cold in the winter quarter, an abundance of rains, floods, and moistures, along with the abundant thriving and growth of food, plantings, trees, and vineyards. **9** And if his latitude was northern, it indicates the intensity of the heat and an abundance of *simooms*. **10** But if it was southern, it indicates the intensity of the coldness of the air. **11** And if he was eastern, it indicates an abundance of moistures, especially in the autumn quarter. **12** But if he was western, it indicates the reverence of kings towards the aged among the people of his house and its administrators, with abundant rains and the moisture of the air. **13** And if he was retrograde, it indicates harms in everything which he indicates. **14** And if he appeared [from under the rays] in it, it indicates illnesses and pains in the head, and there will be coughing along with the movement of bile in their bodies, an abundance of birds, the duration of the blowing of northern winds, the length of the winter, and an abundance of misery[11] [in that], the occurrence of snows, the swelling of rivers, a good summer, the safety of crops [on] even [ground], and an abundance of pressed juices.

♄ **15** And if he was parallel with the sign of Taurus, it indicates death befalling viziers and the nobles, the abundant profession of piety by the people, and their dignity, and sometimes pains of the eyes will befall them, along with a scarcity of birds. **16** And it indicates the intensity of harmful cold, an abundance of rains and earthquakes at the beginning of the winter quarter, an abundance of snows in its middle, the summer quarter will be temperate, and sometimes heat and dryness will intensify in the autumn quarter, with an abundance of food and drink, and the yield will decrease along with the hardship of the tribulation which those sailing the seas will experience. **17** And if his latitude was northern, that indicates the fine mixture of the air. **18** But if it was southern, it indicates the diversity of its mixture and its scarce evenness. **19** And if he was eastern, it indicates a copious amount of rains. **20** But if he was western, it indicates the death of some

---

[11] الاستكانة, lit. "submissiveness, resignation." **BY** read as "foul weather," but I cannot determine why.

of the women of kings, and some of the aged among the nobles, along with the excess moisture of the air. **21** And if he was retrograde, it indicates the stirring up of enemies against kings. **22** And if he appeared [from under the rays] in it, it indicates the death of some famous scholars, the duration of the rains in the winter, with the mixture of the air, the occurrence of snows in the middle [of winter], the raging of the winds, the duration of intense cold at its end, with the goodness of summer, its coldness, and its corruption.

♃♊ **23** And if he was parallel with the sign of Gemini, it indicates an abundance of pains befalling the people in the eyes, and especially children and women, and an abundance of death in them (and the reason for that is the intensity of the heat), and the occurrence of death among livestock. **24** And the summer quarter will be balanced, with the intensity of the cold in the winter quarter (but its scarce harm), the successive blowing of the western winds, and food and drink will be abundant (and especially in the region of the west), with the corruption of seeds and a decrease in waters, and sometimes the waters of springs will increase. **25** And if his latitude was northern, it indicates the blowing of the winds and their evenness. **26** But if it was southern, it indicates the harshness of the summer and the abundance of its *simooms*, and its dryness. **27** And if he was eastern, it indicates an abundance of rains and the intensity of the cold. **28** But if he was western, it indicates the abundance of sorrows befalling kings, and their[12] scarce employment of soldiers. **29** And if he was retrograde, it indicates an abundance of false rumors and alarm. **30** Now if he appeared [from under the rays] in it, it indicates an abundance of pains in the eyes befalling the people, an abundance of death in women, abundant ailments in children, the corruption of the produce of trees, and the scarce waters of springs.

♃♋ **31** And if he was parallel with the sign of Cancer, it indicates the zeal[13] of kings and their might, an abundance of illnesses befalling the people in their mouths and lips, and sometimes bodies will be sound in the autumn quarter, with an abundance of heat and the intensity of the cold (and especially in the region of the east), along with abundant rains and fog, and snows in the winter quarter. **32** And if his latitude was northern, it indi-

---

[12] Lit., "his."
[13] غيرة, which can also refer to one's sense of honor or self-respect. **BY:** "pride."

cates the intensity of the heat and an abundance of *simooms*. **33** But if it was southern, it indicates the same thing. **34** And if he was eastern, it indicates an abundance of rains and the intensity of the cold. **35** But if he was western, it indicates the abundant travels of kings, their shifting [from place to place], the squandering of assets, the occurrence of false rumors, confusion, and derangement among the people. **36** And if he was retrograde, it indicates sorrows entering upon the king from the death of some of the nobles. **37** Now if he appeared [from under the rays] in it, it indicates the intensity of the cold and the blowing of the cold northern winds, with an abundance of thunder, lightning, the swelling of rivers, the fineness of the crops, and the safety of the year, except that pains will befall the people in their mouths and lips in the spring quarter.

2♃ ♌  **38** And if he was parallel with the sign of Leo, it indicates troubles befalling the king, and sorrows and irritation, along with an abundance of pains befalling the people from coughing and winds which occur from the cold, and some of the famous nobles will die, and predatory animals will be sound. **39** And rains will be abundant in the spring quarter, a scarcity of heat in the summer quarter, an intensity of cold in the winter quarter, with the raging of winds uprooting trees, a scarcity of cold in [winter's] middle, with an increase in springs. **40** And if his latitude was northern, it indicates the abundant blowing of the winds, and the harshness of their movement. **41** But if it was southern, it indicates the moisture of the air. **42** And if he was eastern, it indicates an abundance of rains (and their benefit), with the fine mixture of the air of winter, and its evenness. **43** But if he was western, it indicates the abundant anxieties and sorrows which will come to kings, and sometimes illnesses will befall them along with the death of some of the nobles. **44** And if he was retrograde, it indicates abundant travels happening for kings. **45** And if he appeared [from under the rays] in it, it indicates that the winds of hemorrhoids will befall the people, and colds and coughing from the intensity of the cold, and an abundance of incidents among riding animals, with troubles befalling them, with the intensity of the cold in the winter, an abundance of waters and raging winds, a diminishment of the waters of springs, with the warmth of spring, the fineness of the crops, vineyards, and olive trees.

♃ ♍  46 And if he was parallel with the sign of Virgo, it indicates that headaches will befall the people, and the year will be hard for pregnant women, together with the balance of the air in the spring quarter, the goodness of the air of the summer quarter, the intensity of the heat in the autumn quarter (and sometimes the fineness of the mixture of the air in it), and an abundance of rains and snows, and the intensity of the cold in the winter quarter. **47** And if his latitude was northern, it indicates the fine mixture of the air. **48** But if it was southern, it indicates the temperateness of the rains and their benefit. **49** And if he was eastern, it indicates a scarcity of rains. **50** But if he was western, it indicates illnesses befalling kings along with an abundance of anxieties and sorrows coming to the people, and a decrease of meat. **51** And if he was retrograde, it indicates a scarcity of rains along with the goodness of the air and its balance. **52** And if he appeared [from under the rays] in it, it indicates the intensity of the cold of winter at its beginning and end, and the mixture of its middle, and the abundant occurrence of ice and rains, the swelling of rivers, the flooding of the *wadīs*, the intensification of the cold in some places, the existence of rains and illness in the summer quarter along with the fineness of the grasses, the abundant yield of vineyards, and the corruption of the trees.

♃ ♎  **53** And if he was parallel with the sign of Libra, it indicates the people's abundant use of tyranny, arrogance, and pride, along with the spreading of death in cattle, the temperateness of the air of spring, and its inclination towards the cold, and sometimes rains corrupting the food will happen in the summer quarter, along with an abundance of thunder and lightning, an abundance of snows in the beginning of the winter quarter to its middle, along with the warmth of the atmosphere at its end. **54** And if his latitude was northern, that indicates the successive blowing of the winds and the temperateness of their movement (and their benefit). **55** But if it was southern, it indicates an abundance of pains befalling the people, and especially in the eyes, from congestion and colds. **56** And if he was eastern, it indicates an abundance of pains befalling the people in the spring quarter, with troubles befalling ships, with an abundance of grasses and the middling quality of the seeds. **57** But if he was western, it indicates illnesses befalling kings, with a scarcity of rains, the dryness of the air, and its coldness. **58** And if he was retrograde, it indicates the king's marrying a royal woman. **59** And if he appeared [from under the rays] in it, that indicates illnesses befalling the people in their heads, and troubles befalling pregnant women, and there will be rains at the beginning of winter, and there will be a mixture in its middle along with a blowing of the winds in it, and there will be moistures and ice with the mixture of the spring quarter, and an abundance of grasses in the summer quarter, and a decrease of waters.

♃♏  **60** And if was parallel with the sign of Scorpio, it indicates the soundness of people's bodies, and their taking advantage of matters, with a scarcity of harm, an abundance of corrupting rains in all of the regions, the intensity of the cold at the beginning of the winter quarter until one-half [of it], then it will increase; and the air will become thick, and fog will become abundant along with the suitability of vineyards and plowing, and the excellence of the planting of trees. **61** And if his latitude was northern, it indicates the intensity of the heat. **62** But if it was southern, it indicates the moisture of the air and its heat. **63** And if he was eastern, it indicates confusions befalling the leaders. **64** But if he was western, it indicates illnesses befalling kings, or death befalling some of their relatives, with the scarce movement of armies. **65** And if it was retrograde, it indicates a scarcity of rains and the successive blowing of beneficial winds. **66** And if he appeared [from under the rays] in it, it indicates an abundance of pains befalling the people in the spring quarter, with troubles befalling ships, and the beginning of winter will be cold, its middle mild; and the existence of rains, thunder, lightning, a decrease in the waters of springs, an abundance of grasses, the middling [amount] of the seeds, the fineness of vineyards and olive trees, and the incidence of mighty rivers.

♃♐  **67** And if he was parallel with the sign of Sagittarius, that indicates an abundance of illnesses befalling the people from headaches and eye inflammation (and especially in the autumn quarter), the occurrence of death in livestock (and especially in cattle), an abundance of rains, a middling amount of cold in the beginning of winter, and its intensity in in its middle, the occurrence of snows, the corruption of the food and most of the produce, with the intensity of the heat in the summer quarter, and the duration of the blowing of the eastern winds. **68** And if his latitude was northern, it indicates the blowing of the winds and their benefit. **69** But if it was southern, that indicates the appearance of good and benefit among the people, with their calmness and tranquility. **70** And if he was eastern, that indicates pains befalling the people, and especially in the eyes. **71** But if he was western, it indicates anxieties and sorrows befalling kings and leaders, and the death of some of the nobles. **72** And if he was retrograde, it indicates the abundant delight of the subjects in the fairness which appears from kings, with a copious amount of rains at its end, and the mixture of the air of summer, and an abundance of grasses. **73** And if he appeared [from under the rays] in it, it indicates the death of a mighty man, and troubles befalling dogs, the evenness of the air of winter, with the incidence of the blowing of winds and rains at its end, the mixture of summer, an abundance of grasses, the ripening of the produce of plains and mountains, the delaying of the grape harvest, and the fine condition of trees.

♑ **74** And if he was parallel with the sign of Capricorn, that indicates the anger of the king towards some of his administrators, and the death of nobles, with the soundness of the people's bodies, an abundance of rains, the succession of winds in the spring quarter, a scarcity of heat in the summer quarter, the abundance of the eastern winds; and sometimes the death of dogs will occur, with the excellence[14] of the produce, food and drink, and their scarcity. **75** And if his latitude was northern, that indicates an abundance of moistures. **76** But if it was southern, it indicates the same thing. **77** And if he was eastern, it indicates an abundance of illnesses occurring in the people, especially in the eyes. **78** And if he was western, it indicates illnesses befalling kings and leaders, with the abundant occurrence of death, false rumors, and derangement among the people. **79** And if he was retrograde, it indicates confusions befalling kings and the subjects. **80** And if appeared [from under the rays] in it, it indicates that itching and pains in the head and eyes will befall the people, and the abundant agitation of the winds, and the ruin of delicate animals, with the mixture of the air at the beginning of the winter quarter, the incidence of cold and moisture in its middle, the intensity of the cold and an abundance of waters, the blowing of winds and the occurrence of snows at its end, the abundance of thunder and the good-

---

[14] Reading جودة for وجود.

ness of the beginning of the summer quarter, the intensity of heat at its end, with the temperateness of the crops, an abundance of fertility, and the corruption of pressed juices.

♃♒ **81** And if he was parallel with the sign of Aquarius, that indicates the death of some of the nobles, and an abundance of pains befalling the people (and especially in youths), and sometimes their bodies will be sound, with the ruin of birds and predatory animals, an abundance of rains and snows, the intensity of the cold in the spring quarter, and the summer quarter will be full of winds (especially the winds of the east), and rains and winds will be abundant in the autumn quarter, and the beginning of winter will be full of rains, winds, and moistures, and that will spoil the food in the time of the forming of produce and vines, with the abundant submersions of ships on the seas. **82** And if his latitude was northern, that indicates the dryness of the air. **83** But if it was southern, it indicates an abundance of fog. **84** And if he was eastern, it indicates a scarcity of winds. **85** But if he was western, that indicates illnesses befalling the women of kings, the death of some of the nobles, and a scarcity of rains. **86** And if he was retrograde, it indicates illness befalling some of the kings. **87** And if he appeared [from under the rays] in it, it indicates the flight of some of the mighty, an abundance of illnesses befalling the people, the ruin of birds and sea animals, with the submersion of ships in the sea, the raging of winds benefiting the sown crops, with the existence of rains, the occurrence of ice and snows in the beginning of winter, an abundance of good winds in the spring quarter (with their harming the produce), the mixture of the summer quarter and the even blowing of the winds in it (and sometimes rains will rage in it), and the incidence of snows, with rain corrupting grasses in many places, and the fineness of the seeds.

♃♓ **88** And if he was parallel with the sign of Pisces, that indicates the abundance of harm which will find the people (and especially youths, women, and children), and the abundant pains of pregnant women, the successive blowing of cold winds in the spring quarter, the intensity of the heat in the summer quarter, the fine mixture of the air in the autumn quarter, a copious amount of rains at the beginning of the winter quarter, the abundant blowing of the winds in its middle, and the incidence of snow at its end, with the rain corrupting the produce and seeds, and especially vineyards and olive trees. **89** And if his latitude was northern, that indicates the blowing of the winds and their benefit. **90** But if it was southern, it indicates an abundance of rains and the swelling of rivers. **91** And if he was eastern, it indicates a scarcity of rains and the middling quality of the air. **92** But if he was western, it indicates the abundant movement of kings and their shifting [around], and the departure of some armies to the borders of the kingdom. **93** And if he was retrograde, it indicates the badness of the affairs. **94** And if he appeared [from under the rays] in it, that indicates the occurrence of desire in the hearts of the people, and fear, earthquakes, and trepidation, and illnesses befalling women and children in the spring quarter, troubles befalling pregnant women, the intensity of worry and the difficulty of childbirth, and an abundance of rains at the beginning of the winter quarter, an abundance of winds in its middle, the successive blowing of northern winds and the intensity of the cold, and the occurrence of snow at its end, with the intense heat of the summer quarter, and corruption befalling sheep, with the fine condition of the sowing.

**95** Since we have completed what we wanted to explain, let us break off the discussion.

## Chapter V.3: On how to know the indications of Mars in the same way

**1** Since we have set forth in Chapter V.2 how to know the special property of the indications of Jupiter, in this chapter let us state how to know the special property of the indications of Mars in the same way.

**2** We[15] say that if he had the indications which we explained, and he had relevance to the category of people, that indicates an abundance of wars, civil unrest, and rebels against kings, the anger of leaders, and for these reasons sudden, quick, and violent death will befall some of the people, and there will be illnesses with tertian fevers (and especially those advanced in age), and some of them will be afflicted by punishment and degradation, transgression of and departing from the Sharī'ah, with an abundance of highway bandits and their shedding of blood, and the incidence of burning, with epidemics in most of the climes. **3** And if he indicated the category of beasts, and especially those which people use, it indicates their scarcity. **4** And if his indication was for the airy element, it indicates a scarcity of rains, the intensity of the heat, earthquakes, an abundance of lightning bolts, and successive hot, southern, winds. **5** And if his indication was for the earthy element, it indicates the corruption of the produce because of heat burning them, either due to what raging winds do to them, or from their being burned by fire in the places in which they do burn. **6** And if his indication was for the watery element, that indicates the sudden submersion of ships due to harmful, varied winds, or from lightning bolts, and what is like that.

♂♈ **7** Now as for his indication in terms of his mixture with the sign of Aries during his parallelism with it, it is indicative of fighting in the region of the east, with an abundance of pains in the eyes, the swiftness of affairs, and their success at the beginning, the abundant blowing of winds, the intensity of their *simooms*, and a scarcity of rain. **8** And if his latitude was northern, that indicates the dryness of the air. **9** But if it was southern, it indicates the mixture of the air. **10** And if he was eastern, that indicates sorrows befalling the people, and irritation. **11** But if he was western, it indicates the abundant expenses of kings and their squandering, and the scarce movement of armies with the miscarriage of pregnant women. **12** And if he

---

[15] For this whole paragraph, see *Tet.* II.8 (Robbins pp. 183-85).

was retrograde, it indicates an abundance of sorrows and harms which will befall the people. **13** And if he appeared [from under the rays] in it, it indicates an abundance of wars in the region of the east, and illnesses befalling the people in their eyes, with the intense blowing of the winds, and the fineness of the crops.

♂♉ **14** Now if he was parallel with the sign of Taurus, it indicates fighting occurring between the people of the region of the north and the people of the region of the south, and an abundance of pains in the eyes, with the death of women, harms coming to the married ones among them, and the badness of Venusian matters, the death of cattle, and an abundance of sheep with a copious amount of rains, the intensity of thunder, lightning, and fog, the meagerness of the way of life, and an abundance of water. **15** And if his latitude was northern, it indicates an abundance of illnesses [from] smallpox and measles. **16** But if it was southern, it indicates the bad mixture of the air. **17** And if he was eastern, it indicates a scarcity of waters and an abundance of drought. **18** But if he was western, it indicates the illnesses of pregnant women because of their miscarrying, with the corruption of the sown crops and trees, especially vineyards and olive trees. **19** And if he was retrograde, it indicates harms befalling livestock, with their ruin. **20** Now if he appeared [from under the rays] in it, that indicates wars happening between the region of the south and the north, the shedding of blood, and pains of the eyes will find the people of the region of the north, and death will occur in what has four feet (and most of that in cattle and sheep), and vapors, fog, waters, and rains will be abundant, and food scarce.

♂♊ **21** And if he was parallel with the sign of Gemini, that indicates an abundance of pains in the ears which will befall the people, as well as smallpox and measles, and there will be fighting in the region of the north, with an abundance of robbers (and victory over them) and their affairs being made public, and harm will come to the people because of lightning bolts, lightning, and an intensity of cold. **22** And if his latitude was northern, it indicates an abundance of earthquakes. **23** But if it was southern, it indicates the hotness of the air and its stillness. **24** And if he was eastern, it indicates the confusion of the affairs of the general public due to their rulers. **25** But if he was western, it indicates the death of some of the nobles, and sometimes ailments will befall some of the women of kings, and the occurrence of fire in some of the places. **26** And if he was retrograde, it indicates an abundance of illnesses [from] smallpox and measles. **27** And if he appeared [from under the rays] in it, it indicates that death will befall the people, and an abundance of fire, and fighting in the region of the north, with harm from robbers. **28** And if the luminaries were close to him, it indicates that abscesses and pains of the eyes will find the people, and a decrease in the vegetation will happen.

♂♋ **29** And if he was parallel with the sign of Cancer, that indicates fighting occurring in the region of the west or east, and it will overwhelm them, and they will supply the land tax, and illnesses will spread from inflammation of the lung and [in] the chest, daily and tertian [fevers], and pain of the throat, antagonisms will occur between leaders, and death will spread in the region of Jibāl especially, and especially in everything having four feet, with a scarcity of rains and the intensity of the heat. **30** And if his latitude was northern, it indicates the hotness of the air and its moisture, and stillness. **31** But if it was southern, it indicates the same thing. **32** And if he was eastern, it indicates an abundance of anxieties occurring in the people, with the stillness of the air and its dryness. **33** But if he was western, it indicates an abundance of illnesses befalling pregnant women because of their miscarrying, and sometimes it indicates harm and corruption because of movement. **34** And if he was retrograde, that indicates the corruption of the atmosphere, the intensity of the heat, and the blowing of the *simooms*. **35** And if he appeared [from under the rays] in it, it indicates tribulation befalling the people from pains in the throat and chest, chronic illnesses occurring in their limbs, and quartan fever, and death will happen in riding animals, and rain will be scarce, the *simooms* will blow, and locusts will spread, pressed juices will be corrupted, and oil will be scarce.

♂♌ **36** And if he was parallel with the sign of Leo, that indicates an abundance of wars coming to be in the region of the east, with the spread of death (and especially in children), and an abundance of pains in the belly, the incidence of death in riding animals, a scarcity of rains and food, and especially in the region of the east. **37** Now if his latitude was northern, that indicates the blowing of the winds, with the intensity of their *simooms*. **38** But if it was southern, it indicates the dryness of the air. **39** And if he was eastern, it indicates the scarcity of the rains. **40** But if he was western, it indicates the irritation of the king and his scarce activity, the cutting off of hope in most affairs, and the appearance of an enemy along with the intensity of the heat and the *simooms*. **41** And if he was retrograde, it indicates the occurrence of envy and injustice in Rūm. **42** And if he appeared [from under the rays] in it, it indicates the occurrence of death among the mighty, an abundance of pains befalling youths, and worry and pains in the belly will find children and infants, the cold of winter will intensify, and rains and food will be scarce.

♂♍ **43** And if he was parallel with the sign of Virgo, it indicates an abundance of pains in the eyes, an abundance of fighting and bloodshed in the region of the south, an abundance of death in women, and rebels will spread, and the downfall of some of the nobles from their status, with the corruption of the air and its dryness, and an abundance of earthquakes, food, and drink. **44** And if his latitude was northern, it indicates a scarcity of rains. **45** But if his latitude was southern, it indicates the bad mixture of the air. **46** And if he was eastern, it indicates the death of kings. **47** But if he was western, it indicates sorrows and anxieties entering upon secretaries, with the miscarriage of pregnant women, and fatigue affecting the senses. **48** And if he was retrograde, it indicates the dryness of the air. **49** And if he appeared [from under the rays] in it, it indicates that pains of the eyes and long-lasting pains making recovery difficult will come to the people, with the intensity of the cold and the scarce blowing of the winds. **50** And if the luminaries were close to him, that indicates an abundance of rain, the intensity of the cold, and the incidence of wars and bloodshed in the region of the south, and clamor, fears, and terrors befalling the mighty and the nobles, and the removal of some of them from their authority, with the occurrence of much death in the people of the north and south, and the death of sheep.

♂♎ **51** And if he was parallel with the sign of Libra, it indicates a scarcity of troubles and the appearance of safety in the people (and sometimes robbers and highway bandits will appear), and an abundance of fear, false rumors, and evil in the people, and the ruin of many people for reasons of epidemics, and especially in the region of the south, with the scarcity of the rains, clouds, winds, and fog. **52** Now if his latitude was northern, it indicates an abundant succession of winds. **53** But if it was southern, it indicates the scarce mixture of the air. **54** And if he was eastern, it indicates an abundance of rains and thunder. **55** But if he was western, it indicates the tranquility of the solders, and their scarce movements, and illnesses befalling the aged, with the intense dryness of the air in the autumn and a scarcity of rains. **56** And if he was retrograde, it indicates the sudden death of some of the nobles. **57** And if he appeared [from under the rays] in it and Saturn was close to him, it indicates an abundance of death, the raging of robbers, and terrors and infectious disease existing in the world, with an abundance of rains, fog, and clouds, a scarcity of produce, and the growth of grasses and olive trees.

♂ ♏  **58** And if he was parallel with the sign of Scorpio, it indicates abundant pains in the eyes among the people, the appearance of epidemic and illnesses in the people (and especially in youths), and that will be in the region of the north, with an abundance of robbers and highway bandits, the intensity of the cold in the winter and autumn quarters, and the summer quarter, the intense dryness of the air, and that damaging food, drink, trees, olive trees, and sown crops. **59** And if his latitude was northern, it indicates the intense dryness of the air, and an abundance of drought. **60** But if it was southern, it indicates the evenness of the air. **61** And if he was eastern, it indicates a scarcity of rains. **62** But if he was western, it indicates the tranquility of the soldiers, their scarce movements, pains occurring in the eyes, along with miscarriage befalling pregnant women, and the ruin of livestock. **63** And if he was retrograde, it indicates illness befalling the king, from which he will come to the verge of death. **64** And if he appeared [from under the rays] in it, it indicates terrors and fears happening in the people, and death happening in women (and especially the elderly), and particularly in the countries of the north, with many different pains befalling the people for reasons of cold and black bile, with an abundance of poverty, stealing, and sorrows in the people, the rebellion of robbers, and a scarcity of pressed juices and oil.

♂ ♐  **65** And if he was parallel with the sign of Sagittarius, it indicates the occurrence of death in the region of the west and Armenia, and an abundance of fighting there, with illness, harsh coughing, and pains in the eyes (and most of that will be on the sea coasts), and the spring quarter will have bad, corrupted air, with a scarcity of rains, and cold will increase in the winter quarter so that from that, corruption will befall the food and trees, along with the abundant planting of date palms. **66** And if his latitude was northern, it indicates the abundant blowing of the winds along with their dryness, and the scarcity of their moisture. **67** But if it was southern, it indicates the changing of some of the affairs, and their alteration. **68** And if he was eastern, it indicates the intensity of the heat. **69** But if he was western, it indicates hostility befalling the people along with the anger of the king towards some of the nobles, and the abundant miscarrying of pregnant women. **70** And if he was retrograde, it indicates tribulation and evil befalling the soldiers. **71** And if he appeared [from under the rays] in it, it indicates the occurrence of wars and drought in the region of the west, and death befalling kings, skin eruptions, jaundice and pains in the eyes befalling the people in the region of the north, with an abundance of death, the drying up of the waters of springs, a scarcity of rains, the incidence of ice, and cold spoiling the produce, and a scarcity of pressed juices.

♂♑ **72** And if he was parallel with the sign of Capricorn, it indicates an abundance of death and tribulation in the region of the south (especially in the youths of the people), and there will be fighting (and especially in what borders on the region of the east and south), a scarcity of rains and the dryness of the air along with an abundant yield[16] and a scarcity of produce. **73** And if his latitude was northern, that indicates the corrupt mixture of the air. **74** But if it was southern, it indicates the same thing. **75** Now if he was eastern, it indicates the corruption of vineyards. **76** But if he was western, it indicates death befalling the nobles, with anxieties and sorrows befalling the people, and an abundance of rains. **77** And if he was retrograde, it indicates the same thing.[17] **78** And if he appeared [from under the rays] in it, it indicates wars taking place between the people of the east and south, and the occurrence of death in youths and children, with a scarcity of pressed juices and oil.

♂♒ **79** Now if he was parallel with the sign of Aquarius, that indicates the killing of the king of the east (or his death), with an abundance of hardships and tribulation occurring in the people, a copious

---

[16] الغَلّة.

[17] The same as **76**, it seems.

amount of rains, the occurrence of snows, the fine mixture of the air, and an abundance of food and drink and good (but a scarcity of that in the region of the seas). **80** And if his latitude was northern, that indicates the dryness of the air. **81** But if it was southern, it indicates the same thing. **82** And if he was eastern, it indicates the intensity of the heat. **83** But if he was western, it indicates the intensity of fighting happening on the sea, and death and submersion befalling the nobles, with harm entering upon pregnant women and the intensity of the heat. **84** And if he was retrograde, it indicates the poor obedience of the subjects towards the king. **85** And if he appeared [from under the rays] in it, that indicates many evils appearing in the world, the occurrence of wars in the region of the north, a scarcity of rains, a scarcity of locusts, the corruption of the produce, and the expensiveness of food. **86** And if Venus was not viewed by him, that indicates pains befalling the people (and their abundance), along with a decrease in pressed juices.

♂♓ **87** And if he was parallel with the sign of Pisces, that indicates much fighting and killing between kings and the mighty, and the disappearance of a great man's rule for those reasons, the casting down of the nobles from their status and authority, the appearance of daily and tertian fevers in the people of the region of the south and west, the expensiveness of riding animals, and an abundance of rains and snows, with the fine mixture of the air. **88** And if his latitude was northern, that indicates the abundant blowing of the winds. **89** But if it was southern, it indicates an abundance of rains. **90** Now if he was eastern, it indicates fevers befalling the people (like tertian [fevers], and others). **91** But if he was western, it indicates the corruption of the soldiers, and their weakness and fear, with the miscarriage of pregnant women, along with an abundance of cold and ice. **92** And if he was retrograde, it indicates moving and abandonment[18] befalling the people, and the scarce completion of what is hoped of works and affairs. **93** And if he appeared [from under the rays] in it, it indicates the lowering of the status of scholars and the corruption of the authorities. **94** And if Venus was close to him, it indicates an abundance of wars, their intensity, and the presence of thunder and lightning.

---

[18] إعراض. This word has connotations of turning away, shunning, and avoidance, but its meaning is unclear to me here.

☉ **95** As for the special property of the indication of the Sun by himself for [his] victorhood and one of the revolutions, it is harm coming to kings, death befalling the general public, the stirring up of an enemy from all areas, the year will not be successful, riding animals will be abundant and expensive, some of the kings will confide in each other, blood will be shed in the region of the west, fighting will multiply there, the nobles will become impoverished and the poor rich, and fighting will be abundant.

**96** As for his indication in the sense of mixture upon his alighting in the starting points of the revolutionary Beginnings which we described,[19] the planets are relevant to that apart from him, since his parallelism with these positions follows successively in all of the periods.[20] **97** And indeed the distinction in indications is made possible from the Ascendants of the periods, and the different positions of the planets in those Ascendants as well, in accordance with what we set forth. **98** So due to that, we are not stating his indications for lower things from his parallelism with the regions which we mentioned before. **99** But as for the indications of his parallelism with all of the signs, the majority of what that indicates is for alterations of the atmosphere.

---

[19] This would especially be Aries (for the beginnings of years), then the convertible signs (for annual quarters), and finally each sign if one were doing monthly revolutions.

[20] أدوار. This seems to mean that because he will always be in the same signs at each possible revolution (Aries at the beginning of the year, the other convertible signs and the quarters, etc.), it is otiose to discuss his political meanings in the signs because they would be the same every year. Thus we must pay attention to *other* planets when he is the victor, and especially if they're in the Ascendant of a chart, or in the sign of the profection.

## Chapter V.4: On how to know the indications of Venus in the same way

**1** Since we have already set forth in Chapter V.3 the indications of Mars and what is pertinent to the Sun in his own indication by himself, in this chapter let us state the account of the indications of Venus in the same way.

**2** We[21] say that if she had the indications which we described and she was pertinent to the category of people, that indicates the appearance of excellent governance and management, fine teaching in matters of religion, the death of some of the mighty (and especially those of the people of Babylon), the appearance of rulers and the elevation of [their] status, the abundant reverence of the people towards each other, the appearance of delight, the suitability of the matter of marriage, and an abundance of children; and sometimes men will divorce their women, young women will miscarry due to debauchery, and envy and harms to bodies will be abundant. **3** And if that was for the category of beasts which people use, that indicates their abundance and benefiting from them. **4** And if her indication was for the earthy element, that indicates the fine condition of sowing, trees, and produce. **5** And if her indication was for the watery element, that indicates a copious amount of waters and the safety of ships on the sea.

♀♈ **6** And as for her indication in terms of her combining with the sign of Aries during her parallelism with it, it is indicative of drought, with a copious amount of rains (and their benefit), the successive blowing of the winds, and the fine mixture of the air. **7** And if her latitude was northern, it indicates the hotness of the air. **8** But if it was southern, she indicates the intensity of the cold. **9** And if she is distanced [from the Sun] by her greatest distance, it indicates the movement of armies. **10** And if she was retrograde, she indicates an abundance of thunder, lightning, and the intensity of the cold. **11** And if she was under the rays, she indicates derangement befalling the people, with an abundance of false rumors. **12** And if she appeared [from under the rays] in it, she indicates the respect of the cavalry and the people of war, and their strength, the abundant delight of the mighty and the nobles, the appearance of good in the world, an abundance of waters and the in-

---

[21] For this whole paragraph, see *Tet.* II.8 (Robbins pp. 185-87).

crease of water, and the existence of moistures and rains in the winter, the evenness of the air in the summer, and the suitability of the situation of trees.

♀♉ 13 And if she was parallel with the sign of Taurus, she indicates the emergence of rebels, with the disturbance of the people and their confusion, with catastrophes befalling them, an abundance of clouds, rains, thunder, lightning, and fog, and the dryness of the air. 14 And if her latitude was northern, she indicates the fine mixture of the air. 15 But if it was southern, she indicates the jumbled mixture of the air. 16 And if she was distanced [from the Sun] by her greatest distance, she indicates the appearance of safety and good in the people. 17 But if she was retrograde, she indicates the descent of cold, with an abundance of thunder and lightning. 18 And if she appeared [from under the rays] in it, she indicates an abundance of grasses, the fertility of the earth, the safety of vineyards, an abundance of delight, pleasure, cleanliness, tranquility, and amusement in the people. 19 And if she was under the rays, she indicates sorrows and anxieties befalling kings.

♀♊ 20 And if she was parallel with the sign of Gemini, that indicates the moisture of the air, and its corruption. 21 And if her latitude was northern, she indicates the blowing of winds. 22 But if it was southern, she indicates the dryness of the air. 23 And if she was distanced [from the Sun] by her greatest distance, she indicates catastrophes befalling secretaries, as well as distresses and sorrows. 24 And if she was retrograde, she indicates the hotness of the air, and its dryness. 25 And if she was under the rays, that indicates irritation befalling some of the people, as well as alarm. 26 And if she appeared [from under the rays] in it, she indicates fornication, an abundance of debauchery, the moisture of the winter, copious winds, and the abundant propagation of birds.

♀♋ 27 And if she was parallel with the sign of Cancer, she indicates the fine mixture of the air and the abundant blowing of the winds. 28 And if her latitude was northern, she indicates the intensity of the heat. 29 But if it was southern, she indicates the same thing. 30 And if she was distanced [from the Sun] by her greatest distance, she indicates a catastrophe befalling kings or some of the nobles, with the movement of armies. 31 Now if she was retrograde, she indicates catastrophes befalling some of the women of kings. 32 And if she was under the rays, she indicates the harsh demands for the land-tax. 33 And if she appeared [from under the rays] in it, she indicates an increase of water, the flooding of *wadīs*, an abundance of rains, and the safety of the crops, produce, and trees.

♀♌ 34 And if she was parallel with the sign of Leo, she indicates an abundance of illness from smallpox, and the heat of the air (and sometimes its fine mixture, [but] then that will be corrupted), with the scarce blowing of the winds. 35 And if her latitude was northern, she indicates the blowing of the winds, and their hotness. 36 But if it was southern, she indicates the fine mixture of the air. 37 And if she was distanced [from the Sun] by her greatest distance, she indicates that catastrophes will find kings or some of their women. 38 But if she was retrograde, she indicates irritation befalling kings, as well as sorrows and anxieties. 39 And if she was under the rays, she indicates catastrophes befalling the women of kings. 40 And if she appeared [from under the rays] in it, she indicates the abundant respect of kings and nobles, the suitability of the affairs of the authorities, the incidence of illnesses from hotness and moisture, with abundant rumors, wars, and an abundance of predatory animals.

♀♍ 41 And if she was parallel with the sign of Virgo, she indicates the fine mixture of the air, and sometimes it will incline to cold and dryness. 42 And if her latitude was northern, she indicates the fine mixture of the air. 43 But if it was southern, she indicates the same thing. 44 And if she was distanced [from the Sun] by her greatest distance, she indicates the death of nobles along with an abundance of illnesses befalling the people. 45 Now if she was retrograde, she indicates illnesses befalling women, especially in the autumn season. 46 And if she was under the rays, she indicates illnesses befalling women, especially in the autumn season. 47 And if she appeared [from under the rays] in it, she indicates an abundance of ailments and pains in women, with an abundance of alarm and fear in them, the abundant profit of businessmen, the elevation of the leaders of the *diwāns*[22] (and others), with the suitability of the fruits of trees, and the expensiveness of food.

♀♎ 48 And if she was parallel with the sign of Libra, she indicates the good health of people's bodies, with the fine mixture of the air (and its cold), and an abundance of rains. 49 And if her latitude was northern, she

---

[22] This refers to various kinds of administrative registers or bookkeeping (especially financial), or other administrative offices.

indicates the blowing of drying winds. **50** But if it was southern, she indicates illnesses from measles. **51** And if she was distanced [from the Sun] by her greatest distance, she indicates death befalling the women of kings, and the occurrence of derangement and powerful false rumors in the people. **52** And if she was retrograde, she indicates catastrophes befalling the women of kings. **53** And if she was under the rays, she indicates the illnesses of women. **54** And if she appeared [from under the rays] in it, she indicates the appearance of delight in the world, with bodies being safe from troubles, an abundance of birds, successive rains, the greening of lands, and the vigor of grasses.

♀♏ **55** And if she was parallel with the sign of Scorpio, that indicates the harshness of the cold, the abundant blowing of winds, and sometimes the fine mixture of the air. **56** And if her latitude was northern, she indicates the dryness of the air. **57** But if it was southern, she indicates an abundance of rains. **58** And if she was distanced [from the Sun] by her greatest distance, she indicates a catastrophe befalling the nobles, and the shedding of blood. **59** And if she was retrograde, she indicates excitement occurring in the people, with an abundance of false rumors. **60** And if she was under the rays, she indicates the scarce stability of leaders in matters, and their confusion. **61** And if she appeared [from under the rays] in it, she indicates troubles rushing to women, the intensity of the cold of winter, an abundance of rains, cold and snows, the swelling of rivers, and the safety of the growing of herbs.

♀♐ **62** And if she was parallel with the sign of Sagittarius, that indicates the fine mixture of the air, and sometimes it will incline to excess moisture and dryness. **63** And if her latitude was northern, she indicates the successive blowing of winds. **64** But if it was southern, she indicates the abundant alteration of the air, and its moisture. **65** And if she was distanced [from the Sun] by her greatest distance, she indicates illnesses befalling kings, and sometimes they will be miserable. **66** And if she was retrograde, she indicates envy and spite between the leaders. **67** And if she was under the rays, she indicates the death of some of the nobles. **68** But if she appeared [from under the rays] in it, she indicates the victory of kings, the duration of their delight, and their going far away with the rest of the mighty for amusement, and the backsliding of many of the pious from their piety, the suitable condition of riding animals, and an abundance of cultivation.

♀♑ 69 And if she was parallel with the sign of Capricorn, she indicates an abundance of extreme infectious disease, with a copious amount of rains, and sometimes the fine mixture of the air. 70 And if her latitude was northern, she indicates the abundant blowing of the winds. 71 But if it was southern, she indicates an abundance of rains. 72 And if she was distanced [from the Sun] by her greatest distance, she indicates a catastrophe befalling some of the nobles, especially those advanced in age (and sometimes that will be some of the administrators of kings), and the elevation of the status of slaves and the rabble. 73 And if she was retrograde, she indicates sorrows befalling the people, and anxieties. 74 Now if she was under the rays, she indicates illnesses befalling those who are aged among the people. 75 And if she appeared [from under the rays] in it, she indicates the evenness of the year and its fertility, the cold of winter, the goodness of summer, the abundant animosity of women towards their husbands, abundant marriages among the elderly, and women's scarce delight in their husbands.

♀♒ 76 And if she was parallel with the sign of Aquarius, she indicates the fine mixture of the air, the successive blowing of the winds (and their benefit), along with an abundance of rains and fog. 77 And if her latitude was northern, she indicates drought and a scarcity of rains. 78 But if it was southern, she indicates an abundance of griefs.[23] 79 And if she was distanced [from the Sun] by her greatest distance, she indicates the abundant swelling and bursting of springs, along with the submersions which will befall ships on the sea. 80 And if she was retrograde, she indicates illnesses befalling the people from moistures. 81 And if she was under the rays, she indicates the safety of those sailing the sea and the scarce blowing of the winds. 82 And if she appeared [from under the rays] in it, she indicates an abundance of illnesses befalling the people from moisture and phlegm, and an abundance of rains, the raging of the winds, the flooding of *wadīs*, covering by fog, and the descent of ice, with an abundance of fertility.

---

[23] الغموم. But I suspect this should be الغيوم, "clouds, mists."

♀♓ 83 And if she was parallel with the sign of Pisces, she indicates excess moistures along with the intensity of the heat; and sometimes the fine mixture of the air. 84 And if her latitude was northern, she indicates the successive blowing of the winds. 85 But if it was southern, she indicates an abundance of rains. 86 And if she was distanced [from the Sun] by her greatest distance, she indicates a catastrophe coming to some of the [military] commanders and the nobles. 87 And if she was retrograde, she indicates derangement, confusion, false rumors, hardships, and terrors befalling the people. 88 And if she was under the rays, she indicates illnesses befalling the people. 89 And if she appeared [from under the rays] in it, she indicates the suitability of the year for women, and people taking advantage of it; and there will be beneficial rains, the evenness of the air, an abundance of aquatic animals (like fish and what resembles that).

90 Since we have completed what we wanted to explain, let us break off the discussion.

## Chapter V.5: On how to know the special property of the indications of Mercury, in the same way

**1** We[24] say that if he had the indications which we explained and he was relevant to the category of people, that indicates the occurrence of wars and civil unrest, the general public's disparagement of the leaders, and for these reasons death which is sudden will befall some of the people, and illnesses from fevers and vomiting, with the people's separating from the Sharī'ah and committing aggression, killing, captivity, and highway robbery. **2** And if his indication was for the category of beasts, and especially the kind which people use, it indicates that corruption and scarcity will occur in it. **3** And if his indication was for the airy element, that indicates a scarcity of rains, the intense blowing of the winds, and their abundant damage, along with the descent of lightning bolts. **4** And if his indication was for the earthy element, it indicates the corruption of produce by reason of fire, infestation, and locusts, and from the scattering which occurs to it from the winds. **5** And if his indication was for the watery element, that indicates the abundant, sudden submersion of ships on the seas because of the blowing of different, surging winds, and from the occurrence of lightning-bolts, and a decrease in waters will happen in rivers, and dryness in springs.

☿♈ **6** And as for his indication in terms of mixing with the sign of Aries during his parallelism with it, he is indicative of an abundance of death in women, youths, and children, a scarcity of fish with the successive blowing of intense, drying winds, an abundance of fog, the intensity of the heat, a copious amount of waters (and especially in the region of the west), and a scarcity of food and drinks. **7** And if his latitude was northern, that indicates the corruption of the air. **8** But if it was southern, it indicates the mixture of the air. **9** And if he was distanced [from the Sun] by his greatest distance, it indicates the stirring up of fighting in the people, the enemy's conquering most of the regions, and the death of some of the nobles. **10** And if he was retrograde, it indicates illnesses occurring from measles and smallpox. **11** And if he was under the rays, that indicates an abundance of illnesses. **12** And if he appeared [from under the rays] in it, it indicates the

---

[24] For this whole paragraph, see *Tet.* II.8 (Robbins pp. 187-89).

# BOOK V: EACH PLANET AS A TIME LORD, IN ALL SIGNS 255

occurrence of death in the region of the west, the scarce progeny of sheep, the expensiveness of food, an abundance of waters, and the corruption of pressed juice. **13** And if the Moon was there, it indicates an abundance of cultivation. **14** And if Mars and Venus were close to him, it indicates an abundance of wars in the region of the east, and pains of the eyes will befall the people.

♀♉ **15** And if he was parallel with the sign of Taurus, it indicates the occurrence of fighting between the people of the region of the east and the people of the region of the west, an abundance of pains in the eyes among the people of the east, an abundance of death in noble men, the intensity of the heat, the successive blowing of the winds, with the fine mixture of the air, the occurrence of corruption in food and drink, and a copious amount of waters. **16** And if his latitude was northern, it indicates the mixture of the air. **17** But if it was southern, it indicates its confusion. **18** And if he was distanced [from the Sun] by his greatest distance, it indicates the death of cattle. **19** And if he was retrograde, it indicates the fine mixture of the air. **20** And if he was under the rays, it indicates the occurrence of illness in livestock, and the corruption of pressed juices and olive trees. **21** And if he appeared [from under the rays] in it, it indicates wars occurring between the east and the west, and pains in the eyes will befall the people of the east, with an abundance of waters, the dearth of seeds (and their corruption), and a scarcity of pressed juices and olive trees. **22** And if Jupiter was there, it indicates the safety of the people and scarce death, with the existence of terrors befalling the people. **23** And if Mars and Venus were there, it indicates the abundance of wars and their intensity, and the occurrence of death in cattle, and the abundant corruption of olive trees and pressed juices. **24** And if Saturn was there, it indicates the abundant swelling of rivers, the moisture of the lands, the flourishing of the vegetation and grasses, with an abundance of insects.

♀♊ **25** And if he was parallel with the sign of Gemini, it indicates fighting occurring between the regions of the people of the east and north, and death befalling the nobles, an abundance of epidemics and death along with an abundance of terrors befalling the people, the fine mixture of the air, and an abundance of drinks. **26** And if his latitude was northern, it indicates the blowing of the winds and their hotness, and an abundance of *simooms*. **27** But if it was southern, it indicates the dryness of the air. **28** And if he was distanced [from the Sun] by his greatest distance, it indicates death befalling elevated viziers and secretaries, and an abundance of contagious disease befalling the people, with the illness of measles. **29** And if he was retrograde, it indicates that [the year] will not be successful in all of its affairs. **30** And if he was under the rays, it indicates an abundance of illnesses and their malignancy, with the intensity of the heat. **31** And if he appeared [from under the rays] in it, it indicates war and civil unrest in the region of the east, an abundance of killing and death in the region of north, with the occurrence of death among the mighty, the abundant occurrence of ice in the winter, the intense heat of the summer, the strength of food and oil, and an abundance of pressed juices and honey.

☿♋ **32** And if he was parallel with the sign of Cancer, that indicates fighting occurring in the region of the north or from the region of east and west, and death coming to the people, and the pains of abscesses and measles, with an abundance of winds and their coldness, the mixture of the air, a scarcity of food and drink, the corruption of the trees and produce, and especially in the region of the west. **33** And if his latitude was northern, that indicates the blowing of the winds and the abundance of the *simooms*. **34** But if it was southern, it indicates the same thing. **35** And if he was distanced [from the Sun] by his greatest distance, it indicates an abundance of false rumors and derangement in the people. **36** And if he was retrograde, it indicates the death of nobles. **37** And if he was under the rays, it indicates that sorrows will befall the people, with an abundance of heat. **38** And if he appeared [from under the rays], that indicates fighting occurring between the region of the west and south. **39** And if Mars and Venus were close to him, it indicates an abundance of killing occurring in the mighty among the people of the west, an abundance of sorrows and anxieties in the world, with terrors and much death occurring there. **40** And if the Moon was close to him, it indicates that death will multiply in those regions (and especially in the region of the west), food and oil will be scarce, and pressed juices will be dear.

☿♌ **41** And if he was parallel with the sign of Leo, it indicates an abundance of emaciation and pains befalling the people from coughing, pain in the belly and bladder, and an abundance of death (especially in the region of the west), with the downfall of nobles, the death of predatory animals, the scarce mixture of the air, the intensity of heat, scarce rains, the occurrence of corruption in trees, produce, and seeds, and a scarcity of food and drink. **42** And if his latitude was northern, that indicates the blowing of the winds, and their hotness. **43** But if it was southern, it indicates the fine mixture of the air. **44** And if he was distanced [from the Sun] by his greatest distance, it indicates death befalling the mighty among kings. **45** And if he was retrograde, it indicates an abundance of what comes to the people from sorrows, with confusions. **46** And if he was under the rays, it indicates the heat of the air, and its tranquility. **47** And if he appeared [from under the rays] in it, it indicates that ailments, contagious disease, and pains will find the people of the region of the east, and the heat will intensify, rains will be scarce, and it will be feared for the produce, and food will be scarce, as well as pressed juices and oil. **48** And if Mars was there, pressed juices will be fine. **49** And if Venus was there, evil will befall the people. **50** And if Saturn, Mars, Venus, and the fortunes were in his proximity,²⁵ it indicates intense drought, and a scarcity of honey and sugar cane.

☿♍   **51** And if he was parallel with the sign of Virgo, that indicates an abundance of pains (and especially in the eyes), the occurrence of tribulation in the region of the south, with a copious amount of rains, the intensity of the heat and *simooms* (and sometimes the fine mixture of the air) and an abundance of food and drink. **52** And if his latitude was northern, it indicates the dryness of the air. **53** But if it was southern, it indicates the fine mixture of the air. **54** And if he was distanced [from the Sun] by his greatest distance, it indicates the downfall of some of the nobles, and illness befalling the people. **55** And if he was retrograde, it indicates an abundance of false rumors, and derangement. **56** But if he was under the rays, it indicates illness befalling kings, with the ruin of some of the women of nobles. **57** And if he appeared [from under the rays], it indicates that skin eruptions and pain of the eyes will befall the people, and death will be abundant in the region of the south, with an abundance of rains, the lowered price of food, the safety of the seeds, and an abundance of pressed juice and oil. **58** And if Mars was close to him, it indicates war occurring in the region of the west, and pains in

---

²⁵ Reading the more obvious قربه for the text's غربه ("in his west").

their backs will affect the people, riding animals will perish, and the king will become strong.

☿♎ 59 And if he was parallel with Libra, that indicates an abundance of winds and their intensity, with a scarcity of food and drink, and the moisture of the air (and sometimes dryness will occur in it). 60 And if his latitude was northern, it indicates a scarcity of moistures, and an abundance of sterile clouds. 61 But if it was southern, it indicates the corrupt mixture of the air. 62 And if he was distanced [from the Sun] by his greatest distance, it indicates confusions befalling some of the general public (and sometimes they will benefit for some of those reasons). 63 And if he was retrograde, it indicates the same thing. 64 And if he was under the rays, it indicates illnesses coming to the people, along with the alteration of the air. 65 And if he appeared [from under the Sun] in it, it indicates the intense blowing of the winds, and the dearth of food and pressed juices. 66 And if Saturn was close to him, it indicates that pains of the eyes will befall the people. 67 And if Venus was close to him, wars will occur in the west, and some of them will kill each other. 68 And if Mars was close to him, that indicates abundant death befalling the people in the region of the west.

☿♏ 69 And if he was parallel with the sign of Scorpio, that indicates an abundance of fighting occurring in the region of the west and north, the occurrence of snows, a copious amount of rains, the intensity of the cold, the tranquility of the winds, and sometimes the fine mixture of the air. 70 And if his latitude was northern, it indicates the dryness of the air. 71 But if it was southern, it indicates its fine mixture. 72 And if he was distanced [from the Sun] by his greatest distance, it indicates many bad reports and false rumors, and the intensity of fighting. 73 And if he was retrograde, it indicates confusion befalling the soldiers. 74 And if he was under the rays, it indicates sorrows befalling kings, and anxieties coming to the nobles, hindrances in matters, and inquiries into them. 75 And if his appearance [from under the rays] was in Scorpio, that is an indicator that pains will befall the people from much coldness, and pain in the ears and eyes, an abundance of snows and rains, a dearth of water in rivers, an abundance of fighting in the region of the south, along with the corruption of the sown crops, the scorching of the grasses from the cold, and drought befalling the people of the west.

**76** And if Venus was with Mars,[26] the rain will be scarce, and snow and ice will be abundant. **77** And if the Moon was close to him, it indicates safety and a scarcity of death. **78** And if Saturn was close to Mercury, that is an indicator of the occurrence of death in many of the people, along with excessive rains in the region of the south.

**79** And if he was parallel with the sign of Sagittarius, it indicates the suitable condition of kings, the occurrence of tribulation in the region of the west, the existence of war between them and the people of the region of the south, an abundance of selling and buying, with a scarcity of rains, the occurrence of snows, the fine mixture of the air, scarcity will happen in food, and abundance in drink. **80** And if his latitude was northern, it indicates the blowing of raging winds. **81** But if it was southern, it indicates the alteration of the air and its fine mixture. **82** And if he was distanced [from the Sun] by his greatest distance, it indicates the death of some kings or famous commanders. **83** But if he was retrograde, it indicates tribulation happening in the region of Jibāl. **84** And if he entered under the rays, it indicates the soundness of the people's bodies, the calmness and tranquility of the soldiers, with harm coming to the nobles, and an abundance of wrong against them. **85** And if he appeared [from under the rays] in it, it indicates the stirring up of civil unrest in the land of the west, intense pain in the eyes and ears, the intensity of the cold in the year, the occurrence of snow and ice, a scarcity of rains, crops, cultivation, vegetation, and an abundance of pressed juices.

**86** And if he was parallel with the sign of Capricorn, that indicates the existence of fighting and evil which will be in the region of the east, with illness and death befalling youths, an abundance of rains, corruption occurring in the mixture of the air, its inclining to dryness, the abundant blowing of the eastern winds, an abundance of milk and honey, and an abundance of food. **87** And if his latitude was northern, it indicates the fine mixture of the air. **88** But if it was southern, it indicates the same thing. **89** And if he was distanced [from the Sun] by his greatest distance, it indicates the existence of infectious disease and death befalling women and the nobles. **90** Now if he was retrograde, that will be praiseworthy for those sailing

---

[26] This should rather read, "If Venus and Mars were close to him...".

the sea. **91** And if he was under the rays, that indicates the use of leisure and free time, with the strengthening of effective affairs. **92** And if he appeared [from under the rays], it indicates an abundance of civil unrest in the region of the east, the abundance of the people's illnesses from fever and heat, the occurrence of death in children and youths, and the appearance of a portent in the Sun, a scarcity of rains, a dearth of milk and honey, and an abundance of food, pressed juices, and oil. **93** And if Jupiter was close to him, it indicates a scarcity of fighting and death. **94** And if Mars was close to him, it indicates a scarcity of rains in the region of the east. **95** And if Venus was close to him, most of the devastation will be in the region of the north, with the hardship of what comes to them from being besieged.

☿♒ **96** And if he was parallel with the sign of Aquarius, that indicates the intensity of heat, with the fine mixture of the air, and the successive blowing of the winds. **97** And if his latitude was northern, it indicates the dryness of the air. **98** But if it was southern, it indicates an abundance of sterile clouds. **99** And if he was distanced [from the Sun] by his greatest distance, it indicates death occurring in the aged among the nobles and authorities. **100** And if he was retrograde, it indicates abundant illnesses befalling the people. **101** And if he was under the rays, it indicates the scarce travels of the people, and their benefiting from that. **102** And if he appeared [from under the rays] in it, that indicates terrors and fears occurring in the people, and jaundice will find most of them, with a scarcity of rains, a dearth of food, and an abundance of locusts. **103** And if Venus was close to him, skin eruptions and fevers will befall the people, and the occurrence of terror in most of the regions, and troubles in the air will appear, and death will envelop most of the people of the regions, and a portent will appear in the Moon. **104** And if Saturn was close to him, it indicates an abundance of rains, the terror of kings, and fears and harms entering upon the world.

☿♓ **105** And if he was parallel with the sign of Pisces, that indicates the occurrence of death in the region of the south, an abundance of venomous creatures and fish, with the abundant blowing of the winds (and their coldness), the fine mixture of the air, and sometimes inclining towards dryness, with an abundance of waters. **106** And if his latitude was northern, it indicates the successive blowing of the winds, and their moisture. **107** But if it was southern, it indicates the mixture of the air. **108** And if he was distanced [from the Sun] by his greatest distance, it indicates the abundant submersions of ships on the seas and rivers. **109** And if he was retrograde, it indicates harm occurring to the nobles and the masters of authority. **110** And if he was under the rays, it indicates an abundance of rains and thunder. **111** And if he appeared [from under the rays] in it, it indicates an abundance of death in the region of the south, an abundance of waters and the swelling of rivers, and the blowing of the winds. **112** And if Jupiter was close to the Sun, it indicates an abundance of death, and the land's bringing out its flowers and their benefits, an abundance of truffles, the cheapness of food, pressed juices, and oil, and the year will have much good, fertility, and many of the people will desire the good, uprightness, commanding what is good, and prohibiting what is forbidden.

**113** Since we have completed what we wanted to explain, let us break off the chapter.

## Chapter V.6: On how to know the special properties of the indications of the Moon, in the same way

**1** Since we have already set forth in Chapter V.5 the knowledge of the quality of Mercury's indications, in this chapter let us state the indications of the Moon.

**2** We say that if she had the indications which we explained, and she was relevant to the category of people, that indicates fighting occurring between kings and the general public, an abundance of evil in the people, the appearance of robbers, diminishment in all of the cities, an abundance of distresses which will befall kings because of the conflict of the soldiers with them, and their scarce benefit due to the abundant appearance of dishonesty to them, with the recalcitrance of Rūm, the Arabs combating the people of Persia, and abundant harm from predatory animals. **3** Now if her indication was for the category of beasts (and especially those which people use), it indicates the occurrence of death in them. **4** And if her indication was for the airy element, it indicates an abundance of rains. **5** And if her indication was for the watery element, it indicates an abundance of waters and swells. **6** And if her indication was for the earthy element, that indicates the corruption of trees because of swelling [waters].

☽♈ **7** Now[27] as for her indication in the sense of her mixture with the sign of Aries during her parallelism with it, she indicates the swelling of rivers and a decrease of food. **8** And if she appeared [from under the rays] in it, it indicates the appearance of joy, delight, and the good in the world, the release of many people from confinements, the escape of the mighty and the nobles from hardships, and the good favor of kings, along with harm to livestock.

---

[27] In the following interpretations, the second sentence always has the Moon appearing from under the rays, which suggests that the first sentence always has her under the rays. And this especially makes sense if Abū Ma'shar is thinking of the revolutions of months, since she might be under the rays in any of the months. But perhaps these interpretations actually derive from the use of conjunctional and oppositional charts *before* the Sun's ingresses. In that case, the first sentence refers to the Moon's position at the opposition, and the second to her position at the Sun-Moon conjunction (or, where she will be when at 12° from the exact conjunction).

☽♉ 9 And if she was parallel with the sign of Taurus, it indicates an abundance of sorrows, fighting, mildew, drought, and pains befalling the people, with harm coming to the people, and an abundance of rains, the intensity of the cold, and a decrease in food, drink, and produce. 10 And if she appeared [from under the rays] in it, it indicates the fine thoughts of the people, the intensification of their delight and joy in women, an abundance of cattle, the safety of the crops, and an abundance of grasses.

☽♊ 11 And if she was parallel with the sign of Gemini, that indicates an abundance of contagious disease befalling the people, illnesses, and epidemics, with a copious amount of rains, and corruption befalling drinks. 12 And if she appeared [from under the rays] in it, it indicates that melancholic ailments like insanity and obsession[28] will befall the people, with a scarcity of infectious disease, the safety of birds from illness, and the blowing of winds with a bad mixture, along with the intensity of the cold of winter.

☽♋ 13 And if she was parallel with the sign of Cancer, it indicates that movement and travels will befall the king, and the subjects will rejoice in that, and sometimes new rulership will come to a man (fear of whom will intensify), along with drought, hunger befalling the people and a scarcity of rains. 14 And if she appeared [from under the rays] in it, it indicates the safety of those sailing the seas from being submerged, fearful things of the water, an abundance of waters and fish, and the safety of the crops.

☽♌ 15 And if she was parallel with the sign of Leo, it indicates new rulership, and the king will transfer from country to country, along with the suitability of the subjects with him, the abundant perishing of riding animals, and the suitable condition of the produce. 16 And if she appeared [from under the rays] in it, it indicates kings' squandering of assets, with the abundant profits of the general public, and many of the people whose condition had been weak having their needs met, and the liberation of most of them from difficulty.

☽♍ 17 And if she was parallel with the sign of Virgo, that indicates the safety of animals and people, with the cheapness of riding ani-

---

[28] الوسواس. This has connotations of temptation, wickedness, and suspicion, and anxiety.

mals, and an abundance of rains, food, drink, produce, and seeds. **18** And if she appeared [from under the rays] in it, she indicates the easiness of childbirth for pregnant women, and the frequent marrying of virgin women, with the fine condition of secretaries and businessmen, the safety of the trees, and a scarcity of food.

☽♎  **19** And if she was parallel with the sign of Libra, that indicates the occurrence of fighting among the leaders, and confusion in the countries, and fear, death, and sorrow befalling the people, an abundance of civil unrest, the occurrence of locusts, and a decrease in drinks, along with troubles happening in the food. **20** And if she appeared [from under the rays] in it, it indicates the authorities' use of fairness, and the focus of their allies and the rest of the mighty on marriage and clothing, and swelling occurring from blood and winds will befall the people, along with the abundant blowing of the winds, the intensity of the cold, and the evenness of the summer.

☽♏  **21** And if she was parallel with the sign of Scorpio, it indicates an abundance of contentions and confusion, death and lawsuits, civil unrest, and wars befalling the people, along with the scarcity of the water of springs. **22** And if she appeared [from under the rays] in it, it indicates an abundance of waters, delight, the flooding of *wadīs*, and that doing damage to the people, along with an abundance of harmful rains ruining the crops and the seeds.

☽♐  **23** And if she was parallel with the sign of Sagittarius, that indicates the perplexity of kings, the suitable condition of the nobles, and disasters befalling wrongdoers among the people, and illnesses, killing, and diminishment of all the animals, harm will come to birds and the food, and the crops will be corrupted. **24** And if she appeared [from under the rays] in it, it indicates the recalcitrance of robbers, the respect for the mighty, the suitable condition of kings and authorities, and the fine condition of riding animals.

☽♑  **25** And if she was parallel with the sign of Capricorn, that indicates the cheapness of prices, and the suitability of drinks and oils. **26** And if she appeared [from under the rays] in it, it indicates the animosity of women towards their husbands (and the divorce of many of them), with the safety of the crops, an abundance of grasses and the offspring of sheep, and people's benefiting from the vegetation.

☽♒ 27 And if she was parallel with the sign of Aquarius, that indicates the incidence of contagious disease in the people, an abundance of locusts and harms to the yield and the arable land. 28 And if she appeared [from under the rays] in it, that indicates the scarce profits of the general public, the low condition of businessmen, the occurrence of illnesses, ailments, and death in the rest of the people, with an abundance of rains, the blowing of winds, and the intensification of the cold.

☽♓ 29 And if she was parallel with the sign of Pisces, that indicates illnesses befalling the people (and their safety from them), their fertility, the corrupt condition of birds, the abundance of rains, and the cheapness of prices. 30 And if she appeared [from under the rays] in it, it indicates the swelling of waters, abundant floods and rains, the intensification of the cold, and the occurrence of snows and ice.

31 Since we have completed what we wanted to explain, let us break off the chapter.

## Chapter V.7: On how to know the indications of the two Nodes (the northern & southern) & the appearance of the tailed stars, during their parallelism with all of the signs, in the sense of mixture

**1** Since we have already set forth in Chapter V.6 how to know the special property of the indications of the Moon by herself and during her parallelism with all of the signs in the sense of mixture, let us state in this chapter the indications of the Nodes and the tailed stars[29] during their parallelism with all of the signs, since they lack the distinctive properties for indications by themselves (as the rest of the planets have, which we have stated before).

☋ ☊ ♈ **2** We say that if the northern Node was parallel with the sign of Aries, that indicates the elevation of the nobles and leaders above where they had been,[30] along with the death of some of the kings, the alteration of matters, and the occurrence of a [new] king.

**3** And if the southern Node was parallel with it, that indicates the authorities' and kings' doing violence to the subjects, the abundant contrariety of the subjects towards them, with the elevation of people among the underclass, the riffraff, and the wretched from their [former] status, and their shunning of the rulers' command, and sometimes poverty and deception will come to them in matters, and their difficulty, and the death of cattle, sheep, and camels.

**4** And if one of the tailed stars appeared parallel with it, that indicates disasters befalling the king of Babylon, and civil unrest with the occurrence of rancor and wars between the king of Persia and the rest of the kings, the occurrence of wars between the Greeks and the Berbers, the fighting of the people of Italy against the people of Alexandria, the display of arms by Rūm, terrors befalling the people of Persia and the people of Syria (and the abundant shedding of blood for those reasons), and tribulation will find the king of Rūm, and turmoil in his rulership, along with disaster befalling the people of the Turks, and intense drought and pains of the eyes as well as the death of cattle there, the ruin of the mighty, the elevation of the evil and the underclass, an abundance of metals (of gold and silver), and an excess of heat in

---

[29] That is, comets.
[30] ارتفاع...فوق ما عليه.

the summer quarter. **5** And if its appearance was from the direction of the east and the Sun in parallel with the sign of Aries, that indicates the occurrence of rancor between the people of Persia and the submission of most of the countries to the king of Babylon. **6** But if its appearance was from the region of the west, it indicates that detestable things will come to most of the mighty from kings, with disasters and killing befalling the people of the region of the west, an abundance of rains, the swelling of rivers, and the occurrence of snows.

**7** And if the northern Node was parallel with the sign of Taurus, that indicates that that year will be safe from troubles, full of meadows, with moist earth, blooming meadows, preserving the life of grazing animals, sustaining the people and livestock.

**8** And if the southern Node was parallel with it, that indicates the difficult condition of the people, an abundance of *simooms* or hot dusty winds scorching the produce and grasses (and especially in the summer quarter), along with an excess of cold in the winter quarter.

**9** And if one of the tailed stars appeared parallel with it, that indicates the occurrence of civil unrest and false rumors in the land of Rūm, and harsh ailments will befall the people of Babylon (and food will be scarce in it), Ctesiphon will be fertile, tribulation will affect the people of Italy, captivity and hostility will occur among them, and hardship and contagious disease will come to them, and they will do wrong to each other in [the relations] between them, and dry pains like mange and itching will affect the people, and there will be the death of cattle, a disruption in [the production of] metals, and the devastation of some of the land of the mountains,[31] along with the intensity of the cold and the corruption of the sowing there, the scattering of what trees bear, and a scarcity of cultivation and planting in the earth. **10** Now if its appearance was from the region of the east and the Sun is parallel with the sign of Taurus, that indicates the king's fear of his enemies, the occurrence of epidemics in the people (and the duration of that through successive years) along with an abundance of illnesses befalling the people in the summer quarter, and an abundance of death occurring in sheep. **11** But if

---

[31] الجبل. But one would expect الجبال, Jibāl.

its appearance was from the region of the west, it indicates an abundance of rains.

☊♊ **12** And if the northern Node was parallel with the sign of Gemini, that indicates a scarcity of illnesses, the serenity of the air and its moisture, with the good blowing of the winds.

**13** And if the southern Node was parallel with it, it indicates fighting, wars, hunger, difficulty, illnesses, terrors, and fatal infectious disease ruinous to the people.

**14** And if one of the tailed stars appeared parallel with it, it indicates that harsh, detestable things and hardships will come to the king of Rūm, along with troubles befalling the king of Egypt, leading him to death (and his death being for those reasons), and a man not of the family of the king will rule Egypt, along with the occurrence of much illness, death, contagious illness, hunger, the death of children, the miscarriage of pregnant women, the death of birds, the severity of thunder and lightning, an abundance of *simooms*, and their burning the produce. **15** Now if its appearance was from the region of the east and the Sun parallel with the sign of Gemini, that indicates the downfall of many people of the mighty from their status, and the king's killing them, along with the occurrence of epidemics in most of the land of the Arabs. **16** But if its appearance was from the region of the west, that indicates an abundance of captivity and emigration in Persia and the Ahwāz, with an abundance of rains and swells.

☊♋ **17** And if the northern Node was parallel with the sign of Cancer, that indicates the abundant profits of businessmen, and their gaining benefit and much good from the seas, along with the cultivation of land, the moisture of the air, the evenness of rains in their own [proper] times, the scarce swelling of the rivers, and an abundance of fog.

**18** And if the southern Node was parallel with it, it indicates the submersion of ships and the people [on them], an abundance of disasters and troubles befalling the people, with the harm of the water and the expensiveness of fish.

**19** Now if one of the tailed stars appeared parallel with it, that indicates the existence of fighting, much evil, and death in the people, war and bloodshed, harm, submersion, destruction, and the sudden death of [some] people, with fighting occurring among the people of the Ahwāz and their pouncing upon one of their leaders (such as the sons of their kings and what resembles that), and their killing them; then a good king will follow them and die; and it indicates an abundance of rains and a scarcity of fish. **20** And if its appearance was from the region of the east and the Sun was parallel with the sign of Cancer, that indicates anxieties happening in the people, with their scarce obedience to the king, and the cheapness of prices at the end of the year. **21** But if its appearance was from the region of the west, it indicates the occurrence of evil between kings, and some of them setting out against others, and their reconciliation after that.

☊♋ **22** And if the northern Node was parallel with the sign of Leo, that indicates the triumph of the king over his enemies, and his respect and rule, the safety of his body, his abundant delight and scarce anxieties and sorrows, and the suitable condition of his subjects.

**23** And if the southern Node was parallel with it, it indicates that death will be feared for the king, and the underclass, the mob, and the riffraff will pounce upon him, and ruinous pains will afflict [him], and his enemies will triumph over him, and his delight will be scarce.

**24** And if one of the tailed stars appeared parallel with it, that indicates fighting taking place between kings (and especially of Babylon), and some of those will triumph over others, and that will be at the end of the year, with an abundance of wars and bloodshed in the region of the east, and the death of some of the nobles, and sometimes constipation[32] will befall the people, and pains of the belly, with the occurrence of fever in predatory animals, and rabies in dogs. **25** And if its appearance was from the region of the east and the Sun parallel with the sign of Leo, that indicates an abundance of confusions, the occurrence of drought and emigration in the land of the west. **26** But if its appearance was from the region of the west, that indicates many illnesses, and the occurrence of emigration in the region of the north, with the harm of predatory animals and dogs contracting rabies.

☊♍ **27** And if the northern Node was parallel with the sign of Virgo, that indicates kings' making agreements, the incitement[33] of the masters of landed estates, the planting of date palms and trees in them,

---

[32] Or, retention of urine (الحُسر).

[33] حرض. But perhaps this should be حرص, "desire, greed."

their competition for them, the prevalence of good, uprightness, and comfort for all of the people, with the safety of grasses, produce, and grains.

**28** And if the southern Node was parallel with it, that indicates the occurrence of death in livestock, and the year will be barren, dry, with the intensity of cold ruinous for grasses, vegetation, and produce, a scarcity of the herbiage, and the burning of sown crops.

**29** And if one of the tailed stars appeared parallel with it, it indicates an enemy's capture of one of the sons of kings, or one who is within their borders, with the appearance of injustice and wrong, the frequency of what afflicts the people from the pains of shivering fevers, and winds will befall women in their lower parts, and an abundance of abscesses, pustules, and the miscarriage of pregnant women. **30** Now if its appearance was from the region of the east and the Sun parallel with the sign of Virgo, that indicates fighting befalling the people of Persia with the Ahwāz, and their triumphing over them, and the occurrence of rancor between them. **31** But if its appearance was from the region of the west, that indicates fighting befalling the people of Babylon, with an abundance of produce.

☊♉︎♎︎ **32** And if the northern Node was parallel with the sign of Libra, that indicates an abundance of delight, joy, good, and comfortable living in the people, with the nobility of women and the elevation of their importance, the desire of men for [women], the suitable condition of bodies, and people among the subjects making themselves leaders, with an abundance of birds.

**33** And if the southern Node was parallel with it, that indicates the abundant shedding of blood and fatal pains which befall the people, like inflammation of the lung, epidemics, and bad ailments.

**34** And if one of the tailed stars appeared parallel with it, that indicates the anger of the king of Babylon and the harshness of his injustice, the death of some of the kings of the region of the west, the abundant occurrence of death in the leaders and nobles, the shedding of blood, the appearance of death and the interruption of businesses, with a scarcity of rains, an abundance of serene weather, the raging of winds, the dryness of rivers, a scarcity of vegetation, and the corruption of produce. **35** And if its appearance was from the direction of the region of the east and the Sun parallel with the sign of Libra, that indicates an abundance of troubles befalling the king of Babylon, the occurrence of epidemics among them, the perishing of horses and camels, with civil unrest befalling the land of Rūm, and their fighting one another, and harm will come to the people of Mosul. **36** But if its appearance was from the region of the west, that indicates the warring of the people of the Ahwāz against the people of Babylon, the death of some of the kings, the contrariety of slaves against their masters and their scarce obedience, with a middling amount of rain.

☊ ☋ ♏ **37** And if the northern Node was parallel with the sign of Scorpio, that indicates the occurrence of rancor and war between the Arabs, and some of them raiding others, their seeking leadership and victory, and their use of wrong, injustice, and subjugation, along with an abundance of locusts.

**38** And if the southern Node was parallel with it, that indicates an abundance of confusions, disturbance, civil unrest, the Arabs' highway banditry, the blocking of roads (and an abundance of bloodshed for those reasons), and difficulty and detestable things will come to the general public for that reason.

**39** Now if one of the tailed stars appeared parallel with it, that indicates pains of the testicles,[34] bladder, and backs befalling the people, along with rancor befalling kings, their hatred of each other, and detestable things will come to women because of childbirth, and it indicates an abundance of harmful rains, the ruin of the produce from the harshness of the ice and cold, with the darkness of the air and its moisture, a scarcity of waters, the dryness of rivers, and a scarcity of fish. **40** And if its appearance was from the region of the east and the Sun parallel with the sign of Scorpio, that indicates the safety of the people of Babylon and a scarcity of death among them, and that will last for about six years, with the harm of predatory animals and rabies in dogs. **41** But if its appearance was from the region of the west, that indicates the appearance of locusts with a scarcity of their harm.

☊ ☋ ♐ **42** And if the northern Node was parallel with the sign of Sagittarius, that indicates the kings' transferring from country to

---

[34] Reading with **BY** for المذاكر.

country, the lowness of some of the kings and the downfall from their rank in status, with the insignificance of the nobles, the lowness of some of the commanders and soldiers, and their ruin for that reason.

**43** And if the southern Node was parallel with it, that indicates the elevation of the underclass, the respect of the riffraff and disreputable people, the victory of slaves over the ranks of commanders along with their seizure of the ports, their involvement in mighty affairs, and their equality with the leaders in importance and rank, with the ruin of riding animals.

**44** Now if one of the tailed stars appeared parallel with it, that indicates the harshness of the king towards the general public, and his eagerness to collect assets, the lowness of the people and their taking [things] by illegal force, injustice, and wrong, with death befalling the nobles from Isfahān and Jurjān, and drought and death will come to the people of Fārs as well as the ruin of some children of their king, the perishing of riding animals in most of the regions, the intensity of the heat, and the scarce bearing [of fruit] in palms. **45** And if its appearance was from the region of the east and the Sun parallel with the sign of Sagittarius, that indicates the death of kings, the harshness of their illnesses (and that will last for three months), with the appearance of fighting, fear, robbery, people of malice in most of the regions, and the suitability of crops and produce. **46** But if its appearance was from the region of the west, that indicates the abundance of what is suggested to the people in their dreams, with the miscarriage of pregnant women.

**47** And if the northern Node was parallel with the sign of Capricorn, that indicates the suitability of the year, the abundant digging up of metals, the evenness of the air of summer and winter, with the expensiveness of prices, an abundance of grasses, the safety of the sowing, and a scarcity of snow.

**48** And if the southern Node was parallel with it, it indicates poverty, need, difficulty, and an abundance of earthquakes, burning, and devastation occurring because of that.

**49** Now if one of the tailed stars appeared parallel with it, that indicates the occurrence of war between kings, an abundance of tribulation befalling the people of the region of the west due to their king, the occurrence of evil, fear, and false rumors in the region of Fārs, the Ahwāz, Dastī-Maysān, and the people of the south, with an abundance of insanity and obsession befalling the people, the harshness of the situation (and especially in the region of Jibāl), the blocking of roads and the appearance of robbery (and its strength), the insignificance of the people of asceticism, religion, and piety, with the occurrence of death in upright people, the abundant descent of the cold and snows, and its spoiling the vegetation (especially saffron). **50** Now if it appeared from the region of the east and the Sun parallel with the sign of Capricorn, that indicates disasters befalling one of the kings from his enemies, which will be a reason for his ruin and the new rulership of some of the mighty, with an abundance of snows and rains, and the safety of vineyards and the produce. **51** But if it appeared from the region of the west, that indicates the fertility of the year and an abundance of waters.

**52** And if the northern Node was parallel with the sign of Aquarius, it indicates the fine conditions of the general public, the enlargement of their lifestyles, the soundness of their bodies, a scarcity of agriculture and stock farming, the duration of the rains, and the successive blowing of the rains (and their evenness).

**53** And if the southern Node was parallel with it, that indicates an abundance of killing and civil unrest, with troubles befalling snakes, scorpions, and some wild animals.

**54** Now if one of the tailed stars appeared parallel with it, it indicates the death of a king of the region of the east, the setting out of men seeking the rulership, the appearance of disagreement between leaders for those reasons, an abundance of death, epidemics, leprosy, killing, and fighting in the region of the land of the west (and the duration of that for a long time) with darkness occurring in the atmosphere, an abundance of thunder, lightning, and lightning bolts, the ruin of most of the people for those reasons, a scarcity of birds and fish, and the cheapness of prices. **55** Now if its appearance was from the region of the east and the Sun parallel with the sign of Aquarius, that indicates an abundance of fertility. **56** But if its appearance was from the region of the west, that indicates an abundance of false rumors in the land of Persia and the region of Jibāl, and seizing the king's weapons, abundant devastation in the land of the Sawād, and the proceeds from sown crops.

**57** And if the northern Node was parallel with the sign of Pisces, that indicates the people's benefiting from an abundance of waters, the swelling of rivers, and catching fish.

**58** And if the southern Node was parallel with it, it indicates an abundance of submersion befalling the people, the corruption of crops, the death of fish, and an abundance of snows, cold, and ice.

**59** And if one of the tailed stars appeared parallel with it, that indicates the ruin of one of the nations, with an abundance of killing among the leaders of the people of the Sawād and the Copts, and that will be because of religion; and marvelous things will appear, a king will go out of his own accord and burn cities, and [business] associations will be bad for the people, ascetics will fight with each other, and disagreement, disturbances, and tribulation will multiply in the people, poverty and something detestable will appear, death will occur in fish, and the use-benefits of waters will be cut off. **60** And if its appearance was from the region of the east and the Sun parallel with the sign of Pisces, that indicates the harsh contrariety of the commanders and cavalry towards the king, and taking their hands away from obedience, and appropriating some of the king's assets, fear will multiply in most of the climes, and tribulation will happen in Fārs, with a copious amount of rains. **61** But if its appearance was from the direction of the west, that indicates an abundance of the people's anxieties, the occurrence of epidemics and death in most of the climes (especially in the land of the west), the intensity of the dire straits, difficulty, and perplexity (and the duration of that for about three years), and harms and sorrows will befall the people along with an abundance of birds and fish, and the swelling of rivers.

### [Comets in the Ascendants or with their lords]

**62** And when the appearance of one of the tailed stars is in the Ascendants of the roots of the nativities of kings,[35] or the signs of the terminal points, or in the Ascendants of revolutions, or the signs of the distribution (and especially in the bound itself), or it was with the lords of one of them, that indicates an abundance of hardships and wars happening, and that will be because of rebels [attacking] them, and their outrages and wrong towards the people will multiply; and sometimes it indicates their being killed. **63**

---

[35] This must mean that a comet *now* (or, at the revolution) appears in a sign which *was* the Ascendant of some king's nativity.

Now if the native was of the middle [class] of the people, or of the underclass, it indicates the abundance of their enemies and the detestable things which befall them, and tribulation for those reasons.

**64** Since we have completed what we wanted to explain, let us break off the discussion, with the aid of God and His support. **65** Book V is complete, and much praise to God!

# BOOK VI: [THE PLANETS' TRANSITS OVER EACH OTHER, IN ALL SIGNS]

On how to know the special property of lower events from the influences of the upper bodies in the revolutions of years, from the transits of the planets proceeding above one another[1]

*And it is in 12 Chapters:*

**1** Chapter VI.1: On judging the transits of the planets above one another during their parallelism with the sign of Aries.

**2** Chapter VI.2: On judging the transits of the planets above one another during their parallelism with the sign of Taurus.

**3** Chapter VI.3: On judging the transits of the planets above one another during their parallelism with the sign of Gemini.

**4** Chapter VI.4: On judging the transits of the planets above one another during their parallelism with the sign of Cancer.

**5** Chapter VI.5: On judging the transits of the planets above one another during their parallelism with the sign of Leo.

**6** Chapter VI.6: On judging the transits of the planets above one another during their parallelism with the sign of Virgo.

**7** Chapter VI.7: On judging the transits of the planets above one another during their parallelism with the sign of Libra.

**8** Chapter VI.8: On judging the transits of the planets above one another during their parallelism with the sign of Scorpio.

**9** Chapter VI.9: On judging the transits of the planets above one another during their parallelism with the sign of Sagittarius.

**10** Chapter VI.10: On judging the transits of the planets above one another during their parallelism with the sign of Capricorn.

**11** Chapter VI.11: On judging the transits of the planets above one another during their parallelism with the sign of Aquarius.

---

[1] Omitting the prior pious opening: "*In the name of God the Merciful, the Compassionate, and may God bless His prophets.*"

**12** Chapter VI.12: On judging the transits of the planets above one another during their parallelism with the sign of Pisces.

## Chapter VI.1: On judging the transits of the planets above one another during their parallelism with the sign of Aries

**1** Since we have completed in Book V what we wanted to explain about how to know the special property of the indications of the planets by themselves and [in] combination with all of the signs, in this Book let us state how to know the indications of the higher bodies for lower events from the method of the planets' transits over each other at the revolutions of years, since that is one of the things which complete what we have attempted to show about how to know the indications of the conjunctions in this book of ours, by the will of God and His aid.

**2** We say that there is no body in the sphere but that it is higher than the one which follows it in rank. **3** And indeed, one uses the traversing of one over another in the sense that when one of them conjoins with the other and they are equivalent in longitude and latitude, and ascent and descent and evenness,[2] that is the reason for the lower one eclipsing the higher one: and that is one of the fundamental things announcing lower events.

**4** Now as for how to know that for the superior planets and the luminaries, it is that one looks at the mean [position] of whichever of the two you want, and at its equated position. **5** For if [the equated position] is less than its mean one, it is ascending from the middle of its sector to the summit of its sphere. **6** And if its equated position is more than its mean, it is descending from the middle of its sector to the lowest point of its sphere. **7** And if its equated position and its mean one were equivalent in amount, it is in the middle of its sector. **8** Then, after understanding that, one subtracts the lesser of the two from its associate, and multiply what remains by 7, then divide by 22: what comes out from the division is the amount of its ascent or descent, in portions.

**9** As for Venus and Mercury, if one of them was eastern and its equated position was less than the equated position of the Sun, then they are both ascending from the middle of their sectors to the summit of their spheres. **10** And if its equated position was more than the [equated] position of the Sun

---

[2] Here "evenness" means that its position is exactly at the top or bottom of its deferent circle, rather than ascending or descending on either side. See my Introduction.

and it is western, then it is descending from the middle of its sector to the lowest point of its sphere. **11** And if the process of equating it is the same as the equating of the Sun, then the excess between it and the position of the Sun is taken. **12** If there is an excess between them, one operates with it (in terms of multiplication and division) in accordance with how one does it with the superior planets.

**13** And the strongest of the indications of the higher[3] bodies upon [their] transits over each other will appear at [their] conjunctional parallelism. **14** As for oppositions, squares, and the rest of the figures, their indication will be less in manifestation and weaker in effect.

⁂

**15** Since we have set forth what was necessary to do first, let us begin by stating the indications of the transits of the planets over each other in the sign of Aries, and we begin that with the transits of Saturn over the planets, and their transits over him. **16** Then each of the rest of the planets will follow in the order of their centers, if God wills.

**17 The account of the transits of Saturn over the planets. 18** We say that if Saturn was transiting over Jupiter, it indicates the king of Babylon's fighting a number of [his] women, along with what will become evident to him of the bad deeds in the majority of his countries,[4] and the badness of his own conduct, with an abundance of drought, a trivial amount of rains, and an abundance of food and seed. **19** And if he was transiting over Mars, that indicates an abundance of illnesses befalling children, along with an abundance of *simooms* in the season suitable for that, with the turbidity of the atmosphere, and an abundance of dust. **20** And if he was transiting over the Sun, that indicates the establishing of a new king, with wars among the people, and death, with the suitability of the rains, and the people of the Ahwāz attacking Rūm, the occurrence of wars, an abundance

---

[3] I have read this as "higher" rather than "superior," because what matters now is which planet is considered "higher" than the other relative to its own system.

[4] **BY** read this as though what becomes evident is the *king's* bad deeds; but that would be otiose because his bad deeds are mentioned immediately in the next clause.

of death, a copious amount of rains, and the blowing of winds with moderate movement. **21** And if he was transiting over Venus, that indicates the establishing of a new king, the occurrence of wars among the people, and death, with a middling amount of rains. **22** And if he was transiting over Mercury, that indicates the establishing of a new king, and the people of the Ahwāz attacking Rūm, the occurrence of many wars, an abundance of death, a copious amount of rains, and the blowing of winds with moderate movement. **23** And if he was transiting over the Moon, that indicates an abundance of wars, and a copious amount of rains and their benefit.

**24 The account of the planets' transits over Saturn. 25** If Jupiter was transiting over Saturn, that indicates the king's haughtiness towards the subjects, and the scarcity of his enemies, along with an abundance of false rumors and lying, the goodness of the air, the blowing of moderate winds, and the suitability of the seeds and their fine condition. **26** And if Mars was transiting over Saturn, it indicates the grief of the king of Babylon (and sometimes it will bring the new rulership of another), and an abundance of death among the people of Jibāl, with the abundant blowing of the *simooms* and dust, and the good air of summer. **27** And if the Sun was transiting over Saturn, that indicates the entry of Rūm into Armenia, and the occurrence of epidemic among the people of the Ahwāz, with an abundance of rains and seeds (and the suitability of their condition), and sometimes grasses are diminished. **28** And if Venus was transiting over Saturn, that indicates the entry of Rūm into Armenia, and the occurrence of epidemic among the people of the Ahwāz, the successive blowing of the northern winds, and an abundance of waters. **29** And if Mercury was transiting over Saturn, that indicates the entry of Rūm into Armenia, and the occurrence of epidemics and death in the nobles of the people of the Ahwāz, and an abundance of rains with the successive blowing of the northern winds. **30** And if the Moon was transiting over Saturn, that indicates the entry of Rūm into the land of Armenia, and the occurrence of death among the people of the Ahwāz, with a scarcity of rains.

♂♃♈  **31 The account of the transits of Jupiter over the planets. 32** If Jupiter was transiting over Mars, it indicates the death of enemies in Babylon, and an abundance of illnesses and pains in it, with an intensity of cold. **33** And if he was transiting over the Sun, that indicates the suitability of the rains, and their moderateness. **34** And if he was transiting over Venus, it indicates the uprightness of the king of Babylon, and the abundant occurrence of tribulations, illnesses, and death in most of the lands, with the incidence of earthquakes. **35** And if he was transiting over Mercury, that indicates the occurrence of death among the soldiers, an abundance of rains, and the successive blowing of the winds (and their benefit), with the existence of thunder, lightning, and earthquakes. **36** And if he was transiting over the Moon, it indicates the fertility of the year and an abundance of rains.

**37 The account of the planets' transits over Jupiter. 38** And if Mars was transiting over Jupiter, that indicates the death of the king of Babylon, or his killing, or it will bring the new rulership of another, or the death of the king of the people of Jibāl, and the occurrence of death among the people (and especially among the people of Babylon), with a scarcity of rains and a decrease of water. **39** And if the Sun was transiting over him, that indicates a scarcity of rains. **40** And if Venus was transiting over him, that indicates the killing of the king of Babylon, and the majority of their mighty people, and the bad condition of their people, with the arousal of an enemy, an abundance of fighting, the occurrence of rancor between men and women, and an abundance of rains with the increase of mighty rivers, like the Tigris and the Euphrates. **41** And if Mercury was transiting over him, it indicates an abundance of amassing crowds, the amusement of the people of the desert in the countries of Babylon, the safety of their king and his victory over his enemies, with the middling amount of rains and waters, and the successive blowing of the winds. **42** And if the Moon was transiting over him, it indicates the blowing of the rains (and their benefit), the middling amount of rains, and the safety of the people from illnesses.

♂♈ **43 The statement of the transits of Mars over the planets. 44** And if Mars was transiting over the Sun, that indicates the abundant incidence of civil unrest in Babylon, and [the committing of] mutual wrong, lying, the malicious joy of some people towards other, along with a scarcity of heat, the good mixture of the summer quarter, an abundance of lighting, and the raging of winds uprooting trees and date palms. **45** And if he was transiting over Venus, that indicates an abundance of tempting the people of Jibāl against their enemies, an occurrence of death and epidemics in the Ahwāz, the incidence of burning in the rest of the countries, an abundance of detestable things and infirmities, and the suitability of the condition of pregnant women, with troubles befalling their children, [and] with the dryness of the air. **46** And if he was transiting over Mercury, that indicates wars befalling al-Shām, and an abundance of enemies in the land of the Arabs along with a scarcity of clouds and rains, the intensity of the heat, and a trivial amount of the water of springs. **47** And if he was transiting over the Moon, it indicates the death of the king of Babylon and the dispersal of its people, an abundance of fighting and civil unrest in the majority of the lands, and capturing each other, an abundance of death in Persia and Rūm, with the death of a king and bringing the new rulership of another, an abundance of adversities from beasts of prey, the perishing of things having four feet, and a scarcity of moistures.

**48 The statement of the planets' transits over Mars. 49** And if the Sun was transiting over Mars, that indicates the abundance of fighting in Babylon, doing mutual wrong, and the malicious joy of the people towards one another, the intensity of the heat in the summer quarter, an abundance of lightning, and the raging of winds uprooting trees and date palms. **50** And if Venus was transiting over Mars, it indicates the occurrence of illnesses, and especially fevers, in all of the countries, the intensity of fighting occurring among the people, and the existence of fires in most of the countries, along with an abundance of rains and thunder. **51** And if Mercury was transiting over him, that indicates fighting occurring between Rūm and the Turks, and the ruin of the king of Rūm along with an ailment occurring in his eyes, and that soldiers will proceed in the region of the west, corrupting most of it, with an abundance of corruption and illnesses among the people, with mania, fevers, coughing, and the pains of hemorrhoids, with a middling amount of rains and a scarcity of clouds, the intensity of the heat and a trivial amount of the water of springs, fish, produce, and seeds. **52** And if the Moon was transiting over him, it indicates an abundance of moistures.

♄☉♈ **53 The account of the transits of the Sun over the planets. 54** If the Sun was transiting over Venus, that indicates the dryness of the air. **55** And if he was transiting over Mercury, that indicates an abundance of rains and the successive blowing of the winds. **56** And if he was transiting over the Moon, that indicates the existence of lighting, thunder, and thunderbolts.

**57 The account of the planets' transits over the Sun. 58** And if Venus was transiting over the Sun, that indicates the existence of thunder, lightning, and an abundance of rains. **59** And if Mercury was transiting over the Sun, that indicates good coming to the king of Babylon, with the moderation of the rains, and the middling increase of the waters. **60** And if the Moon was transiting over the Sun, that indicates the existence of rains, thunder, lightning, and lightning bolts.

**61 The account of the transits of Venus over the planets. 62** And if Venus was transiting over Mercury, that indicates soldiers attacking the people of Raqqah and what borders on it, the strength of the people of Babylon, with the existence of clouds and rains, thunder, and the blowing of winds (and their moderateness). **63** And if Venus was transiting over the Moon, that indicates an abundance of rains and moistures.

**64 The account of the planets' transits over Venus. 65** And if Mercury was transiting over Venus, that indicates the attack of the people of the Ahwāz against Rūm, with an abundance of clouds and rains, and the fineness of the seed and its flourishing. **66** And if the Moon was transiting over her, it indicates the successive blowing of the southern winds and an abundance of moistures, especially in the summer quarter.

**67 The account of the transits of Mercury over the planets. 68** If Mercury was transiting over the Moon, that indicates good coming to the king of Babylon, along with an abundance of rains, winds, and waters.

**69 The account of the planets' transits over Mercury. 70** If the Moon was transiting over Mercury, that indicates an abundance of rains and the successive blowing of winds.

**71** Since we have completed what we wanted to explain, let us break off the chapter, if God wills.

## Chapter VI.2: On judging the transits of the planets above one another during their parallelism with the sign of Taurus

**1** Since we have already set forth in Chapter VI.1 the statement of the indications of the planets' transits over each other during their parallelism with the sign of Aries, in this chapter let us state the account of the indications of the planets' transits over each other when they are parallel with the sign of Taurus, and their transits over it, then what follows it in order in accordance with what we established in the sign of Aries (and in God is our success).

♄ ♉ **2 The statement of the transits of Saturn over the planets. 3** We say that if Saturn was transiting over Jupiter, that indicates the warring of the people of Armenia against the people of Babylon and Jibāl, and the victory of the king of Armenia against them, and an abundance of drought in most of the climes, with the dryness of the air and the crops. **4** And if he was transiting over Mars, that indicates an abundance of drought, hunger, hardships, and death befalling the people, along with the intensity of the cold and its duration. **5** And if he was transiting over the Sun, that indicates an abundance of wars occurring among the people, with enemies reaching the people of the Ahwāz, and a scarcity of moistures and food. **6** And if he was transiting over Venus, that indicates the death of the king of Rūm, the occurrence of death among women, and the trivial amount of rains. **7** And if he was transiting over Mercury, that indicates the existence of wars among the people, enemies reaching the people of the Ahwāz, the abundant rising [of rivers] and the expensiveness of food. **8** And if he was transiting over the Moon, that indicates the abundance of wars among the people, and enemies reaching the people of the Ahwāz, a scarcity of rains, a copious amount of waters, and the scarcity of food.

**9 The account of the planets' transits over Saturn. 10** If Jupiter was transiting over Saturn, that indicates the corruption of the command of the king of Babylon, ruination happening in the land of Armenia, death befalling some of the mighty, and the incidence of harms in most of the countries, with an abundance of moistures. **11** And if Mars was transiting over him, that indicates the death of the king of the Ahwāz, and the rousing of enemies from two directions, and the occurrence of drought and fire doing damage to the people in most of the countries, along with the existence of earthquakes.

**12** And if the Sun was transiting over Saturn, that indicates an abundance of hunger befalling the people, and an increase in what trees bear, with the moisture of the atmosphere. **13** And if Venus was transiting over him, that indicates the existence of hardships, tribulations, lawsuits, and drought in most of the climes, and an abundance of rains and a scarcity of food. **14** And if Mercury was transiting over him, that indicates an attack by the enemy on the people of Babylon, and the incidence of hardships with the intensity of the cold. **15** And if the Moon was transiting over him, that indicates the miscarriage[5] of pregnant women, a scarcity of seed, and an abundance of rain and winds.

♃♉ **16 The account of the transits of Jupiter over the planets. 17** If Jupiter was transiting over Mars, that indicates ruination occurring in most of the cities, and the abundant occurrence of snows, especially in the cities appropriate for it. **18** And if he was transiting over the Sun, that indicates the dryness of the air and an abundance of *simooms*. **19** And if he was transiting over Venus, that indicates the ruin of most of the Ahwāz, an abundance of harms in the countries of Rūm, and the occurrence of moistures. **20** And if he was transiting over Mercury, that indicates the safety of the people, the corruption of the land of Rūm, the ruination of the desert peasantry[6] with the existence of clouds, and an abundance of rains and a scarcity of waters. **21** And if he was transiting over the Moon, that indicates an abundance of prosperity in Babylon, with the safety of bodies and a middling amount of rain.

**22 The account of the planets' transits over Jupiter. 23** If Mars was transiting over Jupiter, that indicates the ruination of mighty cities, especially in the region of Persia and the Ahwāz, the submission of enemies, the occurrence of illnesses in the region of Jibāl, and the death of some of the mighty, with an abundance of rains, lightning, and thunder. **24** And if the Sun was transiting over him, that indicates the moisture of the atmosphere. **25** And if Venus was transiting over him, that indicates the corruption of the condition of the Ahwāz, the death of its king, the ruination of its villages, an abundance

---

[5] استسقاط. Following **BY**, but the verbal noun of Form 10 is not attested in Lane, who refers to Form 5 instead. That Form means "to try to get another to do something bad," which sounds more like abortion.

[6] البادية. **BY** read, "the nomads" (viz. the Bedouin), but that plural would be البوادِ.

of confusions in the rest of the countries, illnesses, and the power of women over their husbands, with a scarcity of the rains in the cities appropriate for it. **26** And if Mercury was transiting over him, it indicates an abundance of those rising up against the king of Babylon (and his safety from them), an abundance of submersions among the people of villages, and the Arabs' destruction of Dastī-Maysān, along with an abundance of moistures and the blowing of the winds. **27** And if the Moon was transiting over him, that indicates the preparedness of the people of Persia, Rūm, and the Ahwāz against the king of Babylon, and the occurrence of war in Babylon, with drought in the countries of Persia and the Ahwāz, troubles will come to Rūm, and the rains and waters will be abundant.

♂☊ **28 The account of the transits of Mars over the planets. 29** If Mars was transiting over the Sun, that indicates the intensity of the heat and the dryness of the atmosphere. **30** And if he was transiting over Venus, that indicates the death of the king of the Ahwāz, the ruination of most of its land, the occurrence of illnesses and death among them, and an abundance of women's giving birth to females, with an excess of heat in the summer quarter. **31** And if he was transiting over Mercury, that indicates corruption occurring in most of the climes, an abundance of death in the land of Rūm, with an abundance of rains, clouds, and snows, and the intensity of the cold of the winter quarter and the autumn quarter. **32** And if he was transiting over the Moon, that indicates the death of the king of Babylon and the dispersal of its nobles, the death of the king of the Ahwāz and the new rulership of another, an abundance of fighting and civil unrest in most of the climes, the occurrence of death in Persia and Rūm, harm from predatory beasts, and the perishing of riding animals.

**33 The account of the planets' transits over Mars. 34** If the Sun was transiting over Mars, that indicates the moisture of the air. **35** And if Venus was transiting over him, that indicates the death of some of the women of kings, the harshness of the condition of men, the corruption of women, the attack by the people of Iraq against the people of Jibāl, the shifting of most of the armies and the raiding from the region of the Sawād to the region of the mountains, and their destruction of most of the countries along with an abundance of waters and a copious amount of rain. **36** If Mercury was transiting over him, that indicates an abundance of intense fear befalling most of the countries, with the existence of fighting, corruption, disagreement, disturbance, and death in the land of Rūm, and especially in men, with the blowing of winds and an abundance of snows. **37** And if the Moon was transiting over him, it indicates an abundance of moistures and the coldness of the atmosphere.

**38 The account of the Sun's transits over the planets. 39** If the Sun was transiting over Venus, that indicates the dryness of the air. **40** And if he was transiting over Mercury, it indicates the attacks of the people of the cities against one another, an abundance of births, a scarcity of rains, the decrease in grasses, and the swellings of rivers. **41** And if he was transiting over the Moon, that indicates a scarcity of moistures.

**42 The account of the planets' transits over the Sun. 43** If Venus was transiting over the Sun, that indicates an abundance of moistures. **44** And if Mercury was transiting over him, it indicates enemies arriving in the land of Rūm and the occurrence of death in women, with the middling amount of rains and the blowing of the winds. **45** And if the Moon was transiting over him, that indicates a scarcity of rains.

**46 The account of Venus's transits over the planets. 47** If Venus was transiting over Mercury, that indicates an abundance of death and drought, the trembling of the people and their confusions, with a scarcity of rains, thunder, and lightning, and a scarcity of food. **48** And if Venus was transiting over the Moon, that indicates a scarcity of dews and moistures.

**49 The account of the planets' transits over Venus. 50** If Mercury was transiting over Venus, that indicates the people of Armenia attacking the people of Rūm, and an abundance of moistures; and sometimes the air will be temperate with a successive blowing of the winds. **51** And if the Moon was transiting over her, that indicates the existence of civil unrest befalling the people of Persia, and the death of their king in his youth; and it will happen likewise in the Ahwāz, with an abundance of robbers and the totally destitute, the occurrence of warring between the people of Persia and Rūm, the killing of the king of Persia, the miscarriage of pregnant women and the perishing of donkeys, the death of cattle, an abundance of thunder and lightning, and a scarcity of sown crops and seeds.

☿☽ **52 The account of Mercury's transits over the planets. 53** If Mercury was transiting over the Moon, that indicates the attack of enemies against most of the land of Rūm, with an abundance of rains and the swelling of rivers.

**54 The statement of the planets' transits over Mercury. 55** If the Moon was transiting over Mercury, that indicates an abundance of births, a decrease in grasses, and the middling amount of rains.

**56** Since we have completed what we wanted to explain, let us break of the chapter, if God wills.

## Chapter VI.3: On judging the transits of the planets above one another during their parallelism with the sign of Gemini

**1** Since we have already set forth in Chapter VI.2 the statement of the indications of the planets' transits above one another during their parallelism with the sign of Taurus, in this chapter let us state the account of their indications in the same way, when they are parallel with the sign of Gemini.

♈ ♄ ♊  **2 The account of Saturn's transits over the planets. 3** We say that if Saturn was transiting over Jupiter, that indicates the death of the king of Armenia, an abundance of robbers and highway robbery (and especially the Bedouin), and their taking the assets of merchants, with a scarcity of rains and waters, an abundance of aquatic animals (like frogs, and what resembles that). **4** And if he was transiting over Mars, that indications the arousing of the enemy and the occurrence of tribulation in most of the lands, the incidence of locusts, the successive blowing of *simooms*, and a scarcity of moistures. **5** And if he was transiting over the Sun, that indicates the king of Babylon killing some of his women, with the intensity of the heat. **6** And if he was transiting over Venus, that indicates the death of the king of Rūm, an abundance of injustice and tribulation in his land, the occurrence of death in women, and a scarcity of rains. **7** And if he was transiting over Mercury, it indicates the king of Babylon's killing some of his women, with a middling amount of winds and their suitability. **8** And if he was transiting over the Moon, that indicates the king of Babylon's killing of some of his women, with a trivial amount of moistures and their scarcity.

**9 The account of the planets' transits over Saturn. 10** If Jupiter was transiting over Saturn, that indicates the Turks' spoiling most of the land of Jibāl and the traveling of all the people of the Ahwāz to them, and their spoiling most of their lands, along with an abundance of drought in Armenia and its area, the suitability of the seeds in Babylon, the goodness of their produce, the blowing of the winds, and an abundance of moistures. **11** And if Mars was transiting over him, it indicates the movement of the people of Jibāl, and their attack against the people of the west, fighting occurring in the land of Rūm, with an abundance of illness and death in it, and the existence of rains, lightning, and thunder. **12** And if the Sun was transiting over him, that indicates the suitability of the people of the Ahwāz and an abundance of good among them, with the goodness of the air and the middling condition of the rains. **13** And if Venus was transiting over him, it indicates hardships affecting the land of Rūm, with the occurrence of death among them, and an abundance of drought. **14** And if Mercury was transiting over him, that indicates the suitability of the Ahwāz and an abundance of good among them, with the goodness of the air and the middling amount of the rains. **15** And if the Moon was transiting over him, that indicates the suitable condition of the people of the Ahwāz and the abundance of good among them, with a copious amount of rains and moistures.

♃♊ **16 The account of Jupiter's transits over the planets. 17** If Jupiter was transiting over Mars, it indicates the ruin of the people of Yamāmah, and ruination and hardship occurring in the people, with a scarcity of moistures. **18** And if he was transiting over the Sun, that indicates the dryness of the air. **19** And if he was transiting over Venus, that indicates the suitable condition of the king of Babylon, and an attack by the king of Armenia against the people of Iraq, and his devastation of it, the occurrence of death among pregnant women, a scarcity of rains, and an abundance of seeds. **20** And if he was transiting over Mercury, that indicates the warring of the people of India against the people of Rūm, and their devastation of their countries, with the raging of the winds. **21** And if he was transiting over the Moon, that indicates a copious amount of rains and waters.

**22 The account of the planets' transits over Jupiter. 23** If Mars was transiting over Jupiter, that indicates the death of the two kings of Yamāmah and desert peasants, and their devastation (and sometimes that will befall most of the cities); and the occurrence of death in most of the enemies of the king of Babylon. **24** And if the Sun was transiting over him, that indicates the moisture of the atmosphere. **25** And if Venus was transiting over him, that indicates the abundance of fear in the king of Babylon, and the delight of the king of the desert peasants (and the suitability of its people), an abundance of tribulation in Armenia, and the middling conditions of pregnant women, with the darkness of the atmosphere and an abundance of moistures and rains. **26** And if Mercury was transiting over him, it indicates the occurrence of contrariety between most of the people, with the people of villages fighting each other. **27** And if the Moon was transiting over him, that indicates an abundance of moistures.

**28 The account of Mars's transits over the planets. 29** If Mars was transiting over the Sun, that indicates the hotness of the air, and its dryness. **30** And if he was transiting over Venus, that indicates men antagonizing women, the death of pregnant women among them, and the scarcity of dews and moistures. **31** And if he was transiting over Mercury, that indicates the death of some of the children of kings, and the installing of a new king of Babylon who is not suitable for rulership, the departure of armies from Jibāl to Khurāsān, and their fighting each other, an abundance of fears befalling the people, with hostility happening among them, the undermining of churches and synagogues, and the taking of their assets, with the trivial amount of rains and the raging of winds. **32** And if he was transiting over the Moon, that indicates the death of the king of Babylon and the dispersal of its nobles, the spending of its assets, with the death of the king of the Ahwāz, an abundance of fighting and civil unrest in most of the climes, with the dryness of the air and a scarcity of moistures.

**33 The account of the planets' transits over Mars. 34** If the Sun was transiting over Mars, that indicates the moisture of the air. **35** And if Venus was transiting over him, that indicates death occurring among the mighty of the people of Jibāl and their kings, with hostility and rancor occurring among most of the people, and the incidence of death in women and an abundance of rains. **36** And if Mercury was transiting over him, that indicates the attack of the people of Rūm against the people of Jibāl, and there will be civil unrest, damage, and fighting among the people of Jibāl, with the abundant death of sheep, a scarcity of rains, and the intensity of the cold. **37** And if the Moon was transiting over him, that indicates a copious amount of rains and moistures.

**38 The account of the Sun's transits over the planets. 39** And if the Sun was transiting over Venus, that indicates a scarcity of moistures. **40** And if he was transiting over Mercury, that indicates the blowing of winds and *simooms*, and the abundance of winds. **41** And if he was transiting over the Moon, that indicates a trivial amount of waters and a scarcity of moistures.

**42 The account of the planets' transits over the Sun. 43** If Venus was transiting over the Sun, that indicates the moisture of the atmosphere. **44** And if Mercury was transiting over him, that indicates an abundance of drought in most of the climes, and a scarcity of aquatic birds and animals, with a copious amounts of rains and the dryness of the atmosphere. **45** And if the Moon was transiting over him, that indicates the trivial amount of moistures.

**46 The account of Venus's transits over the planets. 47** If Venus was transiting over Mercury, that indicates the appearance of safety, an abundance of alms in the land of Babylon, Persia, the Ahwāz, Iraq, and Rūm, and an increase in their slaves, immovable property, and landed estates, an abundance of disputes of men against women, a scarcity of rains, an abundance of thunder and lightning, a copious amount of waters, and the rising of rivers. **47** And if she was transiting over the Moon, that indicates a trivial amount of moistures.

**48 The account of the planets' transits over Venus. 49** If Mercury was transiting over Venus, that indicates the attack by Rūm against the people of Babylon, with their instilling fear in what is around their land, the occurrence of rancor between Rūm and the Turks, the warring and shifting of armies from the people of Armenia to the people of the Ahwāz, the death of the king of Babylon, and the abundant occurrence of death among pregnant women in Fārs, with an abundance of rains and a copious amount of waters. **50** And if the Moon was transiting over her, that indicates the blowing of winds.

**51 The account of Mercury's transits over the planets. 52** If Mercury was transiting over the Moon, that indicates an abundance of drought in most of the climes, and a scarcity of birds, with a scarcity of fish and the blowing of the winds.

**53 The account of the planets' transits over Mercury. 54** If the Moon was transiting over Mercury, that indicates an abundance of moderation in the rains, and the blowing of the winds.

**55** Since we have completed what we wanted to explain, let us break off the discussion in Chapter VI.3.

## Chapter VI.4: On judging the transits of the planets above one another during their parallelism with the sign of Cancer

**1** Since we have set forth in Chapter VI.3 the account of the indications of the planets' transits over each other during their parallelism with the sign of Gemini, in this chapter let us state their indications for that when they are parallel with the sign of Cancer.

**2 The account of Saturn's transits over the planets. 3** We say that if Saturn was transiting over Jupiter, that indicates the cleverness of the king of Babylon, his control of his kingdom by himself, and his scant reliance on others, an abundance of robbers and people of indecency, a scarcity of rains and the decrease of waters, and an abundance of aquatic animals (like frogs and what is like that). **4** And if he was transiting over Mars, that indicates the stirring up of the Turks and their deceit, the occurrence of hostility among the people, an abundance of locusts, and the copious amount of rains and their steadiness. **5** And if he was transiting over the Sun, that indicates the death of the women of kings, and the occurrence of death in most of the climes, with the dryness of the air. **6** And if he was transiting over Venus, that indicates that death will occur in the lands of Rūm, with an abundance of locusts and a scarcity of moistures. **7** And if he was transiting over Mercury, that indicates the occurrence of death in most of the climes, due to the intensity of fevers befalling the people, along with a scarcity of rains and middling heat. **8** And if he was transiting over the Moon, that indicates the death of some of the women of kings, and the occurrence of death in most of the climes, with the intensity of fevers, along with the trivial amount of rains and a scarcity of waters.

**9 The account of the planets' transits over Saturn. 10** If Jupiter was transiting over Saturn, that indicates an abundance of fighting among kings, the death of the king of Babylon, the pouncing of the people of Jibāl upon the people of Babylon, the devastation of most of the climes, an abundance of reproducing [of children], with a scarcity of rains and moistures, an abundance of sown crops, and the goodness of their beauty. **11** And if Mars was transiting over him, that indicates an abundance of enemies and rebels, and the occurrence of locusts, the middling amount of rains, and a trivial amount of waters. **12** And if the Sun was transiting over him, that indicates a decrease in waters and a middling amount of rains. **13** And if Venus was transiting over him, that indicates the suitability of the rains and their constancy, and an abundance of the locusts' spoiling the sowing. **14** And if Mercury was transiting over him, that indicates the safety of the king of Rūm, and his long lifespan, a trivial amount of rains, and the movement of winds. **15** And if the Moon was transiting over him, that indicates the miscarriage of pregnant women, and a scarcity of seed, a copious amount of rains, and an abundance of moistures.

**16 The account of Jupiter's transits over the planets. 17** If Jupiter was transiting over Mars, that indicates the death of the enemies of the king, an abundance of robbers and their manifesting corruption and folly, with a copious amount of rains and abundant waters, with an increase of the Tigris and Euphrates. **18** And if he was transiting over the Sun, that indicates an abundance of death in the people, and an abundance of wondrous things in the countries of Jibāl, the uprightness of the people of the Tigris and Euphrates, and their safety. **19** And if he was transiting over Venus, that indicates the safety of the king of Babylon and lasting good fortune in his land, an abundance of moistures, and the safety of the seeds. **20** And if he was transiting over Mercury, that indicates the resistance of slaves against kings, lying, uncertainties, the death of the king of Persia, the occurrence of floods and wondrous things in its mountains and the rest of the mountains, the ruination of most of the climes, the corruption of the gatherings of arbitrators, with an abundance of rains in some of the times (and sometimes they will be scarce at [another] time), a scarcity of clouds and thunder, the swiftness of troubles [befalling] the vegetation, and the scarce swelling of the Tigris and the Euphrates. **21** And if he was transiting over the Moon, that indicates the trivial amount of rains and moistures.

**22 The account of the planets' transits over Jupiter. 23** If Mars was transiting over Jupiter, that indicates the stirring up of enemies and their raids against most of the countries, and their attacks on them, the existence of fire in Babylon with an abundance of rains and an increase of the Tigris and Euphrates, and the abundant swelling [of water], especially in the season appropriate for that. **24** And if the Sun was transiting over him, that indicates the wetness of the air and its moisture. **25** And if Venus was transiting over him, that indicates the death of some of the kings and the mighty, and an abundance of delight for the king of Jibāl, with a copious amount of rains and moistures, and a decrease in the water of the sea. **26** And if Mercury was transiting over him, that indicates the death of the king of Babylon, an abundance of wondrous things in most of the climes, the spreading of soothsayers, the people of villages fighting against one another (and their destroying most of them), women's own protecting of themselves, with an abundance of rains and an increase of the waters of rivers. **27** And if the Moon was transiting over him, that indicates an abundance of moistures.

**28 The account of Mars's transits over the planets. 29** If Mars was transiting over the Sun, that indicates the intensity of the heat and the dryness of the air. **30** And if he was transiting over Venus, that indicates an abundance of those rising up against the people of Jibāl, and their attacking them; evil will find the people of the Ahwāz from their enemies, and pregnant women will die, with a scarcity of moistures and an intensity of heat. **31** And if he was transiting over Mercury, that indicates fighting occurring between the sons of kings, the intensity of wars, the destruction of many kingdoms in all countries, and enemies harming the west and its lands, the corruption of the court gatherings of pious kings and their places, with the intensity of heat and its duration. **32** And if he was transiting over the Moon, that indicates the death of the king of Babylon, the dispersal of its nobles, and the spending of its assets; the death of the king of the Ahwāz and an abundance of civil unrest and fighting in most of the climes, and capturing each other, an abundance of death in Persia and Rūm, the intensity of harm from predatory animals, the perishing of beasts of burden among cattle, camels, and others, with a scarcity of moistures and the dryness of the air.

**33 The account of the planets' transits over Mars. 34** If the Sun was transiting over Mars, that indicates an abundance of rains. **35** And if Venus was transiting over him, that indicates the death of some of the children of kings, and their being killed by iron, the attack by the people of Jibāl against the people of Iraq (and an abundance of death among them), the death of the mightiest king, the ruination of most of the countries and the occurrence of fire in them, and an abundance of locusts with the existence of moistures and a copious amount of swelling [of water]. **36** And if Mercury was transiting over him, that indicates the occurrence of death in the people, with the intensity of heat and an abundance of earthquakes. **37** And if the Moon was transiting over him, it indicates an abundance of rains.

**38 The account of the Sun's transits over the planets. 39** If the Sun was transiting over Venus, that indicates the dryness of the air. **40** And if he was transiting over Mercury, that indicates the abundant death of people, with a copious amount of rains, the intensity of the heat in its [proper] time, a scarcity of waters, and the corruption of the rivers. **41** And if he was transiting over the Moon, that indicates the trivial amount of moistures.

**42 The account of the planets' transits over the Sun. 43** If Venus was transiting over the Sun, that indicates an abundance of rains. **44** And if Mercury was transiting over him, that indicates the long lifespan of the king of Rūm, with the intensity of the heat. **45** And if the Moon was transiting over him, that indicates a copious amount of moistures.

**46 The account of Venus's transits over the planets. 47** If Venus was transiting over Mercury, that indicates the destruction of the land of Babylon, the occurrence of death in the countries of Rūm (and especially in women), with an abundance of clouds, rains, thunder, and lighting, and the intensity of the heat in its [proper] time. **48** And if she was transiting over the Moon, that indicates an abundance of rains and a copious amount of moistures.

**49 The account of the planets' transits over Venus. 50** And if Mercury was transiting over Venus, that indicates the people's use of evil, and an abundance of death (and especially among pregnant women), the occurrence of inflammation of the eyes, infectious disease, and wars happening to the people, and especially between the Turks and Rūm, and the Turks' capturing of them, and the existence of corruption in most of the countries, and disagreement in things, with the attack of the king of Babylon against the people of Armenia, and the occurrence of captivity among them, the destruction of churches and synagogues, with an abundance of moistures and fog. **51** And if the Moon was transiting over her, that indicates an abundance of moistures.

**52 The account of Mercury's transits over the planets. 53** And if Mercury was transiting over the Moon, that indicates the long lifespan of the king of Rūm, an abundance of moistures, and an increase in water.

**54 The account of the planets' transits over Mercury. 55** If the Moon was transiting over Mercury, that indicates the blocking of rivers, with a middling amount of rains and the successive blowing of the winds.

**56** Since we have set forth what we wanted to explain, let us break off the discussion in [this] chapter.

## Chapter VI.5: On judging the transits of the planets above one another during their parallelism with the sign of Leo

**1** Since we have set forth in Chapter VI.4 the statement of the indications of the planets' transits over one another during their parallelism with the sign of Cancer, in this chapter let us state their indications for that when they are parallel with the sign of Leo.

♈♄♌ **2 The statement of Saturn's transits over the planets. 3** We say that if Saturn was transiting over Jupiter, that indicates the death of the king of Babylon, the occurrence of death in the people and predatory animals, with a trivial amount of rains and a decrease of seeds in most of the countries. **4** And if he was transiting over Mars, that indicates the intensity of the blowing of the winds and *simooms* in their own [proper] seasons, a scarcity of food and seeds, and the need for both. **5** And if he was transiting over the Sun, that indicates the death of the king of Babylon or some of the people of the Ahwāz, and the occurrence of hardships in Sīstān,[7] with the abundant incidence of locusts, and a copious amount of rains and their suitability. **6** And if he was transiting over Venus, that indicates the death of the king of Babylon or some of the nobles of the people of the Ahwāz, the occurrence of hardships in Sijistān, and abundant heat with a middling amount of moistures. **7** And if he was transiting over Mercury, that indicates the death of the king of Babylon, the abundant incidence of death in the people, and hardships in Sijistān, with the intensity of the heat in its own [proper] time. **8** And if he was transiting over the Moon, that indicates the death of the king of Babylon or some of the nobles of the people of the Ahwāz, and the occurrence of hardships in Sijistān, with an abundance of locusts, the suitability of the rains, and an abundance of moistures.

**9 The account of the planets' transits over Saturn. 10** If Jupiter was transiting over Saturn, that indicates the delight of the king of Babylon and his happiness, the death of some of the kings and the mighty, the ruin of many of the people, and the occurrence of rancor and hostility among them, with the goodness of the air and winds, and the suitable condition of the

---

[7] One would think this should be Sijistān, as in **6-8** below. But **BY** point out that in this instance, some MSS read "Dasti-Maysān."

seeds. **11** And if Mars was transiting over him, that indicates the ruin of the king of Babylon, the intensity of drought in its land, and the ruin of the king of Armenia with the raging of the winds and an abundance of dust. **12** And if the Sun was transiting over him, that indicates an abundance of locusts and the growth of grasses, a scarcity of rains, and the dryness of the air. **13** And if Venus was transiting over him, that indicates an abundance of locusts and grasses, with a copious amount of rains and moistures. **14** And if Mercury was transiting over him, that indicates the occurrence of death in the people, an abundance of drought and locusts, the middling amount of rains, and the abundance of waters and winds. **15** And if the Moon was transiting over him, that indicates the miscarriage of pregnant women, and an abundance of rains, moistures, and winds.

♃♌ **16 The account of Jupiter's transits over the planets. 17** If Jupiter was transiting over Mars, that indicates the death of enemies and the cavalry, and the intensity of the cold. **18** And if he was transiting over the Sun, that indicates the existence of rains, and their suitability. **19** And if he was transiting over Venus, that indicates that harsh tribulation will affect the people of the Sawād, the death of the king of Babylon, and the fine condition of most of the people of the countries, with the existence of earthquakes. **20** And if he was transiting over Mercury, that indicates the king of Babylon's doing good and benefit to his enemies, the killing of the kings of Jibāl and Azerbaijān, and that the people of the east deprive the king of Babylon of his kingdom after an exchange of messengers between them, the occurrence of war, and an abundance of rains, thunder, lighting, winds and earthquakes, with a scarcity of harm and spoiling from that. **21** And if he was transiting over the Moon, that indicates the goodness of the air.

**22 The account of the planets' transits over Jupiter. 23** If Mars was transiting over Jupiter, that indicates the death of the king of Babylon and the ruination of its villages, the victory of enemies over their people and land, a scarcity of rains and a decrease of waters in wells and other things. **24** And if the Sun was transiting over him, it indicates a trivial amount of rains in most of the countries. **25** And if Venus was transiting over him, that indicates the death of the king of Babylon, the abundant delight of the king of the people of the Ahwāz, the stirring up of enemies against kings, the death of the enemies of his children, the pouncing of the people of the Ahwāz upon the Arabs, and the occurrence of death in the people of the Sawād, Iraq, and Jibāl.[8] **26** And if Mercury was transiting over him, that indicates that mighty wars will be in the region of the east and where the east wind blows from, the land of Babylon, and what is around these regions, with an abundance of winds. **27** And if the Moon was transiting over him, that indicates an abundance of moistures.

**28 The account of Mars's transits over the planets. 29** If Mars was transiting over the Sun, that indicates an abundance of lightning. **30** And if he was transiting over Venus, that indicates the death of the king of the Ahwāz and the ruination of its land, the death of some of the women of kings, an abundance of fire, tribulation, hardships, lying, false rumors, and locusts in most of the countries, with a scarcity of rains. **31** And if he was transiting over Mercury, it indicates battling occurring between the people of Khurāsān and Rūm, and the harshness of the affairs in that, with the suitable condition of Rūm, the corruption of the condition of the people of Babylon, an abundance of fire, a scarcity of rains, and excess heat in its own [proper] time. **32** And if he was transiting over the Moon, that indicates the death of the king of Babylon and the dispersal of its nobles, the spending of its assets, the death of the king of the Ahwāz, the abundance of fighting and civil unrest in most of the climes, the capturing of each other, an abundance of death in Persia, Rūm, and the land of Jibāl, with the harm of predatory animals, the perishing of beasts of burden (of cattle, camels, and other things), with the dryness of the air and a scarcity of moistures.

**33 The account of the planets' transits over Mars. 34** If the Sun was transiting over Mars, that indicates a scarcity of rains. **35** And if Venus was transiting over him, that indicates the abundant occurrence of hostility and hatred between the people, with an abundance of rains, thunder, and lighting. **36** And if Mercury was transiting over him, that indicates the people of Babylon fighting against the people of the region of the south, and an abundance of bloodshed between them, the attack of most of the people against the people of Babylon, the death of the king of Persia, the ruin of most of the enemies of kings, sorrow befalling scholars (and the death of some of them), the battling of the people of the region of the east against the people of the

---

[8] Reading الجبال for الجبل ("the mountain").

region of the west, an abundance of loss[9] in most of the countries with the dismissal of the slaves in the houses of worship, an abundance of moistures and the copious amount of rains, and the existence of earthquakes. **37** And if the Moon was transiting over him, that indicates the changing of the air and its variation.

♈☉☊ **38 The account of the Sun's transits over the planets. 39** If the Sun was transiting over Venus, that indicates an abundance of rains. **40** And if he was transiting over Mercury, that indicates the abundant occurrence of death in the people, with the intensity of heat and its duration. **41** And if he was transiting over the Moon, that indicates an abundance of moistures.

**42 The account of the planets' transits over the Sun. 43** If Venus was transiting over the Sun, that indicates the suitability of the air and the blowing of the *simooms*. **44** And if Mercury was transiting over him, that indicates the occurrence of death in livestock, and an abundance of locusts, with the blowing of winds and their hotness. **45** And if the Moon was transiting over him, that indicates a scarcity of moistures.

♈♀☊ **46 The account of Venus's transits over the planets. 47** If Venus was transiting over Mercury, that indicates an abundance of ailments among the soldiers and the nobles from coughing, with an abundance of death for that reason, and the power of women over men, with a scarcity of rains, the intensity of the heat, and the existence of thunder and lighting in its own [proper] season. **48** And if she was transiting over the Moon, that indicates the trivial amount of rains and a scarcity of moistures.

**49 The account of the planets' transits over Venus. 50** If Mercury was transiting over Venus, that indicates the capture of the people of Iraq, and fear and death occurring in most of the climes (especially among the soldiers), an abundance of wars, robbers, and the shedding of blood, with the goodness of the air, the middling amount of moistures, and the intensification of the heat in its own [proper] time. **51** And if the Moon was transiting over her, that indicates the abundance of rains and moistures.

♈☿☊ **52 The account of Mercury's transiting over the planets. 53** If Mercury was transiting over the Moon, that indicates the abun-

---

[9] Or, "damage" (النَّقص).

dant occurrence of death in the people, with the occurrence of locusts and the successive blowing of the winds.

**54 The account of the planets' transits over Mercury. 55** If the Moon was transiting over Mercury, that indicates the occurrence of death in the people, with a scarcity of moistures, the successive blowing of winds, and the intensity of the heat.

**56** Since we have completed what we wanted to explain, let us break off the discussion in [this] chapter.

## Chapter VI.6: On judging the transits of the planets above one another during their parallelism with the sign of Virgo

**1** Since we have completed in Chapter VI.5 the statement of the indications of the planets' transits over one another during their parallelism with the sign of Leo, in this chapter let us state their indications in the same way when they are parallel with the sign of Virgo.

♄♍ **2 The statement of Saturn's transits over the planets. 3** We say that if Saturn was transiting over Jupiter, that indicates the ruination of the land of Armenia, and the duration of that for about three years, with a scarcity of rains, drought, and a copious amount of waters in the seas. **4** And if he was transiting over Mars, that indicates the ruination of most of the regions of the lands, with an intensity of cold and its long lastingness, especially in the two seasons appropriate for it, and an abundance of ruin in most of the trees. **5** And if he was transiting over the Sun, that indicates the dryness of the air. **6** And if he was transiting over Venus, that indicates the movements of the soldiers of Armenia and the suitability of rains and moistures. **7** And if he was transiting over Mercury, that indicates an abundance of warring by the people of the Ahwāz against their enemies, death befalling some of the women of kings, the setting out of a rebel subjugating countries and moving in their borders, with a copious amount of rains, the abundant swelling [of waters] and the intensity of the cold. **8** And if he was transiting over the Moon, that indicates an abundance of rains and moistures.

**9 The account of the planets' transits over Saturn. 10** If Jupiter was transiting over him, that indicates the attack by most of the regions against the land of Rūm, and their laying waste to most of its villages, with the ruination of Armenia, an abundance of illnesses and death in the people, with a scarcity of moistures, the scarce blowing of winds, and the suitability of the condition of seeds; and sometimes drought happens in the countries of the Ahwāz. **11** And if Mars was transiting over him, that indicates an abundance of sexual intercourse, an abundance of heat and cold in the two seasons appropriate for them, with the spoiling of most of the yield by locusts. **12** And if the Sun was transiting over him, that indicates the existence of rains, and their middling amount. **13** And if Venus was transiting over him, that indicates an abundance of disagreement in the soldiers of Armenia, with an occurrence of death and illnesses in the people, the existence of rains and moistures, and their suitability. **14** And if Mercury was transiting over him, that indicates the attack by the people of Armenia against their enemies, with their folly in the countries and their spoiling most of the lands for those reasons, with the intensity of the cold and the swelling of rivers. **15** And if the Moon was transiting over him, that indicates the attack by the people of Armenia against their enemies, and their spoiling most of their land, a copious amount of rains, and an abundance of moistures.

**16 The account of Jupiter's transits over the planets. 17** If Jupiter was transiting over Mars, that indicates the squandering of the assets of businessmen, the suitability of affairs, the ruination of most of the lands of Jibāl, the suitable condition of the people of Babylon, and an abundance of winds in the times appropriate for them. **18** And if he was transiting over the Sun, that indicates the dryness of the air and the trivial amount of rains. **19** And if he was transiting over Venus, that indicates the disobedience of some of [the people of] Rūm towards their king, and his punishing them for that, the suitable condition of the people of Babylon and their delight, harm coming to the people of the Ahwāz and their regions, with an abundance of predatory animals and a scarcity of waters. **20** And if he was transiting over Mercury, that indicates the fighting of the people of Sīstān[10] against the king of Rūm, the safety of the majority of the countries, an abundance of those seeking knowledge, with the successive blowing of the winds. **21** And if he was transiting over the Moon, it indicates a copious amount of moistures.

**22 The account of the planets' transits over Jupiter. 23** If Mars was transiting over Jupiter, that indicates the death of the king of the Ahwāz, the suitable condition of the king of Babylon, the appearance of hostilities and evils in their people, and sometimes fire will occur with a copious amount of rains, lightning, and thunder, and an increase of the waters of rivers. **24** And if the Sun was transiting over him, that indicates the moisture of the atmosphere. **25** And if Venus was transiting over him, that indicates death and hardship in the countries of the Sawād and Babylon, with successive rains in

---

[10] See footnote to VI.5, **5**. Again, two MSS read "Dasti-Maysān."

their own [proper] season, and especially in the countries of Rūm, an abundance of sown crops in Babylon, and the scarcity of the waters of seas. **26** And if Mercury was transiting over him, that indicates the death of the king of Babylon, fear coming to its people, the ruination of some of its countries, the appearance of scholars and their abundance, with a copious amount of rains, a scarcity of seeds and grasses, and the abundant swelling of rivers. **27** And if the Moon was transiting over him, that indicates the alliance of the king[s] of Rūm, Persia, and the Ahwāz against the king of Babylon, the abundant occurrence of war between them, and many harms and drought will afflict them for those reasons, with the shifting of armies and enemies from the region of Jibāl to the region of the Sawād, a copious amount of rains, and abundant waters.

**28 The account of Mars's transits over the planets. 29** If Mars was transiting over the Sun, that indicates the dryness of the air and the scarcity of its moisture. **30** And if he was transiting over Venus, that indicates the death of some of the kings and women's infants, an abundance of lawsuits, the occurrence[11] of locusts, and the intensity of the heat in the season appropriate for it. **31** And if he was transiting over Mercury, that indicates captivity occurring in the land of Babylon and the region of Jibāl, the shedding of blood, the ruination of most of the lands and the corruption of the status of the mighty, an abundance or robbers (and especially in the countries of the Arabs), the wrongdoing of judges, an abundance of people complaining about them, slaves deceiving their masters, the rejection of scholars and soothsayers, the perishing of donkeys and cattle, and an abundance of locusts with the dryness of the air, a scarcity of rains, and an abundance of food. **32** And if he was transiting over the Moon, that indicates a copious amount of rains and an abundance of moistures.

**33 The account of the planets' transits over Mars. 34** If the Sun was transiting over Mars, that indicates an abundance of moistures. **35** And if Venus was transiting over him, that indicates the warring of kings and their fighting one another, an abundance of confusions and harms in most of the countries, an occurrence of death in locusts, with a copious amount of rains and the intensity of the heat. **36** And if Mercury was transiting over him, that

---

[11] Reading as وقوع, for **BY**'s وقوف ("stopping").

indicates alarm befalling Persia and the death of its king, intense fear occurring in most of the countries, and the respect of soothsayers, with the middling amount of the waters in rivers, and their moderation. **37** And if the Moon was transiting over him, that indicates an abundance of moistures.

**38 The account of the Sun's transits over the planets. 39** If the Sun was transiting over Venus, that indicates a copious amount of rains. **40** And if he was transiting over Mercury, that indicates the fear of the people of the Ahwāz towards Rūm, and the appearance of sciences and wisdom, with the dryness of the air and the scarcity of its moisture. **41** And if he was transiting over the Moon, that indicates a scarcity of moistures.

**42 The account of the planets' transits over the Sun. 43** And if Venus was transiting over the Sun, that indicates the copious amount of rains. **44** And if Mercury was transiting over him, that indicates the abundance of the crops as well as locusts, with the abundant blowing of the winds and a copious amount of rains. **45** And if the Moon was transiting over him, that indicates a copious amount of moistures and an abundance of waters.

**46 The account of Venus's transits over the planets. 47** If Venus was transiting over Mercury, that indicates the warring of the people of the Ahwāz against Rūm, and the appearance of the sciences and wisdom, with an abundance of rains, thunder, and lighting, and an increase in rivers. **48** And if she was transiting over the Moon, that indicates the copious amount of rains and an abundance of moistures.

**49 The account of the planets' transits over Venus. 50** If Mercury was transiting over Venus, that indicates the downfall of the king of Rūm and the king of the Arabs from their status, the abundant movement of armies to some of the lands, and the occurrence of false rumors in the people. **51** And if the Moon was transiting over her, that indicates warring taking place between the people of Persia and Rūm, an abundance of the totally destitute and robbers, the miscarriage of pregnant women, the perishing of donkeys, the death of cattle, an abundance of moistures and waters, with a scarcity of seed and sown crops, and especially in the land of Persia and Rūm.

**52 The account of Mercury's transits over the planets. 53** If Mercury was transiting over the Moon, it indicates the successive blowing of winds.

**54 The account of the planets' transits over Mercury. 55** And if the Moon was transiting over Mercury, that indicates the middling amount of rains and moistures.

**56** Since we have completed what we wanted to explain, let us break off the discussion in Chapter VI.6.

## Chapter VI.7: On judging the transits of the planets above one another during their parallelism with the sign of Libra

**1** Since we have set forth in Chapter VI.6 the account of the indications of the planets' transits over each other during their parallelism with the sign of Virgo, in this chapter let us state their indications for that when they are parallel with the sign of Libra.

♈♄♎ **2 The account of Saturn's transits over the planets. 3** If Saturn was transiting over Jupiter, that indicates an abundance of ailments and illnesses occurring from coughing, and an abundance of toil, strain, and plundering (especially in the countries of the Arabs), with a scarcity of rains. **4** And if he was transiting over Mars, that indicates the occurrence of rancor between kings, with the moderation of the winter and the scarcity of its cold. **5** And if he was transiting over the Sun, that indicates an abundance of drought and hunger in most of the lands, with a copious amount of rains (and sometimes they will be moderate), and the death of children. **6** And if he was transiting over Venus, that indicates the uprightness of the people, and the abundance of locusts with a scarcity of rains. **7** And if he was transiting over Mercury, that indicates an abundance of drought and hunger in most of the climes, with a copious amount of rains and the successive blowing of the winds. **8** And if he was transiting over the Moon, that indicates an abundance of drought and hunger in most of the lands, with the existence of moistures and their suitability.

**9 The account of the planets' transits over Saturn. 10** If Jupiter was transiting over Saturn, that indicates the warring of [the people of] Rūm against each other and an abundance of killing among them, the stirring up of enemies and their burning most of the countries, the intensification of drought, the existence of rains (and their suitability), and the fine condition of sowing. **11** And if Mars was transiting over him, that indicates the warring of kings against one another, the death of the women of kings, an abundance of grasses, and a scarcity of rains. **12** And if the Sun was transiting over him, that indicates the warring of kings against one another, the death of some of the women of the king of Babylon, and an abundance of enemies, with the vigor of the grasses and a copious amount of rains. **13** And if Venus was transiting over him, that indicates the warring of kings against one another, and an abundance of herbiage, with an abundance of rains and moistures, and the moderate blowing of winds. **14** And if Mercury was transiting over him, that indicates that disturbances will happen between kings and the mighty, with copious amounts of rains, the middling amount of food and seeds, and the moderate blowing of winds. **15** And if the Moon was transiting over him, that indicates the miscarriage of pregnant women, a copious amount of moistures, and an abundance of seeds.

**16 The account of Jupiter's transits over the planets. 17** If Jupiter was transiting over Mars, that indicates the intense delight of the king of Babylon in the ruin of his enemies, with most affairs moving ahead for him, robbers obtaining the assets of businessmen, and an abundance of clouds. **18** And if he was transiting over the Sun, that indicates the abundant dryness of the air. **19** And if he was transiting over Venus, that indicates tribulation and hardships coming to the people of the Sawād, the fine condition of the people of Babylon, an abundance of confusions in Armenia, and the ruin of the Arabs, with an abundance of earthquakes and the fine condition of the sown crops. **20** And if he was transiting over Mercury, that indicates the existence of safety in most of the countries, and a succession of benefits with the successive blowing of the winds. **21** And if he was transiting over the Moon, that indicates a scarcity of moistures and the dryness of the air.

**22 The account of the planets' transits over Jupiter. 23** If Mars was transiting over Jupiter, that indicates the abundance of the people's fears, and their hostility to one another, the bad condition of businesses, with an abundance of rains, thunder, and lightning. **24** And if the Sun was transiting over him, that indicates the existence of rains, and their moderation. **25** And if Venus was transiting over him, that indicates the suitable condition of business, the abundance of what befalls the people from fevers and melancholic ailments, the expensiveness of food, the corruption of the sown crops in Armenia (but sometimes they are sound), and an abundance of rains and moistures. **26** And if Mercury was transiting over him, that indicates the death of the king of Persia and Rūm, and an abundance of robbers, highway banditry, scoundrels, and Kurds, and killing befalling businessmen from them, fear occurring in most of the climes, and drought along with the raging of the winds. **27** And if the Moon was transiting over him, that indicates a copious amount of moistures, and their abundance.

**28 The account of Mars's transits over the planets. 29** If Mars was transiting over the Sun, that indicates the abundance of civil unrest in Babylon, their wronging each other, lying, the malicious joy of the people towards one another, with the moderation of the air and its inclining to the hot and dry, the excessiveness of the cold in its own [proper] time, and the raging of winds pulling up trees and date palms. **30** And if he was transiting over Venus, that indicates the existence of civil unrest and captivity in the region of the Ahwāz, the abundance of raiding by the people of Jibāl against their enemies, and the appearance of harms and fire, with a trivial amount of rains. **31** And if he was transiting over Mercury, that indicates the death of some of the children of the king, and an abundance of fears befalling the people of the countries, the attack by the people of Jibāl against the people of Khūzistān and the occurrence of war between them, the fighting of the people of the region of the east against the region of the west, and the ruin of most of the nomads of the Arabs and the death of their leaders, the abundant occurrence of death in the people, the perishing of cattle, a scarcity of grazing livestock, the corruption of churches and synagogues, and their plundering, with a scarcity of rains at the beginning of the season appropriate for them, an abundance of clouds, thunder, and lightning, and a decrease of waters in rivers, and their dryness. **32** And if he was transiting over the Moon, that indicates the death of the king of Babylon with the dispersal of their nobles and the spending of their assets, and the death of the king of the Ahwāz, an abundance of civil unrest, fighting, and death in Fārs, Rūm, and the people of Jibāl, an abundance of harm from predatory animals, and the perishing of beasts of burden (like cattle, camels and other things), with an abundance of enemies.

**33 The account of the planets' transits over Mars. 34** If the Sun was transiting over Mars, that indicates an abundance of wrongdoing in Babylon, lying, incitement to rebellion, the malicious joy of the people against each other, with the moisture of the atmosphere and the intensity of heat in its own [proper] time. **35** And if Venus was transiting over him, that indicates the death of some of the women of kings, and an abundance of civil unrest in the countries with a copious amount of moistures. **36** And if Mercury was transiting over him, that indicates the corrupt condition of the people of Babylon, the suitable condition of the people of Rūm, and the occurrence of fire among the nomads of the Arabs, with an abundance of clouds, a copious amount of rains, the existence of earthquakes and thunderbolts at the beginning of the season appropriate for it, and its scarcity at its end. **37** And if the Moon was transiting over him, that indicates an abundance of waters and moistures.

**38 The account of the Sun's transits over the planets. 39** If the Sun was transiting over Venus, that indicates an abundance of clouds and a scarcity of rains. **40** And if he was transiting over Mercury, that indicates catastrophes befalling writers and household managers, with a copious amount of rains. **41** And if he was transiting over the Moon, that indicates the arrival of reports with an abundance of false rumors, and the fine mixture of the air.

**42 The account of the planets' transits over the Sun. 43** If Venus was transiting over the Sun, that indicates an abundance of moistures and the copious amount of rains. **44** And if Mercury was transiting over him, that indicates the successive blowing of the winds and a copious amount of moistures. **45** And if the Moon was transiting over him, that indicates an abundance of moistures.

**46 The account of Venus's transits over the planets. 47** If Venus was transiting over Mercury, that indicates the death of the king of Babylon and the safety of the subjects, the attack by the king of Rūm against the king of the Turks and the countries of the Ahwāz, and his raiding their kingdom and warring against them, a copious amount of rains, and an abundance of waters and the swelling of rivers. **48** And if she was transiting over the Moon, that indicates the moderateness of the air and the scarcity of rains.

**49 The account of the planets' transits over Venus. 50** If Mercury was transiting over Venus, that indicates the occurrence of wars between Rūm and the Turks, and the attack by Rūm and the people of Jibāl against the people of Armenia, and the occurrence of death and lightning bolts in most of the climes, with a copious amount of rains and their moderation. **51** And if the Moon was transiting over her, that indicates the suitability of the rains and an abundance of moistures.

☿☊ **52 The account of Mercury's transits over the planets. 53** If Mercury was transiting over the Moon, that indicates the suitable condition of the rains and an abundance of moistures.

**54 The account of the planets' transits over Mercury. 55** If the Moon was transiting over Mercury, that indicates an abundance of moistures and the swelling [of bodies of water].

**56** Since we have completed what we wanted to explain, let us break off the discussion in Chapter VI.7, if God wills.

## Chapter VI.8: On judging the transits of the planets above one another during their parallelism with the sign of Scorpio

1 Since we have completed in Chapter VI.7 the statement of the indications of the planets' transits over each other during their parallelism with the sign of Libra, in this chapter let us state their indications when they are parallel with the sign of Scorpio.

♈ ♄ ♏ 2 The account of Saturn's transits over the planets. 3 If Saturn was transiting over Jupiter, that indicates the death of some of the kings of Jibāl and the ruination of its land, the ruin of most of the people in it, and the occurrence of death among scorpions and snakes, with a trivial amount of rains and the abundant blowing of the winds. 4 And if he was transiting over Mars, that indicates an abundance of corruption in most of the climes, with the dryness of the air and a scarcity of its moisture. 5 And if he was transiting over the Sun, that indicates the abundant occurrence of death in most of the climes, with excessive heat in its own [proper] time. 6 And if he was transiting over Venus, it indicates powerful illnesses befalling the people in most of the countries, with a trivial amount of moistures. 7 And if he was transiting over Mercury, that indicates the occurrence of death in most of the climes, with a trivial amount of rains and an abundance of waters. 8 And if he was transiting over the Moon, that indicates a scarcity of rains and waters.

9 The account of the planets' transits over Saturn. 10 If Jupiter was transiting over Saturn, that indicates the death of some of the kings of Jibāl, and good will come to the king of Babylon there, with an abundance of rancor and hostilities happening in most of the climes, and the occurrence of fire in them, with a copious amount of rains. 11 And if Mars was transiting over him, that indicates an abundance of civil unrest in the region of Jibāl, corruption occurring in most of the climes, the incidence of locusts doing damage to sowing, and the existence of rains, thunder, and lightning. 12 And if the Sun was transiting over him, that indicates the occurrence of wars between kings, an abundance of epidemics and death in the people, the goodness of the air, and the moisture of the atmosphere. 13 And if Venus was transiting over Saturn, that indicates anxieties and sorrows befalling the king of Babylon, and his downfall from his status, and death happening

among women, things crawling on the earth, and flies, with an abundance of moistures. **14** And if Mercury was transiting over him, that indicates combat happening between kings, the occurrence of epidemics and death in most animals and livestock, with a copious amount of rains and an abundance of unhealthiness. **15** And if the Moon was transiting over him, that indicates the incidence of combat between kings, and the occurrence of epidemics and death in most venomous animals, with an abundance of moistures.

♈♃♏︎ **16 The account of Jupiter's transits over the planets. 17** If Jupiter was transiting over Mars, that indicates death occurring among the children of kings, the ruin of the nobles of Babylon, the frequent appearance of their enemies, and the occurrence of fire in it with the fertility of the countries and a scarcity of rains. **18** And if he was transiting over the Sun, that indicates the dryness of the air. **19** And if he was transiting over Venus, that indicates the confusion of the affairs of the king of Babylon, and his transferring to the Sawād, the warring of the people of the Ahwāz against each other, and the killing of gatherings of women for those reasons. **20** And if he was transiting over Mercury, that indicates fear coming to the king of Babylon and its people, and the attack of armies belonging to the people of the south, war befalling the people of Jibāl, and defeat happening to them (and their safety from that), an abundance of griefs, hardships, and wars befalling the people of the region of the east, the ruination of most of their villages, the fertility of the villages of Rūm, with an abundance of clouds, and a copious amount of rains, especially in the season appropriate for it. **21** And if he was transiting over the Moon, that indicates a scarcity of waters and rains.

**22 The account of the planets' transits over Jupiter. 23** If Mars was transiting over Jupiter, that indicates the occurrence of fears in the land of Babylon and the ruination of most of it, and the capture by the people of Jibāl over against the people of the Ahwāz, with an abundance of death in most of the climes, a scarcity of rains, the decrease of waters in rivers and of fish, and especially in Babylon. **24** And if the Sun was transiting over him, that indicates the moisture of the air. **25** And if Venus was transiting over him, that indicates anxieties befalling the king of Jibāl, the occurrence of confusions and the killing of the king of the Ahwāz by the sword, and an abundance of death in most of the climes with a copious amount of rains. **26**

BOOK VI: PLANETS TRANSITING OVER EACH OTHER, IN ALL SIGNS   315

And if Mercury was transiting over him, that indicates corruption happening in the land of Babylon, the occurrence of fears and civil unrest in most of the climes, the warring of the people of the region of the east against the people of the region of the north, the conquest of many cities and fortifications, the attack by most of the people of Khurāsān against the people of the region of the south and east, with the successive blowing of the winds. **27** And if the Moon was transiting over him, that indicates the copious amount of rains and an abundance of waters.

♂♏ **28 The account of Mars's planets over the planets. 29** If Mars was transiting over the Sun, that indicates the dryness of the air, and its hotness. **30** And if he was transiting over Venus, that indicates the death of the women of kings, and the pouncing of the people of Jibāl upon the people of Khurāsān, with a scarcity of moistures. **31** And if he was transiting over Mercury, that indicates the death of the king of the Arab nomads, and the pouncing of the people of Jibāl upon them, and their victory over most of their land, and the occurrence of death among the people and cattle, with the successive blowing of the winds. **32** And if he was transiting over the Moon, that indicates the death of the king of Babylon and the dispersal of their nobles, the spending of their assets, the death of the king of the Ahwāz, with an abundance of fighting and civil unrest in most of the climes, and their capturing one another, the occurrence of death in Persia, Rūm, and the land of Jibāl, with harm from predatory beasts, the perishing of beasts of burden (like camels and cattle, and what resembles that), with the existence of thunder, lightning, and lightning bolts.

**33 The account of the planets' transits over Mars. 34** If the Sun was transiting over Mars, that indicates the moisture of the atmosphere. **35** And if Venus was transiting over him, that indicates new kingship in the land of Rūm [by a man] having no importance, the death of some of the children of kings, and the frequent appearance of abominable things in the people of the Sawād, with a copious amount of rains. **36** And if Mercury was transiting over him, that indicates the pouncing of the people of the king of Babylon upon their own king, and their fighting their enemies, fears befalling the people of Jibāl and their killing of their king, and the occurrence of locusts and corruption in it, with an abundance of clouds and rains in the season appropriate for it, and the intensity of the heat in its own [proper] season. **37**

And if the Moon was transiting over him, that indicates the existence of thunder, lightning, and lightning bolts.

☉♏ **38 The account of the Sun's transits over the planets. 39** If the Sun was transiting over Venus, that indicates a scarcity of rains. **40** And if he was transiting over Mercury, that indicates a copious amount of moistures. **41** And if he was transiting over the Moon, that indicates a scarcity of moistures and waters, and the trivial amount of rains.

**42 The account of the planets' transits over the Sun. 43** If Venus was transiting over the Sun, that indicates a copious amount of rains. **44** And if Mercury was transiting over him, that indicates a copious amount of rains and the successive blowing of winds. **45** And if the Moon was transiting over him, that indicates the copious amounts of rains and a scarcity of waters.

♀♏ **46 The account of Venus's transits over the planets. 47** If Venus was transiting over Mercury, that indicates the death of the king of Babylon, the ruination of most of Iraq, and the capturing by the people of grazing livestock in most of the lands, an abundance of fighting and its intensity, with the copious amount of rains, and the existence of thunder, lightning, and the incidence of earthquakes, and the abundant swelling of waters. **48** And if she was transiting over the Moon, that indicates the existence of moistures and rains.

**49 The account of the planets' transits over Venus. 50** If Mercury was transiting over Venus, that indicates the advance of armies from the land of India to the region of Babylon, and their abundant [numbers] in that, and their attacking the land of Armenia (and their safety), an abundance of robbers, and the dispersal of soldiers within the east to the region of the south, the attack by the people of Jibāl against Armenia, the bad condition of the Greeks, the safety of Jibāl, an abundance of births, and a copious amount of rains. **51** And if the Moon was transiting over her, that indicates a copious amount of rains and an abundance of moistures.

☿♏ **52 The account of Mercury's transits over the planets. 53** If Mercury was transiting over the Moon, that indicates the warring of Rūm against the people of the Ahwāz, and the abundant occurrence of death in women, with a copious amount of rains and the abundant blowing of the winds.

**54 The account of the planets' transits over Mercury. 55** If the Moon was transiting over Mercury, that indicates a copious amount of rains, the abundance of waters, and the appearance of shooting stars and fires in the atmosphere.

**56** Since he have completed what we wanted to explain, let us break off the discussion in Chapter VI.8, if God wills.

## Chapter VI.9: On judging the transits of the planets above one another during their parallelism with the sign of Sagittarius

**1** Since we have set forth in Chapter VI.8 the statement of the indications of the planets' transits over each other during their parallelism with the sign of Scorpio, in this chapter let us state the account of their indications for that during their parallelism with the sign of Sagittarius.

♈♄♐ **2 The account of Saturn's transits over the planets. 3** If Saturn was transiting over Jupiter, that indicates the occurrence of tribulations and hardships in most of the climes, an abundance of wars in Babylon and the death of its king, and the occurrence of false rumors and ruination in it. **4** And if he was transiting over Mars, that indicates the occurrence of wars between kings, and an abundance of death in some of the climes with the intensity of the *simooms* in their own [proper] season. **5** And if he was transiting over the Sun, that indicates the occurrence of death in livestock with a copious amount of rains (and sometimes they will be moderate), and a scarcity of sowing. **6** And if he was transiting over Venus, that indicates the death of some of the women of kings, and their being taken as booty, with a trivial amount of rains and the fine condition of the crops. **7** And if he was transiting over Mercury, that indicates the occurrence of death among livestock and civil unrest in most of the climes, with the successive blowing of the winds and the scarce flourishing of the sowing. **8** And if he was transiting over the Moon, that indicates the occurrence of death among livestock, with the suitability of moistures and their successive [occurrence], and the scarce rise [in the prices] of seeds.

**9 The account of the planets' transits over Saturn. 10** If Jupiter was transiting over Saturn, that indicates tribulations, hardships, and civil unrest befalling the king of Babylon, and the intense drought among its people, an abundance of enemies, rancor, and wars happening among the people, with an abundance of rains and their moderation. **11** And if Mars was transiting over him, that indicates an abundance of illnesses in most of the climes, the successive blowing of the winds, and an abundance of dust and the cheapness of food. **12** And if the Sun was transiting over him, that indicates the occurrence of wars between kings, and the death of the king of Babylon, with a copious amount of rains. **13** And if Venus was transiting over him, that indicates the death of the women of kings, or their being killed by poison, with a trivial amount of rains and the fineness of the seeds. **14** And if Mercury was transiting over him, that indicates the occurrence of warring between kings, and the rising up of a rebel with the middling amount of rains, an abundance of waters, and the successive blowing of winds. **15** And if the Moon was transiting over him, that indicates the warring of kings against one another, with a copious amount of rains and an abundance of moistures.

**16 The account of Jupiter's transits over the planets. 17** If Jupiter was transiting over Mars, that indicates the death of the king of Rūm, the occurrence of death among the nobles of his land, an abundance of fire in it, with the intensity of the cold in its own [proper] time. **18** And if he was transiting over the Sun, that indicates an abundance of rains and their benefit. **19** And if he was transiting over Venus, that indicates an abundance of false testimonies among the people of the Sawād, with the pouncing of the mighty upon (and his[12] victory over) them, and his killing them, the harshness of the king of the Ahwāz against his subjects and his killing some of his children, the ruin of some of its people, an abundance of earthquakes, and the suitability of the seeds. **20** And if he was transiting over Mercury, that indicates a copious amount of rains, the successive blowing of winds, an abundance of thunder, lightning, earthquakes, and snows (with their benefit), and especially in the season appropriate for that, with an abundance of seeds, and especially in the Ahwāz. **21** And if he was transiting over the Moon, that indicates the middling amount of moistures.

**22 The account of the planets' transits over Jupiter. 23** If Mars was transiting over Jupiter, that indicates the ruination of most of the villages of Babylon, and anxieties and sorrows befalling the people of Rūm, and the occurrence of death among the rich, with a scarcity of rains. **24** And if the Sun was transiting over him, that indicates the dryness of the air and the occurrence of death in most of the climes. **25** And if Venus was transiting over him, that indicates an abundance of lying and false rumors in the regions, the warring of the people of Babylon against the Ahwāz, the occurrence of rancor between them, with the death of women, a copious amount of rains, and an increase in the Tigris and Euphrates. **26** And if Mercury was transiting

---

[12] Apparently, the king.

over him, that indicates the ruination of the king of Babylon, and his shifting from land to land, his attacking his enemies and his subjugating them, with hardship coming to them from him, an abundance of drought and devastation in his land, and his victory over robbers; and there will be fighting and damage in the region of Jibāl, the people of the south will fight the people of the east, the houses of assets will decrease, and fire will happen in the houses of worship, and the generality of the countries will be devastated, with an abundance of rains, the successive blowing of the winds, and the swelling of rivers. **27** And if the Moon was transiting over him, that indicates an abundance of moistures and a copious amount of waters.

T♂♐ **28 The account of Mars's transits over the planets. 29** If Mars was transiting over the Sun, that indicates an abundance of lightning. **30** And if Mars was transiting over Venus, that indicates the death of the king of Babylon, and the abundant opposition of enemies against them, with a copious amount of rains. **31** And if he was transiting over Mercury, that indicates the fighting of the people of Babylon against one another, their mutual shedding of blood, the intensity of anger, and an abundance of pains and death among the people, with an abundance of clouds and rains. **32** And if he was transiting over the Moon, that indicates a trivial amount of waters and rains.

**33 The account of the planets' transits over Mars. 34** If the Sun was transiting over Mars, that indicates the moisture of the atmosphere. **35** And if Venus was transiting over him, that indicates safety and uprightness appearing among the people of Egypt, and the bad condition of the nobles, with a copious amount of rains. **36** And if Mercury was transiting over him, that indicates the fighting of the people of the region of the east against the region of the west, an abundance of death among them, the descent of locusts, with a copious amount of rains, the blowing of winds, and the corruption of the crops. **37** And if the Moon was transiting over him, that indicates the appearance of waters and moistures.

T☉♐ **38 The account of the Sun's transits over the planets. 39** If the Sun was transiting over Venus, that indicates the dryness of the air. **40** And if the Sun was transiting over Mercury, that indicates the death of some of the kings of the cities which are on the coasts of the sea, with a copious amount of rains and the abundant blowing of the winds. **41**

And if he was transiting over the Moon, the indicates a trivial amount of moistures.

**42 The account of the planets' transits over the Sun. 43** If Venus was transiting over the Sun, that indicates an abundance of moistures. **44** And if Mercury was transiting over him, that indicates the occurrence of rancor among the people, with the existence of winds and a copious amount of rains, and an abundance of moistures. **45** And if the Moon was transiting over him, that indicates a copious amount of waters and an abundance of moistures.

♈︎☿♐︎ **46 The account of Venus's transits over the planets. 47** If Venus was transiting over Mercury, that indicates the attack by the king of Babylon and his children against the king of Armenia, and the attack of his enemies against his land, the occurrence of war between them and the king of Iraq, an abundance of civil unrest in border towns and cities, with hardship occurring in the countries, the abundant stirring-up of black bile in the people as well as insanity, with a copious amount of rains and the occurrence of thunder. **48** And if she was transiting over the Moon, that indicates an abundance of moistures.

**49 The account of the planets' transits over Venus. 50** If Mercury was transiting over Venus, that indicates civil unrest occurring in most of the climes, and the assembling of people in Babylon, and their attacking the countries of Rūm and their corrupting some of their land, their ruining many of the border towns in Rūm, and their king being defeated, and tribulations, hardships, death, and harms will be abundant in Fārs, with the existence of rains and winds, and their moderateness. **51** And if the Moon was transiting over her, it indicates the existence of moistures and rains.

♈︎♀︎♐︎ **52 The account of Mercury's transits over the planets. 53** If Mercury was transiting over the Moon, that indicates the occurrence of rancor among the people, with a copious amount of rains.

**54 The account of the planets' transits over Mercury. 55** If the Moon was transiting over Mercury, that indicates the death of some of the kings of cities which are on the coasts and waters, with the existence of moistures.

**56** Since we have completed what we wanted to explain, let us break off the discussion in [this] chapter.

## Chapter VI.10: On judging the transits of the planets above one another during their parallelism with the sign of Capricorn

**1** Since we have set forth in Chapter VI.9 the account of the indications of the planets' transits over each other during their parallelism with the sign of Sagittarius, in this chapter let us state their indications for the same thing during their parallelism with the sign of Capricorn.

**2 The account of Saturn's transits over the planets. 3** If Saturn was transiting over Jupiter, that indicates the perishing of donkeys and the death of sheep, the scarcity of moistures, and a decrease in waters, especially in rivers. **4** And if he was transiting over Mars, that indicates the perishing of donkeys, and the intensity of cold and its duration. **5** And if he was transiting over the Sun, that indicates the dryness of the air. **6** And if he was transiting over Venus, that indicates the perishing of donkeys, with a trivial amount of moistures and a decrease in waters, especially in the sea. **7** And if he was transiting over Mercury, that indicates an abundance of death in the Ahwāz, and women of some of the kings killing some of their own relatives (such as their mother, and what is like that), with a copious amount of rains, an abundance of swelling [in waters] and the intensity of the cold. **8** And if he was transiting over the Moon, that indicates a scarcity of moistures and waters.

**9 The account of the planets' transits over Saturn. 10** If Jupiter was transiting over Saturn, that indicates the death of some of the kings of Jibāl, the ruin of most robbers, the hardship of the predatory animals, and a scarcity of locusts, with a scarcity of moistures and the flourishing of the sown crops. **11** And if Mars was transiting over him, that indicates an abundance of donkeys and sheep, with an intensity of heat and cold and their duration in the two seasons appropriate for that. **12** And if the Sun was transiting over him, that indicates the attack by Rūm on Armenia and an abundance of illnesses and death befalling the people, with an abundance of rains. **13** And if Venus was transiting over him, that indicates a copious amount of rains, the attack by Rūm on Armenia, and an abundance of death and illnesses befalling the people. **14** And if Mercury was transiting over him, that indicates the occurrence of death in the women of kings, the abundant appearance of epidemics in things having four [feet], with an abundance of rains and the successive blowing of the winds, and a decrease in grasses. **15** And if the Moon was transiting over him, that indicates an abundance of moistures and a copious amount of waters.

**16 The account of Jupiter's transits over the planets. 17** If Jupiter was transiting over Mars, that indicates the occurrence of death among most of the enemies of Rūm, the death of predatory beasts and harmful creeping things, and the death of aquatic birds, with an abundance of clouds, rains, and waters. **18** And if he was transiting over the Sun, that indicates the moderation of the air. **19** And if he was transiting over Venus, that indicates the triumph of the king of Babylon over his enemies, the year will be suitable, death will take place in sheep and cattle, and many fish and delicate birds (like sparrows and what is like that), with the abundant incidence of earthquakes and a scarcity of rains. **20** And if he was transiting over Mercury, that indicates the attack by the king of Rūm against his enemies, and his victory over them, an abundance of soothsayers and magicians, with the intensity of destructive cold, a copious amount of rains, the flourishing of the sown crops and the fineness of their condition. **21** And if he was transiting over the Moon, that indicates an abundance of moistures and a copious amount of waters.

**22 The account of the planets' transits over Jupiter. 23** If Mars was transiting over Jupiter, that indicates an abundance of captivity in most of the climes, the occurrence of death among sheep, a scarcity of rains, and the intensity of cold in the season appropriate for it, and a trivial amount of rainwater. **24** And if the Sun was transiting over him, that indicates the confusion of the king of Babylon, with the moisture of the atmosphere. **25** And if Venus was transiting over him, that indicates that there will be infectious disease in Babylon, the king of Rūm's killing his own mighty [people] and the downfall of those of them who survive, an abundance of death in sheep, with a trivial amount of rains in the time appropriate for it, and a scarcity of food, especially among the people of the Sawād. **26** And if Mercury was transiting over him, that indicates wars befalling the king of Babylon, the downfall of the king of Rūm from his status, and the king of Arīn will turn away from his kingdom (and his enemies' pouncing on him, and the scarcity of his helpers), and the occurrence of disturbances in most of the countries, with an abundance of epidemics and death in cows and sheep, with a copious amount of waters, the intensity of destructive cold in the season appropriate for it, with snows, the incidence of earthquakes, and lightning bolts, especially in Persia. **27** And if the Moon was transiting over him, that indicates the abundance of waters and moistures.

**28 The account of Mars's transits over the planets. 29** If Mars was transiting over the Sun, that indicates the dryness of the air. **30** And if he was transiting over Venus, that indicates the death of the king of the Ahwāz, the miscarriage of pregnant women, with the safety of women and the occurrence of death in sheep with the intensity of the heat in the season appropriate for it. **31** And if he was transiting over Mercury, that indicates the death of the king of Rūm, an abundance of illnesses, ailments, and death befalling the people, with the incidence of civil unrest and captivity, the perishing of donkeys and the death of sheep, a scarcity of pressed juices and oils, with a scarcity of rains in the first quarter of winter, an abundance of civil unrest and the middling amount of rains at the end of the winter quarter, and the intensity of the cold. **32** And if he was transiting over the Moon, that indicates the death of the king of Babylon, the dispersal of its nobles, and the spending of its assets, the death of the king of the Ahwāz, the abundance of fighting and civil unrest in most of the climes, the capturing of some by others, an abundance of death in Fārs, Rūm, and Jibāl, and the appearance of harm from predatory animals, the perishing of beasts of burden (of cattle, camels, and other things) with a trivial amount of rains and a scarcity of waters.

**33 The account of the planets' transits over Mars. 34** If the Sun was transiting over Mars, that indicates the moisture of the atmosphere. **35** And if Venus was transiting over him, that indicates an abundance of fire in the land of the Ahwāz, and an abundance of rebels in the land of Jibāl, with a copious amount of rains. **36** And if Mercury was transiting over him, that indicates intense fear happening in most of the countries, an abundance of epidemics and death in the land of Rūm, the appearance of alms, the conflict between sons and their fathers, the perishing of donkeys, and death taking place in sheep, with an abundance of clouds, the middling amount of rains, the intensity of the cold, and an abundance of snows. **37** And if the Moon was transiting over him, that indicates an abundance of waters and swelling [of waters].

♈☉☿ **38 The account of the Sun's transits over the planets. 39** If the Sun was transiting over Venus, that indicates the dryness of the air. **40** And if he was transiting over Mercury, that indicates an abundance of death in the Ahwāz because of epidemics, with the middling amount of rains and the swelling [of waters]. **41** And if he was transiting over the Moon, that indicates a scarcity of moistures.

**42 The account of the planets' transits over the Sun. 43** If Venus was transiting over the Sun, that indicates the moisture of the atmosphere, the abundance of moistures, and the intensity of the heat. **44** And if Mercury was transiting over him, that indicates the occurrence of epidemics among things having four [feet], with a copious amount of rains and the successive blowing of the winds. **45** And if the Moon was transiting over him, that indicates the copious amount of moistures.

♈♀☿ **46 The account of Venus's transits over the planets. 47** If Venus was transiting over Mercury, that indicates kings' concluding a truce with the king of Babylon, the victory of the people of Babylon over one who is hostile to them, the death of the king of Rūm, the appearance of robbers, fears, and sorrows in most of the countries, death befalling donkeys and camels, with the intensity of the cold in the season appropriate for that, a trivial amount of rains, and the existence of communicable diseases and thunder. **48** If she was transiting over the Moon, that indicates a scarcity of moistures.

**49 The account of the planets' transits over Venus. 50** If Mercury was transiting over Venus, that indicates the death of the king of Rūm, the existence of epidemics, captivity, and death in most of the lands, the gathering of the villages and their fortification, the miscarriage of pregnant women from the intensity of the cold, and the death of the king of Arīn with an abundance of clouds and rains, the decline of foreigners,[13] and the existence of floods. **51** If the Moon was transiting over her, that indicates the occurrence of wars between the people of Persia and Rūm, the death of the king of Persia, an abundance of the totally destitute and robbers, the miscarriage of pregnant

---

[13] Or perhaps, "the falling of strange things [from the sky]," as **BY** read it ( سقوط الغرباء).

women, the perishing of donkeys, the death of cattle with the dryness of the atmosphere, and a scarcity of seeds and sown crops.

♄☿♂ **52 The account of Mercury's transits over the planets. 53** If Mercury was transiting over the Moon, that indicates an abundance of moistures, swellings [of water], and rains.

**54 The account of the planets' transits over Mercury. 55** If the Moon was transiting over Mercury, that indicates the dryness of the atmosphere and a scarcity of rains.

**56** Since we have completed what we wanted to explain, let us break off the discussion in [this] chapter, if God wills.

## Chapter VI.11: On judging the transits of the planets above one another during their parallelism with the sign of Aquarius

1 Since we have completed in Chapter VI.10 the transits of the planets above one another during their parallelism with the sign of Capricorn, in this chapter let us state their indications for that during their parallelism with the sign of Aquarius.

2 **The account of Saturn's transits over the planets.** 3 If Saturn was transiting over Jupiter, that indicates hardships taking place among the people, and drought in most of the countries, with a copious amount of rains, a scarcity of waters, and the dryness of rivers. 4 And if he was transiting over Mars, that indicates the intensity of the heat and cold in their own [proper] times. 5 And if he was transiting over the Sun, that indicates the abundant occurrence of death among women, with the dryness of the air. 6 And if he was transiting over Venus, that indicates that alarm and confusion will enter upon kings, and sometimes the king of Babylon will die, with a scarcity of moistures. 7 And if he was transiting over Mercury, that indicates the people's engaging in sins, and especially in the land of Armenia and the regions of Jibāl, the occurrence of epidemics and death in the people, the death of some of the children of kings or his relatives, with a copious amount of rains, an abundance of waters, the intensity of the cold, a scarcity of thunder and lightning, and the corruption of the seeds. 8 And if he was transiting over the Moon, that indicates hardship taking place in the land of Armenia, with a trivial amount of rains and a scarcity of waters.

9 **The account of the planets' transits over Saturn.** 10 If Jupiter was transiting over Saturn, that indicates the fine condition of the people of Babylon, their fertility,[14] and the fertility of most of the countries, with a copious amount of rains, an abundance of snows and waters, and the swelling of rivers and their safety. 11 And if Mars was transiting over him, that indicates the frequent pouncing of enemies upon the countries of the Arabs, with a scarcity of waters and a trivial amount of rains. 12 And if the Sun was transiting over him, that indicates hardships taking place in the land of Armenia, with the moisture of the atmosphere. 13 And if Venus was transiting over

---

[14] Or, "abundance" (خصب).

Saturn, that indicates ailments befalling the people from coughing, and the abundance of waters, with the moderateness of rivers. **14** And if Mercury was transiting over him, that indicates a copious amount of rains, an abundance of ice, an increase of rivers in the rivers, a scarcity of thunder and lightning, and the flourishing of sown crops. **15** And if the Moon was transiting over him, that indicates the occurrence of hardships in the land of Armenia, with an abundance of moistures and waters.

**16 The account of Jupiter's transits over the planets. 17** If Jupiter was transiting over Mars, that indicates the attack by the people of Jibāl against the people of Babylon, enemies triumphing over most of the countries, and the appearance of delight, bliss, and safety after that, with a scarcity of rains and waters. **18** And if he was transiting over the Sun, that indicates the dryness of the air, darkness occurring in the atmosphere, with a copious amount of waters, and an abundance of fish and delicate birds. **19** And if he was transiting over Venus, that indicates the suitability of the affairs of the Turks, few pains happening in most of the countries, with an abundance of waters and the darkness of the atmosphere. **20** And if he was transiting over Mercury, that indicates the victory of the king over his enemies (and sometimes he is made unfortunate at their hands), and the strength of his allies and subjects, and the submissiveness of the people of the east, west, and south towards him, the occurrence of rancor between the king of Rūm and his enemies, the death of the king of Persia and the ruination of most of it, and an abundance of earthquakes in it, and clouds with a copious amount or rains and the intensity of the cold. **21** If he was transiting over the Moon, that indicates an abundance of moistures.

**22 The account of the planets' transits over Jupiter. 23** If Mars was transiting over Jupiter, that indicates assets coming to the king of Babylon, the moderate amount of waters, and the flourishing of vegetation. **24** And if the Sun was transiting over him, that indicates the moisture of the atmosphere. **25** And if Venus was transiting over him, that indicates tribulation coming to the king of Babylon [who] will come close to ruin from it, catastrophe will afflict the king of Armenia, some of the kings will kill their[15] children, and drought will befall most of the countries, with a trivial amount

---

[15] Lit., "his" children.

of rains, a decrease of waters and rivers, and a scarcity of food, especially in the land of the Turks and what borders on that. **26** And if Mercury was transiting over him, that indicates the killing of the king of Persia and the ruination of most of its cities, the king of Babylon's pouncing on some of his brothers, the killing of some of his children by the sword, an abundance of drought, the king of Rūm's killing some of his relatives, with a copious amount of rains (and sometimes they will be middling), the intensity of the cold, an increase of rivers, the suitability of the crops, and the existence of earthquakes. **27** And if the Moon was transiting over him, that indicates an abundance of moistures.

**28 The account of Mars's transits over the planets. 29** If Mars was transiting over the Sun, that indicates the intensity of the heat and the dryness of the air. **30** And if he was transiting over Venus, that indicates the death of some of the mothers of the children of kings, with hardship happening in the land of Babylon, the fighting of the Arabs, hardships, and locusts will be abundant in their land and in the rest of the countries, drought will be abundant, and the expensiveness of food, a scarcity of rains, and a decrease of waters. **31** And if he was transiting over Mercury, that indicates the gathering of the people of the coasts of Rūm at its extreme parts, and their attacking the people of Babylon, and their desire for their land, the death of the king of Babylon and the dispersal of its nobles, the spending of its assets, the death of the king of the Ahwāz, an abundance of fighting and civil unrest in most of the climes, and [the people's] capturing one another, with an abundance of death in Persia and the land of Jibāl, the abundant harm by predatory animals and the perishing of beasts of burden (of cattle, camels, and other things), with an abundance of hunting, a trivial amount of rains and moistures, a scarcity of waters in rivers, and the expensiveness of food. **32** And if he was transiting over the Moon, that indicates a trivial amount of rains.

**33 The account of the planets' transits over Mars. 34** If the Sun was transiting over Mars, that indicates the moisture of the atmosphere. **35** And if Venus was transiting over him, that indicates the abundant occurrence of fire in most of the countries, with the attack by the people of the Sawād against the people of Jibāl, the occurrence of death among them, and a copious amount of rains and an abundance of locusts. **36** And if Mercury was transiting over Mars, that indicates an abundance of moistures and thought,¹⁶ the occurrence of death among the people and the burning of most of the countries of the Arabs, the pouncing of enemies on them, with the perishing of donkeys, a copious amount of rains, the successive blowing of rains, and an abundance of seeds. **37** And if the Moon was transiting over it, that indicates a copious amount of moistures.

**38 The account of the Sun's transits over the planets. 39** If the Sun was transiting over Venus, that indicates the dryness of the air. **40** And if he was transiting over Mercury, that indicates the warring of the people of the Ahwāz against Rūm, with successive rains, the suitability of crops, and the swelling of the rivers. **41** And if he was transiting over the Moon, that indicates the existence of thunder, lightning, and lightning bolts.

**42 The account of the planets' transits over the Sun. 43** If Venus was transiting over the Sun, that indicates the existence of moistures. **44** And if Mercury was transiting over him, that indicates the attack by Rūm against the people of Iraq, with a copious amount of rains and the successive blowing of the winds. **45** And if the Moon was transiting over him, that indicates the existence of thunder and lightning.

**46 The account of Venus's transits over the planets. 47** If Venus was transiting over Mercury, that indicates the attack by Rūm against the people of the Turks and the Ahwāz, with the middling amount of rains and the existence of lightning and thunder. **48** And if she was transiting over the Moon, that indicates the existence of moistures.

**49 The account of the planets' transits over Venus. 50** If Mercury was transiting over Venus, that indicates the attack by the Turks against the people of the regions, with a copious amount of rains, an abundance of thunder, lightning, swellings [of water], and the flourishing of the sowing. **51** And if the Moon was transiting over her, that indicates the copious amount of rains and an abundance of lightning flashes.

**52 The account of Mercury's transits over the planets. 53** If Mercury was transiting over the Moon, that indicates the attack by Rūm against the people of Iraq, a trivial amount of rains, and the successive blowing of the winds.

---

¹⁶ والفكر. This usually has connotations of "negative thoughts."

**54** The account of the planets' transits over Mercury. **55** If the Moon was transiting over Mercury, that indicates the warring of the people of the Ahwāz against Rūm, and a successive blowing of the winds.

**56** Since he have completed what we wanted to explain, let us break off the discussion in [this] chapter, if God wills.

## Chapter VI.12: On judging the transits of the planets above one another during their parallelism with the sign of Pisces

**1** Since we have set forth in Chapter VI.11 a statement of the indications of the planets over each other during their parallelism with the sign of Aquarius, in this chapter let us state their indications in the same way, when they are parallel with the sign of Pisces.

♈♄♓ **2 The account of Saturn's transits over the planets. 3** If Saturn was transiting over Jupiter, that indicates the occurrence of death in most of the climes, the stirring up of enemies in Babylon and Jibāl, the occurrence of rancor in what is between them, a scarcity of fish and delicate birds (like sparrows and what is like them), and an abundance of locusts, with a copious amount of rains, snows, and waters. **4** And if he was transiting over Mars, that indicates an abundance of fish and delicate birds (like sparrows and what is like them), with the intensity of the heat of the atmosphere. **5** And if he was transiting over the Sun, that indicates the dryness of the atmosphere and the scarcity of its moisture. **6** And if he was transiting over Venus, that indicates the death of pregnant women, especially the women of kings, with a copious amount of rains, an abundance of thunder, and the intensity of the cold. **7** And if he was transiting over Mercury, that indicates the abundance of birds and fish, the swelling of rivers, an abundance of moistures, and the darkness of the atmosphere. **8** And if he was transiting over the Moon, that indicates a scarcity of moistures and waters.

**9 The account of the planets' transits over Saturn. 10** If Jupiter was transiting over Saturn, that indicates the ruin of the king of Babylon and the seating of his son [on the throne] after him, the fine condition of the people of the climes (and sometimes drought will find the majority of them), an abundance of fish and delicate birds (like sparrows), with a copious amount of rains. **11** And if Mars was transiting over him, that indicates the occurrence of tribulations in most of the climes, an abundance of fish and delicate birds, with a copious amount of rains, and an abundance of thunder and lightning. **12** And if the Sun was transiting over him, that indicates the moisture of the atmosphere. **13** And if Venus was transiting over him, that indicates the conflict of the people of Armenia and Jibāl against the king of

Babylon, with the intensity of the cold, a copious amount of rains, and abundance of thunder and lightning. **14** And if Mercury was transiting over him, that indicates the attack by the king of Rūm against the people of the region of the east, a scarcity of birds, a decrease of waters, and the successive blowing of the winds, with a copious amount of rains. **15** And if the Moon was transiting over him, that indicates the miscarriage of pregnant women, a scarcity of seeds, a copious amount of rains, and an abundance of moistures.

T♃⯯ **16 The account of Jupiter's transits over the planets. 17** If Jupiter was transiting over Mars, that indicates the abundant shifting of the king of Babylon and his dwelling in another country, his producing benefit for his subjects, with the abundant appearance of wondrous things and portents, the occurrence of fear in the people (with [their] safety and being cured of that), and the hotness of the air and its dryness. **18** And if he was transiting over the Sun, that indicates the dryness of the air. **19** And if he was transiting over Venus, that indicates the prevalence of safety for the people of the countries, the occurrence of death in pregnant women, an abundance of fish and delicate animals (like sparrows), with a copious amount of rains and the intensity of the cold. **20** And if he was transiting over Mercury, that indicates an abundance of fish and delicate birds, with a copious amount of rains and the intensity of the cold. **21** And if he was transiting over the Moon, that indicates a scarcity of moistures.

**22 The account of the planets' transits over Jupiter. 23** If Mars was transiting over Jupiter, that indicates an attack by enemies against the people of Babylon and Jibāl, the appearance of joy in most of the countries, the conflict of those with relatives against their relatives, kings killing one another, and the authority of women over men, with a copious amount of rains and an abundance of lightning. **24** And if the Sun was transiting over him, that indicates the moisture of the atmosphere. **25** And if Venus was transiting over him, that indicates the existence of civil unrest in the land of Mosul and the ruin of most of them, the suitability of their situation after that, the death of women, the decrease of birds (and specially delicate ones), with an abundance of moistures and seeds. **26** And if Mercury was transiting over him, that indicates the killing of the king of Persia (or the killing of one of his children) by the sword, and the king of Rūm's killing his own relatives, and an earthquake will befall the people of Persia, drought and hunger will multiply in Babylon, and sometimes the people of the desert nomads will pounce upon the people of Jibāl, with an abundance of rains and winds, and powerful swells. **27** And if the Moon was transiting over him, that indicates a copious amount of rains and waters.

♂ ♃  **28 The account of Mars's transits over the planets. 29** If Mars was transiting over the Sun, that indicates the dryness of the air. **30** And if he was transiting over Venus, that indicates the suitability of most of the countries, the people's abundant demands on one another, an abundance of fish and delicate birds (like sparrows). **31** And if he was transiting over the Mercury, that indicates the arousing of the king from his place and the occurrence of many disasters, and the attack by Rūm against the people of Babylon, and their warring against them, with Rūm's gathering in their outskirts on the coasts of the sea, troubles occurring to medical doctors, killing and an abundance of hunting, fertility in the region of the west, with a copious amount of rains, the middling amount of waters in rivers and seas, and the expensiveness of food. **32** And if he was transiting over the Moon, that indicates the death of the king of Babylon and the dispersal of its nobles, the spending of its assets, and the death of some kings, the occurrence of death in Fārs and the land of Jibāl, abundant harm from predatory animals, and the perishing of beasts of burden (of cattle, camels, and other things) with a trivial amount of rains.

**33 The account of the planets' transits over Mars. 34** If the Sun was transiting over Mars, that indicates a copious amount of rains and the existence of thunder and lightning. **35** And if Venus was transiting over him, that indicates the death of the king of Babylon, an abundance of death in the people, and a copious amount of rains and waters. **36** And if Mercury was transiting over him, that indicates the death of the king of Babylon, an abundance of death in the people, a copious amount of rains, the warring of Rūm against the people of Babylon, and their laying waste to most of their countries, the people of Babylon fighting against one another, and their submission into their hands unto [their] ruin, an abundance of apostasy and defamation, the occurrence of death among the people, an abundance of childbirth, the perishing of donkeys and the death of sheep, an abundance of seeds, and a copious amount of rains and winds. **37** And if the Moon was transiting over him, that indicates an abundance of moistures.

# BOOK VI: PLANETS TRANSITING OVER EACH OTHER, IN ALL SIGNS    335

T☉♓    **38 The account of the Sun's transits over the planets. 39** If the Sun was transiting over Venus, that indicates the dryness of the air. **40** And if he was transiting over Mercury, that indicates an abundance of birds and fish, the swelling of rivers, and a middling amount of moistures. **41** And if he was transiting over the Moon, that indicates an abundance of moistures, and the existence of thunder, lightning, and lightning bolts.

**42 The account of the planets' transits over the Sun. 43** If Venus was transiting over the Sun, that indicates an abundance of moistures. **44** And if Mercury was transiting over him, that indicates the attack by Rūm against the people of the east, the killing of some of the kings by the sword, a scarcity of birds and fish, a copious amount of rains, and the successive blowing of the winds. **45** And if the Moon was transiting over him, that indicates an abundance of moistures, thunder, and lightning.

T♀♓    **46 The account of Venus's transits over the planets. 47** If Venus was transiting over Mercury, that indicates the suitable condition of the people, the fairness of scholars, and an abundance of soothsayers. **48** And if she was transiting over the Moon, that indicates the moderation of the air, an abundance of fish and delicate birds, with an abundance of rains, and the existence of thunder, lightning, and moistures.

**49 The account of the planets' transits over Venus. 50** If Mercury was transiting over Venus, that indicates the attack by the Turks against the people of Khurāsān, and death will occur in the winter quarter, the people of the Ahwāz will transfer to the east, and death will multiply in the people, a copious amount of rains, and the blowing of the winds. **51** And if the Moon was transiting over her, that indicates a copious amount of rains and the abundance of moistures.

T☿♓    **52 The account of Mercury's transits over the planets. 53** If Mercury was transiting over the Moon, that indicates the attack by Rūm against the people of the east, a decrease of waters, and a trivial amount of moistures.

**54 The account of the planets' transits over Mercury. 55** And if the Moon was transiting over Mercury, that indicates an abundance of birds and fish, the copious amount of rains, and the swelling of rivers.

**56** Since we have completed what we wanted to explain, let us break off [the account] in Chapter VI.12, if God wills. **57** Book VI is completed, with the aid of God and His support. **58** Book VII follows.

# BOOK VII: [PROFECTED OR REVOLUTIONARY ASCENDANTS, ON PLACES OF PRIOR CHARTS, & PLANETS IN THEM]

On how to know the indications for lower events of the sign of [1] the terminal point, or [2] one of the Ascendants of annual revolutions, when one of the two coincides with some house of one of the foundational Ascendants of the preceding Beginnings, or the sign of the conjunctions, or [3] the direction, or [4] one of the upper bodies is in it or in the revolutionary divisions[1]

*And it is in 12 Chapters:*

**1** Chapter VII.1: On the indication of the sign of the terminal point or the Ascendant of the revolution for lower events, if it was the Ascendant of one of the preceding Beginnings, or the sign of the conjunction, or the direction, or one of the upper bodies is in it or in the Ascendant of the revolution.

**2** Chapter VII.2: On the indication of the second house, in the same way.

**3** Chapter VII.3: On the indication of the third house, in the same way.

**4** Chapter VII.4: On the indication of the fourth house, in the same way.

**5** Chapter VII.5: On the indication of the fifth house, in the same way.

**6** Chapter VII.6: On the indication of the sixth house, in the same way.

**7** Chapter VII.7: On the indication of the seventh house, in the same way.

**8** Chapter VII.8: On the indication of the eighth house, in the same way.

**9** Chapter VII.9: On the indication of the ninth house, in the same way.

**10** Chapter VII.10: On the indication of the tenth house, in the same way.

**11** Chapter VII.11: On the indication of the eleventh house, in the same way.

**12** Chapter VII.12: On the indication of the twelfth house, in the same way.

---

[1] Omitting the prior pious heading: *In the name of God the Merciful, the Compassionate, and may God bless His prophets.*

**Chapter VII.1: On the indication of the sign of the terminal point or the Ascendant of the revolution for lower events, if it was the Ascendant of one of the preceding Beginnings, or the sign of the conjunction, or the direction, or one of the upper bodies was in it or in the Ascendant of the revolution**

**1** Since we have already set forth in Book VI how to know lower events from the influences of upper bodies in the revolutions of years from the perspective of [the planets'] transits over each other, in this Book let us state how to know the indications for lower events of [1] the sign of the terminal point or [2] one of the Ascendants of the revolutions of years we have set forth, when one of the two matches some house of one of the foundational Ascendants of the preceding Beginnings or conjunctions, or the directions, or one of the upper bodies was in them, or in the revolutionary divisions.

**2** So, we say that sometimes the spherical divisions are divided among two houses, so the indication discovered will be from the house in which the distribution is, if the directions are directed from it, rather than the other house.[2]

**3** And[3] when the parallelism of the upper bodies differs in the place which is relative to the Ascendant of the root, the position of the conjunction, and the Ascendant of the revolution, then one should use a blend [of them] in accordance with their parallelism with the divisions, and speak in accordance with that, if God wills.

---

[2] This seems to mean that if the mundane distribution through the bounds is in the degree of some sign, use the quadrant division in which it falls to interpret the topical meaning, rather than the whole sign. Thus if the distribution is in the third sign but the fourth quadrant division, interpret it in terms of land, ancestors, etc.

[3] This sentence seems to have two different interpretations. One is that it is about comparing planets *across* the three charts mentioned, so that one constructs a story involving, e.g., the 5th of one chart, the 12th of another, and the 3rd of some other: and this is what Abū Ma'shar does in *PN4* (using only quadrant divisions). But it might also continue the thought of **2**: if *a* planet in *any* chart is in some position, and it is likewise in one whole-sign place relative to a previous Ascendant, but another by division, then favor the division and then blend it all together. I favor the first interpretation, but Abū Ma'shar muddies the water by ending the sentence with the statement about the bodies' "parallelism with the divisions."

**4** Now if it happens that the sign of the terminal point or the Ascendant of the revolution is [the Ascendant of] one of the preceding Beginnings, or the sign of the conjunction, or the directions are in it, or one of the upper bodies are in it or in the Ascendant of the revolution (in accordance with what we have described), it is an indicator that a fine way of life will appear in the countries whose indicator that sign is, as well as initiatives in works, innovation in things, their completion and increase, and the use of reason, discussion, and knowledge in the sciences, much zeal for foods and drinks, associations, buying and selling, and that most of their desire for colors will be for the dusty and the dark.

**5** Then one looks at its lord, and judges from it in accordance with its own proper position in the circle. **6** For if it was in [the Ascendant],[4] that indicates an abundance of good in that year.

**7** And if the conjunction was alighting in it,[5] it indicates the hardship of the subjects' conditions, the existence of epidemics and illness, the ruination of most of the countries, and a scarcity of assets, especially in the first year.

**8** And if Saturn was alighting in it and he is in a fine condition, that indicates that the king will have gentleness and a regard to the matter of the subjects, and their favorability towards him, along with a far-reaching voice and name for him. **9** But if he was in a bad condition, that indicates his abundant dissatisfaction, malice, and deception, the intensity of his greed and avarice, his scarce praise and repute, the insignificance of his assets and good fortune (along with harm coming to him), and the corruption of assets in that year.

**10** And if Jupiter was alighting in it and he is in a fine condition, it indicates the abundance of the king's assets and the goodness of his soul, his rejoicing and delight, the easiness of his disposition, and the safety of the people in that year. **11** But if he was in a bad condition, that indicates the weakness of his body and his scarce stability in matters, along with his committing outrages, and his being well known for that.

---

[4] Would this also include the sign of the year?
[5] The revolutionary Ascendant or the sign of the year.

**12** And if Mars was alighting in it and he is in a fine condition, that indicates the safety of the king and his well-being. **13** But if he was in a bad condition, that indicates his crudeness, roughness, and use of violence, his scarce stability in matters, his fall in status, disgrace, and the abundance of his enemies along with the shedding of blood.

**14** And if the Sun was alighting in it and he is in a fine condition, that indicates the justice of the king and his piety. **15** But if he was in a bad condition, that is an indicator of the antithesis of that.

**16** And if Venus was alighting in it and she is in a fine condition, that is an indicator of the abundance of the people's joy, and their happiness. **17** But if she was in a bad condition, that is an indicator of the antithesis of that.

**18** And if Mercury was alighting in it and he is in a fine condition, that indicates the fine condition of judges and businessmen. **19** But if he was in a bad condition, that indicates the antithesis of that.

**20** And if the Moon was alighting in it and she is in a fine condition, that indicates the suitability of the matter of the subjects in all of their actions and their bodies. **21** But if she was in a bad condition, it indicates the antithesis of that.

**22** Since we have completed what we wanted to explain, let us break off the discussion in [this] chapter, if God wills.

## Chapter VII.2: On the indication of the second house, in the same way

**1** Since we have set forth in Chapter VII.1 a statement of the indications of the Ascendant if it is in the way we described, in this chapter let us state the account of the indications of the second house in the same way.

**2** We say that if it happens that the sign of the terminal point or the Ascendant of the revolution <of the year> is the second [house] of one of the preceding Beginnings or the conjunctions, or the direction or one of the bodies is in it or in the second of the revolution, it indicates that, in the countries whose indicator that sign is, there will appear an abundance of selling and buying, acquiring assets and collecting them along with their storing, and entering into partnerships in them, and an abundance of contention among the people because of them, along with an abundance of thinking [about] the future, and that the majority of their desire for colors will be for the green.

**3** Then one looks at its lord, and judges about it in accordance with its own proper position in the circle.[6] **4** For if it was in the Ascendant, that indicates the abundance of the people's profits due to assets, and an abundance of silver and gold.

**5** And if the conjunctions were alighting in it, that indicates the bad condition of the subjects in their way of living, and the victory of ignorance over them, the scarcity of their desire for the sciences, and the abundant occurrence of death in the second year, among the nobles and others.

**6** And if Saturn was alighting in it and he is in a fine condition, that indicates the king's use of justice at the beginning of his command, and his shifting after one-half of his lifespan to hypocrisy and conflicting with what he began with. **7** But if he was in a bad condition, that indicates [his] seeking of assets and spending them, and his squandering them on wars, the contrariety of the soldiers towards him and their hatred, and the harshness of what he encounters from his subjects, along with an intensity of desolation and a scarcity of winds.

---

[6] The text adds, "and the Sun," but the other chapters lack this statement and so I omit it here.

**8** And if Jupiter was alighting in it and he is in a fine condition, that indicates an abundance of business profits. **9** But if he was in a bad condition, it indicates the antithesis of that.

**10** And if Mars was alighting in it and he is in a fine condition, that indicates the suitability of the affairs of riding animals, and their abundance. **11** But if he was in a bad condition, that indicates their perishing and the death of everything having claws.

**12** And if the Sun was alighting in it and he is in a fine condition, that indicates the king's collecting of assets. **13** But if he was in a bad condition, that indicates the antithesis of that.

**14** And if Venus was alighting in it and she is in a fine condition, it indicates the fine condition of kings, and an abundance of dates, and their expensiveness. **15** But if she was in a bad condition it indicates the antithesis of that.

**16** And if Mercury was alighting in it and he is in a fine condition, that indicates the respect of scholars and science. **17** But if he was in a bad condition, that indicates the antithesis of that.

**18** And if the Moon was alighting in it and she is in a fine condition, that indicates the appearance of good in the subjects. **19** But if she was in a bad condition, that indicates the antithesis of that.

**20** Since we have completed what we wanted to explain, let us break off the discussion in [this] chapter, if God wills.

## Chapter VII.3: On the indication of the third house, in the same way

**1** Since we have set forth in Chapter VII.2 a statement of the indications of the second house in just the way we described, in this chapter let us state the indications of the third house in the same way.[7]

**2** We say that if it happens that the sign of the terminal point or the Ascendant of the revolution was the third of one of the preceding Beginnings or the conjunctions, or the direction or one of the bodies was alighting in it, or in the third of the revolution, that indicates that in the countries whose indicator that sign is, there will appear an abundance of people's charity towards those having a [kin] relationship (and especially towards women), the abundance of their travels, and employing justice, calm, and dignity, the creation of houses of worship, an abundance of reports,[8] correspondence, messengers, and dreams, the appearance of [serious] thought in the matter of divinity and prophets, looking into religion, jurisprudence, and piety, and an abundance of disagreements

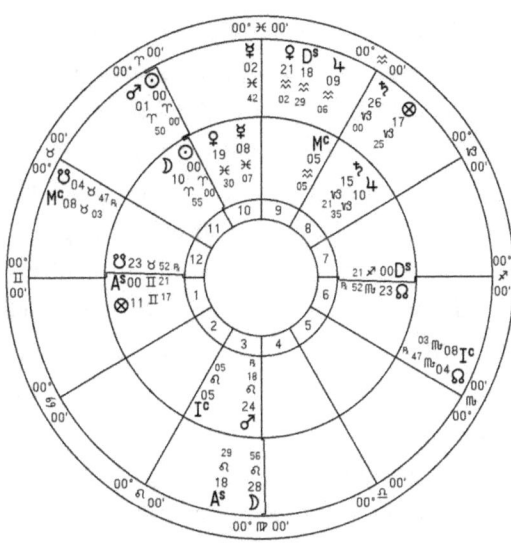

Figure 51: 1902 ingress Ascendant (outer) on 1901 conjunction third (inner)

---

[7] The figure here illustrates the situation in **2**. The inner chart is that of the 1901 Saturn-Jupiter conjunction in Sarajevo, Bosnia. In 1902, the Ascendant of the Aries Ingress (outer chart) was Leo, which was the 1901 third place. This means that third-place topics are activated in 1902, in accordance with Leo's condition in the original chart and the Moon's transiting in it at the revolution. And if there had been an ingress planet transiting in Libra (the ingress third), that would also have indications for third-place matters.

[8] Or, "rumors" (الأخبار).

and contention in them, and that the majority of their desire for colors will be for the yellow.

**3** Then, one looks at its lord and judges it in accordance with its own proper place in the circle. **4** For if it was alighting in the Ascendant, it indicates an abundance of travels and movements.

**5** And if the conjunction was alighting in it, that indicates the strength of the conditions of the king, his squandering of assets, and the ruination of the houses of worship in the third year.

**6** And if Saturn was alighting in it and he is in a fine condition, that indicates the suitability of the condition of kings, and their use of kindness towards their subjects, and their fine piety, the excellence of their understanding, their leaving hypocrisy behind in any of their deeds, along with abundant consideration of the affairs of the kingdom. **7** But if he was in a bad condition, that indicates the difficulty of kings' collaboration in their works, and their seeking them,[9] and the abundance of their changing [place] and their travels.

**8** And if Jupiter was alighting in it and he is in a fine condition, that indicates the good fortune of the condition of businessmen. **9** But if he was in a bad condition, it indicates the antithesis of that.

**10** If Mars was alighting in it and he is in a fine condition, it indicates an abundance of familiarity with relatives. **11** But if he was in a bad condition, it indicates an abundance of lawsuits between brothers, sisters, and parents.

**12** And if the Sun was alighting in it and he is in a fine condition, it indicates an abundance of kings' devotion to the subjects. **13** But if he was in a bad condition, it indicates the antithesis of that.

**14** And if Venus was alighting in it and she is in a fine condition, she indicates the scarcity of the people's movement. **15** But if she was in a bad condition, she indicates an abundance of travels happening to the people for the sake of seeking knowledge, along with the affairs of joking around.

**16** And if Mercury was alighting in it and he is in a fine condition, that indicates an abundance of the people's travel for the sake of seeking knowledge. **17** But if he was in a bad condition, it indicates the antithesis of that.

---

[9] وتفقّدها.

**18** And if the Moon was alighting in it and she is in a fine condition, it indicates an abundance of the people's travels for the purposes of the good, benefit, joy, and delight. **19** But if she was in a bad condition it indicates the antithesis of that.

**20** Since we have completed what we wanted to explain, let us break off the discussion in [this] chapter.

## Chapter VII.4: On the indication of the fourth house, in the same way

**1** Since we have set forth in Chapter VII.3 a statement of the indications of the third house in the way we described, in this chapter let us state the account of the fourth house in the same way.

**2** We say that if it happens that the sign of the terminal point or the Ascendant of the revolution was the fourth of one of the preceding Beginnings or the conjunctions, or the direction or one of the bodies was alighting in it or in the fourth of the revolution, that indicates that in the countries whose indicator that sign was, there will appear a desire to build mosques, occupy lands and real estate (in terms of assets and commodities), and a scarcity of moving, an abundance of looking into outcomes, death and destruction (and its causes), the honoring of fathers and elders, and that the majority of their desire for colors will be for the red.

**3** Then, one looks at its lord and judges it in accordance with its own proper position in the circle. **4** For if it was alighting in the Ascendant, it indicates grief entering upon the people at the end of the year.

**5** And if the conjunction was alighting in it, that indicates an abundance of moving, travels, and the ruination of countries and cities in most of the climes in the fourth year.

**6** Now if Saturn was alighting in it and he is in a fine condition, that indicates the piety of kings and their gentleness, along with their involvement in buildings and gardens. **7** But if he was in a bad condition, it indicates the weakness of kings and their assigning the kingdom to some of those of old age from among their relatives[10] (of those who are the oldest of them), an abundance of troubles happening among their relatives and in those of old age and their associates, and griefs befalling people in prisons.

**8** And if Jupiter was alighting in it and he is in a fine condition, that indicates the cheapness of food, and travels. **9** But if he was in a bad condition it indicates its expensiveness, and especially if it was an earthy sign.

**10** And if Mars was alighting in it and he is in a fine condition, that indicates the scarcity of kings' enemies, and the suitability of the regions

---

[10] This sounds like the situation after the death of Muhammad in 632 AD, when his elderly father-in-law Abū Bakr was chosen to be the first of the Rashidūn Caliphs which immediately followed. He ruled from only 632-34, dying from natural causes.

belonging to them. **11** But if he was in a bad condition, it indicates an abundance of Khārijites and Exchangers,[11] and their rising up at the end of the year.

**12** And if the Sun was alighting in it and he is in a fine condition, he indicates the amusement of kings, and their delight. **13** But if he was in a bad condition, he indicates the antithesis of that.

**14** And if Venus was alighting in it and she is in a fine condition, she indicates the people's manifesting abstention, worship, and seeking the good. **15** But if she was in a bad condition, she indicates the antithesis of that.

**16** And if Mercury was alighting in it and he is in a fine condition, it indicates the suitability of writers and businessmen in that year. **17** But if he was in a bad condition, it indicates the antithesis of that.

**18** And if the Moon was alighting in it and she is in a fine condition, that indicates the joy of the people. **19** But if she was in a bad condition, it indicates the people's griefs.

**20** Since we have completed what we wanted to explain, let us break of the discussion in [this] chapter.

---

[11] These are two names for a schismatic movement in early Islam. Certain groups of Muslims got up and "left" (Khārijites) the discussions about choosing a new rightful ruler (as they thought one was not needed), and thereby separated themselves from the mainstream. The name "Exchanger" is related to Qur. 2:207, and means that these same types of people wanted to exchange the merely worldly (and political) life for a higher one with God. Generically, the Arabic word for Khārijites also means simply "rebels." See also III.2, **2**.

## Chapter VII.5: On the indication of the fifth house, in the same way

**1** Since we have set forth in Chapter VII.4 the indications of the fourth house if it was as we explained, in this chapter let us state the indications of the fifth house in the same way.

**2** We say that if it happened that the sign of the terminal point or the Ascendant of the revolution was the fifth of one of the preceding Beginnings or the conjunctions, or the direction or one of the bodies was alighting in it or in the fifth of the revolution, it indicates that in the countries whose indicator that sign is, there will appear an abundance of fornication, gifting [things], a desire for women, children and friends, joy and delight, joking, humor, and looking into old matters, the building of cities, the taking of revenues, the abundant sending of messengers, and that the majority of their desire for colors is for the white.

**3** Then one looks at its lord and judges it in accordance with its position in the circle. **4** And if it was alighting in the Ascendant, it indicates an abundance of children in that year.

**5** And if the conjunction was alighting in it, it indicates an abundance of troubles occurring in children and vegetation, and that that will pervade much of the climes in the fifth year.

**6** And if Saturn was alighting in it and he is in a fine condition, it indicates the abundance of kings' children and their love for the subjects. **7** But if he was in a bad condition, it indicates [his] assigning the kingdom and the rest of his affairs to his children, along with an abundance of death in them, and in youths and children.

**8** And if Jupiter was alighting in it and he is in a fine condition, it indicates the safety of the children in that year. **9** But if he was in a bad condition, it indicates the antithesis of that.

**10** And if Mars was alighting in it and he is in a fine condition, it indicates the safety of pregnant women in that year. **11** But if he was in a bad condition, it indicates the antithesis of that.

**12** And if the Sun was alighting in it and he is in a fine condition, he indicates the amusement of kings and their delight. **13** But if he was in a bad condition, it indicates the antithesis of that.

**14** And if Venus was alighting in it and she is in a fine condition, she indicates the fine conditions of youths and adolescents. **15** But if she was in a bad condition, she indicates the antithesis of that.

**16** And if Mercury was alighting in it and he is in a fine condition, it indicates an abundance of children. **17** But if he was in a bad condition, it indicates the antithesis of that.

**18** And if the Moon was alighting in it and she is in a fine condition, that indicates the abundance of the people's delight and the cheapness of prices. **19** But if she was in a bad condition, it indicates the antithesis of that.

**20** Since we have completed what we wanted to explain, let us break off the discussion in [this] chapter.

## Chapter VII.6: On the indication of the sixth house, in the same way

**1** Since we have set forth in Chapter VII.5 the indications of the fifth house, in this chapter let us state the indications of the sixth house in the same way.

**2** We say that if it happens that the sign of the terminal point or the Ascendant of the revolution was the sixth of one of the preceding Beginnings or the conjunctions, or the direction or one of the bodies was alighting in it or in the sixth of the revolution, it indicates that in the countries whose indicator that sign is, there will appear apostasy, an inclination to the worship of idols and what is like that, and the matter of the underclass will become powerful as well as the masters of the bad trades, slaves, servants, corrupted women, ailments, illnesses, travels, and the emigration of most of the people from their homeland, shifting, toil, an abundance of trouble and debauchery, forgeries, the occurrence of envy and accusation, losses in business, rising up against the authorities, a removing of one's hand from obedience, breaking agreements, an abundance of those imprisoned, and that the majority of their desire for colors is for the black.

**3** Then one looks at its lord and judges it in accordance with its own proper position in the circle. **4** Now if it was alighting in the Ascendant, it indicates an abundance of illnesses and ailments.

**5** And if the conjunction was alighting in it, it indicates an abundance of illnesses in the sixth year.

**6** And if Saturn was alighting in it and he is in a fine condition, it indicates the love of kings for acquiring horses and riding animals. **7** But if he was in a bad condition it indicates his vileness towards his servants, servant girls giving birth to his children, and his closeness to slaves and his beardless youths, along with the abundance of his illnesses, the scorn of his subjects towards him, and an abundance of emaciation as well the harm of riding animals.

**8** And if Jupiter was alighting in it and he is in a fine condition, it indicates the suitability of the affairs of the people. **9** But if he was in a bad condition, it indicates pains and fevers befalling the people.

**10** And if Mars was alighting in it and he is in a fine condition, it indicates the scarcity of the people's illnesses. **11** But if he was in a bad condition, it indicates ailments befalling the people, and especially to children; and that will be from pustules, smallpox, measles, and pains in the head.

**12** And if the Sun was alighting in it and he is in a fine condition, he indicates the delight of the king. **13** But if he was in a bad condition, he indicates griefs befalling the king.

**14** And if Venus was alighting in it and she is in a fine condition, she indicates the safety of the people and the soundness of their bodies. **15** But if she was in a bad condition, she indicates ailments befalling the people in their noses and faces.

**16** And if Mercury was alighting in it and he is in a fine condition, it indicates the good health of children. **17** But if he was in a bad condition, it indicates ailments befalling children in their faces.

**18** And if the Moon was alighting in it and she is in a fine condition, that indicates a scarcity of pains in the eyes among the people. **19** But if she was in a bad condition, it indicates an abundance of inflammation and pains in the eyes befalling the people.

**20** Since we have completed what we wanted to explain, let us break off the discussion in [this] chapter.

## Chapter VII.7: On the indication of the seventh house, in the same way

**1** Since we have set forth in Chapter VII.6 the indications of the sixth house in the way we described, in this chapter let us state the indications of the seventh house in the same way.

**2** We say that if it happens that the sign of the terminal point or the Ascendant of the revolution was the seventh of one of the preceding Beginnings or the conjunctions, or the direction or one of the bodies was alighting in it or in the seventh of the revolution, that indicates that in the countries whose indicator that sign is, there will appear an abundance of marriage, a desire for women, weddings, banquets, and impoverishment for these reasons, travel, moving, emigration, the downfall of [some] people and the elevation of others, an abundance of lawsuits and prosecutions, the evasion of things, an abundance of despising the people, the killing of some by others, an abundance of loans,[12] and the desire for hunting, buying and selling, and an abundance of worry about death and its causes. **3** And it indicates that the majority of their desire for colors will be for things which are mixed with a little black.

**4** Then one looks at its lord and judges it in accordance with its own proper position in the circle. **5** For if it was in the Ascendant, it indicates an abundance of weddings in that year.

**6** And if the conjunction was alighting in it, that indicates the harshness of kings towards their subjects, along with the badness of their conditions for those reasons; and the duration of that (if there was an acceder) is a term of <seven>[13] years from the beginning of his accession.

**7** And if Saturn was alighting in it and he is in a fine condition, it indicates kings' openness towards the subjects, and their becoming close to them. **8** But if he was in a bad condition, that indicates the combat of his subjects against him, and their hatred of him, their coveting of his rule, and his moving from the land of his rule to another; and troubles befalling women, especially the women of kings, and their[14] doing wrong to those older than they are.

---

[12] Reading tentatively for معارات.
[13] Adding with one of the MS sources, in parallel with the other chapters.
[14] This is in the masculine, suggesting that we are back to what the kings are doing.

**9** And if Jupiter was alighting in it and he was in a fine condition, that indicates the abundance of kings' collecting assets as well as their dispersing them in their regions and places, and an abundance of dates and goodness in the middle of the year. **10** But if he was in a bad condition, it indicates the abundance of the king's anxieties, his expenses, his squandering, the obscurity of his voice,[15] and his administrators will be from among the people of fornication and the underclass.

**11** And if Mars was alighting in it and he is in a fine condition, that indicates the suitability of the people and their turning away from corruption. **12** But if he was in a bad condition, it indicates a scarcity of piety and an abundance of fornication.

**13** And if the Sun was alighting in it and he is in a fine condition, he indicates the king's openness towards the people and his becoming close to them. **14** But if he was in a bad condition, he indicates the king's withdrawing from the people.

**15** And if Venus was alighting in it and she is in a fine condition, she indicates the fine condition of women and the prosperous among men. **16** But if she was in a bad condition she indicates the antithesis of that.

**17** And if Mercury was alighting in it and he is in a fine condition, it indicates the suitability of the people. **18** But if he was in a bad condition, it indicates an abundance of corruption and debauchery.

**19** And if the Moon was alighting in it and she is in a fine condition, it indicates an abundance of marriage. **20** But if she was in a bad condition it indicates the antithesis of that.

**21** Since we have completed what we wanted to explain, let us break off the discussion.

---

[15] That is, of his fame and influence.

## Chapter VII.8: On the indication of the eighth house, in the same way

**1** Since we have set forth in Chapter VII.7 the statement of the indications of the seventh house in the way we explained, in this chapter let us state the indications of the eighth house in the same way.

**2** We say that if it happened that the sign of the terminal point or the Ascendant of the revolution was the eighth of one of the preceding Beginnings or the conjunctions, or the direction or one of the bodies was alighting in it or in the eighth of the revolution, that indicates that in the countries whose indicator that sign is, there will appear an abundance of illnesses, death, the drinking of poisons, killing, looking into the matters of ancestors and inheritance, profit and assets, things entrusted for deposit, the protection of assets and their spending them in incorrect ways and their wasting, poverty, intense need, roughness, and what profit is possible will be from travel, an abundance of laziness, idleness, stratagems and cunning, contention over trivialities, wars, an abundance of espionage[16] and much fear, sorrow, and stupidity, and that the majority of their desire for colors will be for the black.

**3** Then one looks at its lord and judges it in accordance with its own proper position in the circle. **4** For if it was alighting in the Ascendant, it indicates an abundance of death in that year.

**5** And if the conjunction was alighting in it, it indicates an abundance of death in the eighth year.

**6** And if Saturn was alighting in it and he is in a fine condition, it indicates the king's scanty lifespan and the goodness of his way of living. **7** But if he was in a bad condition, it indicates the abundance of his anxieties, expenses and squandering, the obscurity of his voice, and his administrators will be from among the workers of the underclass and the people of fornication, along with an abundance of death among the cavalry and slave girls.

**8** And if Jupiter was alighting in it and he is in a fine condition, it indicates the long lifespans of the people. **9** But if he was in a bad condition, it indicates the sudden death of the people.

---

[16] التّجسيس. I do not find an entry for this Form 2, but following **BY** in treating it like Form 5.

**10** And if Mars was alighting in it and he is in a fine condition, it indicates the safety of the people in that year. **11** But if he was in a bad condition it indicates hot, harmful ailments, along with which death will multiply.

**12** And if the Sun was alighting in it and he is in a fine condition, he indicates the survival of kings. **13** But if he was in a bad condition, he indicates the death of kings if the lord of the opposite[17] looked at him.

**14** And if Venus was alighting in it and she is in a fine condition, she indicates the safety of the people. **15** But if she was in a bad condition, she indicates an abundance of death, and especially in the young.

**16** And if Mercury was alighting in it and he is in a fine condition, it indicates the good health of the people and livestock. **17** But if he was in a bad condition, it indicates death occurring to children and donkeys.

**18** And if the Moon was alighting in it and she is in a fine condition, it indicates a scarcity of death. **19** But if she was in a bad condition, it indicates an abundance of death.

**20** Since we have completed what we wanted to explain, let us break off the discussion in [this] chapter.

---

[17] النَّظير. Normally this would be the lord of the seventh; but I could also see it being the lord of the sign "opposite" the Sun, namely the lord of the second.

## Chapter VII.9: On the indication of the ninth house, in the same way

**1** Since we have set forth in Chapter VII.8 a statement of the indications of the eighth house in the way we described, in this chapter let us state the account of the indications of the ninth house in the same way.

**2** We say that if it happened that the sign of the terminal point or the Ascendant of the revolution was the ninth of one of the preceding Beginnings or the conjunctions, or the direction or one of the bodies was alighting in it or in the ninth of the revolution, that indicates that in the countries whose indicator that sign is, there will appear an abundance of illnesses and death, and looking into the divine sciences and the conditions of prophets, messengers and reports; renunciation, devoutness, mortification, a zeal for houses of worship, and looking into the stellar sciences and philosophy, stratagems,[18] skillfulness of the hand, and skilled managers,[19] along with an abundance of travels, being occupied,[20] the raging of the winds, and that the majority of their desire for colors will be for the white.

**3** Then one looks at its lord and judges it in accordance with its position in the circle. **4** For if it were alighting in the Ascendant, it indicates the *jihād*, the Hajj, and renunciation.

**5** And if the conjunction was alighting in it, it indicates the strength of the king's conditions, and his squandering of assets; and the majority of that will be in the ninth year.

**6** And if Saturn was alighting in it and he is in a fine condition, that indicates the piety of the king and his devoutness, and the abundance of his travels for reasons of worship, and his being well known for [his] understanding, opinion, and seeking wisdom, the abundance of his messengers to the regions, along with the flourishing of palm fruit. **7** But if he was in a bad condition, it indicates his moving, travels, the abundance of his enemies, his killing, his pursuing war by himself, and his coarseness and confusion.

---

[18] حيل. **BY** read this as "engineering," perhaps drawing on the other sense of this word for tools and instruments.

[19] المخاريق, following the sense of Lane, p. 729 col. C (entry مخراق).

[20] الشغل. Or, being "preoccupied" and otherwise busy with many things.

**8** And if Jupiter was alighting in it and he is in a fine condition, it indicates an abundance of pilgrimages. **9** But if he was in a bad condition, it indicates the antithesis of that.

**10** And if Mars was alighting in it and he is in a fine condition, that indicates the safety of the people. **11** But if he was in a bad condition, it indicates an abundance of robbers and highway bandits.

**12** And if the Sun was alighting in it and he is in a fine condition, that indicates the scarcity of kings' movement. **13** But if he was in a bad condition, it indicates the badness of his condition and its corruption.

**14** And[21] if Venus was alighting in it and she is in a fine condition, she indicates the suitability of the condition of scholars. **15** But if she was in a bad condition, she indicates the antithesis of that for scholars and astrologers.

**16** And if Mercury was alighting in it and he is in a fine condition, it indicates the suitability of the condition of scholars. **17** But if he was in a bad condition, he indicates the antithesis of that for scholars and astrologers.

**18** And if the Moon was alighting in it and she is in a fine condition, that indicates the people's manifesting mortification and renunciation, and especially if it was a house of Jupiter. **19** If it was a house of Mercury, that indicates the corruption of religion. **20** But if she was in a bad condition, it indicates the antithesis of that.

**21** Since we have completed what we wanted to describe, let us break off the discussion in [this] chapter.

---

[21] Note that the significations in this paragraph are the same as for Mercury (**16-17**): I suspect the significations for Venus have been lost and accidentally replaced by those of Mercury.

## Chapter VII.10: On the indication of the tenth house, in the same way

**1** Since we have set forth in Chapter VII.9 the indications of the ninth house in the way we described, in this chapter let us state the indications of the tenth house in the same way.

**2** We say that if it happened that the sign of the terminal point or the Ascendant of the revolution was the tenth of one of the preceding Beginnings or the conjunctions, or the direction or one of the bodies was alighting in it or in the tenth of the revolution, that indicates that in the countries whose indicator that sign was, there will appear authoritative kings, masters, the proud, and the celebrated among the people, those having courage and valor, exceeding bounds,[22] and fame; the seeking of leadership and reputation, praise, commendation, respect, influence, and an intuitive grasp of propriety; the elevation of people for those reasons, marvelous and astonishing arts, and things will take place in them which had not been before, and the people will be friendly to their leaders and masters, and that the majority of their desire for colors will be for the red.

**3** Then one looks at its lord and judges it in accordance with its own proper position in the circle. **4** For if it was alighting in the Ascendant, it indicates the [new] existence of a king in that year.

**5** But if the conjunction was alighting in it, it indicates the hardship of the condition of kings, and that more than one of them will be afflicted in that conjunction; and the worst of it will be in the tenth year.

**6** And if Saturn was alighting in it and he is in a fine condition, that indicates the mildness of the king, and his gravity, reverence, and eminence among the people of his house and leadership (and if the king was suitable for it), and his attacking many cities, and the surrender of the kings of many people of his time, and he will have a determination to contrive [new] affairs and crafts.[23] **7** But if he was in a bad condition, that indicates an abundance of contention against his enemies, his emaciation, and the emergence of one contending with him in his rulership, along with his own weakness in his house, and harm coming to his household managers and administrators.

---

[22] الفتك. Following one of the senses of Lane, for the usual "assassination."
[23] Or, "skills."

**8** And if Jupiter was alighting in it and he is in a fine condition, it indicates the cheapness of food. **9** But if he was in a bad condition, it indicates its expensiveness.

**10** And if Mars was alighting in it and he is in a fine condition, that indicates the toil of the cavalry and the commanders in delegations and the ways of war. **11** But if he was in a bad condition, it indicates <*missing*>.

**12** And if the Sun was alighting in it and he was in a fine condition, that indicates the justice of the king towards his subjects, along with his piety. **13** But if he was in a bad condition, he indicates the antithesis of that.

**14** And if Venus was alighting in it and she was in a fine condition, she indicates the cheapness of food. **15** But if she was in a bad condition, she indicates its expensiveness and a lack of it.

**16** And if Mercury was alighting in it and he is in a fine condition, that indicates kings' seeking the crafts. **17** But if he was in a bad condition, it indicates the antithesis of that.

**18** And if the Moon was alighting in it and she is in a fine condition, that indicates an abundance of works. **19** But if she was in a bad condition, it indicates the antithesis of that.

**20** Since we have completed what we wanted to explain, let us break off the discussion in Chapter VII.10.

## Chapter VII.11: On the indication of the eleventh place, in the same way

**1** Since we have set forth in Chapter VII.10 the indications of the tenth house if it was as we described, let us state the indications of the eleventh house in the same way.

**2** We say that if it happened that the sign of the terminal point or the Ascendant of the revolution was the eleventh of one of the preceding Beginnings, or the conjunctions, or the direction or one of the bodies was alighting in it, or in the eleventh or the revolution, it indicates that in the countries whose indicator that sign was, there will appear renown, thoughtfulness, an abundance of agreements, buying and selling, taking and giving, generosity, an abundance of habitations and gifts, messengers, passion, love, skill in the professions, the sincerity of[24] their hopes, their protection, the fulfillment of their good fortune, and that the majority of their desire for colors will be for the yellow.

**3** Then one looks at its lord and judges it in accordance with its own proper position in the circle. **4** For if it was alighting in the Ascendant, it indicates the people's engagement in things which bring them closer to God (mighty and honored).

**5** And if the conjunction was alighting in it, it indicates kings' collection of assets and their taking of treasures, and the majority of that will be in the eleventh year.

**6** And if Saturn was alighting in it and he is in a fine condition, that indicates new rulership for the king,[25] his fairness and justice, the abundance of his children, and the intensity of the subjects' love for him. **7** But if he was in a bad condition, it indicates the antithesis of that, in the sense of his neglecting his subjects and squandering the stated assets.[26]

---

[24] صدق. **BY** read this as "realization of," in the sense that one's hopes turn out to be "correct."

[25] تجدّد الملك للملك. In other passages this has seemed to mean "new rulership" for someone else, not the current king.

[26] See **5**.

**8** Now if Jupiter was alighting in it and he is in a fine condition, it indicates the profits of businessmen. **9** But if he was in a bad condition, it indicates the antithesis of that.

**10** And if Mars was alighting in it and he is in a fine condition, it indicates the suitability of the soldiers, and a rise in their awards. **11** But if he was in a bad condition, it indicates the antithesis of that.

**12** And if the Sun was alighting in it and he is in a fine condition, he indicates an abundance of growth[27] and the suitability of the period and of women. **13** But if he was in a bad condition, he indicates the antithesis of that.

**14** And if Venus was alighting in it and she is in a fine condition, she indicates the cheapness of grain. **15** But if she was in a bad condition, she indicates their expensiveness.

**16** And if Mercury was alighting in it and he is in a fine condition, it indicates the king's encouragement of the scholars. **17** But if he was in a bad condition, it indicates the antithesis of that.

**18** And if the Moon was alighting in it and she is in a fine condition, it indicates an abundance of raiding and the hostility of the people of debauchery. **19** But if she was in a bad condition it indicates the antithesis of that.

**20** Since we have completed what we wanted to explain, let us break off the discussion in Chapter VII.11, if God wills.

---

[27] This root also connotes building and manufacturing, not merely crops and other things.

## Chapter VII.12: On the indication of the twelfth house, in the same way

**1** Since we have set forth in Chapter VII.11 the indications of the eleventh if it was as we described, in this chapter let us state the indications of the twelfth in the same way.

**2** We say that if it happened that the sign of the terminal point or the Ascendant of the revolution was the twelfth of one of the preceding Beginnings or the conjunctions, or the direction or one of the bodies was alighting in it or in the twelfth of the revolution, it indicates that in the countries whose indicator that sign is, there will appear wrong, fear, grief, bad thoughts, lawsuits, the elevation of slaves and the underclass, an abundance of confusions and engagement in base, mean affairs, and violators and rebels against the authorities will be abundant, bail money, emigration, isolation, insanity, injustice, bad thinking, robbery, an abundance of those held in custody,[28] illnesses, chronic illnesses, and their desire for colors will be for the green.

**3** Then one looks at its lord and judges it in accordance with its own proper position in the circle. **4** For if it was alighting in the Ascendant, it indicates an abundance of enemies in that year.

**5** And if the conjunction was alighting in it, it indicates the resistance of the king towards his subjects, his bad opinion of them, and the hardest trouble will be in the twelfth year.

**6** And if Saturn was alighting in it and he is in a fine condition, it indicates the love of the king for slaves and riding animals, and a preference for pleasures, along with the fineness of his situation among his subjects, and the suitability of their affairs. **7** But if he was in a bad condition, it indicates the abundance of his wars, the impugning of his affairs, the harshness of the harm coming to him from his enemies, along with the occurrence of death in the people of the Sawād.

**8** And if Jupiter was alighting in it and he is in a fine condition, it indicates the suitability of the produce, the safety of the people, and their delight. **9** But if he was in a bad condition, it indicates the antithesis of that.

---

[28] Reading with MS **N** for المحتسبين ("those who reckon debts").

**10** And if Mars was alighting in it and he is in a fine condition, it indicates the safety of the people and their delight. **11** But if he was in a bad condition, it indicates the antithesis of that.

**12** And if the Sun was alighting in it and he was in a fine condition, he indicates the delight of the king. **13** But if he was in a bad condition, he indicates the antithesis of that.

**14** And if Venus was alighting in it and she is in a fine condition, she indicates the fine condition of the people along with[29] the king. **15** But if she was in a bad condition, she indicates the antithesis of that.

**16** And if Mercury was alighting in it and he is in a fine condition, that indicates an abundance of scholars and businessmen. **17** But if he was in a bad condition, it indicates the antithesis of that.

**18** And if the Moon was alighting in it and she is in a fine condition, it indicates the suitability of the regions. **19** But if she was in a bad condition, it indicates an abundance of enemies and people in [a state of] disagreement.

**20** Since we have completed what we wanted to explain, let us break off the discussion in Chapter VII.12, with the help of God and His support.

**21** Book VII is completed, and praise be to God greatly! **22** Book VIII follows it.

---

[29] Or perhaps, "in relation to" (مع).

# BOOK VIII: [DISASTERS, WARS, FOUNDATIONAL CHARTS, & FARDĀRS]

### On the sum of how to know the indications of the upper bodies for lower events, from the terminal points of the years & conjunctions[1]

*And it is in 2 Chapters:*

**1** Chapter VIII.1: On knowing lower events from the revolutions of years.

**2** Chapter VIII.2: On knowing the terminal points in the transit of the years from the Ascendants and the positions of the conjunctions, and how to know the *fardārs*, their lords, and their indications for lower events.

---

[1] Omitting the prior pious phrase: "*In the name of God the Merciful, the Compassionate, and upon Him and <...>, and in Him one seeks help.*"

## Chapter VIII.1: On knowing lower events from the revolutions of years

**1** Since we have set forth in Book VII how to know the indications of the sign of the terminal point, or one of the Ascendants of the annual revolutions, when one of the two coincides with one of the houses of the foundational Ascendants of the preceding Beginnings, or the conjunctions or directions, or one of the upper bodies was alighting in it or in the revolutionary divisions, in this Book let us state the sum of how to know the indications of the upper bodies for lower events from the terminal points of the years or conjunctions,[2] and what pertains to them. **2** In this chapter let us provide the knowledge of universal events from the revolutions of years.

**3** We say that the way of examining that is divided into different indications:

**4** One of them is seeking information about [1] upper effects, like fires, shooting stars, those having tails,[3] and what is like that.

**5** The second is for [2] lower events, like earthquakes, sinkholes, floods, and what is like that.

**6** The third is for [3] universal things affecting a class [of beings], like unhealthy air, fertility, drought, rains, and what is like that.[4]

**7** The fourth is for things which are [4] peculiar to one of the types of a class, like war and what is like that.

**8** And the planets, too, have a special claim on every one of these types, and some of them have a [special] claim apart from others: and that is at the terminal points of turnings,[5] the directions, the distribution and rays, and the Ascendants of the times pertaining to their assembling, squares, oppositions, and victorships over one of their Ascendants.

---

[2] Namely, profections from the conjunction itself.
[3] That is, comets.
[4] That is, drought affects all members of a class (at least, in some region), such as humans. But war affects only some people (7).
[5] That is, profections (أدوار).

## [1: Indications for upper events]

**9** As for discovering how to know the occurrence of fires, shooting stars, and those having tails, that is known from the indication of Mars in conjunctional years as well as others, and especially if his rays were in the airy signs, or he had the turning[6] and the rays and was alighting in the airy signs, and the Moon was made unfortunate in an airy sign,[7] and especially if he[8] ruled the tenth.

## [2: Indications for lower events]

**10** As for how to know the occurrence of earthquakes, sinkholes, and floods, that is known from the indications of Saturn, and especially if his rays were in the earthy and watery signs, and he had the turning[9] and the rays, or he alighted in the earthy signs and the Moon was made unfortunate by him: for if it was like that, sinkholes will occur. **11** And if he was in the watery ones, floods will occur; in the airy ones, snows and killing, corruptive hail along with the cold, the darkness of the atmosphere, raging winds, and what is like that.

## [3: Indications for universal things affecting a class]

**12** And[10] as for the quality of universal things affecting a class, like unhealthy air, epidemics, fertility and sterility, and rains, that is known from the Ascendants of the universal Beginnings which are before the greater luminary's being parallel with the spring tropic, and at the time of [his] being parallel, and from the two positions of the Moon (the portion of the meeting and of the fullness) in the years of conjunctions as well as others. **13** For if

---

[6] I take this to mean he is the lord of a profection (دور) and not the Turn, although I could be wrong. For example, if he had the turning (profection) and the rays, this could mean he rules the sign of the year by profection and is the partner of the mundane distribution. See also **10**.

[7] Presumably, by Mars (as with Saturn in **10**).

[8] Grammatically this could be either the Moon or Mars.

[9] See footnote above (دور).

[10] For **12-21**, cf. *Forty Chapters* Ch. 39, **1-11**. (See Appendix A.)

everything of what I described was safe from misfortunes, it indicates safety. **14** And if it was not like that, it indicates unhealthy air.

**15** And if the lords of the two Ascendants (or one of them) or the Moon had misfortune [and was] connecting with the lord of its own eighth, that indicates an abundance of death because of unhealthy [air]. **16** And if it was to the contrary, the unhealthy air will not have excessive death even if there was much unhealthy air: for this reason it will not affect the [whole] class [of people]. **17** And if these indicators (or the majority of them) were connecting with the lord of their own eighth, that indicates an abundance of sudden death without illnesses.

**18** And if the lords of their own sixths were proceeding towards them, unhealthy airs will follow in succession, and illnesses will be abundant, and their duration will be long. **19** But if they were quick [in motion], the illnesses will multiply but not last long.

**20** And if the one causing misfortune was Mars, and he is in the hot signs, and especially if he was quick [and] powerful, that indicates hot illnesses. **21** But if the one causing misfortune was Saturn, the illnesses will be Saturnian, chronic, and especially if he was slow [and] powerful, in the cold, dry signs.

**22** And as for the years indicative of epidemics, they are the years in which the distribution terminates at the bounds of Mercury, and especially if Mercury was combining with Saturn.

**23** As for the years indicative of fertility and sterility, it is that you look at the Ascendants of the conjunctional or full-Moon Beginnings, and at their portions: for if [1] the portion of the meeting or fullness was connecting with Jupiter (especially if he had a claim in it), and if [2] the lord of the Ascendant was made fortunate along with [3] the safety of the lord of the fourth, and [4] the terminal point of the year from the Ascendant of the religious community or of the shift of the triplicity had reached the position of Jupiter or Venus (by aspect or ray), fertility will occur in that year—and especially if the lord of the second was providing good fortune to the lord of the Ascendant or connected with it, or looked at it from a praiseworthy position, and especially if the Lot of Fortune witnessed it: for it is an indicator of an increase in fertility.

**24** As for the sterile years, they are those in which Saturn is governor over the meeting or fullness, by connection or by rulership, and especially if he ruled the Ascendant or made it unfortunate, or alighted in the chief posts,[11] and the lord of the fourth was corrupted by the infortunes (and especially by Saturn); and it is harsher for that if he was parallel with Mercury.

**25** And if Saturn was in the stakes of the Beginnings whose mention was set forth,[12] and especially the lunar posts, that is an indicator of expensiveness; and likewise if the Moon handed over to him at the time of her being released from the Node.[13] **26** And if Saturn was rising up, it indicates the same thing.

**27** And whichever one of the two infortunes had the misfortune, that is more difficult if Mercury was combining with them.

**28** And if misfortune from the lord of the Lot of Fortune befell the second, the Lot of Fortune, and the Ascendant, it will be greater in sterility.

**29** And the misfortune which is from Saturn in this matter is more difficult than the misfortune of Mars; and likewise the good fortune of Jupiter in the matter of fertility is more powerful than the good fortune of Venus.

**30** As for rains, if Mars was in the houses of Saturn in the revolution of the year of the world, it indicates a scarcity of rains. **31** But if he was in his own houses, it indicates their abundance. **32** And if he was in the rest of the planets' houses, it indicates their middling [amount].

---

[11] المراكز الرّئيسية. The "posts" are equivalent to the stakes, according to al-Rijāl VIII.2, 4; the "chief" ones would certainly be the Ascendant and Midheaven, just as Firmicus Maternus routinely calls those the "principal pivots." But Abū Ma'shar sometimes uses it to mean certain angular distances from the Moon, as he is about to do in **25**.

[12] See **24** and its footnote about the "chief posts."

[13] That is, the degree of the pre-chart lunation (the meeting or fullness). Since "Node" means "knot" in both Latin and Arabic, when she leaves it she is being released or loosened from it. Of course the lunation will rarely happen exactly on the Node (in which case an eclipse would take place). I suspect that this ambiguous rule and formulation has been copied by Abū Ma'shar from some other author, just like the rare use of "post" as an equivalent to "stake" in **24-25**.

## [4: Indications for particular things, like war]

**33** As for the years indicative of wars and civil unrest, they are distinguished by some of the species of the genus:[14] for you discover the knowledge of them from the time of Jupiter's assembling with Saturn, or his square or opposition, or from the stakes of the Ascendant of the year.

**34** And as for when in that year it is, it will be at the greater luminary's being parallel with the degree of Saturn, by assembly or aspect; but if it went beyond that, then at the Ascendant's reaching the position of the infortunes by direction, a month or year for every degree.

**35** And likewise if the Ascendant terminated at the conjunction which occurs in the positions of the infortunes by the assembly, square, or opposition, or at the Ascendant of the year's terminating at the position of the infortunes: for the events because of which there are wars, will be in these times.

**36** And if Mars too was in one of the stakes of the Ascendant of the year or of the Sun, the war will be in the direction of the world in which is the sign of that planet which is looking at [Mars] from the square or opposition. **37** And one may also operate apart from the square and opposition, especially if he was in the fiery triplicity: for the war will be in the region of the east. **38** And the statement on the rest of the triplicities is in this manner.

**39** And [a sign] is said to be on the "right" of the places and their "left" in accordance with the locations of the signs: because each sign rises before a sign which is on its left, and each sign rises after one which is on its right.

**40** And the sign of every clime may be divided into seven divisions, each clime getting 4° 17' 08" 35'''[15] and something. **41** The beginning of the first division will belong to the clime of the sign, and the second which follows it in position, until it terminates at the seventh clime from that clime. **42** So, where the infortunes alight in these divisions, it indicates that the events and misfortunes will occur in that clime; and where the fortunes alight it indicates good fortune for that clime, and the comfortableness of the way of life. **43** And the alighting of the infortunes in the eighth indicates the same thing.

---

[14] Abū Ma'shar's use of this philosophical language made more sense in *Gr. Intr.*, but is awkward and strained here.

[15] More correctly, 34'''.

### [Two Lots for war]

**44** And one may look at the Lot of prosperity, taken from the degree of the Sun to the degree of the west, cast out from the Ascendant, and where it terminates, there is the Lot of prosperity.[16] **45** And [one may look] from the Lot of battle, taken from Mars to the Moon, cast out from the position of the Sun, and where it terminates, there is the Lot of battle.[17] **46** When Mars is with one of the two [Lots] in the revolutionary periods, especially if he was in one of the fiery signs, that is an indicator of the occurrence of wars in that year. **47** Now if the Lot of prosperity was strong, not corrupted, it indicates that victory will belong to the people of truth (of the two sides between which the wars are arising); and if it was weak, it indicates the victory of the people of falsity (of the two of them).

### [Other rules for war]

**48** And one may discover the times in which the wars come to be from the distance which is between the two infortunes and the stake, and it is cast out from the Ascendant (and every 2 1/2° between them is a month).[18]

**49** And[19] the time in that is also known from the perspective of their motion. **50** For if it was direct, it indicates that the events will be at its retrogradation. **51** And if it was retrograde, it indicates that the events will be when it mixes its light with the light of the indicator of the king. **52** And at the mixing of its light with the indicator of the subjects, it indicates an abundance of wrongdoing and robbers.

**53** And[20] if [an infortune] is not in a stake and it is retrograde, it is more harmful for that in the land of the sign which it is parallel with, but it will not be universal among the people unless it mixes its light with the lord of the

---

[16] This Lot does not appear in *Gr. Intr.*, but the use of the Descendant does not make sense to me either.

[17] This Lot does not appear in *Gr. Intr.*

[18] But what is the point of casting out from the ASC, if it's the distance between the infortunes that gives the time?

[19] For this paragraph, see *Scito* Ch. 80, **2-3**; and Sahl's *Revolutions* Ch. 1.2, **40-41**.

[20] For this paragraph, see *Scito* Ch. 80, **4-5**; and Sahl's *Revolutions* Ch. 1.2, **43-45**.

Ascendant or the light of the lord of the Midheaven (if it was the indicator of the king). **54** And if it was not looking at the Ascendant, it does not indicate harm in that year unless it was the lord of the year or the indicator of the king.

**55** And if Mars was in the stakes, and the distribution reached his bound, and the turning[21] terminated at his position in the new conjunction and the shift of the transit,[22] the wars will be in the direction which belongs to that sign which the direction[23] terminated at, or in the countries whose Ascendants are that sign.

**56** And[24] likewise too if Mars was opposing Saturn or squaring him, and he[25] is received, that indicates wars. **57** And if Mars was not received but Saturn was received, that is an indicator of a scarcity of wars.

**58** And if he was in the revolutionary stakes, under the rays, that indicates the existence of wars in that revolution; and it is harsher for that if it was in the convertible signs. **59** If it was in the embodied signs, it will not be completed. **60** And if it was in the fixed ones, that indicates that the wars will be for trivial reasons and shielding [oneself][26] from the truth.

**61** And[27] if Mars was in the Midheaven in the revolution of years, and especially in Gemini, that indicates an abundance of crucifixion in that year. **62** And if he was in the Ascendant or the Setting, it indicates the cutting off of hands. **63** And if he was in the stake of the earth, it indicates the cutting off of hands and feet.

**64** And that may also be known from the conditions of Jupiter in terms of [his] being received or not, and the aspect of Mars towards him.

---

[21] Probably, a profection (دور).

[22] In this case, Mars is dynamically advancing in some chart, is the distributor of the mundane distribution, and the profection has reached him at the time of a new conjunction (thus activating his promise at a time which already shows change).

[23] Or perhaps, the profection.

[24] For this paragraph, see Sahl's *Revolutions* Ch. 8.1, **44-45**. *Scito* Ch. 38, **16-18** is close but not as exact as Sahl.

[25] In Sahl's *Revolutions* this is Mars, who is being received by a planet *other than* Saturn, which makes sense.

[26] الانزواء.

[27] For this paragraph, see *RYW* Ch. 36, **2-4**; *Scito* Ch. 74, **29-30**; Sahl's *Revolutions* Ch. 5.3, **88-90**.

**65** And[28] one also looks at the lord of the Ascendant and of the ninth: for if it was in the fourth, it indicates an abundance of captives in that year. **66** And if the lord of the fourth was in the ninth, it indicates the opening of prisons, and the freeing of most of the captives from the jails.

**67** And when Jupiter conjoins with Saturn or is in his square or opposition, that warns of rebels setting out in that year: and the time in that is Jupiter's being parallel with his[29] house or exaltation, or the time of his alighting in one of the stakes, or in his power. **68** But if he did not appear in these stakes, then that will be when the direction[30] from that year arrives at the positions of the infortunes from the Ascendant, or their opposition, the measurement of each sign being a month or year.

**69** And[31] if the year from the current conjunction or from the Ascendant of the religious community terminated at the position of the infortunes, their conjunction, or opposition, that will be one of the feared times in which the rebels' motion and setting out is.

**70** And it is necessary that one look at the Ascendants of the annual Beginnings, mention of which we have set forth [earlier]. **71** For if they were convertible, the quarters of the year are revolved, and one judges the quarters of the year from their Ascendants in accordance with what we have set out, because the Ascendants of their revolutions do not have power if the sign of the year was convertible, since that is an indicator of an abundance of changes in the year, according to the revolving of its quarters. **72** But if they were embodied, then its halves should be revolved instead of its quarters, because embodied Ascendants indicate two times of the year. **73** And if they were fixed, operate according to the Ascendant of the year, because [it is] stronger than the rest of its parts, and especially if the lords of the Ascendants [of the quarters] alight in signs of like figures[32] as its Ascendant.

**74** Now as for how to know the time of the appearance of the indications in the parts of the year, and their strength, it is discovered from the lords of the Ascendants: because if they were in convertible signs, it indicates the

---

[28] For this paragraph, cf. *Scito* Ch. 71, **1-4**; Sahl's *Revolutions* Ch. 7, **63**.

[29] This is most likely Jupiter's own house or exaltation, not Saturn's.

[30] Or more likely, profection.

[31] For this sentence, cf. Sahl's *Revolutions* Ch. 8.4, **11**.

[32] That is, its quadruplicity.

coming-to-be of the events and their time in the first quarter of the year; but if they were embodied, it will occur in its middle; and if they were fixed, it will occur at its end.

**75** And it is also necessary that one sees when one of the signs is made unfortunate by the infortunes being parallel with it or the casting of their rays to it from the square or opposition, in whichever area they are. **76** If they were in the region of the east, it indicates that the majority of what [harm there is] is had (from the land of those signs) is in the region of the east; and the statement about the west is likewise. **77** But if they were in the Midheaven they indicate that the trouble will extend over the eastern and western land, especially that which is from it in the region of the north.[33] **78** And if they were in the stake of the earth, it indicates that the trouble which is had from the lands is in the region of the south.

**79** Since we have completed what we wanted to describe, let us break off the discussion in Chapter VIII.1, if God wills.

---

[33] I should think this ought to be "south," and the stake of the earth the north in **78**.

## Chapter VIII.2: On knowing the terminal points in the transit of the years from the Ascendants, the positions of the conjunctions, & their indications, & how to know the fardārs, their lords, & their indications for all lower events

**1** Since we have set forth in Chapter VIII.1 how to know universal events from the method of annual revolutions, in this chapter let us sketch out the sphere's positions[34] by the calculation of the *Canon* at [the time of] the universal Beginnings if the direction was from them, and the turning[35] of terminal points; and after that follows how the terminal points and *fardārs* work. **2** For what we have summarized in this book of ours on the sum of the conditions of conjunctions and their indications, is close to rounding out what of the years is revolved, with the help of God.

**3** We say that the dates for which the planets are properly set up in the three images by the *Canon*, are for three times. **4** One of them is for the revolution of the year in which is the conjunctional shift indicating the religious community. **5** The second is for the revolution of the year indicative of the shift of the rulership to the Sawād of Iraq. **6** The third is for the revolution of the year in which the conjunction shifted from the watery triplicity to the fiery triplicity. **7** And the times encompassed in that are according to what is written next to the images of their charts, if God wills—and He is who is called on for help.

---

[34] Or, "foundations" (الأوضاع): these are the three foundational charts for Abū Ma'shar's time: see **3**.

[35] الأدوار.

BOOK VIII: DISASTERS, WARS, FOUNDATIONAL CHARTS, FARDĀRS   375

[Foundational chart #1]

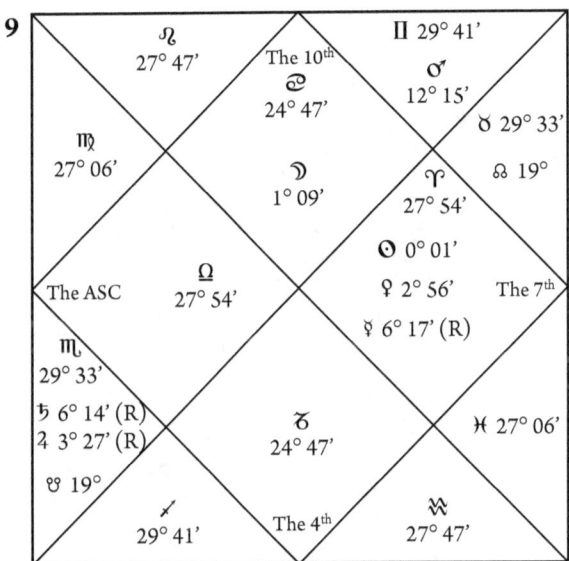

**8** The date of the revolution of the year of the conjunction indicative of the religious community: this is the chart of the religious community [itself].[37]

**10** From the Ascendant of the conjunction indicative of the Flood, this year terminated at the Ascendant of this year (which is

Figure 52: Triplicity shift to Islam (571 AD)[36]

Libra), and from the sign of the terminal point of the turning[38] to Gemini, and from the position of the conjunction of the Flood to Sagittarius, and the distribution arrived from the beginning of Aries (having come to be in it at one of the conjunctions at the time of one of the Turns[39] whose mention we set forth),[40] to the 20th portion of Pisces without the rays of any of the planets. **11** The parallelism of the greater luminary with the spring convertible point in the year of the shift indicative of the religious community was at the second hour of the night, whose morning was the 23rd day of Bahman Māh.

---

[36] This chart of Abū Ma'shar's can be dated to March 19, 571 AD JC, around 7:45PM (LAT) at the latitude 4N31 and longitude 39E (the rough longitude of Mecca).

[37] I have counted the chart as sentence **9** for accurate citing.

[38] دور. See my footnote to II.4, **99** for a possible explanation of this, as a profection from the Ascendant of the Flood. See a similar reference in **30** below.

[39] أدوار. Or perhaps, "cycles."

[40] This probably means the Flood. The Saturn-Cancer Turn, the profections, and the direction all begin at that Aries conjunction. Thus the ecliptical direction around the zodiac began at 0° Aries and has now reached 20° Pisces.

**12** And the Ascendant and the positions of the planets in order, according to the *Canon* and the date, are as we have drawn them here.

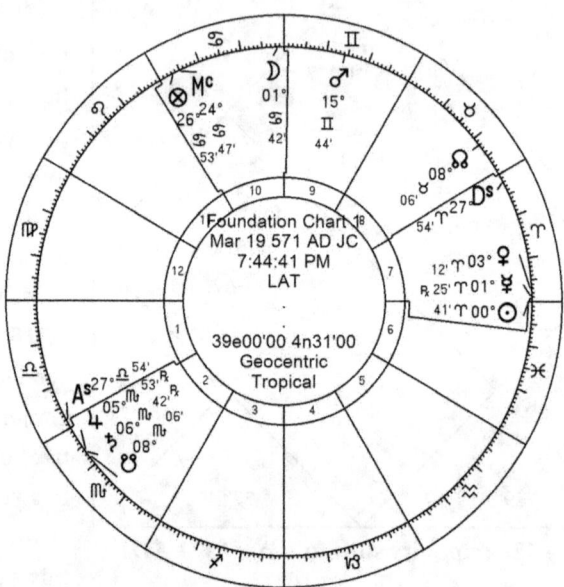

**Figure 53: Modern approximation of Abū Ma'shar's shift to Islam**

*[Foundational chart #2]*

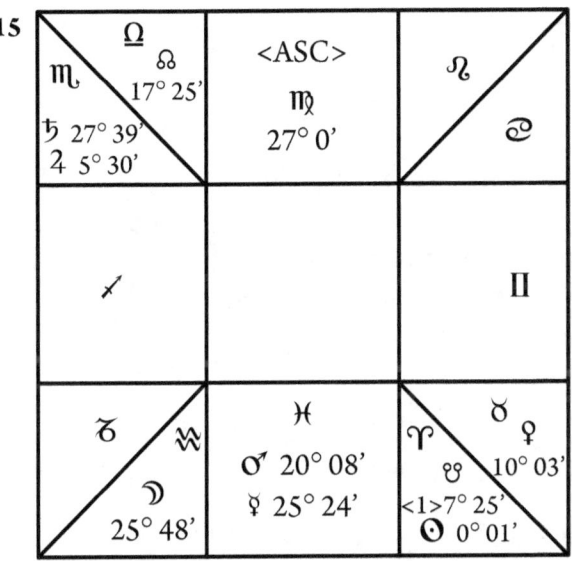

Figure 54: Dynasty shift to 'Abbāsids (749 AD)[41]

**13** The date for this image is <*missing*>. **14** This is the chart of the shift of the dynasty to the Sawād of Iraq.[42] **16** From the Ascendant of the conjunction of the religious community,[43] this year terminated at Cancer, and by distribution to the 19th portion of Virgo (and in it are the rays of Saturn, Mars, and Mercury by retrogradation), and from the position of the conjunction to Leo. **17** And the parallelism of the greater luminary with the point of the spring equinox, in this year of the shift indicative of the dynasty, was at the end of the 12th hour of the 17th[44] day of Bahman Māh, of year 117 of Yazdijird. **18** The Ascendant and the positions of the planets, and the date by the *Canon*, are according to what is established in this image, if God wills.

---

[41] This chart of Abū Ma'shar's can be dated to March 20, 749 AD JC, around 5:36PM (LAT) at the latitude 4N31 and longitude 39E (the rough longitude of Mecca).
[42] I have counted the chart as sentence **15** for accurate citation.
[43] Namely, Foundational chart #1 above (**9**).
[44] This should be "7th".

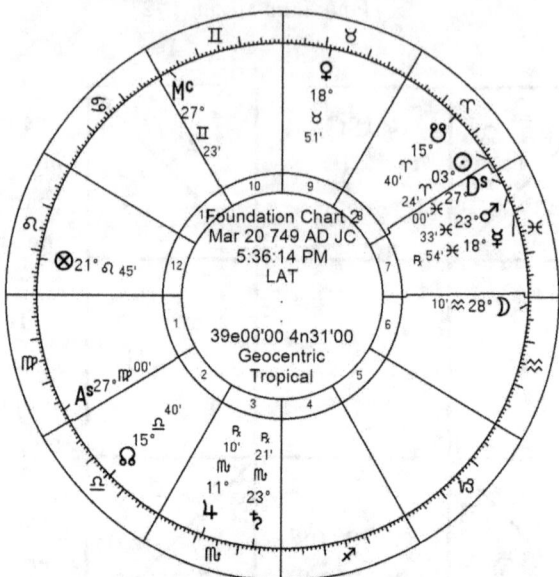

**Figure 55: Modern approximation of Abū Ma'shar's dynasty shift to 'Abbāsids**

## [Foundational chart #3]

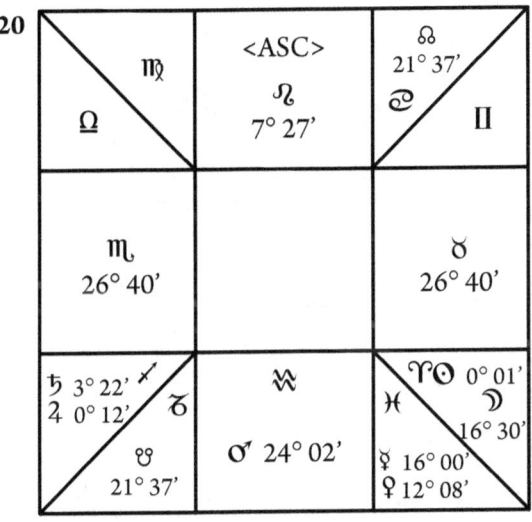

Figure 56: Triplicity shift to fire (809 AD)[45]

**19** This is the chart of the shift of the conjunction from the watery triplicity to the fiery triplicity.[46]

**21** And from the Ascendant of the conjunction of the religious community,[47] this year terminated at Cancer; and from the position of the conjunction to Leo; and from the distribution to the 19th portion of Scorpio. **22** And the parallelism of the greater luminary with the spring convertible point in this year was at 7 ½ hours of the 22nd day of Bahman Māh, in the year 177 of Yazdijird. **23** The Ascendant and positions of the planets by the *Canon* and in order are according to what is in this image, and the date properly set for it is written in its center, if God wills.

---

[45] This chart of Abū Ma'shar's can be dated to March 20, 809 AD JC. However, the chart as it stands is impossible, because there is no northern latitude at which the MC can be 26° 40' Taurus and the ASC at 7°27' Leo. However, if we assume a scribal error and make the ASC **27° 27'** Leo, the chart can be timed to around 3:24PM (LAT) at the latitude 22N55 (just north of Mecca) and longitude 39E (the rough longitude of Mecca).

[46] I have counted the chart as sentence **20** for accurate citing.

[47] Namely, Foundational chart #1 above (**9**).

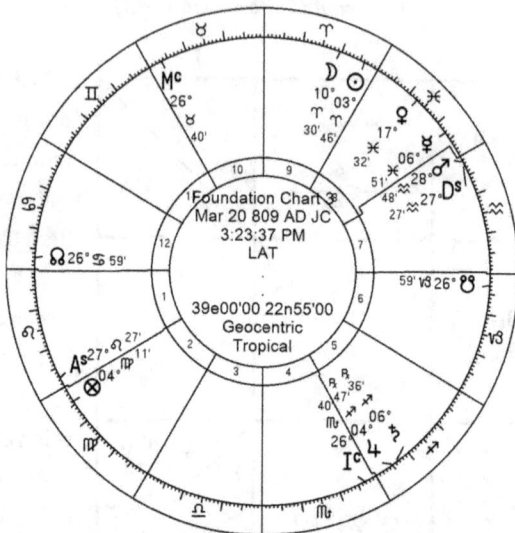

Figure 57: Triplicity shift to fire (809 AD)

*[Calculation shortcuts]*

**24** Since we have sketched out the positions of the sphere at the times of the three Beginnings in relation to their universal influences, and the directions from them to the positions of the terminal points in the transits of the years, it is most necessary that we be fully acquainted with the number of Persian years which are between the year in which the transit was, and the first day of the years of Yazdijird, so that one may facilitate how to know the terminal points in whatever time period one wants knowledge of that; and the knowledge of the quality of the terminal points and the *fardārs* follows that, by the will of God (be He respected and honored!).

**25** We say that the times enclosed by [1] the first day of the year in which the greater luminary was parallel with the spring convertible point of the year of the shift of the transit indicative of the religious community, and [2] the first day of the Hijrah, was 51 Persian years, 3 months, 3 days, 16 hours. **26** And from the first day of the Hijrah to the first day of the rule of Yazdijird b. Shahriyār, was 9 Persian years, 11 months, 9 days. **27** The sum of that is 61 years, 2 months, 12 days, 16 hours.

**28** So, if you wanted to know the sign of the terminal point from the Ascendant of the shift of the transit from the airy triplicity to the watery triplicity (indicating the religious community) at the transit of years, then always add to the years of Yazdijird the amount [in time] between the first day of the year of the religious community and it, and begin to cast out from Libra: and where it terminates, there is the sign of the terminal point from the Ascendant of the religion.

**29** And if you wanted the terminal point from the sign of the conjunction of the religious community, then let the casting out be from Scorpio.

**30** And if you wanted the terminal point from the sign of the Turn,[48] then let the casting out be from the sign of Gemini.

**31** And if you wanted the terminal point from the degree of the direction, then let the casting out be from degree 20 of Pisces, a year for each degree, and where it terminates, there is the degree of the distribution.

**32** When[49] you have understood the degree of the terminal point at the time of the greater luminary's being parallel with the first portion of the spring convertible, it is most necessary that 10" be added for every degree of the sphere which the Sun has marked off: the sum of that when each of the signs has been marked off is 5'. **33** And you should use this arrangement of marking [degrees] off for all of the spherical divisions, until you come to the end of its divisions (which is the end of Pisces). **34** So what is necessary to add to the degree of the terminal point is according to what we set forth: for every sign, 5' of a complete degree.

---

[48] دور. This sounds like a profection from the sign of the current Turn (Venus-Gemini). But see **10** above, and my footnote to II.4, **99**.

[49] The purpose of this paragraph is to calculate how far to move the mundane direction (**20**) for units of time less than a year. (This is not very useful since we have already seen that this ecliptical direction is only approximate.) So, we first find out where the degree is at any particular Aries ingress. Since the direction moves 1° per year, it will move 5' in longitude every month, namely the length of time it takes for the Sun to move through a sign (1° / 12 months = 5'). Each month/sign has 30°, which is equivalent to the Sun taking 30 days to move through it, which means each day is worth 10" of longitude (5' / 30 = 10"). Thus, we move this "directed" Ascendant 10" per day, 5' per month, and 1° per year.

**35** And[50] in this way one knows the Ascendants of the *fardārs* extracted from the method of the twelfth-parts of the terminal sign, and its stakes from the Ascendants of the transit and its stakes, and the coinciding of the degree of the terminal point and its stakes with the sign of the transit, which reveals the soundness of the Ascendants of the times in which individual things truly happen.

**36** And if you wanted the terminal point from the Ascendant of the dynasty, then you subtract 117 years from the complete years of Yazdijird, then begin to cast out from Virgo.

**37** And if you wanted the terminal point from the conjunction of the dynasty, then let the casting out be from Scorpio.

**38** And if you wanted the terminal point from the Ascendant of the shift of the transit from the watery triplicity to the fiery triplicity, then let 177 years be deducted from the years of Yazdijird, then you begin the casting out from Leo.

**39** And if you wanted the terminal point from the sign of the conjunction of the transit from the watery triplicity to the fiery triplicity, let the casting out be from Sagittarius.

### [Fardārs]

**40** Now as for how to know to which of the upper bodies the *fardār*ship belongs, one turns to the complete years of Yazdijird, and 18 are always cast off from them first;[51] then one divides the remainder by 75, and whatever remains which is not a complete 75, one casts off from it the years of the planets in succession, in the order of the *fardārs*. **41** Begin by casting off from Saturn, and the planet which it terminates at, whether it has no remainder or if some number remains, it is the lord of the *fardār*. **42** And[52] what has al-

---

[50] This paragraph is confusing. It seems to suggest that *fardārs* actually have Ascendants, somehow derived from the twelfth-parts of profection signs. But it is so convoluted I can't make sense of it. **BY** seem to quietly ignore it, too.

[51] This tells us that Abū Ma'shar begins a new set of *fardārs* from the year 632 AD, the beginning of the Islamic calendar.

[52] **BY** note that they don't quite know what to make of this sentence. It seems to be poor mathematical explaining by Abū Ma'shar.

ready elapsed of its *fardār* is in the same manner as the number remaining: then one repeats in the future year for the year which follows that number.

**43** Now as for the *fardārs* set down for the planets: the *fardār* of the Sun is 10 years, the *fardār* of the Moon 9 years, the *fardār* of the Head 3 years, the *fardār* of Jupiter 12 years, the *fardār* of Mercury 13 years, the *fardār* of Saturn 11 years, the *fardār* of the Tail 2 years, the *fardār* of Mars 7 years, and the *fardār* of Venus 8 years.

**44** As for the way of knowing the indication of the *fardār* of each planet for lower events, it is that you should see if it was one of the three *fardārs* belonging to the Sun:[53] for that is an indicator of delight occurring to the king of Babylon, along with an increase in their respect, kingdom, and victory, and their devising customs which did not exist [before], and their abundant moving [around] and their travels, support for them, the submission in obedience towards them by the people of the regions, along with an abundance of their conquests of those in cities, their victory over enemies, a prevalence of delight in the subjects, and an abundant rise in the yield.

**45** If the *fardār*ship belonged to the Moon, that indicates an abundance of disorder in the kings' management of the people of Babylon in their administration, and the small influence of their command; they will employ justice and become famous for that, and the conditions of their women will be fine, the land-tax will increase, and assets be plentiful.

**46** If the *fardār*ship belonged to the Head, that indicates the expansion of the kingdom of the people of Babylon, and books reaching them from regions having submission and obedience to them, along with the good which will come [to them] from the kings of the rest of the regions, and their building cities and villages, their attacking their enemies and victory over them, the intensity of their awe among the kings, and an abundance of fertility in the whole of its *fardār*; but sometimes illnesses will befall its kings in their heads, like headaches and what is like that.

**47** Now if the *fardār*ship belonged to Jupiter, that indicates the increase of the kings of Babylon in respect, skill[54] in their rule, victory over their ene-

---

[53] This may refer to mundane *fardārs* of different sizes, as described in *AW2*, my Introduction §9. Nevertheless I do not understand Abū Ma'shar instructions here. See my Introduction to this book.

[54] Or perhaps, the "extension, spreading" of it (بسطة).

mies (and [the enemies'] submissiveness towards them), their command to dig rivers, the flourishing of populated areas, the abundance of the land-tax, the thriving of the yield, an abundance of plowing and vegetation, and the endurance of the matter for the whole of his *fardār*—except that distresses will befall them by reason of their relatives, and they will be blessed with children and put them in charge of works, they will have good fortune and will rejoice in their kinfolk, they will attack the land of Rūm, and killing will be abundant, and captivity in it, and the condition of the people of Persia and the Arabs will be fine.

**48** And if the *fardār*ship belonged to Mercury, that indicates the prevalence of health in the kings of Babylon and their children, and their increase in respect, nobility, and authority, and the kings will put their children in charge, they will perform beneficial things for their slaves, attendants, and servants; and sometimes they will imprison some of their attendants and punish and fine them, [but] then they will be released after that. **49** And it multiplies the travels of the kings of the people of Babylon, and they will be victorious over their enemies where they face them, and they will attack cities, and scholars and the people of asceticism will multiply, as well as diviners, astrologers, and writers, and the people will have harm because of demanding the land-tax from them, and the roughness of elders towards them, and reports and false rumors will multiply at the doors of the kings, and the people of the climes will have tribulation—except for the people of Persia, because they will increase in the good. **50** And anxiety, sorrow, [worried] thinking, debauchery, treachery, and betrayal will be abundant, and the people will have difficulty in what is needed, justice and benefit will spread among the people, kings will order the digging of rivers and the building of cities, business will be brisk in the land of Babylon, and watery things like pearls and fish will be abundant, as well as aquatic birds; and sometimes kings will be worried about hidden matters.

**51** And if the *fardār*ship belonged to Saturn, that indicates an abundance of sorrows and anxieties in the land of Babylon, and troubles befalling the land of Persia, and the lowliness of its people, and their defeat and moving around, the appearance of fearful portents and signs in the atmosphere will multiply, the people will become impoverished, false rumors will be abundant, kings will raid each other, and the war between them will intensify, and emaciation and death will befall the people, tribulation and death will be general among most of the people of the climes (but the people of Babylon will be freed from that), and sowing and the produce will thrive for them, and their land will be fertile.

**52** And if the *fardār*ship belonged to the Tail, that is an indicator of the appearance of debauchery, the difficulty of matters for the people, and the fine condition of the people of Persia, India, and Rūm.

**53** And if the *fardār*ship belonged to Mars, that is an indicator of the fine condition of the people of Persia for the term of two years of his *fardār*, and their might, and submissiveness and troubles befalling the people of Rūm, and respect will come to the people of Babylon, along with [their] safety from troubles and infirmities, with an abundant rise[55] [in prices] and fertility, an attack by the people of Persia against the people of Rūm, with an abundance of fighting between them, the people of villages acting [in concert] with each other, with an abundance of malice; and sometimes illnesses and abscesses will befall them.

**54** And if the *fardār*ship belonged to Venus, that indicates the existence of safety and delight in most of the climes for the whole of her *fardār*, and the fine condition of the people of Babylon, the Arabs, and Rūm, and the people's practice of thankfulness, fidelity, and love, forgiveness and asceticism, working hard in worship, along with the appearance of suitable portents and signs in the atmosphere and the land, and womens' abstinence, kings will exchange gifts, and books and letters will flow between them, and what is raised on[56] the land will flourish, and its cultivated land will prosper, kings and subjects will rejoice in their assets and children, pearls and the catch of the sea will be abundant, as well as aquatic birds, the offspring of sheep, and fertility. **55** And justice, safety, and well-being will appear, as well as uprightness and piety. **56** And tribulation, evil, and injustice will affect the people of India, and kings will order the digging of a mighty river.

---

[55] **BY**: "yield" (الرَّفع).
[56] الرَّفع.

## [Predictive principles for fardārs and other charts]

**57** And for all of what we have stated of the indications of these planets, if they were in a fine condition they indicate increase in all of the praiseworthy matters that they indicate. **58** And if the situation was the antithesis of that, they indicate a decrease in all of the praiseworthy matters that they indicate. **59** And sometimes the evil is complete, with the nullity of most of the beneficial matters.

**60** And [for] everything that we have explained in this chapter about these judgments of these *fardārs*, and in the rest of the chapters of the other Books, if the testimony of the higher bodies in the spherical positions at the times of the universal Beginnings and the particular revolutions matches these indications, that is one of the reasons expressing the truth of the indication. **61** But if the matter was to the contrary of that, the matter in the judgment will incline in accordance with what we have described of the position of the upper bodies at the revolutionary times,[57] rather than these judgments.

**62** And an example of that is if one of the *fardārs* had victorship or the indication of kings' changing [house] and their movements, and the conjunction in the revolution (or the greater luminary), was in positions indicative of standing still (like the stakes and what resembles them), if the matter was like that, it is necessary that, in stating the judgment about moving, it should incline towards holding that back.[58]

**63** And likewise, if Venus was in a fine condition in one of the revolutions, and any of the indicators indicates the badness of Venusian things, then the indication inclines towards the middling quality of the matter in condition, <in its badness>[59] or its goodness. **64** And likewise the statement about the indications of the rest of the upper bodies for all of the indications attributed to them.

**65** But when one of the upper bodies in the revolutionary periods matches the testimonies of the indicators of the *fardārs* and other things, that is

---

[57] That is, prefer the ingress charts to these more general *fardār* indications.
[58] That is, restraining the movement.
[59] Following **BY** by adding this with the Latin.

more powerful in indication and more truthful, by the will of God (mighty and lofty) and His help.

**66** Since we have completed what we wanted to explain, let us complete Chapter 2 of Book VIII, with our completing the whole of the book, with the help of God and His support; and praise be to God alone, and the prayers of God and salvation be upon our master Muhammad, his family, and companions.

# APPENDIX A: AL-KINDĪ'S *FORTY CHAPTERS*

For the reader's interest, I include here two chapters of al-Kindī's *Forty Chapters*, from several sources:
- **J:** Jerusalem, al-Khalidi Ar. 1856 f. 51.
- **N:** (Nuruosmaniye 2776), from al-Rijāl's Book VIII.6 and VIII.31.
- The two Latin versions (Hugo of Santalla and Robert of Ketton), which were the basis of my *Forty Chapters* (2011).

BRD includes Ch. 39 in its VIII.1, **12-21**.

### Chapter 39: On a year of infectious disease, & safety [from it]

**1** Erect the Ascendant of the year and the Ascendant of the meeting and[1] fullness which was before the Sun's entry into Aries. **2** Then, look: for if the two Ascendants and the Moon were cleansed of the infortunes, and [also] the lord of the portion of the meeting <or fullness>[2] (that is, the victor), and its[3] connection with was a fortune, and the luminaries looked at it (or that one of the two which had the shift), the year will be safe from infectious disease, by the aid of God. **3** And if the lord of the Ascendants[4] and the Moon, and the lord of the portion of the meeting and fullness, were made unfortunate (or most of them), that indicates infectious disease in accordance with the misfortunes, their difficulty,[5] and the nature of the infortune, and the position in which the misfortune is.

**4** Now if you saw the two lords of the Ascendants (or one of them) and the Moon having misfortune, connecting with the lord of their own eighth,[6] it indicates infectious disease and an abundance of death. **5** But if it was contrary to that, there will be infectious disease but not excessive death. **6** And if the infectious disease did multiply, death in this ailment will be scarce. **7** And

---

[1] This should be understood as "or."
[2] Adding with **N**.
[3] I take this to be the victor over the degree of the lunation.
[4] Reading with **N** for "Ascendant."
[5] Reading وصعوبتها with **J** for "its witness/spectator" (معاينها).
[6] Reading with **N** and the Latin versions, for **J**'s "the eighth."

if among these indicators there was a planet connecting with the lord of its own eighth, the death will be abundant, sudden, [and] without illnesses.

**8** And if the lord of the sixth of each of them was proceeding to it, from the stakes, and it was slow, the illnesses will multiply and last a long time. **9** And if it was fast, the illnesses will multiply but will not last long.

**10** And if the one making [it] unfortunate was Mars, the illnesses will be hot, especially if he was easternizing, strong, in hot, dry signs. **11** But if the one making [it] unfortunate was Saturn, the illnesses will be Saturnian, chronic, and especially if Saturn was slow, strong, in cold, dry signs.

## Chapter 40: On the revolution of the year of the world, and what occurs in the matter of prominent people[7] & the general public

**1** If you wanted a revolution of the year of the world, erect the meeting and fullness which was before the Sun's entering Aries, and calculate exactly the stakes and the positions of the planets. **2** Then look at which of the planets the Moon connects with when she separates from the meeting and fullness, whether it is a fortune or infortune, strong or weak, and speak in accordance with that about the condition of the general public.

**3** For if the Moon was advancing and she was in her shares, and connected with a strong, advancing fortune in its own shares, the condition of the general public will be fine in that year, and they will have abundance and comfort in their way of life, and they will shift from comfort to comfort, and [from] good to good. **4** And if the one which she connects with is Jupiter, they will have fairness, loyalty, and health, and an abundance of offspring, purity, and respectable morals. **5** But if the one she connects with is Venus, they will have comfort, delight, and incidents of sexual intercourse, and delighting in marriage.

**6** But if the matter was to the contrary of that, such as if the Moon is falling, not in her own shares, it will also be according to what we described of

---

[7] Tentatively reading for العلیّة.

good fortune,[8] except that they will not pass over to good fortune from difficulty and languor, nor from weakness to strength.

**7** But if the Moon was advancing and she is as we described in terms of a strong condition and alighting in her shares, and her connection was with a *falling* fortune in its own shares, they will pass over from comfort and strength to the comfort of a weaker condition than it, and to languor.

**8** And if the fortune was western [and] alien in addition to its falling, there will be hindrances to the good fortune, and comfort that is mistaken and not complete, even though in themselves they will be in good health and [have] safety from illnesses.

**9** And if the Moon was weak, in alienation, and connects with advancing, strong infortunes, that indicates the bad condition of the general public, their decline, the weakness of their conditions, difficulty in their subsistence, the abundance of their illnesses, and medications used for them.

**10** Now if the infortune with which the Moon connects was the lord of the Moon's eighth, or it had a strong share in the eighth of the Moon (if she was not its lord), death will multiply among them. **11** But if the infortune was not like that but the lord of the eighth of the Moon was looking at[9] the Moon, that also indicate an abundance of death.

**12** Now if the infortune which the Moon connects with was Saturn, the illnesses will be Saturnian, cold; and the reasons for the death will be that. **13** And instead of Saturn it was Mars, the illnesses will be hot and bloody. **14** And if the sign [of the infortune] was of the signs of people, there will be killing along with that, and the shedding of much blood, and especially if the year[10] had terminated at the position of Mars.

**15** So begin [the profection] either to his position in the shift of the transit[11] or to his place in the [most recent] conjunction which was before the revolution: for these two years indicate wars and the shedding of blood. **16** And the wars will be in the areas which are attributed to the sign in which

---

[8] This would only make sense if she was still applying to fortunes.
[9] ناظر إلى. This suggests especially the opposition.
[10] That is, from the Ascendant of a previous conjunction: see the next sentence.
[11] That is, the triplicity shift.

Mars is in the revolved year, and the earlier places[12] which we determined; and the conclusion of the war will be in the revolution[13] of the year (by the permission of God) upon Mars's burning of his entering his own fall, and the burning of Jupiter. **17** Then look in addition to that at the position of Mars: for if he was eastern or western, or northern or southern: for the victory <will belong to that direction>.[14]

---

[12] الرّؤوس. This may mean, "the areas attributed to the sign in which Mars *was* in the *earlier* conjunction chart.
[13] Tentatively reading حلل for لل.
[14] Adding with the Latin versions.

# Bibliography

Abū Ma'shar, *On Historical Astrology: The Book of Religions and Dynasties (On the Great Conjunctions)*, Keiji Yamamoto and Charles Burnett trans. and ed., Vols. 1-2 (Leiden: Brill, 2000)

Abū Ma'shar, *Persian Nativities IV: On the Revolutions of the Years of Nativities*, trans. Benjamin N. Dykes (Minneapolis: The Cazimi Press, 2019)

Abū Ma'shar (attr.) *Scito horam introitus*, in *AW2*

Abū Ma'shar, *The Flowers of Abū Ma'shar*, in *AW2*

Abū Ma'shar, *The Great Introduction to the Science of the Stars*, trans. Benjamin N. Dykes (Minneapolis: The Cazimi Press, 2020)

'Alī b. Abī al-Rijāl, *The Book of the Skilled* (in *AW2*)

Al-Kindī, *The Length of Arab Rule* (in Appendix III of *BY*)

Al-Qabīsī, *The Introduction to Astrology*, eds. Charles Burnett, Keiji Yamamoto, Michio Yano (London and Turin: The Warburg Institute, 2004)

*Al-Qur'ān*, Ahmed Alī trans. and ed. (Princeton: Princeton University Press, 1984)

Al-Ṭabarī, *The History of Prophets & Kings*, 40 vols. (Albany: The State University of New York Press, 1989-2007)

Aristotle, *The Complete Works of Aristotle* vols. I-II, ed. Jonathan Barnes (Princeton, NJ: Princeton University Press, 1984)

Dykes, Benjamin N. trans. and ed., *Astrology of the World* vols. 1-2 (Minneapolis: The Cazimi Press, 2013-14)

Firmicus Maternus, *Mathesis*, trans. and ed. Benjamin N. Dykes (Minneapolis: The Cazimi Press, 2023)

ibn Bishr, Sahl, trans. and ed. Benjamin N. Dykes, *The Astrology of Sahl b. Bishr Volume I: Principles, Elections, Questions, Nativities* (Minneapolis, MN: The Cazimi Press, 2019)

Kennedy, Edward S. et al, "Al-Battānī's Astrological History of the Prophet and the Early Caliphate," in *Suhayl* v. 9 (2009-10), pp. 13-148.

Lane, Edward, *An Arabic-English Lexicon* (Beirut: Librairie du Liban, 1968)

LeStrange, Guy, *The Lands of the Eastern Caliphate* (London: Frank Cass & Co., Ltd, 1966)

Leopold of Austria, *A Compilation on the Science of the Stars*, trans. Benjamin N. Dykes (Minneapolis: The Cazimi Press, 2015)

Māshā'allāh b. Atharī, *On the Revolutions of the Years of the World*, in *AW2*

Mūsā b. Nawbakht, *The Book of Fulfilment*, trans. Benjamin N. Dykes (*forthcoming*)

Mūsā b. Nawbakht, *The Book of Periods & Epochs*, trans. Benjamin N. Dykes (*forthcoming*)

Pingree, David, *The Thousands of Abū Ma'shar* (London: The Warburg Institute and University of London, 1968)

Ramesey, William, *Astrologie Restored* (1653)

Sahl b. Bishr, *On the Revolutions of the Years of the World*, trans. Benjamin N. Dykes (*forthcoming*)

Schmidt, Robert trans. and Robert Hand ed., *Dorotheus, Orpheus, Anubio, & Pseudo-Valens: Teachings on Transits* (Berkeley Springs, WV: The Golden Hind Press, 1995)

Ptolemy, Claudius, *Tetrabiblos*, F.E. Robbins trans. and ed. (Cambridge and London: Harvard University Press, 1940)

# INDEX

This is a standard index of topics and names, but I direct the reader to the entry for "Advice," which points largely to my own summaries of how Abū Ma'shar approaches chart interpretation, as well as some of my own ideas.

'Abbāsids...35, 47-48, 52, 54, 65-66, 68-69, 88, 114, 132, 165, 181, 377-378
'Abd al-Malik (Caliph) ........... 132
'Alī (Caliph) ..................... 103, 132
'Alī b. Muhammad the "'Alawite" ................ 3, 35-36, 56, 103-104
'Umar I (Caliph) ..................... 132
'Umar II (Caliph) .................... 132
'Umayyads...54, 65, 68, 88, 114, 133, 167
'Uthmān b. 'Affān (Caliph) .....54, 132, 154, 167
Abthnūs (unknown astrologer) ................................85
Abū Bakr (Caliph)...48, 132-33, 181, 346
Abū Ma'shar... 1-7, 10-11, 13-16, 19, 21-22, 25, 28-38, 40, 42-49, 51-58, 64, 67-70, 79-86, 88-89, 92, 98, 100-01, 115, 126, 132-33, 135, 138-39, 141, 143, 146-47, 153-55, 158-59, 163-64, 167-68, 182, 185-86, 188, 262, 338, 368-69, 374-75, 376-79, 382-83, 392
  natal predictive theory ..4-5, 38
  theory of mundane astrology 7, 39, 73-76, 81
  types of mundane chart . 77, 82

Abū Muslim ...48, 54, 167, 180-81
Abū Qumash ........................2-3, 23
Adam................................85
Advice...23-26, 29-34, 37-41, 48-49, 51, 73
Ahwāz...268, 270-72, 279-80, 282-7, 289, 291-92, 295, 298-300, 303-04, 306, 310-11, 314-16, 319, 322, 324-25, 329-31, 335
al-Amīn (Caliph) ................. 35, 55
al-Battānī........................17
Alexander the Great...........46, 182
Alexandria................. 266
al-Kindī...4, 38, 52-53, 55, 57, 64-65, 132, 162-63, 166-68, 388
al-Ma'mūn (Caliph) ..... 35, 55, 68
al-Mu'tadid (Caliph)...................56
al-Mu'tamid (Caliph) ................56
al-Mu'tasim (Caliph) .. 55, 68, 157
al-Muhallab........................54, 167
al-Muktafi........................ 6
al-Musta'īn (Caliph) .........56, 168
al-Mutawakkil (Caliph) .......... 154
al-Nadīm ........................... 3
al-Qabīsī..................... 107
al-Rijāl, 'Alī b. Abī...10-11, 368, 388
al-Saffāh (Caliph) .............. 132-33
al-Shām........................ 282

al-Ṭabarī (historian)...55, 103-04, 157
al-Walīd I (Caliph) .................. 132
al-Walīd II (Caliph)..54, 132, 167
al-Wāthiq (Caliph) .................. 154
al-Zubaydah............................55
al-Zubayr........47-48, 54, 167, 181
Ana Labarta ................................. 3
Applying/separating aspects. 199
Arabs...2, 38, 52, 64-65, 84-87, 123, 154, 162, 164-66, 169-71, 178, 183, 203, 218, 231, 262, 268, 271-82, 286, 300, 305-306, 308-11, 315, 327, 329-30, 384-85
Ardashīr b. Bābikān ..........46, 182
Arīn..................... 323, 325
Aristotle................................ 7, 9, 74
Armenia...169, 203, 206, 232, 244, 280, 284, 287, 289-90, 292, 296, 299, 303, 309, 311, 316, 321-22, 327-28, 332
Ascensions ....................... 119, 144
Aversion...37, 110, 118, 128, 136-37, 143-44, 151, 164-65, 167-68, 171-78, 181-82, 371
Azerbaijān.............................26, 299
Babylon...30, 50, 64, 123, 170, 172-73, 203-04, 206, 208, 210, 212, 216-17, 222, 231, 248, 266-67, 269-71, 279-86, 289-96, 298-300, 304-05, 308-11, 313-16, 318-21, 323-25, 327-29, 332-34, 383-85
Babylon............................... 1, 6
Baghdad............ 36, 55-56, 68, 104
Bahrain ....................................... 103
Basrah .......................36, 103-04

Bedouin ........................... 285, 289
Berbers.............................. 170, 266
Besieging..................................... 125
Blair, Tony......................................37
Burnett and Yamamoto...1, 5-6, 38, 45, 69, 76-77, 82, 87-88, 93, 95, 99-100, 112, 119-20, 134-36, 140-41, 144, 147-49, 152, 156-57, 160, 162-63, 169, 178, 183-85, 194, 199, 202-03, 206, 209, 219, 232-33, 271, 279, 285, 298, 305, 325, 354, 356, 360, 382, 385-86
Buyids .............................................56
Chicago ..........................................26
China.............. 26, 37, 60, 123, 171
Chorography...1, 26-27, 29-30, 53, 64-65, 162
Christianity.................66, 106, 182
Comets (tailed stars)...71, 221-22, 266-74, 365-66
Copts.............................. 170, 274
Covington Kids ...........................63
Ctesiphon ............................. 267
Damascus................................... 114
Darius the Great...................... 182
Dastī-Maysān .................. 272, 286
Daylam ...................... 178, 216
Directions...5, 33, 38, 43, 45, 87, 90, 139, 147-48, 154, 156-57, 166, 174, 187, 203-04, 207-10, 212, 214, 216-19, 337-39, 341, 343, 346, 348, 350, 352, 354, 356, 358, 360, 362, 365, 369, 371-72, 374-75, 380-81
Distributions...2, 31, 38-39, 42, 90-91, 139, 148, 156, 274, 338,

365-67, 371, 375, 377, 379, 381
Dorotheus of Sidon ....... 24, 30, 60
Dynasties...2, 8, 25, 28-29, 36-38, 47, 51-52, 54-57, 70, 73-76, 83-84, 87-89, 95, 105, 107, 109-16, 118-19, 124, 132, 148, 154, 156-57, 162-64, 167-68, 180-85, 187-89, 377-78, 382
Eclipses...1-3, 7, 25, 48, 68, 157-58, 368
Egypt, Egyptians...7, 123, 190, 268, 320
Emptiness in course........... 129-30
Epicycles......................7, 32
Equant ..................32
Equation of the center................32
Escape.................. 126
Ethiopia ...................... 170
Euphrates ........ 218, 281, 294, 319
European Union.......................... 37
Exchangers........................ 192, 347
*Fardārs*...2, 35, 49-50, 142-43, 364, 374, 380, 382-86
Fārs...30, 66, 203-04, 272, 274, 292, 310, 321, 324, 334
Firmicus Maternus.......... 105, 368
Fixed stars ..................... 123
Flood...41-42, 44, 49, 84-86, 111, 132-33, 375
   indicator conjunction..... 43-44, 84, 86
Germany ......................... 27
Greeks.............................. 266, 316
Hajj................................56, 356
Head/Tail (Nodes)...49, 100, 123, 125, 129, 157, 222, 266-74, 368, 383, 385

Hijrah...49-50, 53, 68, 163-64, 166, 380
House-master........................... 147
ibn al-Bāzyār.............................. 6
Ibrāhīm b. al-Hasan al-'Alawī ... 55
India, Indians2, 3, 7, 21, 42-44, 65, 81, 123, 162, 170, 203, 290, 316, 385
Inferior planets...8-9, 29, 73, 75-76, 95, 114, 135-37, 140, 143, 187-88
Ingresses (revolutions of years)... 1-4, 11-12, 15, 25-27, 29-30, 33-34, 39-41, 45-46, 48-49, 51-52, 57, 68, 70-71, 77, 82-83, 87, 104, 117, 155, 164, 186-87, 262, 276, 278, 338, 343, 364-65, 381, 386
Iraq...30, 35, 53-54, 65, 103, 162-64, 167, 286, 290, 292, 295, 300-01, 316, 321, 330, 374, 377
Isfahān .............................. 206, 272
Islam, Muslims...1, 7, 35, 49-50, 53, 56, 68, 105, 112, 165, 192, 347, 382
Italy....................................27, 266-67
Jerusalem..............................36, 388
Jesus................................ 36, 46, 182
Jibāl...169, 242, 259, 267, 273, 280-81, 284-86, 289, 291, 293-95, 299-300, 304-05, 310-11, 313-16, 320, 322, 324, 327-29, 332-34
*Jihād* ............................61, 192, 356
Judaism..............................66, 105
Jurjān................................. 272
Ka'aba .............................48, 180-81

Khārijites .......................... 192, 347
Khurāsān...26, 55, 173, 232, 291, 300, 315, 335
Khusrau II ................................ 53
Kūfa .............................. 171, 219
Kurds .............................. 173, 309
Los Angeles ........................... 26
Lots ....................................... 58
   authority (Sun to MC) ...... 107
   battle .................................. 370
   body marks ........................ 99
   elevation ............................ 58
   elevation, victory ................ 158
   exaltation ............................ 58
   Fortune.... 24, 58, 98, 123, 129, 367-68
   king's involvement ............. 131
   life ..................................... 143
   lifespan (Jupiter-Saturn-ASC) .................................. 143
   lifespan (Jupiter-Saturn-conjunction) ..................... 146
   lifespan (Sun-Saturn) ......... 145
   lifespan A ........................... 145
   lifespan B ........................... 145
   livelihood .......................... 143
   prosperity .......................... 370
   prosperity and aid ................ 58
   rulership (from ASC of conjunction) ................... 107
   rulership (from I.4) ............. 116
   rulership (undefined)...118-20, 125, 127, 131, 160
   rulership and authority 106-07
   victory ................................. 58
Lunations...100, 113, 144, 366-68, 388-89
Manī ............................... 46, 182

Marwān I (Caliph) ................. 132
Marwān II (Caliph) ......... 132, 154
Mary (mother of Jesus) .......... 182
Māshā'allāh... 3-4, 10, 42-44, 57, 67, 69, 84-85, 101, 114, 133, 140-42, 146, 152
Mazdaism ................... 66, 105, 182
Mecca ................. 54, 375, 377, 379
Merv ............................... 66, 108
Mesopotamia ............................ 30
Mongolia .................................. 26
Mosul ........................... 271, 333
Mu'āwiya I (Caliph) ................ 132
Mu'āwiya II (Caliph) .............. 132
Muhammad (prophet of Islam)... 9, 35, 46, 48, 54, 57, 132-33, 163, 180-82
Muhammad b. al-Hasan al-'Alawī ........................................... 55
Mūsā b. Nawbakht... 2-3, 6, 10-15, 23, 25, 27, 37, 38, 40, 42-45, 47-50, 52, 56, 58, 60-62, 64, 67, 69, 84-87, 92, 94, 100-01, 155-56
Nihāvand, Battle of ........... 53, 166
Nile River .................................. 7
Nubia .................................. 170
Persia, Persians... 2, 4, 7, 9-10, 28, 34, 46, 49-50, 53, 60, 65, 146, 156, 164-166, 170-71, 182-83, 262, 266-68, 270, 273, 282, 285, 286-87, 292, 294-95, 300, 305-06, 309, 315, 324-25, 328-29, 333, 380, 384-85
Persian theory of politics...7, 10, 130, 153
   Arrows and Sword..10-11, 125, 146-47

Philip of Macedon.................... 182
Pingree, David .............................. 3
Places
   colors.......................................... 67
   mundane significations..... ...63-64, 179, 339, 341, 343, 346, 348, 350, 352, 354, 356, 358, 360, 362
Planetary years...94, 102, 104, 118-20, 140-43, 152, 168, 183, 185, 203, 210
Planets
   and animals........................... 108
   and clothing.......................... 107
   and religion..................... 105-06
   appearing from under the rays ....... 223-30, 232-39, 241-46, 248-65
   eastern/western...31, 111, 121, 123, 126, 131, 145, 206, 208-09, 214, 217-19, 224-30, 232-46, 259, 278-79, 373, 390-91
   easternizing/westernizing... 31, 90, 127, 142, 223, 389
   in own exaltation. 117, 122-23, 127, 129-31, 144, 165
   latitude...31, 223-30, 232-37, 238-46, 248-60
   mundane significations....8-10, 61-62
   under the rays.... 128, 151, 248-58, 260-61
Profections...2, 4-6, 25, 29-31, 33-34, 36, 38-42, 48-49, 51, 53, 57, 70, 88-89, 95, 97-98, 101-02, 104, 111-12, 114, 124, 132-33, 135, 139-40, 147-48, 156, 187, 201, 247, 365-66, 371-72, 374-75, 381-82, 390
   types of................................88-89
Prophets...2, 28-29, 35-36, 45, 61, 70, 72, 88, 97, 100, 103, 110, 188, 212, 276, 337, 343, 356
Ptolemy, Claudius....1, 4, 6-7, 30, 32, 231
   *Tet.* 7, 30, 203-04, 207-10, 212, 214, 216-19, 222, 231, 240, 248, 254
Qarmatians................................56
Quadrant divisions vs. whole signs...25, 101, 104, 109, 119, 121, 125, 140, 172, 179, 338, 365, 381
Quadruplicities
   convertible ...8, 49, 77, 82, 112-13, 127, 166, 171, 181-82, 184, 247, 371-72, 375, 379-81
   double-bodied...8, 36, 49, 97-98, 101-04, 113-14, 119, 143, 154-55, 171, 371-73
   fixed.. ...8, 49, 112-13, 128, 130, 166, 171, 185, 371-73
Quarters...43, 45, 84, 86-88, 95, 114, 148, 153-54, 157, 187
Quhistān..............................66, 108
Ramesey, William........................61
Raqqah...................................... 283
Rayy........................................... 103
Releaser ................................... 147
Religious communities ........28-29, 36-37, 51, 57, 64-65, 74-76, 83-89, 91, 105, 108-10, 112-14, 116, 118, 120-21, 124, 132, 135, 139, 145, 147, 154, 156-

57, 162, 180-82, 184, 187-88, 189, 191, 367, 372, 374-75, 377, 379-81

Retrogradation/direct...7, 16-17, 31, 41, 82, 119, 155-56, 172-78, 223-30, 232-39, 241-46, 248-61, 370, 377

*Revolutions* (Sahl)...2, 4, 24, 64, 146, 171, 173, 175-76, 178, 370-72

Rome.................................................53

Rūm...65, 123, 162, 169-70, 183, 195, 203, 206, 208, 216, 218, 231, 243, 262, 266-68, 271, 279-80, 282-97, 300, 303-06, 308-11, 314-16, 319, 321-25, 328-31, 333-35, 384-85

*RYW* (Māshā'allāh).........3-4, 371

Sahl b. Bishr... 2-4, 10-11, 23-24, 48, 58, 64-65, 123, 146-47, 166, 171, 173, 175-76, 178, 370-72

Samarra..........................55-56, 114

San'ā'..................................................65

Sarajevo.................. 40, 48, 51, 343

Sasanian Persians...26, 46, 50, 164, 182

Saturn cycles...22, 29, 45-47, 81, 181-82, 185

Saturn-Jupiter conjunctions...2, 4, 11, 22, 28-29, 32, 34, 39, 42, 44, 47, 52, 83, 134, 135, 180, 185, 343

and direction of power..........92
and elements ...........................22
and longevity.....................93-95
and social rank .......................96
and strength............................92
and timing of effects ..............93
conjunctional distance.. 16, 22, 78-79
conjunctional period 16, 18-19, 22, 51, 78
in all signs................................83
in the places....... 339, 341, 344, 346, 348, 350, 352, 354, 356, 358, 360, 362
mean conjunctions... 16-18, 21, 40, 48, 54, 166, 181
Sixties...12, 14-15, 22, 25, 29, 37, 47-48, 69, 93, 98, 180-81
triplicity shifts...2, 12-16, 19, 22-23, 25, 29-30, 35-37, 44, 47-48, 51-52, 54-55, 59, 68, 77-78, 80-81, 83, 87, 89-91, 93, 95-98, 103, 105-16, 118, 121-22, 132, 138, 141, 146, 152-54, 163, 168, 178, 180-82, 188, 367, 371, 374-82, 388-90
true conjunctions....... 16-17, 52, 54
Twenties...11-15, 29-30, 118, 187

Saturn-Mars conjunctions...29, 38, 52-53, 56, 83, 162, 166, 185, 189
in all signs......................29, 169
in Cancer...29, 38, 52-53, 56, 77, 83, 162, 167-68
in exaltation signs..........29, 171
in the places......................... 179

Sawād...167, 171, 180, 273-74, 286, 299-300, 304, 309, 314-15, 319, 323, 329, 362, 374, 377

*Scito horam introitus*... 4, 10, 370-72
Sect...61, 122, 127-29, 137, 143-44, 158
   *halb* .......................... 98, 123, 136
   *hayyiz* ....................... 98, 131, 137
   sect light ................. 121-22, 137
Shīʿa ................................................ 56
Sidereal zodiac...19-22, 38, 42-43, 52-53, 69, 117, 166
Signs
   airy...92-96, 222, 231, 240, 254, 262, 366, 381
   colors ........................................... 67
   earthy ...... 13-14, 16, 19, 22, 92-94, 96, 98, 223, 231, 240, 248, 254, 262, 346, 366
   fiery... 12-13, 19, 22, 56, 80, 92-94, 96, 103, 369-70, 374, 379, 382
   royal ................................. 33, 127
   watery 22, 31, 80, 92-93, 95-96, 103, 116, 190, 219, 223, 231, 240, 248, 254, 262, 366, 374, 379, 381-82, 384
Sijistān ........................................ 298
Sirius .............................................. 7
Sīstān ................................... 298, 304
Solomon ..................................... 105
Soviet Union ............................... 37
Spear-bearing ............................ 123
Sulaymān (Caliph) .................. 132
Superior planets...4, 8-10, 23, 29, 34-35, 73-77, 83, 95, 97, 101-02, 135, 140-43, 146, 162, 187-88, 278-79
Syria ..................................... 54, 266

Tabaristān ................................. 178
Theophilus of Edessa ................ 30
Thunberg, Greta ......................... 63
Tigris ............... 218, 281, 294, 319
Time lords...2, 6, 30-31, 38-39, 41-43, 49, 57, 84
Transits (of one planet over another) .................................... 31
Trepidation ................. 29, 184, 239
Tropical zodiac...17-21, 45-46, 53, 166
Turks...55, 65, 123, 162, 168-70, 173, 178, 266, 282, 289, 292-93, 296, 311, 328-30, 335
Turn (the 360)...6, 12, 37, 42-43, 83-88, 90, 95, 110, 112, 114, 120, 133, 366, 375, 381
Twelfth-parts ................ 50, 91, 382
ʿUmar al-Ṭabarī ......................... 11
Vettius Valens ............................. 24
Victors
   indicator of the acceder ....... 57, 132, 155, 158, 160
   indicator of the king ...... ...4, 57, 160, 175, 370-371
   indicator of the subjects ....... 57, 370
   lord of the year 57, 172-78, 371
War (limited indications) 369-73
Washington, DC ........................ 26
Yamāmah ................................. 290
Yazdijird III 53, 166, 184-85, 377, 379-82
Yazīd I (Caliph) ........................ 132
Yazīd III (Caliph) .................... 132
Zanj ....................... 35, 103-14, 170
Zikrawayh b. Mihrawayh ........... 56

www.ingramcontent.com/pod-product-compliance
Lightning Source LLC
Chambersburg PA
CBHW050328230426
43663CB00010B/1774